D1472528

FOUNDATIONS
of Learning
in
CHILDHOOD
EDUCATION

FOUNDATIONS
of Learning
in
CHILDHOOD
EDUCATION

Edith M. Leonard
Professor of Education
University of California, Santa Barbara

Dorothy D. VanDeman
Professor of Education
University of California, Santa Barbara

Lillian E. Miles
Educational Consultant and
formerly member of the San Bernardino,
California Board of Education

CHARLES E. MERRILL BOOKS, INC.
COLUMBUS, OHIO

Library of Congress Catalog Card Number: 63-9027

PRINTED IN THE UNITED STATES OF AMERICA

PREFACE

Helping children learn through successive experiences to make wise choices is one of the basic responsibilities of the teacher in a democracy, and the first precept of the authors of this book. The authors believe that each child is constantly becoming something more than he was before and, slowly or rapidly, is passing through the phases of growth characteristic of all children.

Perceptive teachers know this, but they also recognize each child as a separate personality with initiative and creative abilities. Each has an inner drive to succeed, to understand, and to direct his efforts toward what for him are worthwhile endeavors. This is the teacher's mighty challenge: to make democracy a way of life for his group of junior citizens; to create a classroom where the contributions of individuals can be in keeping with their abilities, and where each child may enjoy the recognition and appreciation of the group. Here, every child is a universe within himself, while still retaining his buoyant interest in the life about him and reflecting his joy in living, growing, and learning.

When the teacher, too, is living, observing life, and guiding children's growth, the room climate stimulates creativity, one of the basic aspects of childhood education. A classroom where this type of learning is possible becomes in itself a foundation upon which all else must rest.

A study of the table of contents will reveal the authors' purposes. Each topic discussed describes how a skillful and creative teacher assures continuity of learning for his group in early childhood. Through a unique, "custom-built curriculum," every teacher is led to encourage language expression, foster wholesome social relationships, and lay the foundation for reading, writing and numbers. He is directed to recognize sensory impressions as avenues of learning, and to see in the child's inherent love of exploration and discovery the real budding of a life-long interest in science.

The theme of this book is faith—faith in childhood; in teachers, to

v

develop resources from within themselves; in administrators and boards of education, to support the open-minded seeking of the teacher; in the value of inter-personal relationships within a democratic classroom; in the individual child, to respond as a person in his own right; in the quality of learning that takes place in every member of the group, including the teacher.

This book is dedicated to teachers, administrators, parents, boards of education, and citizens everywhere who recognize childhood as the now of the future; who see within the day by day learning of each individual the foundation for all his future learning.

Edith M. Leonard
Dorothy D. VanDeman
Lillian E. Miles

Santa Barbara, California

ACKNOWLEDGMENTS

Grateful acknowledgment is made to the many teachers and student teachers, both named and unnamed, who have generously shared with us interesting anecdotes, verbalizations, and revealing comments of children.

We are deeply indebted, also, to the following teachers for the classroom experiences which are incorporated herein: June Brouhard; Lois Cardona; Judy Marshall Diaz; Clarence George; Jane Hefflefinger; Gerry Jones; Gertrude Bishel Kiskadden; Irene Lansing; Margaret Leonard; Sally Loyd; Ethel Moulton; Pauline Sanders; Frances Seger; Betsy Vigus; Clarita Thompson Williams, Inez Williams and Una Wyatt.

Special gratitude is due June Holman for the many uniquely interesting activities which are so much a part of the learning situations constantly evident in her classroom, as she lives and works with her children.

We wish to express our appreciation, also, to Burbank, California, City Schools for reference to their exemplary Advanced First Grade Program.

Finally, our sincere thanks go to Mrs. R. W. Evans of the First Community Church Day School, Columbus, Ohio, for her cooperation and assistance in setting up the photographs, and to Amy, Candy, and Danny Martinez, the charming models pictured in them.

CONTENTS

Part Three.   MAJOR INFLUENCES ON
LEARNING IN THE CLASSROOM

Part Four.   SENSORY IMPRESSIONS IN
CHILDHOOD EDUCATION

Part Nine. SOCIAL DEVELOPMENT THROUGH CENTERS OF INTEREST AND AREAS OF EXPERIENCE

Part Ten. A PHILOSOPHY TOWARD SELECTIVE HOMEWORK

INTRODUCTION

Education is life and therefore consists of all the experiences which make up the life of the individual from birth through the adult years. In *Foundations of Learning in Childhood Education*, democracy is presented as a way of life, a way of feeling, thinking, and acting upon foundations laid down in the early experiences of childhood. Therefore, education for democracy is a continuous process.

In all the experiences of living, from infancy on through life, the individual is forming attitudes and habits, gaining knowledge and developing skills which influence his thought and his actions. The experiences of the early home and school years are determined by the nature of the environment which is provided by adults, who are for the most part the child's parents and teachers. Their own way of life, their feelings of self worth, their respect for the self of each child in their care will to a very large extent influence the education of those for whom they have responsibility.

In infancy and toddlerhood, foundations are laid for trust in oneself and one's environment and for the beginnings of self-direction, if the conditions are right for such learning. In an environment of safety, of intelligent permissiveness, of warmth and unpossessive love, trust grows and feelings of "I can" emerge.

School life continues the education which begins in the home. To the extent that parents and teachers work together to provide experiences which help each child continue in the building of a good self-image, will education be good. It is this self-image that projects into all new experiences. If the self-image is a growing, trustful one, one that means I can do, I can take responsibility, I can make choices, I can experiment and explore, I can find out things for myself, I can share with and learn from others, we can be assured that it is the self-image of a child who is truly laying a firm foundation for democratic living.

The authors of *Foundations of Learning in Childhood Education* present in a simple, direct way the principles and the classroom practices which foster the preservation of a democratic way of life. Their subtle analysis of characteristics inherent in democracy sets the stage for their enlightening discussion of the schools' responsibility for providing an environment in which these characteristics are nurtured. Every principle enunciated, every method described is so well illustrated with examples from actual situations that no parent, teacher or student can fail to grasp the full significance of the authors' meaning.

The authors also discuss subject matter and skills as necessary facets of the child's education, at the same time stressing the importance of the atmosphere in which the child learns skills, gains knowledge and forms attitudes which result in action. The discussions of the teacher's part in providing a favorable atmosphere for learning are significant contributions to teacher education.

Every thoughtful student will find in *Foundations of Learning in Childhood Education* new insight and understanding. This is only one of several important contributions which these authors have made to education, theory and practice. It is a culminating summation of their faith in democracy, and in education as a means of fostering democracy as a way of life.

Laura Hooper
Program Coordinator
Association for Childhood
  Education International
Washington, D.C.

FOUNDATIONS
of Learning
in
CHILDHOOD
EDUCATION

DEMOCRACY IN

Part One

CHILDHOOD EDUCATION

I. IMPLICATIONS OF DEMOCRATIC LIVING FOR THE INDIVIDUAL CHILD

The ideal democracy is a "government of the people, by the people, for the people," but before this ideal can be attained the people concerned must have had practice in democratic living.

One of the school's major responsibilities, parallel with the teaching of the skill subjects, is to afford children the opportunity to learn that democracy is more than a mode of government. It is a way of thinking and living, a way of making decisions and carrying them out unselfishly every hour of the day, not only at school but at home, at work, and in leisure hours. Wise decisions make for growth, and at the same time take into consideration the rights of others.

Many an adult flounders and errs in his decisions because in the formative years of childhood he had no part in deciding what to do, either at home or at school. Parents and teachers directed how everything was to be done without giving him an opportunity to weigh and make choices between one eventuality and another. Now, beyond

3

the portals of parental and teacher influence he finds it difficult to make thoughtful decisions; he is often impulsive and acts on the basis of his own likes and dislikes. The outcome is that he seldom does much on his own initiative, but is prone instead to follow the dictates of the loudest speaker, or the one who caters to his tastes.

On the other hand, those who during the formative years participate in democratic group decisions learn that good citizens cannot follow every wayward impulse. They become aware that law and authority apply to them as individuals at all times, and their motto is, "We are free only so long as we ourselves are growing and are not interfering with the growth of others." This attitude is the very foundation of a democracy.

Home Backgrounds for Democratic Living

Few teachers have a group in which the children are truly homogeneous from the standpoint of parental control and home background. One child may have experienced parental indifference, over-indulgence or laxity; another,such autocratic rule and forced compliance with parental authority that "the lid blows off" and he does bizarre things when he is released from such rigid control.

As their teacher, you will necessarily guide these children in a different manner, but each will need your help. You will be gratified indeed to note the development of each individual child under your democratic regime, regardless of contrasting home situations. Democratic action in a school situation exerts a strong influence on individuals.

Michael is the product of a home ruled by force. His automatic response to everything is "No!" During rhythms Martha, a classmate, said, "Let's all go walking together."

Michael's response was, "No, I won't go walking. No one can make me do what I don't want to do!"

Martha's suggestion was an invitation, not a command. Miss Thompson, the teacher, realized this, and remarked, "We'd enjoy having you walk with us, Michael, but if you would rather watch this time, it will be all right. Some things *have* to be done, but this is a matter of choice."

Michael will grow from this experience. He is being treated like a person, a real personality. His teacher, who insisted that he follow through on essential issues, was nevertheless willing to offer *bona fide* opportunities for him to decide one way or another when a choice was justified.

The opposite extreme is typified by a father who said, "*My* father had his own idea of discipline and I follow after him. When he said to me, 'Jump,' I would say, 'How high, Dad?' "

On the other hand, children who come from democratic homes have had the opportunity to take part in family planning according to their maturity. Sharon lives democratically at home and at school. She has excellent self-control and automatically says, "I'd like to help you."

Sharon can grow, and help others to grow also. She can help others through her automatic use of democratic behavior patterns. For example, during clean-up time Sharon and four boys, one of whom was Michael, were working together. To Philip's complaint, "Michael won't help clean up," Sharon replied, "Oh yes he will. Everyone helps clean up, don't they Michael." And Michael went to work without delay.

Democratic parents and teachers are always eager to help each other see the value of encouraging and guiding children to think things through rather than imposing decisions upon them. The democratic teacher realizes that counseling with parents is an important phase of her responsibility. Parents and teachers can find many ways to implement their philosophy that children who learn to practice democracy are the nation's insurance for perpetuating the great principles for which their forefathers worked and fought.

Various Types of Control

Control of the individual within the group is achieved in different ways. Each type of control needs to be evaluated in terms of the child himself.

Individual Child's Viewpoint

Ideas of what constitutes acceptable behavior vary from one situation to another, and as the child is shifted about from home to school, and from teacher to teacher, he must often remember what is permissible in one place is not in another: in one situation he must wait to be told; in another he must ask; in another he may show initiative, plan his time, and exercise control over his own actions. Through these varying experiences he gradually acquires a negative or positive attitude toward authority, discipline, and self-control.

The Individual Child—Asset or Liability?

Ralph and George were in different upper primary rooms. A similar incident which occurred in each of these groups of eight- and nine-year-old children shows the difference between autocratic and democratic procedure. One day Ralph caught a beam of sunlight in a pocket mirror and sent it dancing on a picture that hung on the opposite wall. His teacher, who was autocratic in her government, asked, "Who did that?"

Ralph held up his hand, "I did. My dad and I used reflector mirrors this week-end when we went hiking. I know what makes the light reflect."

Ignoring this, the teacher said, "Ralph, we have work to do now. This is not a hike. If it happens again you will be sent out of the room."

Ralph put his mirror away and went on with his work; but later the sunlight was coming in from another place, and he spontaneously took out his mirror and tried to reflect it on the same picture from the new angle. The teacher sent him out and Ralph stood at the entrance of the room for the rest of the morning.

About the same time, by coincidence, George first used *his* mirror, but his teacher, Miss F., saw the serious interest which the boy was showing in the refraction of light, and encouraged him to explain it to the group, "while the sunlight is just right." Various children took turns trying it, and George drew an illustration on the chalk board to show how the light was bent at a sharp angle where it struck the reflecting surface. "We had intended to finish discussing the ripening of wheat, our topic for today," said Miss F. "This experiment with light has taken ten minutes of our time. However, we have learned several things," she explained. She and the children then summarized what had been presented.

Unlike Ralph's teacher, Miss F. had guided the children into a constructive learning situation based on George's diversion, and George remained with his group to make a worthwhile contribution. The mirror was placed on a shelf where others might work with it later as an independent activity, and George offered to make a poster at another time to explain the principle of the experiment. The group went back to their discussion of grain, and although there was not time to finish it, as originally intended, they reorganized their plan to continue it into the next day. Miss F. was obviously a democratic teacher. She was also a spontaneous individual who was able to capitalize upon unforeseen events.

On the other hand, when Ralph was punished by the teacher who acted in an autocratic manner, the children were resentful and rebellious. His teacher might have said, "Ralph, that is an interesting experiment and we would like to hear about it, but it is time for reading and other activities now. You just show us how it works and then put it away and explain it to us later." Ralph could then have anticipated the joy of sharing his experience with the other children and the teacher could have planned to use his demonstration later as a basis for a reading experience, or for arithmetic or spelling or some other learning. Had this course of action been followed, a spirit of good fellowship would no doubt have been encouraged, and much more could have been accomplished with the children.

Institutional Viewpoints

Ways of controlling children have been discussed and varied for as long as schoolrooms have been in existence. Some of these are:

Discipline by Compulsion

The type of control that has remained firm for all time is that of compulsion, the restraining by physical force or coercion; the "you do it because I say so, or else" approach. The child is seldom given any reasonable explanation, and punishment meted out by the one in authority is often to vent his own feelings. Threats and scoldings are used to chastise, and strict penalties are imposed. Such a child, raised in fear, is like a robot. He has no feeling for what he does and has no personal sense of right or wrong. He is expected in the years ahead to go out into the world and become a part of it. It is assumed that he will understand and live by the ideals of democracy. How can he? He has never lived democracy.

Lack of understanding causes fear and distrust. In a nation built upon the principles of democracy, it is up to every teacher to keep democracy the living, vital idea it is, by guiding his group so that the natural remark to a problem will be, "Let's talk it over," rather than, "I hate you and you can't make me do it."

It is only when the teacher is present that the child ruled by compulsion does the right thing. Mrs. X.'s room, for example, climaxes the old standard of classroom behavior. Everyone can hear a pin drop when she is present with her pupils. But let her be called from the room and there is immediate bedlam. Children whistle and call to each other; some of them run around the room; some of the boys stage a wrestling match; the girls write forbidden notes; erasers and paper wads are thrown. By the time Mrs. X. returns, the room looks as if a small cyclone had struck it, even though the children are all sitting absorbed in their books, hoping to give a convincing appearance of innocence. They know severe punishment awaits the unfortunates who may be caught.

Mrs. X. is also a martinet when the children go over to the auditorium to attend a program. She lines them up and marches them two by two, heads erect, eyes straight ahead. One day Paula saw a lovely butterfly on a flower. Involuntarily she paused to enjoy it.

Mrs. X.'s voice barked out, "Stop!"

Every child stopped as if he had been struck. Mrs. X. glared at Paula. "I said that anyone who got out of line would go back to the room. Now you go back to your room and put your head on your desk."

Force and coercion will make the child obey, and will undoubtedly bring deep satisfaction to the disciplinarian. However, it is evident that there is no democracy within the situations described. Deceitfulness, negativism, rebellion, or cowardice may result. The child's idea often becomes one of trying to "get by" without being caught; he may defy threats and test the adult to see just how far he can go. On the other hand, submission and blind obedience may lead to dependence upon authority, and confusion in the absence of it; or the individual may become too easily influenced by others and be weak in making decisions and taking responsibility.

Discipline by Rule

Some teachers are "Rule Makers." They set up rules on the chalkboard for both conduct and learning, with penalties for their transgression, as:

> Any pupil caught whispering will be required to write, "I will not whisper," 100 times.
>
> Two words missed in spelling—remain fifteen minutes after school.
>
> Four words missed—remain one-half hour.
>
> If caught out of seat without permission, stand in corner with nose in ring. (Teacher draws a circle on the chalkboard, and the child must stand facing the chalkboard with his nose in the center of the circle.)

Rules like the above are not only associated with long ago, but are all too common today. Recently seven-year-old Carl spent the major portion of his weekend painstakingly copying one hundred times the following erroneous sentence written by his teacher: "Chalk and paint *is* not to be used on my face; I am not an Indian."

Carl's transgression is obvious; the teacher's grammatical error, though equally obvious, is harder to explain. Carl's mother said (but not in the boy's hearing), "Well, poor thing, she is not very well, and she is leaving at the end of the year. Carl has made her enough trouble—why should I make more?" But big brother was less magnanimous. While Carl worked away in his careful beginner's writing, out of ear shot, big brother was heard to remark scornfully, "What dumb punishment! I could figure out something better than that myself." Oblivious to these comments, Carl had his own solution. After filling several pages with his repeated sentence, he found an interesting way of breaking the monotony of the assignment, just as most bright children would do. On the next page, he wrote the first word of the sentence in a column all the way down the page, and then started at the top and wrote the second word next to it all the way down, and so on across the page. When he discovered he could not get the whole sentence on the paper in this manner, he attached another sheet to the edge and continued adding pages. He fulfilled his task to the letter.

Sometimes children are punished for lack of understanding about something they should, but do not know. Later they may be punished for not remembering a rule. The reason a child does not remember is often because the rule is an adult one that has been imposed upon him. It is not a rule that he has participated in making.

"I can't play there. Teacher says so," remarks a child.

"But why?" asks his friend.

"I don't know. She just says I can't."

Discipline by Approval

There is also the discipline by approval. Children learn and grow under approval, but it is the *type* of approval that determines whether growth is temporary or permanent. If the mother's or the teacher's personality is the controlling force, the child's conduct stems from his wanting to please. Often the child has respect and affection for the teacher who says, "I am delighted with your block house," or "I am proud of the way you are working today, Lewis."

The teacher *is* proud, but will Lewis do what teacher is so proud of when *she* is not around? Her approbation seems to be the ruling force. How much better for the teacher to say when Lewis has worked carefully and well on a painting, "What a lovely painting, Lewis! Your painting shows how carefully you worked." The teacher's approval is implied here, but not stated. Or, if she can truthfully say so, she might comment, "What lovely colors! Your work shows that you planned well."

In a similar way she makes evaluations impersonal. She doesn't say, "I am happy that John is working hard on his boat." Instead, she says, "John is working hard to finish his boat." In place of saying, "I'm pleased that Bill is remembering to put away the blocks," she says, "Bill is remembering to put away the blocks when he isn't using them."

The child's satisfaction in the doing of the deed is the important thing, rather than the favor and approbation he might win by doing it for the teacher. He may sense the approbation, but it is not the motive for his efforts.

Approval should be honest and sincere. If the child has made a real effort, there is always something that is worthy of commendation, even if it is nothing more than "You've worked hard today."

A child accustomed to adult approval finds life a dull place when no one is present to say, "I'm so proud," or "I like the way . . ." When he reaches adulthood he finds it hard to assume responsibility. Many times he becomes lazy and lacks ambition because he is incapable of working without approbation.

While the discipline of approval is more nearly democratic than discipline by fear or by adult rule, it is a far cry from meeting the requirements of training for democratic living. The children from such a group, when placed under a teacher whose personality is less winning, will "try her out," and if they find her indifferent will soon produce the bedlam that reigned in Mrs. A.'s room during her absence.

Another serious result of this type of discipline is that the child unable to live up to expectations may feel inferior, or he may be too easily influenced by flattery and become a victim of unscrupulous persons. Then, too, individuals vie with each other to find favor in the eyes of those in a position of power. Tattling and informing on peers may be done for approval. Under these circumstances, there can be no true sense of values.

Discipline of Routine Plus Rigid Schedule

This sort of discipline is illustrated by the teacher who takes all the responsibility for the child's actions, dictates what he shall or shall not do, and tells him how to do it. Little or no opportunity is given the child to think through plans as an individual or as a member of a group.

The teacher who maintains a rigid routine and schedule is usually enslaved by her course of study and her plans for the day. She may have an excellent background of knowledge and yet fall short as a teacher because of failure to secure child interest and cooperation.

In her plans for the day a teacher had written, "Tell the story of a walk about the neighborhood." When the time came she asked the children if they had ever gone for a walk.

"Oh, yes," said Danny. "I went for a walk in San Diego. I walked in the big zoo."

Sara said, "I went for a walk in the redwoods. We were at Williams Grove."

Those children had a real contribution to make to the group, but the teacher did not capitalize on it. "A walk around the neighborhood was what I meant," she said, and proceeded to tell her story. That teacher was enslaved by her plans.

In a group where a schedule is rigidly followed, the next thing is done because it is done at that time every day. If an emergency arises or there is any change in the program, the group disintegrates.

The child who is so directed will undoubtedly lack the ability to make judgments, to set up a goal and work reliably toward it. He may become submissive to the dictates of a leader who makes false promises;

or he may be driven to "cover-up" actions and feelings, becoming two-faced, hypocritical, and deceitful. There is also the danger that he may seek outlets and release from adult dictates, ganging up with others against those in authority, or becoming shiftless and irresponsible when on his own.

Routine is a stabilizing force in the child's life. When understood and accepted by the individual or group as a good way of getting things done, it has a valid place in democracy. For example, a child learns to pick up the large blocks first because they belong on the bottom part of the shelf, the middle-sized ones next, and so on in the order in which they fit best. He realizes that "this is the way to do the job effectively." Throughout life the child needs to be alert to discover procedures that will expedite necessary routine so that he can be released for more pleasurable activity.

To live successfully in a democracy the individual must be able to cooperate in carrying out routines, but he must also be able to think, plan, and evaluate.

Planning and Evaluation: Democracy in Action

This method combines adult guidance and the child's own initiative. It is democracy in action, with participation the keynote. The adult recognizes the child's growing abilities in self-direction. Teacher and children plan together, discover the need for standards, make the rules, and then apply them to everyday problems. There is provision for group as well as individual discussion; there is reasoning and consultation. Feelings are recognized and controlled, and children are "in the know" and respond accordingly with informed obedience to law and authority. Possible results of various choices are recognized when more than one plan of action is open. Individual differences are considered, mutual interests are discovered, committees are set up for definite purposes, contributions of individuals are welcomed in terms of ability and effort, appreciation is expressed and commendation given. Consideration for others grows with practice. Privileges and responsibilities are recognized as such and children learn to face disappointments and profit by them. The ability to face a situation objectively, to recognize the issues and adjust behavior accordingly, is gradually developed.

> Miss Thompson's six-, seven-, and eight-year-olds had discussed the need for self-control, and as a result, had developed several rules which they considered essential. The children desired to keep the rules, but practice was needed.
>
> Later in the day some of them began working independently in the patio, using paint and clay, while others remained in the room to read. Shortly

after these activities had begun, noise and confusion were heard on the patio. Miss Thompson recognized at once that here was an opportunity for the children to use their newly-made rules for self-control. She stepped outside and asked the children which rule they needed to use. Alastair said, "Think about others."

Then after a brief discussion, Miss Thompson went back to the reading group. However, the noise in the patio resumed, and Miss Thompson went out again. She explained the children's responsibility to the other groups that were working. Then she said the privilege to work in the patio any more that day had been lost.

"Those children who were making a disturbance need to come inside and think about self-control," she said. "Each of you knows if you were disturbing the others, and now you know what to do about it."

No one responded at first. Then Alastair said, "I was making noise, and I'm going inside."

Mark said, "Yes, Alastair made noise."

Alastair turned to Mark and said, "You don't have to tell on me. I made noise and I said so, and now I'm going in the room."

Soon Mark and Tommy joined him. Susan said, "Bobby, you need to go in, too."

"No," Bobby said, "I didn't make any noise." Then he thought a moment and said, "I really did, so I'm going inside, too."

In this type of program the outcomes are measured in human values and the product in character and personality. The raw material is the personal resources within the individual and the group. There is in the child who has reached this stage of development, a deep appreciation of the physical, human, and spiritual resources which are his heritage from the past, his opportunity for today, and his responsibility to the future.

There are some precautions which must be recognized in order to safeguard this program. Tolerance should be taught for others whose ideas are not in accord with the individual's; and the child needs to be fortified against his own possible impatience with other situations. Evaluations without ethical standards can become not only selfish but dangerous.

Autocratic Discipline in Contrast to
Democratic Planning and Evaluation

A certain school in a residential area is located on a piece of land in such a way that there are areas of the grounds which are out of sight of other areas. The children all know that they must stay on the south lawn, front lawn, or driveway areas when they are in the yard.

During recess one day a dozen children were found playing out of boundaries away from the view of the yard teacher. Six of the children happened to be from one of the primary groups, and six were from another classroom.

The teacher of the latter made all six stay after school and do ten additional pages of arithmetic as a "punishment."

The other teacher called her entire class together to discuss and evaluate the playground situation and the needs of the six who had gone into forbidden territory. The class as a group, under the guidance of the teacher, decided it would be well to make a map of the play yard so all could better understand where to play. The group discussed what the map should contain, and decided to include the south lawn, front lawn, and driveway in relation to the areas where the yard teacher could see the children.

After thorough class discussion and an experiment at the chalkboard, the children who had forgotten the rules were appointed to make the pictorial map in colors.

The six children were asked to study the map before going out to the yard for each intermission. The result was a better understanding of the playground rule and one hundred percent cooperation from the entire group.

Fulfillment—Self-Directed Cooperative Behavior

Finally, there is control from within, which is the ultimate goal. As someone has so aptly said, "Willing conformity to law gives man his greatest freedom." Here the child gradually *learns* to do the right thing because he *knows* it is the right thing to do. He feels better about being his *best self* than in responding in any other way. What he does is not done from fear or rule or love of approbation or routine. He does it because through experience he has come to appreciate values. He finds a balance between his own interests and those of others. He has friends and interests which help bring out the best in him. He has acceptable outlets for his unacceptable feelings, and he recreates in his daily round of living. Controls are built into him, self-control is a firm part of his character, and he lives the abundant life. Day by day he learns to make decisions in the light of findings, developing the fortitude to abide by them and the humility to recognize his limitations in relation to his abilities. He has the courage to change what he can in his environment, and to accept what cannot be changed. He has the patience to make his own contribution to democratic group action on the basis of his ever-widening background of experience.

The active toddler can feel a certain amount of self-direction in accordance with his ability to understand a need he can do something about. Even at this early age he is learning that freedom is not license, that there are things which belong to him which he may use, and there are things which belong to other people which he must not use without permission. The child of school age is faced with numerous situations where he must apply what he has previously learned in ever-widening spheres of action.

Robert, who had just celebrated his sixth birthday, said with great enthusiasm, "I love the idea first graders are big enough to do things for themselves and take care of themselves."

How a child at any age may be helped to achieve this control from within is one of your major concerns as a teacher.

Understanding Democratic Control Through Experience

Miss Holman's middle primary group of children was studying community helpers. The children's interest in the baker led them to experiment with bread dough. They watched it rise to the top of the pan and then spill over the edges.

Miss Holman used this idea as an illustration of the need for controls. She made two pictures, one showing the bread in a loaf, the other a mass of limp dough spreading out in all directions. The children and Miss Holman discussed the experiment, and as they talked they saw the comparison between the way the bread acted without boundaries and their own need for limitations on their conduct.

During their discussion Miss Holman made notes on the chalkboard. Afterward, she and the children decided to put the notes on large stiff cards so they might refer to them again and again. "When we see something like this it will help us remember that we are a little like that bread dough," said William. "It will help us think to keep our actions within the boundaries," added Albert.

The series of notes was taken seriously by this group of children. "Liberty within the law" had a definite meaning for them. Their notes, each on a separate piece of tagboard with a picture above it, read as follows:

This bread
has no boundaries.

This bread
has boundaries.

We need boundaries
and limitations, too,
so we can have order
in our lives.

We will try to make
good habits our boundaries,
to help give us order.

We will come quickly
and quietly when called,
even when we would like
to keep on working or playing.

We will use tools
and instruments
at the proper times.

We will handle our chairs
quietly.

We will plan game time
briefly and orderly,
so we will have longer
to play.

When we remember
the right thing to do,
we feel happy.

Meanings for Teacher and Child

In initiating and carrying through a program of democratic control, it is of primary importance that you know what you are attempting to do. Some teachers, with little or no understanding of how it may be achieved, have tried to adopt a democratic program. The result was chaos, and in many instances brought the idea of democracy in the schoolroom into disrepute. Merely to use the "jargon" is not enough. One child's reaction brought this fact home forcefully to a teacher who was attempting to work along these lines:

> Willard, age 6/6 (six years and six months), took home his report card which the teacher had prepared. It was the type that indicates "plus" if the child is considered above average by the teacher, a check mark if he is average, and an "N" if the child is lower than low. Willard's only "N" was after "Practices Self-Control." The child was humiliated and uncommunicative about it. His mother called the teacher and found that Willard's problem had its roots in his talking too much during discussions, but by the end of the day, this busy parent had not found opportunity to go over the problem with her son. In his prayers that night his mother heard Willard say, "Dear God, help me to do better in that 'practices self-conscious.' "
>
> Neither the teacher nor the mother had realized how much Willard felt the stigma of the report, and how little he understood the terminology.

That children can and do understand is shown again and again in groups where control from within is stressed.

Non-social behavior is often prevalent among young children who are learning in their first years of school to make adjustments to group living. The use of physical force in face-to-face relationships is usually replaced with verbal communication as the child learns better ways of getting along with others.

> Seven-year-old Greg had much difficulty in keeping his hands to himself. At first he would continually punch and pummel other children. Gradually he was improving.
>
> One day Milton came up to him and unexpectedly hit him. Greg started to retaliate, and just as he was about to swing his hand into Milton's face he stopped and said, "Milton, you know how hard I am trying, and you know how hard it is for me to have self-control. Now get out of here and don't bother me any more, or I'll lose my temper and really hit you hard."

As children grow in self-understanding, they will be able to cooperate in an honest, objective evaluation of their own growth, as seen in statements such as:

"I am strong in honesty."

"I need help in being courteous."

All statements should be positive rather than negative.

"I can remind myself to be a good sport," is a better statement than, "I forgot to be a good sport."

The evaluation needs to be in terms of goals the child may achieve in the not too distant future, and in words that he understands. It seems best to include only a few items, rather than too many items in each statement.

Sammy made his own list of points to evaluate his growth and took them very seriously. "I need help," "Improving," "Tried very hard," "Doing the best I can," were each marked with a different color. He included such things as: "I have tried to be a good sport," "I have cooperated with the group," and "I have finished my work on time."

Sammy and his teacher talked earnestly about honest effort. The child would indicate the color of the mark that should follow each item. At given intervals he would discuss the evaluation chart with his teacher. In one instance, Sammy said he thought he should have both a blue line for trying very hard and a red line for needing help, because, as he said, "I have really tried, but I haven't done the *best* I could."

Many a beginning teacher expects to be an artist in developing self-control in children long before she has had enough experience to attain the skill she has seen demonstrated by a master teacher. The teacher, no less than the children, must grow gradually. There is a delicate balance between the degree of control exercised by her and that which comes from within the child. It is this balance which must be maintained, with a gradual increase in the responsibility which the children assume.

Confidence Begets Confidence

A visitor at a certain school was talking with the principal. He said, "You should drop by and see the art work in Miss S.'s room. She is a wonder with those children, all boys, ages eight to twelve. They were the rough necks, you know, and we gave them to her because no one else could handle them. They reminded me of wild young colts fresh off the range. Now they fairly eat out of her hand."

The visitor "dropped by" and stood in the classroom doorway. The children were so absorbed in their work that they did not see her, but the teacher was nowhere in sight. One boy left his seat, took his drawing and went over to confer earnestly with another child. On his return he glanced up and saw the visitor in the doorway. "Oh, how do you do," he said politely. "Won't you come in. I didn't notice that Miss S. had left the room, but I'm sure she'll be back in a few minutes. Maybe you'd like to look around and see the work we are doing."

As he talked with the visitor, Miss S. returned. "We were running low on poster paint," she explained after she greeted the visitor pleasantly, "and every one of the children was so intent upon his work I thought it best that I go myself to the supply room. Thank you, Ramon, for taking over."

Soon it was lunch time. One boy said, "Miss S., couldn't we stay and work just a little longer?"

Miss S. promptly asked the group, "How about it, boys? Should we lose our place in the cafeteria line and hold up others?"

The boy who had made the request shook his head, and one or two of his companions gave him a friendly grin. They all put their work away with dispatch and quietly left the room.

"The boys have been so busy this morning," explained Miss S. "We call ourselves the Art Service Club. We do the dozen and one small services about the school that no one particularly likes to do. For example, almost everyone likes to put up an exhibit in the hall, but no one likes to take it down. We do that because our boys are among the taller ones. If there are flowers in the hall we empty and wash the containers. We keep a hammer and nails and a good strong step ladder right on hand in the closet, so we are always ready to help if anyone wants us. We do many other things, too. Today, the boys are busy getting ready to decorate the children's ward at the County Hospital for the Thanksgiving holidays. That was why Ramon wanted to work longer. I thought it was so sweet of him, because boys of his age have a bottomless pit for a stomach.

"When we, the committee and I, first went to see the supervisor at the hospital about decorating the ward from time to time, she was very doubtful. She thought our boys would be noisy or cause a disturbance, but she said we could try the experiment. Now she often calls the committee to talk about what we will do next. Only this morning she called to ask about the Thanksgiving decorations. This time they've made table favors, too," and she opened a closet to show a flock of strutting turkeys ingeniously constructed from pine cones and colored paper.

"Am I detaining you?" the visitor asked. "Do you need to be with your children in the cafeteria?"

"Oh, no," said Miss S. "Lee and his committee are in charge. We never have any trouble there. I am so glad you came," she continued earnestly. "It makes these poor boys realize that someone is interested in them. These aren't the most promising children from the standpoint of intellectual endowment or home background. I think one of the important things for them is to learn the satisfactions that come from being of service, and appreciating what we have here in our democracy. It is surprising, too, what wonderfully good material we uncover in the group."

"But how," asked the visitor curiously, "do you build up the attitude I have seen here this morning? The principal said these children were the roughnecks."

"They're like any other children," said Miss S. almost indignantly. "For my part, I just love them and listen to them and their suggestions. Really, ninety-eight percent of the time they themselves decide what they should do."

So it was as simple as that!

The Consequences of Actions

Practicing democracy in the classroom is an implementation of the age-old tenet, "We learn to do by doing." Yet some teachers say, "I would certainly like to teach democratically, but there are a few individuals who just won't let me."

What about such children, the ones who need individual guidance measures? Is there any reason why the group should lose the privilege of deciding what to do and how to do it because a few children have not attained enough self-control to conform? Isn't it the teacher's problem to find a way to guide these individuals, so that they will gradually develop into participating members of the group, rather than penalizing everyone by rejecting group thinking as impractical? Shouldn't you find a means of controlling these few during the process of group thinking so that the success of the other children will not be jeopardized?

It is important that children comprehend that they are given as much freedom as they are able to manage, but that they are free to do what they wish and to have a happy time at school, only when they are doing what will help them learn and grow and will in no way interfere with the learning of their friends and classmates. If said in all seriousness, this will become meaningful to the children. This means that each child must take care of himself and let his friends take care of themselves.

The maturity of the group must, of course, be taken into consideration, but regardless of the age for which you are responsible, your problem as teacher is not only to see that group control works on a democratic principle, but also to help those children who are used to "bossing," who lack emotional stability, who cannot yet take part in a democratic group. Approval and disapproval can work pressure on these individuals. What his peers think of him means more than physical punishment to the child.

There is a place for retributive punishment when violation of the rights of others persists. The offense should be talked over frankly, in an objective and impersonal way. Obedience must be demanded when the child's thinking or lack of thought causes him to ignore the right thing to be done. It is important that the child understand that what might otherwise be thought of as punishment is really a logical result of his own actions, and not superimposed upon him by another individual.

Cooperative Group Control

The child himself may suggest a means by which he can be helped to remember, or the group may impose the judgment. In a democratic situation, when it is necessary to send a child away from the group, he himself states when he feels he is ready to come back. His friends may ask him questions to find out if he is really ready to return, and, if they think he is, they accept him back under democratic teacher guidance. This procedure proves effective throughout the early childhood years.

Individuals react to this practice in different ways. Ricky, in upper primary, when sent away, was invited to return to the group whenever he felt he was ready to cooperate. After thinking it over for some fifteen minutes he returned quietly and showed by his actions that he knew how to be a cooperative member of the group. After such an experience it would be hours and sometimes even days before Ricky forgot and interfered with another. Then he would voluntarily leave the group and for a time would think things over alone. Whenever isolation became necessary, Ricky knew why he was in solitude.

Everett, on the other hand, was the wiggly, energetic type who frequently disturbed others, and when given the choice between leaving or staying, would elect to stay. However, the effort of keeping to himself would prove too much, and the opposite choice would be made for him by his own actions. Whenever it became necessary to send him away, it was made clear to Everett why he was being excluded.

When he was sent away, Everett would wait a few minutes; then he would return and ask for a chance to tell the group he was ready to help. He made sure everyone knew he was back.

Firmness and Understanding

Under your guidance, even young children can sense the need to meet infringements with firmness. Baldwin presented such a need. The democratic action of his five- and six-year-old peers did more to make him compliant than any external restrictions could have done.

> Baldwin usually wanted everything for himself. He was always striving to be first. When individuals were talking, he would interrupt and disturb the group. Time and again he had been given a choice to stay and listen or go away and think over his actions. Always he had decided he wanted to stay, and then he would forget and have to go away. After thinking in isolation he would decide he could remember and would return of his free will. This time Mrs. Bishel said, "We like you, Baldwin, and we want you to be with us, but these boys and girls just don't want to be disturbed. When you are ready to come back and show us what a fine listener you can be, you will have to ask the boys and girls what they think about it."
>
> After a few minutes in isolation Baldwin said, "I want to talk to the boys and girls."
>
> Mrs. Bishel: "All right, Baldwin."
>
> Baldwin: "Boys and girls, I've been sitting over there in that chair. I'm ready to come back and listen. Put up your right hand. How many of you kids want me back?"
>
> Not one hand went up.
>
> Baldwin: "Mrs. Bishel. What's the matter with those kids? I said I'm ready to listen."
>
> Frank: "Yes, but Baldwin, we can't trust you. You've told us that before."
>
> Baldwin went back to his chair and waited until the children went home. Then he said to Mrs. Bishel:
>
> "If they won't believe what I say, I'll just have to *show* them I mean what I say."
>
> The next day Baldwin took his place in the group and listened. Paul said to Mrs. Bishel after the group discussion, "Did you see Baldwin? He surely is remembering today, isn't he?"
>
> Mrs. Bishel smiled as she said, "Don't you think Baldwin would like to hear you say that?"
>
> Baldwin beamed when Paul told him.
>
> "I said I'd show them," Baldwin told Mrs. Bishel as he helped her move the heavy furniture afterward.

Later that day, when the group met again, Baldwin said, "Mrs. Bishel, I want to talk to the boys and girls. They have to believe me now."

Frank: "We believe you when you do what you say."

Baldwin: "All right. I can do what I say. You just watch and see."

Paul: "We're sure glad, Baldwin. Really we are."

Actions Can Be Changed

It is important that the child know it is not he as a person whom the group is rejecting. It is *what* he has done. You may say to him in all sincerity, "We like you, but we don't like what you do. You can change that, you know."

Thus he comes to realize that the problem is one he can do something about. The group's confidence in him as an individual has much to do with his ability to control and redirect his own behavior.

Parents sometimes feel indignant because they think other children are sitting in judgment on their child. They may fail to take into account that if what a child does concerns the group, the group's attitude toward him is important. It is true that without guidance children are often inclined to be more severe in their judgments than adults. The group should be led to be interested, not in punishing the offender, but in helping him to become a cooperative member of the group and a well-adjusted individual. Many teachers make the mistake of actually letting children decide the way a child should be punished, rather than saying, "What could Ricky do that would help him remember next time?"

Edward had recently come into the group from an unhappy school experience. He was always finding new ways to annoy the other children. This time he was brought in by the yard teacher with the report, "What do you think he was doing this time? Running on the lunch tables."

The group talked over the problem. "What could Edward do that would help him remember next time?"

"These tables are for us to eat on," Arthur explained.

"We don't want feet on them 'cause it gets the tables too dirty," said Mary.

Other comments were, "There are other places to run." "If Edward wants to put his feet on the tables he should go out and scrub the tops clean again afterward."

So Edward, with the help of a committee of two other children, scrubbed the tables. There was no more climbing on them. Edward had the experience of working cooperatively with a committee.

A Growing Sense of Responsibility

As children grow older and have increasing ability to evaluate their growth in terms of good citizenship, they need to realize that each has a certain responsibility regarding his influence on others. An individual child may be able to engage in some activity with no ill effects to himself, but by doing so he might influence a weaker or younger child who has a different background. Thus an older child remarked, "Let's sit in the swings when we swing. We probably could stand up and not get hurt, but the younger children might try it and they would be sure to have an accident."

A measure of growth of the children in a specific room is to note the contrast in standards of behavior between the regular members of the group and a new child who comes in, either from another community or from another room or school within the system. His orientation to the group becomes a matter of pride and satisfaction both to the children and the teacher. The case which follows illustrates this point. It also shows how children who have already established standards of working together in a democratic way, can be led to understand the position of the child who needs opportunity to grow in this respect.

Earl was the son of parents who openly rejected him: he was the terror of the community. He could not be left alone even at the noon hour, and had been in every school in town.

After Earl's first few days in Miss McCullough's room, something had to be done. Miss McCullough sent Earl to the library on an errand and talked the situation over frankly with the other children. She reiterated that some members of the group were strong in some things and needed help in others.

This group of children had experienced enough of the described behavior procedures to be objective and impersonal in their evaluations. Each knew his own unique strengths and needs for improvement. Miss McCullough used the same type of approach now: some of the children were strong in reading, some in writing, some in music, but they were not up to standard in all things. She solicited their assistance in helping Earl in his behaviors. When he did wrong things, instead of telling on him they might try to help make it easier for him to do the right things. The children responded whole-heartedly. One child volunteered, "We have our qualifications for president of our group. Earl doesn't have those qualifications. Can't we make him president anyway? It might help him to know we trust him and want him to be one of us. He has to be good to be president."

The children were unanimous in their acceptance of this plan. Upon his return from the library Earl was given a warm welcome and told by the children that they wanted him to be their leader for the next month. Earl was completely overcome with joy and a certain humiliation. He struggled valiantly during the next month, and with the children's help, confidence, and reassurance, came through triumphantly.

Permanent Impressions

Years later when Earl was in high school, Miss McCullough met him while she was searching in vain for an address in a suburban area. Earl was on his bicycle on his way to an appointment. When he saw Miss Mc-Cullough, he jumped off his bicycle, greeted her enthusiastically, and when she told him of her plight, he said, "I'll be delighted to take you to that address. I want to talk to you anyway. I've never had a chance to tell you how much your kindness and faith meant to me when I went to school to you. It made me a decent citizen and I don't know whatever would have become of me if I hadn't landed in your room when I was in upper primary. You know, Miss McCullough, you were really the only friend I had until you got the other kids to try to see I had a few good points."

QUESTIONS ON IMPLICATIONS OF DEMOCRATIC LIVING FOR THE INDIVIDUAL CHILD

1. What are some of the responsibilities of the individual child in a democratic classroom?

2. Discuss the difference in responsibilities to be assumed by children of varying abilities within your group. Be concrete.

3. What knowledge of children must you have in order to guide them toward self-directed, cooperative behavior? Illustrate.

4. How does participation in a democratic classroom develop resourcefulness: a. in the child; b. in the teacher?

5. How can children be taught to abide by the decisions of the majority and yet respect the rights of the minority? Give examples from your own experience.

6. What is expected of children by various adults of your acquaintance? Discuss and illustrate.

7. Recall your own childhood and discuss the various types of control to which you were subjected in different situations. Discuss the control exercised by your teachers whom you recall and cite examples to illustrate your points.

8. How will you teach your children to respect law and authority and yet establish the policy that each child is responsible for his own actions?

9. What is the function of retributive punishment in the democratic classroom? Illustrate with examples drawn from your own experience.

II. DEMOCRATIC GROUP ACTION

Freedom of Speech

Socially acceptable adults know when they can speak freely, and in most situations they wait until they have the proper opportunity. Children who are training for adult citizenship also need this experience. The privilege of freedom of speech carries with it certain responsibilities. This is particularly true of children in the classroom. The important things for them to learn are to think before they speak, to speak to the point, and to avoid interrupting others. These are difficult learnings, but under artistic and diplomatic guidance, even young children can master them.

From the beginning, hand raising is discouraged by the democratic teacher, as is illustrated in the following positive remarks:

"Think first, then talk."

"It is better to keep your hands down. You can show by your face that you know."

"Listen around you to see when it is your turn to talk."

"When someone else is talking, listen to him. Talk only when he is through."

The only way to be sure that everyone in the group is thinking is to insist on individual answers. Questioning showed that a number of children who had been answering in chorus with others had not heard what one child had been saying. "What shall we do about this?" the teacher asked. This time there was no answer. So the teacher led on thus: "Edward, when you have something to say, and someone else is talking, what do you do?"

> "I wait," he said, and Sue remarked spontaneously, "All the children should wait until it's their turn."
>
> Bill added, "You rest your lips when someone else has a turn."

In every class there seems to be at least one child who tends to monopolize the conversation. This child must see that the fair thing to do is to allow everyone to have an opportunity to speak. On one of the many occasions when this fact was demonstrated to Stella, a prize monopolizer, the teacher asked, "How many friends do we have in the group, Stella?"

After Stella had counted the children, the teacher gave the master stroke, "Your friends like to talk, too. And do you know! Meredith hasn't had even one turn!"

Every individual should learn to look directly into the face of the person he is addressing. He can thus command the individual's attention.

In Miss Thomas' room there had been considerable discussion of giving alert attention to the person who is addressed. The children gave many suggestions as to the best way to abstain from interrupting. Wayne finally summarized the discussion beautifully when he said, "I just ask myself, 'Is your name Harry? No. Is your name George? No. Then keep still until someone says 'Wayne.'"

Keeping still when he has something to say is one of the most difficult problems in self-control for a child to master. On the other hand, listening when someone else is speaking requires almost equal powers of self-mastery. This is influenced by the fact that, although it is difficult for him to do so, the child *can* learn to concentrate his attention upon a concrete presentation of the problem at hand, and by using self-control, avoid disturbing others by his actions or voice. Positive suggestions such as the following help to focus group thinking:

"Bobby, we need you because you have such good ideas."

"Joe, remember how polite your friends were when you were telling us about your baby rabbits?"

"Everyone is quiet because that helps Bennie to think."

"Tell Roberta again, Lucy. Her ears are listening now."

"Look at your friends and see what they are doing."

"Why isn't this the time to play with our friends?"

If the attention of the entire group seems to be wandering, your problem is how to relax the children and focus their attention and thinking. This requires a calm teacher and a low, confident tone of voice. It sometimes helps to ask the children to cup their palms over their closed eyes and visualize something definitely related to the discussion. The "Now-let's-talk-this-over" technique helps to start the group thinking profitably again.

At other times when the children are overstimulated, it takes a well-told story, one that is almost whispered, to get attention again.

Physical exertion is a basic need of children. You cannot expect children to remain passive and to listen attentively unless you provide frequent opportunities for large muscle activity. Varying the active and passive in a group discussion is a necessary procedure in cultivating the ability to listen cooperatively.

Learning to Vote

Democracy comes to life for the child when he is given the privilege of voting on issues that arise in the classroom. This is particularly true for the child who in his home has had perhaps not only one, but several "bosses," or who has experienced autocratic authority both at home and at school.

Children in the early primary will need to be taught how to make their preferences known, but a child old enough to be in school is old enough to express a preference by vote when given opportunity.

Exceedingly great care is necessary to make sure the younger children really understand the meaning and purpose of voting. The following illustrations emphasize this point. A beginning primary group went for a walk around the neighborhood to look at the abundance of flowering trees.

When Arthur was telling his mother about it later, he said enthusiastically, "We saw lots of trees this morning! One was a jacaranda and it was covered with beau-ti-ful lavender-blue flowers!"

His mother asked him how they knew what kind of tree it was. Arthur answered, "Miss Roberts knew it was a jacaranda tree and we talked all about it. Then we saw a magnolia and it had big white blossoms on it and it smelled sweet."

"How did you recognize this tree?" asked his mother.

"Oh, Howard knew that tree because it was in front of his house."

"We saw an acacia tree, too, with yellow blossoms, only the blossoms were just about gone from it. Miss Roberts knew that tree, too," explained Arthur.

The next day Arthur was again telling his mother about school. "When Bert and Bob and I were walking home we saw another flowering tree. It is a eucalyptus tree."

"How did you identify this tree?" his mother asked.

"We weren't sure. Bert and I thought it was a eucalyptus and Bob said it was a bottle tree, but we took a vote on it and Bert and I won. So it's a eucalyptus tree."

It was apparent that Arthur's faith in democratic voting surpassed his knowledge of scientific classification.

The next day Miss Roberts received a friendly note from Arthur's mother describing the conversation.

The children took another walk and observed the bark and the leaves as well as the blossoms on the trees.

"I found out something today, Mom," said Arthur. "You know about that voting we did. There are some things you can decide by voting and some things that just *are* a certain way, and voting won't change them. It's a funny thing about trees. If you find out what's alike about them, and what's different, you can be sure what they are, but you really have to know your trees first."

One lower primary group had early in the year converted a crate into a barn for the farm they were constructing. Some wanted to paint it red and others green. They were arguing among themselves. To the surprise of the teacher, who thought they were not old enough to understand the intricacies of democratic government, one child said, "Let's take a vote on it." The children suggested each would stand to vote, but the teacher observed that some children voted each time, for both red and green. She explained that each was to vote once, but some of the children said they changed their minds during the voting, so they voted for both colors. Others said they didn't care, so they didn't vote. This led to a discussion of why people vote. The children decided that when anyone voted twice or not at all, they were letting others choose for them. They agreed it would be better to vote for one color or the other rather than to let someone else decide for them.

A Democratic Program of Safety

The child's observance of safety measures depends in large part upon his attitude toward them, and this, in turn, reflects the type of guidance he has received.

In a certain school the teachers had made a concerted effort to put a safety program into effect, but there continued to be many accidents; so many, in fact, that the Parent-Teacher Association made official inquiry. A joint meeting was arranged for parents and teachers to see what could be done to reduce accidents. Some teachers felt that the program might be a success if the children could be brought into the planning rather than for the safety rules to be imposed upon them. It was decided to try the proposal!

The children were called together to talk over the situation and to suggest safety rules. A student council was set up in each of the rooms. A student court, made up of two representatives from each council was also formed. The chief responsibility of the court was to suggest what might be done in case of infringement of the rules. Of course the program was not entirely turned over to the children. A teacher guide was always present to give counsel as needed.

In a very short time the changed approach reflected more effective safety practices. The children took great pride in their safety program.

Some of the problems the children formulated in the council meetings were presented in charts. For example one day a chart read:

We need to discuss:
>   how to take care of our toys
>   bumping each other on the rings
>   climbing on the bars

and on another day:

> We need to discuss:
>> playing tag in a fair way
>> so that our clothes are not torn

With experience came more skill in expressing problems in a constructive way. "We can just as easily say what to do about it as to say what we need to discuss," was a suggestion that came from the children. That day the chart read:

> How to Be Safe in the Corridors:
> Walk carefully when carrying milk.
>
> Keep away from room doors
> (Someone might open a door and
> strike one of us when carrying
> milk or a vase or paint.)
>
> Always walk in the corridors.

Several days later came the following:

> What to Remember About the Magnifying Glass:
> Use the magnifying glass carefully.
>
> Keep it away from the direct rays
> of the sun or it will burn.

The children developed their own rules concerning running on the walks, in the halls, or in the rooms, playing on the slides and where to stand when waiting for their turn on the swing.

Their program not only cut down the number of accidents; it was a start toward making better citizens. Through voting and making their own rules, and through governing themselves with teacher counsel, they were forming useful patterns of democratic living that would carry over into adult life. They were learning how the place where they lived, worked, and played could become a better place for all because they assumed the responsibility of making it a safe place to be.

QUESTIONS ON DEMOCRATIC GROUP ACTION

1. Discuss the privileges and obligations of freedom of speech in the classroom. How can you prepare your children for group discussion?

2. What are the pros and cons of hand raising? How can children in the classroom learn to speak in a group without raising hands? Discuss the value of this.

3. Discuss ways you can make sure the children understand the significance of voting in a democracy. Cite examples.

4. What are your responsibilities toward children in a classroom where each child is expected to exercise self-control? Discuss such matters as a. interest and attention span; b. alternating of active and passive; c. making discussions concrete; d. following through on requests; e. adapting assignments to individual differences in ability; f. recognizing diverse home backgrounds.

5. What does democratic group action demand of a child in your classroom?

6. What types of situations are the responsibility of the group to decide?

7. What types of problems are for the individual to decide? Why?

III. INDIVIDUAL DIFFERENCES IN A DEMOCRACY

Individual Viewpoints, Interests, and Needs

In a democratic group, the individual finds opportunity to express his viewpoints and desires in many ways. He can also develop interests which may vary from those of the other group members. Ann, age eight, expressed this beautifully in a chart she herself made toward the end of the school year when this topic was under discussion in Miss Holman's middle primary group:

Being Different

I'm glad
we're all different
and do not have
the same names.
I am different
from everyone in the class.
I can do different skills
and projects.
I'll always be different.

Ann

The school frequently provides opportunity for the development of these special interests, which is one of the virtues and privileges of a true democracy. How this is to be done is a question for each teacher to work out according to the needs of her group.

Beyond the usual differences in opinion, tastes, aptitudes, and interests will be the unique needs of children who stand out because of circumstances beyond their control. These needs may arise from differences in economic, social, or racial status, or from unusual physical, mental, or emotional conditions.

A child may have an extremely low mentality or a highly superior intellect or an unusual aptitude in a given direction that sets him apart from the group. There may also be the child from another locality, or one who has not had a fair chance at home and whose behavior is unacceptable to the group. Whatever the difference, it is your responsibility to do everything possible to help these individuals adjust and be accepted by the group.

In teaching the younger children to accept differences in individuals, your task will be less difficult. Often answering a few questions will satisfy their curiosity, and thereafter they will accept people as they are, which is a delightful characteristic of early childhood. However, if the children do feel disturbed over a child who is different, it is much better to seek the group's cooperation in his behalf at a time when he is not present.

The Newcomer

Any child who moves from one environment to another, even to a new neighborhood in the same city, may have a feeling of loneliness and of being an outsider when he enters the new school. For a time, at least, he is "different." In the past, and occasionally today, a boy finds entrance to a new school an occasion for testing his ability to hold his own in a fight. He has to prove himself before he is accepted. In earlier times, the luckless one who was less skilled in fistfighting was often the subject of bullying and petty persecutions throughout the year, unless he was continually under the teacher's eye.

In a democratic classroom the child is made to feel that he is welcome in the group and that he has something of interest to impart to his classmates.

Sometimes a special committee visits with the new pupil and tries to make him feel at home. They find out where he lives; how far his old school is from the new; whether he came to his new home by car, bus, train, or airplane; how many brothers and sisters he has; and other personal data of interest he may care to share with the group.

After this preliminary "interview," the committee introduces him to the other children in the room, who give him a hearty welcome. One child might give him a copy of the school song, another an issue of the school newspaper, still another a guest lunch ticket for the first day.

The special committee has the pleasant duty of taking the new pupil for a tour of the building. They point out the lavatories, the auditorium, the location of the different rooms; they explain about buses and bus tickets, about lunch tickets, about the student council. He is invited to share in their games.

In an older group, one of the students had a small camera and was named the room photographer. He took a picture of each new child, and as soon as the picture was developed he put a pin on the map where the child had formerly lived, tied a string to the pin and extended it to the edge of the map where he attached the new child's picture. Needless to say, within a short time the newcomer no longer felt himself to be "different."

Sometimes children who have lived in another country enter school. In this case, there will be differences in clothing, language, customs, or economic status. A woman who became one of California's great educators used to tell how she and her brothers and sisters came to this country from Czechoslovakia. They were happy to be in America and anxious to accept the ways and customs of their adopted country, but everything was so different! They didn't know the traditions and customs here, and she and her sisters suffered agony because their dresses were ankle length and other little girls' dresses were short; they had long braids tied with string, and others had bobbed hair with huge bows; they couldn't form the sounds of the new language properly, even when they knew the meaning of the words. Had it not been for their eager desire to learn, school for them would have been a nightmare.

Children can be helped in such a situation if the teacher stresses the positive aspects, so that the new children share the traditions and customs of their native land with the group, and the American born children share theirs with those of foreign birth. The newcomers will be able to talk about their games if their language handicap is not too great, or tell the group about how they celebrate Christmas or other holidays. Perhaps they will describe the special foods such as goulash or pizza or tamales which their mother makes. Often non-English-speaking children are particularly gifted in art and pen craft, or in music. Special attention and appreciation on your part is warranted in such cases, so that the group, also, may catch this spirit of friendliness and acceptance. You will find there are many opportunities to discuss what really makes a good American.

Much is being done by television and travel to bring about an exchange of ideas between peoples of varying cultural and geographic backgrounds. Newcomers in the classroom can bring firsthand acquaintance and lifelong understanding.

Economic Differences

Frequently there are children whose parents receive aid from governmental agencies. This constitutes a delicate problem. If the child is issued "free lunch" or "free milk" tickets, the matter should be handled so inconspicuously that other children are not aware of the situation. Children whose parents receive such aid are sometimes deeply sensitive about it. In the hands of an artist teacher they will maintain their sense of personal worth, which is most essential to their growth and development.

Sometimes children come to school poorly clad. Many school systems have a "Clothes Closet," often operated by the Parent-Teacher Association, where the parents of children who are in need of clothing may supply their children's needs. Those who are to benefit from this generosity are often cleared by the welfare agency of the school. In many instances groups of mothers repair the surplus clothing and see that it is in condition for distribution. Sometimes the mothers who are to be recipients of aid are eager to assist in repairing the clothing, feeling that in this way they can make return.

Whenever a "Clothes Closet" is established, it is a good policy to make sure that clothing collected from one area is redistributed in some other locality. A child might feel himself disgraced before his associates should another unthinkingly remark, "That used to be my dress you are wearing. My mother sent it to the Clothes Closet."

Sometimes children come to school with body and clothing in a sad state of uncleanliness. When such conditions exist, the school that has bathing facilities available to younger as well as older children is indeed fortunate. You, as a teacher, can magnify personal cleanliness, and when cleanliness is stressed at school, it may finally carry back to the home.

Other Handicaps

Children who have had counseling and guidance may be sympathetic and thoughtful in their relationships with those who have a mental or physical handicap.

When a child is of unusually small stature in comparison to his group, the others are inclined to mother him and be tender with him. However, it is important that neither children nor adults over-indulge any child who is "different" by showing him too much consideration, just as a mother must guard against spoiling a handicapped child. In no case should the group be so considerate that the "different" individual comes to think the world owes him special treatment. Often there is something *he* can do which is a contribution to the others.

Acknowledging individual differences, and recognizing the place of each member of the group, no matter what his unique characteristics may be, is something which only democratic participation in a group can bring to the individual.

> Willa was born with an unjointed stub arm just elbow length, to which were attached two short little fingers. At first the mother and father bemoaned the tragedy that made their child so different from others. There was a relative in the family who had only one arm, and always her carefully pinned back empty sleeve was mute evidence of her handicap and her limitations. But Willa's parents were able to realize that for their daughter this need not be the case. Instead of pity they gave her courage.

Developing a Constructive Philosophy

> Because her parents, her teachers, and her playmates helped her accept her deformed arm as one she could learn to get along with and use, Willa was able in later years to undertake whatever a person with two normal arms could do. She tackled anything and worked until she learned how to make the stub serve her in whatever way she wanted to use it. She did not even consider her arm a handicap. She took part in team sports, and learned to play every musical instrument competently except the piano and organ. These she played with one hand.
>
> Willa attributed much of her success to the way she was accepted by the school groups to which she belonged during the formative years of her life, and to the teachers who guided these groups. Her own attitude and courage, in turn, were largely responsible for her acceptance in a true, democratic spirit, and for the admiration and love she evoked wherever she went. By the time Willa reached college she had developed a positive and constructive philosophy toward the problems faced by a child with a physical handicap. Because of this, she was able to help many people better understand and assist such a child in making a successful adjustment to life.

Individual Worth

Belonging to a democratic school group helps the individual child to realize his own worth. It should also help him to adjust in a society in which his color or race may sometimes be discriminated against. The child must come to know this, at the same time recognizing his own value as a person and citizen, and the contribution he can make as an accepted member of the democratic community. By watching your children at their work and play you may become aware of opportunities to help them recognize the contributions of each group member.

QUESTIONS ON INDIVIDUAL DIFFERENCES IN A DEMOCRACY

1. Discuss the viewpoint that it is your responsibility as a democratic teacher to do everything within your power to help individuals to be accepted by the group. How can you do this and yet respect: a. the individuality of the children and b. the family preferences and traditions?

2. What adjustments are you justified in expecting individual children to make in order to function as members of your classroom group? Give examples.

3. How can you gain the cooperation of a class group in behalf of a child who is different? Discuss. Why is it sometimes best to do this at a time when he is not present? Illustrate.

4. If you believe in the rule of the majority, why should you concern yourself with the few children who deviate from the average in your group? Discuss the implication of the term "average" in this connection.

5. How could these children benefit from having enrolled in your classroom: a. a newcomer; b. a child with a physical handicap (specify what) ; c. a child whose mentality is below the others; d. a child endowed with a special talent or intellectual gift; e. a child from a different economic bracket; f. a child with some other difference beyond his control.

6. In each instance in question No. 5, what measures would you suggest be followed for the good of the other children?

7. What would you do to help each child concerned to develop a constructive philosophy?

IV. PATRIOTIC ASPECTS OF DEMOCRACY FOR THE YOUNG CHILD

The Flag as a Symbol of Patriotism

Even young children are capable of appreciating their country and its democratic form of government.

When Tina was five years and eleven months old, she said,

"I know why the children all stop walking when they 'pledge' the flag. It's to show respect to the flag because it means our country. And if you move around it would bother somebody else."

A visitor in a group of six- and seven-year-old children was told by one of them:

"We know how to say our *Pledge of Allegiance* just the way our mothers and fathers do. We have our own songs, too, that help us understand what it means to 'pledge allegiance' to our country and to our flag."

The children sang for the visitor:

Our Flag Song

Originated by
Upper Primary Group

Certainly children should learn to pledge allegiance to the flag, but the formality of repeating it parrot-like must never be allowed to become merely routine.

An upper primary teacher who hoped to teach patriotism through a daily salute to the flag made an informal study to determine how many children in her group really understood the *Pledge of Allegiance*. At the beginning of the year only ten percent had any conception of what they were saying, and although emphasis was placed on word meaning throughout the year, at the end there were still a number who had not been able to grasp the significance of the *Pledge*. This was a group of children with a range in intelligence quotients from eighty to one hundred.

On occasion the *Pledge*, said with meaning, has a real message to bring, but for the child who pledged "allegiance to the United States and to the Republic of Richard Sands," the salute was nothing more than mumbo jumbo. The end goal is to have the child love his country and live so as to honor it. The flag symbolizes this goal. "The Star-Spangled Banner" and the *Pledge of Allegiance* give homage to the flag. A song or poem which tells in the children's own words what the flag means to them may be a stepping stone toward developing an appreciation of their country and its blessings. In this respect their own song may have more meaning to the young child than the daily exercise of pledging allegiance or singing the national anthem.

Your group will sing with understanding a song which they help create, for example:

1 | 3 3 4 5
Our | flag says to you,

5 | 6 5 3
"Be | true, be true

1 2 | 3 3 3 2 | 1   -- ||
To our | flag and coun try, | too."

A song such as the following may make democracy more meaningful to
children of seven and eight or older:

THE LAND WE LOVE

A - mer-i-ca, A - mer-i-ca, The land we love, so fair!

A - mer-i-ca, A - mer-i-ca, With free-dom ev'-ry-where.

We can be free,   As long as we re - mem-ber,

Lib - er-ty with - in the law, Our flag, our land, our home!

The type of patriotic activities which call for a certain maturity before
they can be comprehended should not be required of young children as
a regular routine, but be reserved for special occasions so that when the
children do take part in them they can do so with understanding.

Democracy in Daily Activities

Those who pledge allegiance to flag and country must at the same time
learn what kind of living true allegiance entails. Even young children,
as they grow more aware of their own rights and those of others, begin to
realize that even though people think and act in many different ways,
they are still able to live together in mutual liking and respect. There are

many things you can do day by day in the early childhood years to enrich children's backgrounds for sincere citizenship and loyalty. You can call their attention to how much each person enjoys belonging to a group where he may do as he likes as long as he respects the privileges of others. Finding ways to carry this out in daily activities captures the child's interest and becomes a way of looking at life. Each may pursue a different activity, yet all are friends. For example, in choosing equipment to work with, John decides to use the easel, Mary Lou the autoharp, and Wayne the magnet; if someone else wants these things, they talk it over together and decide who shall use what, and when. Then each has his turn, according to the agreement. In this way, each is learning to regard his friends' and neighbors' rights, while safeguarding his own.

This is one way of clarifying individual rights and responsibilities in a democracy, at the child's level of comprehension.

Rights and Obligations in Using Public Property

A sense of belonging is bound up in the child's growing concept of citizenship. There are numerous ways you can make this real for him in his present life rather than in some distant future.

A group of primary children lived in an area where wild flowers were abundant. While admiring and discussing the carpets of gold and purple the question of public property came up. "The flowers belong to the public," explained Mr. James, their teacher. "That means they belong to all the people—you and me and your neighbors—everyone."

The following weekend, Wayne, one of the boys from that group, went with his father and his younger brother Jack, for a picnic in the mountains. They found a public camp ground and roasted hot dogs in the outdoor stove. After they had eaten, the boys insisted they would clean up while the father rested. He settled back in the camp chair with his book, but his thoughts were diverted by the boys' chatter. He heard Wayne say to the younger boy, "No, no, Jack. Don't throw those food scraps in the stream. Put them in the garbage can over there."

"Why not put stuff in the stream?" asked Jack.

"Because," said Wayne, "this camp belongs to the public and we are the public. We want to keep the stream clear so we can all enjoy it."

On the way home from the area Jack and Wayne noticed that a group of careless picnickers had left papers strewn on the ground. The boys were concerned about the apparent lack of interest.

The following Monday, Wayne gave an account of his excursion with his family. Other children verified his observation of apparent unconcern on the part of the public. Mr. James was quick to capitalize on the interest of the group. The following chart was the result:

Our Public Property

Our area has many
beautiful spots.
Many of these belong
to the public.
We are part
of the public.
So are you.
Help us keep
our public property lovely
so we can all
enjoy it.

This attitude of personal interest in helping to care for public property must spring from a recognition of the value of commercial as well as natural resources. As children learn to respect school property, you may also help them gain a concept of how community needs are supplied through tax money that father and mother and other people pay.

Fundamental Concepts

In a broader sense, children can begin to understand how the parks, the libraries, the post office, and the fire departments are maintained for the enjoyment, the convenience, and the safety of everyone who wishes to use them.

Classroom talks by the postman, the policeman, the fireman, and others will do much to impress upon children the importance and the dignity of the services they represent. Community workers might come to the schools dressed in the uniform of their occupations.

In such ways you are helping the children become sensitive to some of the factors that go to make up a happy neighborhood, a desirable community, and a united nation. Little by little the groundwork is being laid for a lasting love of country. Gradually you can develop in your children an appreciation of public facilities and the responsibilities that go along with these privileges. In this way fundamental concepts of citizenship, liberty, and public responsibility can be established. The flag may come to symbolize this and much more for the child as he grows older. Gradually children develop a readiness to participate in the *Pledge of Allegiance* with the understanding born of experience.

Historical Aspects of Democracy for Older Children

Experiences and discussion relating to an appreciation of democracy should be progressively more challenging as children grow and their thinking matures.

Dramatization offers wonderful possibilities for making democracy live for the older child. For example, intermediate boys and girls will enjoy learning how the old-time schools were conducted. Grandparents may relate stories, and old books furnish much information about the schools of another day. Both ideas are full of dramatic possibilities. The rote recitation, the dunce stool, the floggings for the slightest misdemeanor, the crime of drawing a picture on one's slate—all help older children of the present day to appreciate their own democratic classrooms.

The word *tyranny* creeps into the vocabulary of today, but many children have little idea of its meaning. Here, again, dramatization helps to make their forefathers' struggles to overcome the cruelties and injustices of bad government more real. When children reach an age where history is meaningful, they might write a simple historical play somewhat like the following: the first scene might depict a family's concern about food, because it must all go to the Crown for payment of taxes. The second scene might show the arrival of the bailiff, who takes both the family's wheat crop and the father, who must go to prison for debts. The third scene might present an announcement that laws have been made that will no longer permit these bad practices. Such a play would not only impress upon children the evils of poor government, but would help them realize that good government is achieved by working for it, and by constant watchfulness. History teems with incidents that can be dramatized to emphasize these truths.

Children beyond the early years may also gain a concept of service and devotion to their country through hearing and reading the stories of men like Washington, Hamilton, Franklin, Jefferson, and Lincoln, as well as of the patriots of other lands.

Proper stress on an appreciation of good government and the part each citizen must play in its realization is of vital importance in our chaotic times. Liberty, like health, is to be prized and guarded, and those who have always known liberty may fail to realize its priceless blessing until it is lost. The teacher has a major responsibility to perform in helping children to realize that some day they will be the ones to "carry on"; you, the teacher, must fit them for the task by making each day in the school-room an experience in democratic living.

QUESTIONS ON PATRIOTIC ASPECTS OF DEMOCRACY FOR THE YOUNG CHILD

1. Suggest what you would do to help your children develop a wholesome respect for the flag.

2. How can you make the meaning of the flag concrete for your children? Give examples.

3. How would you explain patriotism to a child in terms of his everyday experiences? Illustrate.

4. What is the value of clarifying individual rights and responsibilities in a democracy, at the child's level of comprehension? How would you make this understandable to him? Suggest concrete examples from daily experiences of the children.

5. What can you do as a teacher to help your children develop a sense of civic responsibility? With what aspects of this responsibility can a child be concerned? Give classroom examples.

SELECTED REFERENCES

Association for Supervision and Curriculum Development, GROUP PROCESSES IN SUPERVISION, Washington, D.C.: National Education Association, 1948, Chapters I and II.

Beasley, Christine, DEMOCRACY IN THE HOME, N. Y.: Association Press, 1954.

Bode, Boyd H., DEMOCRACY AS A WAY OF LIFE, N. Y.: The Macmillan Company, 1959.

Byers, Loretta, and Elizabeth Irish, SUCCESS IN STUDENT TEACHING, Boston: D. C. Heath, 1961.

Dewey, John, DEMOCRACY AND EDUCATION, N. Y.: The Macmillan Company, 1916.

Horne, Herman R., THE DEMOCRATIC PHILOSOPHY OF EDUCATION, N. Y.: The Macmillan Company, 1932.

Hullfish, H. Gordon, EDUCATIONAL FREEDOM IN AN AGE OF ANXIETY, Chapter II, N. Y.: Harper Brothers, 1953.

Laski, Harold, THE AMERICAN DEMOCRACY, N. Y.: The Viking Press, Inc., 1948.

Lindberg, Lucile, THE DEMOCRATIC CLASSROOM: A GUIDE FOR TEACHERS, N. Y.: Bureau of Publications, Teachers College, Columbia University, 1955.

Lindsay, A. B., THE ESSENTIALS OF DEMOCRACY, N. Y.: Oxford University Press, 1935.

McKown, Harry C., THE STUDENT COUNCIL, N. Y.: McGraw-Hill, 1949.

Miel, Alice, and others, COOPERATIVE PROCEDURES IN LEARNING, N. Y.: Bureau of Publications, Teachers College, Columbia University, 1949.

Mursell, James L., PRINCIPLES OF DEMOCRATIC EDUCATION, N. Y.: W. W. Norton & Company, Inc., 1955.

Redl, Fritz and David Wineman, CONTROLS FROM WITHIN, Glencoe, Illinois: The Free Press, 1952.

Rees, Elinor, OUR FLAG, Chicago, Ill.: Melmont Publishers, Inc., 1960.

Ritholz, S., CHILDREN'S BEHAVIOR, N. Y.: Bookman Associates, 1959.

Sheviakov, G. V., and Fritz Redl, DISCIPLINE FOR TODAY'S CHILDREN AND YOUTH, Washington, D.C.: Association for Supervision and Curriculum Development, 1956.

Weston, Grace, and associates, DEMOCRATIC CITIZENSHIP AND DEVELOPMENT OF CHILDREN, Detroit, Michigan: Detroit Public Schools, 1949.

THE GOALS OF

Part Two

CHILDHOOD EDUCATION

THE SIX GOALS: I. WHOLESOME ATTITUDES

The curriculum from the earliest years onward must be built in terms of what is known about the children it is to benefit. Important as are the buildings, equipment, and materials at hand, the most influential factor in the elementary school is the teacher's ability to guide children toward the attainment of certain constructive goals. These goals have been variously classified by educators, but in the final analysis resolve themselves into the following:

1. Wholesome Attitudes
2. Automatic Behavior Patterns
3. Deep Appreciations
4. Creative Expression
5. Independent Thinking and Problem Solving
6. Widening Understanding, Knowledge, and Skills

A child's progress toward any one of these goals contributes to the realization of each of the others. Academic learning, in its true perspective, is one of the important outcomes of these goals rather than a goal in itself. When the maximum development of the individual is the major emphasis of the school, each child is helped toward satisfactory relationships with people and the world around him. Achievement in academic subjects follows as a vital part of these relationships.

Satisfactory human relationships are basic to successful living in the world today. Wholesome attitudes toward people, toward things, toward situations, and toward activities are the foundation of democratic living. Children demonstrate by their attitudes the impact of any given situation upon them. Do they go about things eagerly or reluctantly? What are their attitudes toward each other, toward you, their teacher, toward their room and school, toward each activity or study? Are they characteristically cooperative or antagonistic? The honest answers to these questions reveal much.

Facing a Common Threat

The underlying attitude of an entire group may be affected by an external circumstance which threatens to take away something of special value. This can be met with a counter interest which challenges the children's enthusiasm and stimulates them to express their reactions constructively.

Miss Holman's middle primary group at Hope School loved the "Hollow," a natural depression that adjoined their playground. It was shady and cool on hot days and a perfect spot for outdoor work and play.

Hope School enjoyed an ideally small enrollment until expansion of the city made the district a desirable residential area. Then came the problems of enlarged enrollments and the need for more buildings.

One day the children were greeted by the noise of heavy machines at work, and to their horror saw their beloved Hollow being desecrated. Disconsolate, Miss Holman and her children watched their pepper and eucalyptus trees being felled. Excavating and filling in were in progress, and their Hollow was no more.

As the days passed, the noise, dirt and confusion grew more intolerable. The children became almost belligerent in their revolt, and even their clever, creative Miss Holman found it difficult to placate them.

At the most crucial point Peter saved the situation by awakening a passive interest in his painting of the mighty machines at work. When Marshall said, "Let's make a chart to go with Peter's picture," everyone agreed.

Mighty Machines at Work

Urnk! Urnk!
Push! mighty machines.
You look like monsters
taking giant bites
out of the earth.
Pull, pull, powerful scraper.
Fill your stomach
like an enormous elephant.

The children's interest in the machines and their work brought a whole new point of view. Many creative rhythms, songs, stories and even poems followed and were recorded in chart form. This developing interest brought back the old *esprit de corps* of the group. By finding something constructive and interesting to observe day by day, the thing that had seemed so devastating at first became a source of inspiration.

Their favorite chart during these days of adjustment reflected their attitudes before and after "the invasion" of what they considered to be their own domain:

Our Sad Hollow

The city is coming
day by day.
Our hollow
used to be so gay.
Now the trees
are coming down.
Crish! Crash!
All around.
It makes us sad
to see them go.
But there is a reason
we all know.
Our school is growing
day by day.
It will be better
in every way.

Recognizing Feelings

If you are sensitive to a child's feelings about himself and others, and wish to guide him effectively in a given situation, you will let him know you recognize how he feels but you will always try to help him build positive attitudes. The child who does not like his work, or who for some other reason is unhappy, should feel free to discuss his reactions with you.

Perhaps a young child is crying over a hurt knee. You might say, "Of course it hurt when you fell down and skinned your knee, Joan. We'll wash it off and put some disinfectant on it. It really won't make your knee better to cry, but if you think it helps you, it will be all right to cry for a little while. If you are brave, though, you can stand the hurt, and you won't need to cry at all." This attitude brings a response of cooperation from the child as he realizes you recognize what he is going through. He is less inclined to display his feelings unduly when he knows they are understood.

Even a young child can be helped to recognize that the way he feels, though perhaps not always acceptable, is a perfectly natural reaction to whatever he faces. Moreover, he may learn how to release his feelings in a way that *is* acceptable. Seeing the situation in its true perspective sometimes requires more judgment than he has yet acquired, but it is a goal toward which he may grow. He can always try first to understand things as they really are; next, develop a more wholesome attitude toward his immediate problem; and finally, learn to act in a desirable way about it. Failure in any one of the above steps can dissipate whatever chance of success the child might have in overcoming a poor attitude which springs from conditions that are difficult for him to meet.

Five-year-old Mike cried for nearly half an hour the first day he was left at school. When his beloved Aunt June called for him, his teacher mentioned the crying to her, but nothing was said to Mike at that time.

As they drove home together, Mike told Aunt June what he did at school.

"We sang some songs. I worked with clay, and I cried."

Aunt June said, "You must have been missing your mother. Did it make you feel better to cry?"

Mike said, "Yes."

The next day Mike cried again when left behind.

As he and his aunt drove home together, Aunt June said, "What did you do at school today, Mike?"

Mike said, "We worked with blocks and painted. And I cried again, too."

Aunt June said in a matter of fact tone, "You must have been missing your mother again today."

Mike nodded.

His aunt asked, "Did it make you feel better to cry?"

"Yes."

"Maybe some day you won't even need to cry at all," Aunt June suggested. "There are so many other things you can do to make you feel better."

Mike and Aunt June talked over some of the other things and Mike said, "I think I'll cry just a little teeny bit, but not so long tomorrow."

The next day and in the days ahead Mike was able to meet his school world without the insecurity which caused his tears. By frankly facing his feelings he had been helped to overcome them.

Uncovering Hidden Roots

Sometimes attitudes that are not relieved will be pushed into the background where, instead of being dissipated, they remain long after the situation which caused them has ceased to exist. This is one reason why it is urgent that the child learn how to face his own feelings and find some acceptable means of releasing them, redirecting them, or otherwise controlling them so that they do not lead to undesirable attitudes that persist.

Seven-year-old Eddie would recoil every time he heard a dog bark, even when the animal was on a leash or behind a fence. His teacher learned from Eddie's mother that when he was twenty months old he had been bitten by a dog. Although he did not remember the incident it probably accounted for his terror of barking dogs.

The teacher and Eddie's mother planned to give the child a very young pup as a means of helping him acquire a more wholesome attitude toward dogs.

Eddie brought his new pet to school to show the other children, and was pleased when the group made a reading chart about his pup.

Eddie still reacted unfavorably to other dogs that barked, until one day the children, under Miss V.'s guidance, began discussing the meaning of the sounds made by various animals. Eddie reported on what his dog was trying to say when he whined and barked. The child's old attitude disappeared following this experience, and he gradually came to trust dogs in general.

Some children are able to recognize their feelings and maintain emotional stability even when the odds seem against them.

Jackie's family was struggling financially. He was thinly clad, and one of his toes showed through a hole in his shoe. His teacher noticed the child shivering in spite of himself, but Jackie's smile was bright. One morning Miss A. told the children a story about a happy child. At its conclusion, one six-year-old said, "I think Jackie is the happiest one in our room."

Jackie said, "Maybe I don't always want to smile inside, but I just smile anyway."

Teachers must realize that not all children are able to resolve their difficulties with the equanimity Jackie exhibited. He undoubtedly found happiness in his acts of service to others and in his round of daily activities. Much of his attitude may have reflected a brave facing of realities by his family or by an influential member of it.

Exchanging One Attitude for Another

Young children who are intense in the expression of their loves, their hates, and their frustrations should not be censured for feeling as they do. It is well to help them face the fact that they may not always feel happy inside, but instead of taking their feelings out on another person, they can find acceptable ways to release these mean feelings when they exist. Resentments and attitudes of antagonism are very real, and must be faced and overcome by children, rather than denied because they are not acceptable. Individuals find their unique ways of relieving tensions legitimately, and the result is a much more wholesome attitude toward life in general, and toward situations and associates in particular.

Howard, though only five, took life very seriously. The teacher had mentioned this earlier to a visitor, who was nevertheless somewhat surprised by the reaction the child exhibited when the group was dismissed to go outside. The teacher said to the children, "If you have a happy smile today and feel all happy inside, then you are ready to go outdoors."

Every child went quickly out except this serious-faced boy who remained seated on the rug. The teacher said, "Howard, how do you feel today? Do you feel like going out and giving "Mr. Puncho" a good punching? If you have unhappy feelings you would like to get rid of, and you think it would help to do some punching, then you are ready to go outside, too."

Howard went into the yard, and in a few minutes the visitor saw him giving well directed blows to a large bag of sand suspended by a rope to the limb of a tree. When Howard was beyond hearing range, the teacher explained that this child had a feeling of resentment toward other children who attempted to be friendly toward him. He never quarreled with them, but would simply draw away and remain aloof and uncommunicative. When the punching bag was placed in the yard, Howard had been the first to discover it, and since then he made more use of it than any of the other children. These bouts with the bag seemed to be the one way he had found to relieve the pent-up feelings that he was unable to express even in negative ways.

In another group, a leather punching bag containing an air bladder was placed near the door. The children learned to go to it when they felt antagonistic. Burt was heard to remark often, "I think I'd better go give that bag a punch. Then I'll feel better."

The group discussed how they might exchange feelings they needed to get rid of for ones they wanted. "We throw away our unhappy feelings," as Ricki remarked, "and then happy ones come back again."

"Punching the bag is a way that can't hurt anyone else, and it helps us a lot," explained Russell.

The children discussed other things that helped them. "Clay is good, too," said Arthur.

"Yes, and easel painting."

"I like to get out and just run," said Dick.

"But you can't always do that," said Annie.

"Music helps me," said Elsie, "especially when I can move to it."

The group tried these various suggestions and decided they did not have to be cross to people just because they felt cross inside. "You can't always help feeling cross," said Esther, "but you can do something about it. You can get rid of your feelings some other way."

"Then the cross feeling is gone, and you haven't hurt anybody either," added Bruce.

Opportunities for Guidance

The real challenge in teaching comes in seeing the day-to-day growth within individual children, and in guiding them toward attitudes that may not at first be evident to the casual observer. Sometimes opportunities of this nature are overlooked.

One morning in a group of five- and six-year-olds Marcia had built a fireman's truck from blocks, and as she worked with it she was oblivious to everything around her. She was driving the truck and talking to herself. Suddenly, Danny came up and took one of the large blocks out from under the base of the truck, which left a big hole. Marcia protested, "Danny, you spoiled my truck, and I was on the way to a fire, and now we will have an accident. You hurry up and put that back or the building will burn down and everything will happen!"

Danny paid no attention.

Marcia got out of the truck, put her hands on her hips and said, "That beats all. Now, what am I going to do?" Then she said to the teacher, "Miss B., Danny took a piece out of my truck and I can't go on to the fire, and the whole town will burn down."

The teacher looked at Marcia but did nothing. Marcia finally stalked over to the home area and said in an undertone, "Danny won't give back the base of my truck, and Miss B. won't help me, so I guess I just won't be a fireman anymore, and the town can burn up."

There would have been an entirely different attitude on the part of both children if the teacher had entered in, had called Danny and Marcia over—not taking Marcia out of the role of fireman—and said, "That isn't fair, Danny. You will have to hurry and repair the truck as fast as you can. This fireman has to get to the fire at once."

Meeting a Child's Basic Need

Children learn to cooperate and readily acquire wholesome attitudes if given sufficient opportunity. The teacher must be willing to go more than halfway to be fair and just. Adverse reactions are often caused from a negative inference or experience. Your guidance may help remove the child's need to react in an undesirable way and may cause him to behave more cooperatively in the future. Your understanding of a child's basic need, and your ability to meet it, determines the type of guidance that will bring effective changes in his attitudes.

No one trusted Harold. He took many things that did not belong to him. His mother said when she registered him for school, "Don't leave anything around where Harold is. He will steal it."

Miss Kelly, his teacher, held to the philosophy that if you give a child the name he will play the game. In other words, this teacher of seven- and eight-year-olds believed that expecting cooperation and giving the child every opportunity to respond in an acceptable manner creates a desirable attitude.

Miss Kelly put her theory into practice in the case of Harold. She found an old purse with a broken clasp that would not stay shut and filled it with quarters, dimes and nickels. She said to Harold, "I have to go on an errand. I'll be gone part of the noon hour, and I would appreciate your taking care of my purse while I am away. You will notice it needs to be held together because the clasp is not tight. This is the money I have to buy my food with for the rest of the week. I can trust you, Harold, so I am leaving my money in your care."

When Miss Kelly came back in half an hour Harold was exhausted because he had held the purse so tightly against his chest. His teacher had trusted him and he had responded to that trust.

Attitudes Toward Property

Children observe whether or not their teacher is meticulously careful of other people's money and property. When a child brings lunch or milk money or other miscellaneous funds which are so often a part of the school program, it is exceedingly important that you be careful and consistent in its handling.

The teacher who leaves money around, whether it is her own or is entrusted to her by the children, is not only running the risk of losing it, but of giving the children an impression of carelessness in its handling.

An attitude of trust and confidence in the children is certainly to be commended, but carelessness in leaving money about, or in accounting and caring for funds is not to be mistaken for confidence. By this token, it is unwise for a teacher to leave a purse or other personal belongings out in the open. It presents a temptation to the children and may mean a losing battle for honesty. Naturally, you should not borrow or remove something from a child's locker or desk without his knowledge, and you should expect the children to respect the things on your desk or table in the same way.

This philosophy also applies to the care of any object that may be in your hands temporarily, whether it is in your possession because you felt called upon to remove it from someone who was causing a disturbance, or because it was voluntarily placed in your custody by some child.

> Occasionally a teacher may unwittingly encourage a child to take what is not his by being too enthusiastic about gifts or flowers brought to her by other children. Miss Blake, for example, was teaching in one of the lowest economic districts in her community. The children scarcely had enough clothes to keep warm, and many were undernourished. Yet every Monday morning Aaron brought her a beautiful bouquet of two dozen red carnations. Miss Blake was enthusiastic in her acceptance, never once giving a thought to the source of the contribution. One day her principal saw the flowers and said, "They are lovely, but where did Aaron get them?"
>
> Miss Blake questioned Aaron, who replied, "Off'n the graves"!
>
> It was then Miss Blake remembered that Aaron went through the cemetery on his daily route to school.

The Child's Word

You should always know the circumstances behind a child's statements before either doubting his word or questioning an unusual occurrence.

> Five-year-old Daniel and his mother followed his father from one military base to another. It was necessary for the mother to work and to find someone to care for her son. The father's last base before being shipped overseas was in Florida. Here the mother placed the boy with an elderly couple who lived near a swamp. Daniel spent many happy days with these friends whom he fondly called "Grandpa" and "Grandma." Grandpa sometimes went to the edge of the swamp to look for alligator eggs, and whenever he went he took Daniel with him. Daniel enjoyed digging in the soft mud, and found it a thrill to uncover the creamy white alligator eggs.
>
> When Daniel and his mother returned to their home in one of the northern states, the boy entered school for the first time. During the first week the teacher asked each child to tell what he liked to do best. Daniel said, "I like to hunt alligator eggs better than anything else."
>
> The teacher said, "Now, Daniel, we are telling true stories. We want you to tell what you really like to do."

Daniel insisted, "I really do like to hunt alligator eggs. I hunted them all summer."

The teacher was indignant. "Sit down, Daniel. We don't even want to hear from you if you can't be truthful."

Daniel went home heartbroken. "But I did love to hunt alligator eggs best of anything," he sobbed on his mother's shoulder.

The mother's visit to the teacher and an explanation of their sojourn in various parts of the country seemed not to please the teacher, who was cool in her response.

Could this experience have had something to do with the fact that in after years, Daniel had an attitude of disinterest in school?

The Positive Approach

Important as it is for you to be consistent in guidance measures and to follow through on requests, it is essential that the child know that you expect him to do the right thing and infer that he is doing it. For example, Johnny is always slow in getting to the group or going to work. Miss J. does not say, "We are waiting for Johnny." Instead, she says, "Johnny is almost ready," and Johnny responds by being ready.

The positive suggestion takes effect. In time, this attitude is caught by the children, as was evidenced when Gilbert was carrying a chair incorrectly and another child said in an attitude of friend to friend, "There's a better way to carry the chair, Gilbert. Carry it like this," and she demonstrated the proper way.

This is further exemplified in the viewpoints expressed by a group of children who had had much experience in the positive approach. The following chart was an outgrowth of one of their council meetings:

> 1. We are remembering
> to put papers in cans,
> and to wash our hands
> before lunch.
>   2. We need to think more about
> where to play
> where to climb
> staying off of fences
> kicking balls away from the fence.

Personal Resources

Another group had been thinking and talking about how people in a democracy work and share together.

Betty brought her kitten. Wayne brought his toy truck for the sand box. Sue brought her doll for the home center.

José was sad because he thought he had nothing to share. Miss Holman helped him think through his problem. He thought and thought.

Then he said, "Why, I've got *me!* I'll share *myself.*"

The first thing José decided to share with his friends at school was his smile. All day he wore a happy smile.

Next, he shared kind words, "please," "thank you," "you're welcome."

Third, José put his sharing into active service and did many things to help both teacher and children.

Finally, he and Miss Holman made a song about all this, and José sang it as a surprise to his delighted group of friends:

I'LL SHARE MYSELF

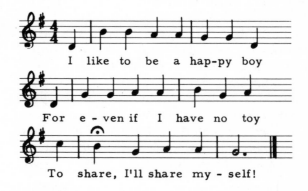

In another group which had also discussed sharing and working to-gether, two children were having trouble. One child had built a hospital of blocks. She wanted some people for her hospital. Another child did not wish to relinquish these accessory materials. Allen, who had just turned five, said, "I will give him some of *my* people. *I* remember 'good' to divide up the toys."

Allen's response, couched as it was in immature English, was as sig-nificant for him as José's creative song was for the more gifted child.

It is as important—perhaps even more important—to the child who has a meager endowment, that you accept his sincere effort as fully as you do that of the child more richly endowed. There may be a higher ratio between accomplishment and potential in the case of the slower child than in his more gifted classmate.

Patience

An attitude of patience, so important in teaching, is particularly needed in the case of the slow learner. There are successive steps in any learning process, and you must recognize the differences in children's ability and rate of progress in mastering these steps. Endless repetitions are often necessary with slower children, whereas the bright child may learn with the first or second hearing. Holding everyone to the same level of accomplishment discourages the slow learner and bores the fast one, but because the fast learner is not challenged is no reason to condemn the retarded child for holding the other back. Impatience or pressure only serves to confuse him and may block his learning process completely.

It has often been said that "there is nothing that succeeds like success." Knowing this, you can build within children an attitude of confidence rather than of failure. In the case of the less gifted child this viewpoint offers you a challenge. He, too, may come to realize that he can make progress and be successful when he sees his own growth measured against his past achievements rather than in comparison to a more gifted individual. This means that if a child has difficulty in any endeavor, you will try to help him to help himself, rather than passing him by in order to work with the more alert child where results will be more quickly seen.

Efforts to understand and help the mentally retarded child have aided educators in teaching all children. Even individuals with extremely low mental endowment can learn when the teaching is geared to very simple things, with many unhurried repetitions at the child's own slow tempo. Those who have dedicated their lives to the education of exceptional children have proven that even the mongolian idiot can learn when pressures are removed and he is placed in an atmosphere of loving care and sympathetic understanding of his unique problems. The attitude of all those who come in contact with him must be essentially one of patience, hopefulness, and acceptance of him as he is, without censure or blame.

The Child's Attitude Toward His Own Potential

Children of average endowment, as well as those of superior ability, need to realize they cannot expect to excel in everything; that the important thing is to make the most of their potentialities and their circumstances. This is largely a matter of attitude. Fortunate indeed is the child who recognizes his strengths and accepts his needs and then does something about them. Betsy (6/8) said, "I never could tie a bow, but I just did."

Peter, who had felt insecure because he could not skip with both feet, evidenced his attitude toward his own development when he came to his teacher with stars in his eyes and said, "Maybe I can't skip, Miss Barrett, but I can tie my shoes."

This attitude is commendable at any age. Usually behind such reactions is the quiet influence of the understanding teacher who guides each child into an appreciation and development of his own unique potentials and resources.

John Ruskin put it this way:

> The weakest among us
>   has a gift,
>   however seemingly trivial,
>   which is peculiar to him,
>   and which,
>   worthily used,
>   will be a gift also
>   to his race forever.

Modern Painters

William was the youngest of a family of bright children. Even as a young child he could always be found in the orchard or around the barn, and whenever there was work to be done William was there in the midst of it, doing his bit. He didn't care for school. He was never one for "book learning" as he put it, and as he grew older William accepted his position in the family as being "rather dumb, but oh, so helpful!" That he had a reliable memory for detail was evidenced by the fact that he could be sent for any errand and without writing out his list would always return with the needed materials. He worked around the cars, and when anything was wrong he was always the one who could readily find the difficulty. William knew what others thought he could do and what they thought he couldn't do, and accepted these estimates of his own abilities. Somehow, he never had a teacher who fully understood him. William failed to realize his strengths and never learned how to take advantage of them. He imposed standards upon himself in the traditional fields of learning, and because he could not measure up in these he felt inferior to other members of his family who could. This attitude remained with him throughout life.

Milton was a superior academic student, but his muscular coordination was extremely poor. He faced this frankly with his teacher. "I'll probably never be very good in athletics," he said, "but I'll work at it hard."

"Probably you won't excel," agreed his teacher. "No one is superior in everything. Some of us do one thing well and some another. But you can work at athletics and perhaps you'll do as well as the average player. And you can enjoy sports with your friends."

The boy accepted this and worked diligently through the years to become "average" in sports, while he continued to be outstanding in the academic field. By the time he reached high school he was a solid, average player in a variety of athletics, and he thoroughly enjoyed the activities that he might have avoided had he hesitated to develop what he knew was not his strongest field.

The highly intelligent child offers a challenge all his own. Sarah Ann and her group were no exception. In the lower primary, Sarah Ann had read avidly, but when she was in the upper primary she had a miserable attitude toward numbers. She would find all kinds of excuses when the time came to do arithmetic. Parents and teacher worked together to find how to reach Sarah Ann in this respect, but to no avail. It was agreed that a change of attitude was probably all that was needed, as the child gave every indication that her superior mentality could function in this field as well as in any other. The real question was what could be done to challenge her to exert herself to overcome her mental block. Finally, her teacher, Miss A., said, "Sarah Ann, I am going to give some tests a week from today. You are such a good leader, you could take charge of the group while I am busy. I am telling you in advance because I know you are the kind of person who will want to make plans."

Sarah Ann was delighted with the idea and said, "I'd like to be in charge of the group while you are gone, but of course we won't do arithmetic that day."

Miss A. said, "Go home and talk the idea over with your mother and father. You decide what you think would make a good, well-balanced plan for the day. Do you think it would make a good day's plan without arithmetic? If you decide not to do it we will get someone else."

(In the meantime Miss A. had secured the cooperation of Sarah Ann's parents, who encouraged their young daughter to make plans to take over the class.)

The next day Sarah Ann told Miss A., "I have decided I will take the class for you, arithmetic and all. I made a teaching plan just the way you do. I decided if I was going to teach the boys and girls, I would have to know how to do it. These are the problems we will have in arithmetic." She handed Miss A. her plan.

Because Sarah Ann would have to know the answers she had worked the problems carefully and put the solutions in her notebook for ready reference. In doing this the child became so interested that in a short time she

had mastered the principle involved. (The teacher had secured the cooperation of the principal, who was available for any emergency that might present itself.)

Sarah Ann and the other children had so much fun that some of them
asked if they might each have a turn at being teacher. This plan was followed, and the pupil-teacher was responsible for making out the teaching
plan and conducting the class. As for Sarah Ann, she never had any more
trouble with arithmetic.

Attitude and Effort

The child's willingness to exert energy stems chiefly from attitude.
For example, Clifford had to copy a poem for an imposed "lesson."
He looked out the window and bit the end of his pencil; he turned the
leaves of his book aimlessly; he did everything but write the poem. It
took him forty-five minutes to accomplish the task.

Later, he and some other children were on a committee to write invi-
tations to their parents to come to a school assembly. The children were
planning a scrapbook of things to show their parents. They needed examples of the stories they had been reading, some creative poems and songs,
some of their spelling work, and some arithmetic problems. Clifford became so interested that he copied numerous examples for the book, completing over five times the amount of work in the same period it had
taken him to do one poem the day before.

Attitudes by Imitation

The child of course acquires many of his attitudes through direct imitation. While using the telephone in the home center at school, he may go
through the whole process of calling the market or he may call a friend.
His conversation often reveals the attitudes of those with whom he associates. Even the way he picks up the receiver may be indicative of an
acquired attitude. He may say, "There goes the phone! Wonder who it
can be! Maybe it's for me. Oh, good!" Or possibly he will remark, "Oh,
there is that old phone again." He is really delighted with the phone
call, but in his dramatic expression he is often carrying out the pattern
that his elders have set before him.

If a child has a cooperative social environment he will usually manifest an attitude of trust and faith in people and in situations all through
the day. These things have probably not been taught him directly. He
has for the most part imbibed them.

On the contrary, association with people who have a lust for power or material possessions will usually be reflected consistently in the child's attitudes and reactions. Attitudes of complaint, wrangling, dissatisfaction, and disapproval are also carried over.

There are many opportunities at school for a child to acquire attitudes through imitation and association. Randy had a naturally loud voice, but with his teacher's encouragement he was trying to curb it out of respect for others. Sometimes he still forgot, and when he did, Miss B., with a knowing smile, would soften her own down almost to a whisper in addressing him. Immediately he would tone his voice to match hers . One day when thus reminded, he said, "My voice is sorry about that shouting."

Marie was the busybody type, always quick to correct another child while often overlooking her own shortcomings. Miss B. told little stories and drew pictures to illustrate how each child could learn to take care of himself. That Marie was growing under Miss B.'s quiet influence was evident when the child said to her one morning, "We should take care of ourselves, first, and then other children."

Mark, age seven years, was a born philosopher. He imbibed many of his attitudes from Miss B.'s stories and the class discussions, and his remarks indicated that he saw more deeply than many of his peers, as when he said, "I see it is best to do what you are supposed to do first, and then if you have spare time, to do what you *want*."

Incidental comments made by their teacher during the day impress children deeply. This was brought forcefully to Miss B.'s attention when she heard one of her own casual remarks coming from Lee out on the playground. Lee said to Peter, "Don't be sad. It's fun when you lose, and fun when you win."

Influence of Home Attitudes

There is in any group, of course, extreme contrast in the attitudes that have been built up at home. Teddy showed he had a fine home background, and parents who were willing to let him grow into maturity, when he said to his mother as she left him in the school room the first day, "Goodbye, Mommy Girl. I will try to bring you something when I come home."

Wilbur, on the other hand, revealed his possession by a mother who did not want to release her baby. He clung to her skirts and cried, and refused to be left alone at school.

Kathy was ten years old and in the upper elementary school. Her mother could not understand why she would sit around and refuse to participate in many of the school activities. When the mother talked with the child's teacher, the latter found that the mother was concerned because Kathy had brought home so many "idiotic" things from school—pine cones, butterflies, an Indian loom with weaving on it. When the teacher went into the background of it, she found Kathy had at one time or another been very interested in all these things. The mother reported disgustedly how cluttered Kathy's room had been, and how she had said nothing to Kathy about it, but had waited patiently to throw things out until the child was away from home during spring vacation. When Kathy returned, the room would be in perfect order. Kathy had apparently accepted the change without visible protest; but the mother now wondered why her daughter was no longer interested in school projects.

Many young children are confronted with the problem of reconciling the conflicts in the attitudes they encounter at home and at school. For example, in dramatic expression, Albert, who was taking the part of a motorist arrested by a traffic officer, paid a bribe instead of taking a ticket for "unsafe driving." "Daddy did that," said Albert.

Before attempting to change the impression made on the group of children by Albert's remark, the teacher had to ponder the whole question of home versus school influences, and children's respect for parental attitudes.

One child was impersonating the mother in the home center. "You have been very naughty," she said to the children. She took off her belt and began flaying them. When the teacher remonstrated the child said, "My Mommy whips me like that when I'm bad."

Three five-year-old boys were working in the home center. Ann, the same age, came up and wanted to work, too. She begged and beseeched, but the boys were adamant in their reaction that they wanted to work without her. Ann said, "Every family needs a mother," to which the boys replied, "Ours doesn't. We are three bachelors living on the county."

Eleanor, a brilliant nine-year-old, was a natural leader. At home she was pampered and indulged. Though her attitudes were exceedingly self-centered she was well liked by her peers. When Eleanor suggested forming a club, all her friends were enthusiastic and everything went well until it came to the election of officers. Naturally, Eleanor was made president. However, when other names were recommended for the remaining officers, Eleanor was indignant. She would be president, vice-president, secretary, and treasurer or they just wouldn't have a club. The club was dissolved!

Some of your children may exhibit other undesirable attitudes which are attributable to home influences. If unchanged, these attitudes will tend to hinder well-rounded character development. It is unwise to censure parents. Even though you may believe a child's family background is detrimental to him, your help for him and his family is more effective if you refrain from an openly critical attitude toward the home. Yet such behaviors in children pose real problems. Each problem is different and each requires judgment, patience, and tact in handling. If you can help the individual realize that he has a problem to face and that he can choose to do for himself what no one else can do for him, the battle is half won. In the final analysis there is no remedy more efficacious than precept and example.

QUESTIONS ON THE SIX GOALS:
I. WHOLESOME ATTITUDES

1. Give your own illustration of the positive approach to a situation in the classroom in contrast to a negative approach. Compare the influence of each of these on children's behavior.

2. Justify the inclusion of a punching bag in the requisition for an elementary classroom. What other acceptable ways would you provide for your children to work off undesirable feelings?

3. Discuss the philosophy that expecting cooperation from the child creates a desirable attitude that carries over into action. What justification would you have for following this philosophy in your classroom even though a few individuals might fail to respond to it during the first six weeks of school?

4. How does the child's attitude toward his own ability affect his progress? Give illustrations.

5. What opportunities are there at school for a child to acquire attitudes by imitation and association? What is your responsibility in this respect as a teacher?

6. What bearing has attitude upon academic learning? Give specific examples in the area of arithmetic; reading; writing.

7. Discuss the relationship of attitude to growth in art; music; carpentry; physical education.

THE SIX GOALS:
II. AUTOMATIC BEHAVIOR PATTERNS

There are many things which the adult does every day without giving any particular thought to the process. The young child, in order to do some of these same things, has to give complete attention to each motion. In the beginning, he must concentrate on such everyday occurrences as dressing, washing his face and hands, and brushing his teeth.

Patterns of behavior are built up through participation. However, merely going through a routine of doing the same thing in the same way many times does not guarantee that the pattern will become completely automatic unless the child enters into it wholeheartedly, both at home and at school. Developing behaviors is a complex and intricate process, and each one must be built separately. The child must be guided; he needs to be supervised; and until a behavior pattern becomes automatic for him, he must continually realize how important it is to accomplish the task at hand.

Automatic Behavior

Unless a response occurs as the result of understanding the reason for it, the automatic behavior may trigger into an awkward situation.

Daniel was a child who might charitably be termed a slow learner. This was noticeable all through his first year at school. With patience Miss T. was able to teach him a few routine procedures. She solicited the help of the other children, who took keen satisfaction in seeing him establish first one behavior pattern and then another. Responding to the fire drill bell was one of the last learnings to come, no doubt due to the infrequency of the occurrence. Miss T. was interested in helping Daniel to develop independence in as many tasks as possible. She kept working with him until, no matter what he was doing when the fire bell rang, he would leave in the midst of it and go outside with the others. Miss T. was justly proud of her accomplishment in teaching Daniel to respond automatically to the bell.

Then one day, just as the children were leaving for home, Daniel, who usually rode the schoolbus, accidentally slipped in some mud and soiled his clothing. Miss T. sent the other children home and went with Daniel into the nearest lavatory. She helped him to remove his trousers and then said to him, "Miss T. has to go and get some clean clothes for you. You stay right here until she gets back."

While she was gone the fire bell rang. The principal was walking in the corridor with two dignitaries who were visiting the school. All at once, one of the visitors said, "What do I see coming down the breezeway?" Mr. S., the principal, turned and looked in the direction indicated and said, "Oh, no, it can't be!"

There was Daniel coming down the corridor, dressed only in his shirt, holding out his dripping, muddy garments at arm's length. The automatic behavior had held even in an emergency. Daniel had remembered that "when the fire bell rings you go outside no matter what you are doing."

Constructive Automatic Behaviors

You will do well to provide time in your program each day for the development of constructive automatic behavior patterns until they become routine. Many of them need to be developed from the first day of school. Which patterns are needed will vary from one group to another, but time taken out to build behavior patterns, even though they may consume the major part of the first weeks of school, will reap a saving of much time later.

Take, for instance, the way the children come into the room. After the behavior pattern is established, each one watches where he is going without interfering with the others. They neither march in, nor run in, nor push. They walk. At the beginning of the year you can help them to think of how to enter the room properly, and why they need to remember this for themselves. They do not just passively acquiesce because you demand it, or from fear of punishment; instead, they realize it is their problem to be worked out by them. They demonstrate how it is done, and they do it that way. Gradually, behavior becomes automatic with the children. After this has been fully established you seldom have to give it further consideration, unless a new child comes in who has not had that background, or unless the group regresses.

When entering the room in the right way finally becomes automatic, examples such as the following will not be unique or unusual:

Kenneth, starting to run into the room, stopped with one foot in the air and said thoughtfully, "Oh, you don't need to tell me what to do, Miss Holman. I'm remembering, myself."

Here, the quiet influence of the teacher is beginning to evidence itself in Kenneth's behavior. The children in her class have an opportunity to express themselves vociferously out of doors, and have learned to enter the room quietly. As Miss Holman explained to one visitor, "From the first day, the children learned that this is our 'school home,' and as such it deserves certain respect and consideration. They have acquired an appreciation for the room and its furnishing. They are aware of sounds that may disturb other people, and will soften their voices when they come inside."

Responsibility Gradually Assumed

Unfortunately, interruptions in the child's learning are often caused by the adults in his environment who are the most interested in him. The side-tracking which his development often suffers is a tremendous factor. He may attempt to fasten his own sweater and fumble over the task. The admiring or impatient adult may take over the task without thinking how to help him learn to do it. The fact that mother or father always does this for him may give the young child the attitude that he cannot do such things for himself, or may prevent him from trying again.

The child who has had his shoes put on for him every day at home has had no opportunity to learn how to put them on, even though he may have watched an adult do it for him dozens of times. When that child arrives at school, there are many things he needs to learn to do automatically. He may have to learn not only to tie his shoes and button or zip his clothing, but to manage his over-shoes and raincoat as well. He must also learn to take care of his own things, and to assume responsibility for his toilet routine and his eating. He must give attention to these until doing them acceptably becomes automatic.

Care of his own possessions is one of the first important behavior patterns that need guidance. Hooks within the child's reach and his own locker tags provide for wraps, as do coat hangers or large tape loops sewn in the neck of the garment. Cooperation of parents can be secured in marking the child's belongings for identification before he brings them to school.

Another behavior children must early make automatic is to locate, put on, and tie an apron for work in which clothing needs protection, as with paint or clay. A child may ask a friend to fasten his apron until he learns to do this himself. And in turn, he may learn to fasten another child's apron for him. At first he will be very awkward, but he will persevere until putting on an apron becomes an automatic behavior pattern.

When behavior patterns are started early, and consistent attention is given them, the children will gradually take over responsibility for their own actions, and will progress to a point where they are able to list their own standards, such as in the chart on the following page.

Felt figures may be cut to represent the apron, the jar of paint, the paper, the picture being painted, the table. These may be displayed on a felt board while the child tells a creative story about someone hand-painting. This concrete illustration helps establish the behavior patterns desired in getting out materials and caring for equipment and clothing.

Hand Painting

What to do:

1. Put on an apron.
2. Get out paint.
3. See that name and date are on paper.
4. Apply three or four tablespoons of paint.
5. Use whole hand and arm in painting.
6. When picture is finished make another if there is time.
7. Put paint away.
8. Clean table.
9. Wash hands.
10. Put apron away.

Cleaning up after work, lunch, or independent activities will become automatic with the children only if you guide the experience consistently for a number of weeks.

The children may have a part in the planning of what is to be done. In time, it becomes the accepted procedure for each child to put away whatever materials he has been using before beginning another activity, so that the next person will know where to find them. It also helps take care of the materials so they will last longer. Eventually the children will come to evaluate themselves consistently to see if they have really cleaned up adequately.

Constant reminding by the teacher is of no permanent value in setting up behavior patterns. Your guidance must be such that when it is removed, the child is able to continue "on his own." Ann's voluntary comment gave evidence of a constructive behavior pattern in the process of being developed when she said, "I almost went off without wiping the little box where the paints are, but I remembered and went back and did it."

Enthusiastic Response

If a clean-up job is being done lackadaisically, the children are not doing acceptable work. Children may enter into the job of cleaning up with as much enthusiasm as they show for any other activity. Andrea expressed it delightfully when she voluntarily exclaimed, "Sometimes it's even more fun to clean up than to work!"

You may occasionally ask each child to evaluate his own clean-up and then report to the group.

One group of children developed a song that was extremely popular with them. Often it would be heard coming from first one part of the room, then another, as individuals or committees worked. (The repetitions were often sung as an echo.)

WORK SONG
(Composite Song, Upper Primary)

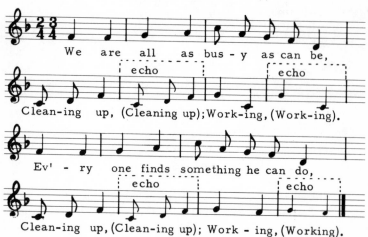

How different is the above approach to one in which the 'teacher's approbation is the ruling force, or in which the teacher is continually reminding the children, "This is a messy place. Clean it up at once."

Such reminders will not be needed if you think in terms of the principles behind cleaning up. The point is not just to get things tidy, but to guide the children into the constructive behavior pattern of keeping things in efficient working condition, no matter what the job they are doing. If the children feel they are wholly responsible in clean-up, it will become a natural response following every activity.

Automatic Care of Equipment

Before they begin a task, the children may plan how they will safeguard the furniture or floor if it needs protection from the kind of work they may be doing. Some tables have a hard surface especially made to withstand moisture. Others are injured by dampness or are easily marred or scratched. For work jobs it is desirable to have a durable surface, but the child must learn, too, to adapt himself to the situation, wherever he is working.

Establishing Patterns of Behavior

Children are quick to follow your example. They imitate many of the things you do automatically. If by chance they see you stand on a chair to reach something without protecting the chair, they too, may exhibit the same undesirable behavior.

Mrs. Samuels was a beginning teacher, but a very intelligent and superior person. One day the principal came into Mrs. Samuels' room and found her standing on a chair which had no protective covering over it. After the children were dismissed and the principal and Mrs. Samuels were in conference, the principal called attention to this and discussed behavior patterns at some length.

Two weeks later the principal returned to Mrs. Samuels' room. She noticed that it was Alvin's responsibility that day to check and report the number of children who would have lunch in the cafeteria. Sixteen children stood up and remained standing while Alvin went from one to the other, counting. He held his hand directly over the head of each as he counted so there would be no mistake. When he had finished, he wrote the number down on a pad, and turned to Mrs. Samuels to ask if she expected to eat in the cafeteria, also. She indicated that she did. Alvin added one to his total.

Then he took a chair and placed it beneath the inter-communication speaker. He procured an old newspaper from a stack in the closet, placed the paper on the chair, stood on the chair, and pressed the communicating button. When the office responded he said, "Reporting on cafeteria lunches for Room 2. There will be sixteen children and one teacher eating lunch in the cafeteria today."

Alvin got down carefully, put the paper away in the cupboard, and returned the chair to its place. Mrs. Samuels thanked Alvin and he returned to his seat.

This incident shows how quickly the teacher profited from the suggestion, and how readily the behavior pattern had been established with the children.

Making the explanation concrete is important with young children, as with any age group. Instead of saying, "Wash your hands before you take a book," it would be better to go with Billy to the wash basin when his hands are dirty, talk with him while he washes them, and have him discover how he can spread the soap suds all over the back of each hand and in between his fingers and up onto his wrists; then how he can rinse his hands with just a small stream of water that will take the soap away and keep his clothes dry. When he comes back, he can tell the others about it. He can pantomime how he washed his hands and show how he used the soap and smoothed it all over his fingers. The other children can try it in pantomime also, and talk about how it helps to get the hands clean, and then well rinsed and dry before touching a book.

This will carry over into action, and illustrates a positive approach that leads to understanding of what can be done, rather than nagging every time the child's hands are dirty.

A drop of hand lotion from an automatic dispenser may add a finishing touch to the cycle of washing hands. This helps keep the hands in good condition and gives the child a wholesome satisfaction in having hands that are really clean and ready for the next activity. This is particularly desirable in preparation for lunch or the handling of food.

Eating Together

The noon lunch period is an occasion for the development of permanent behavior patterns, desirable or undesirable, depending upon the guidance offered.

Many schools have a mid-morning or mid-afternoon snack in the room. This, too, can be the opportunity for establishing standards of eating that will carry over throughout life. Behavior patterns here, as always, are dependent upon attitudes. Children need to develop the feeling that clean hands are fit to handle food, soiled hands are not. Thus they will always proceed to wash their hands before touching food.

It is a good procedure to have waxed paper or another type of material available when children serve food that has to be handled, so that those serving it can pick it up with clean paper rather than the hands. Attitudes toward preserving food and preventing it from falling, or when it does fall, washing it if possible, are important. Any food that drops on the floor or ground and cannot be used can be discarded with great ceremony so that the children learn contaminated food must not be eaten.

If a child spills milk or other liquid, he should wipe it up. Sponges or rags should always be available for the purpose, and if no sink is close at hand, a container of clean water may be in readiness.

Wisely guided, the snack time can be rich in learning. It may be a ritual which the children anticipate from day to day. Hosts and hostesses may carry the responsibility for setting up the tables and guiding the procedures. You may stress clean tables, with dainty bouquets or other attractive centerpieces. There can be a free discussion of happy experiences and situations. At first, you will have to initiate this, but later the children will carry on without your leadership, although you are always a participating member of the group. If a guest is present, the children in charge will invite him or her to participate in the snack, even though nothing but a glass of water is served.

In situations where there is no provision made by the school for mid-morning or mid-afternoon snacks, each child may bring a small amount of food, such as one-fourth of an apple, a few raisins, or something else light and easily eaten. It should be made clear to parents how small a quantity is desirable—just something so there can be an experience in eating together and sharing ideas, with opportunities for growth in language expression, attitudes, and appreciation.

How to pass food, and the handling of foods and napkins needs to be stressed. Children can be encouraged to break crackers in two, to take small bites, and to eat slowly. By a nod of the head or other signs of approval you can help children realize the different standards that are expected.

The principle of consideration for others can be furthered by stories, pictures, conversation and films, as well as by commendation for acceptable behavior.

Toilet Procedure

There is a definite pattern of behavior for toilet procedures. During the first days of the child's experience in school, he needs to be carefully guided into the complete cycle. Flushing the toilet after use, fastening or pulling up his own clothing, washing hands, and getting a drink of water are all a definite part of this procedure.

Consistent guidance and supervision are needed to establish these permanent behavior patterns in the early childhood years. The routine can be presented in many ways that will make it challenging to the children to follow the acceptable procedures.

You can present the picture or silhouettes in story form as you place them on the felt board, and the children can talk about them afterward. This procedure may be varied by using the chalkboard or easel and making stick figures. Another way is to use a series of pipe cleaner dolls showing the various steps in the toileting process. These may be called to the children's attention and then mounted on colored construction paper and fastened to the lavatory wall.

It takes constant guidance and supervision to make these procedures become automatic, but they finally do, and are henceforth a lifelong achievement in which hands are consistently washed after using the toilet.

In connection with behavior patterns in toilet procedure comes the question of toilet terminology. At school there is a "toilet" or "lavatory" rather than a bathroom. Some prefer to call it a "washroom." Regardless of the terminology children may have become accustomed to use at home, they can learn the correct terms for urination and defecation, and for the various parts of the body without embarrassment, but with deference for the feelings of others. The use of the same toilet room and facilities by all the children in the immediate school group, under the teacher's supervision and guidance, is encouraged by many educators and parents for the young child in the primary school, as well as in the nursery school. When this is done during these early years, and the toilet procedures introduced as suggested above, there is no deep mystery about the toilet process, and the physiological differences between the sexes is accepted as a fact as natural as any other phenomenon and not to be set apart as something to receive undue attention or to be mysteriously ignored.

Older children who have not had this early training need just as careful supervision and guidance on their own maturation level in order that wholesome attitudes as well as acceptable behavior patterns may be developed.

Sometimes when there is only one toilet, more than one child will attempt to go in, a practice which should be prohibited. Children should observe how many toilet accommodations there are, and how many children may therefore be accommodated at one time. They should learn to conserve toilet tissue and to avoid throwing anything into the toilet that might cause difficulty with the sewer.

They must establish the behavior pattern of entering the toilet, going directly through the necessary routine, including washing their hands, and leaving at once to release the facilities for the use of someone else. This helps prevent the problem of loitering and silliness before it has an opportunity to develop.

Rest

To avoid interruption at rest time it may be wise to put a permanent note on the outside of the door above the children's eye level, such as,

"Rest is part of our day's program. When the children are resting a picture card will be hung on the doorknob. Please do not enter until the card is removed, except in case of emergency."

If a rest card is used it is essential that it be removed immediately after rest. It is a simple matter to have one particular child take over this responsibility every day.

One consultant whose time was limited slipped unobtrusively into a room where there was such a sign. She sank quietly onto the window seat and joined the resters, thinking no one had seen her. Later, Richard came over to her and asked, "Have you seen our sign?"

With considerable humility the consultant said, "Oh, Richard, thank you for bringing me the sign to read. I apologize for coming in while you were resting." (She looked with admiration at their new pictorial rest card.)

"Oh, did you come in while we were resting? We didn't even know that," Richard said, smiling. "Anyway, you are our friend. You would never disturb us." His interest and pride in the new sign revealed the attitude toward resting which had been established.

It is sometimes wise to have various children show each other how to rest. Individuals or small groups may dramatize going to their resting places in a manner that suggests the relaxation which is to follow. There are many different ways which are good. These may be discussed with the children. Their attitude toward rest is the determining factor in developing the patterns of behavior desired.

Standards firmly established should be consistently observed. It is to be remembered that a few moments of complete relaxation are much more effective than a longer unit of time in which the children become restless.

There should be an attitude of repose and consideration established from the first day of resting at school. The physical environment can be conducive to this type of attitude. Perhaps it means drawing the blinds, walking on tip-toe, getting out blankets, mats or cots, depending on the plan to be followed. There should be no confusion. You will move almost stealthily, and speak in a low quiet voice. The children will catch the spirit and respond in like manner. This pattern of quiet in getting ready for rest should be built up anew each day until it becomes automatic.

If the entire group learn to leave the previous activity together in a quiet mood, and lie down at the same time, it helps to assure a good rest. A tranquil poem at the end of snack-time, a song, or a story may help create the necessary atmosphere before the children prepare for rest.

Children need to understand the reason for finding a location where they will not breathe in each other's face. Flannel board cutouts of children resting may be used to show the positions in which the children should lie. Some teachers have the children lie in alternate positions, that is, one child with his head in one direction, the next child with his feet in that direction. You may present the entire resting procedure in story form on the felt board.

The superactive children may rest better if located in the area near you, but away from each other. If those who are special friends find they are inclined to talk when they lie near each other, they can agree to rest in different parts of the room. Commendation of thoughtfulness and consideration shown by individuals and by the group as a whole will go far toward bringing about desirable responses.

Occasionally a soft lullaby may be sung, a lovely composition played on the piano, autoharp, harmolin, or other instrument, but care must be taken to avoid overstimulating the children during rest or conditioning them to expect music during every rest period.

One of the main objectives is complete relaxation of body muscles, and where there is no provision for the children to stretch out completely, other means of relaxation may be substituted. Leaning head and arms on a table or desk is a strain on body muscles and is therefore not considered as desirable as sitting in a relaxed "rag doll" manner.

Immediate Needs

Although many behavior patterns established in the early years will be lifelong, others will last only during school days. There are certain behaviors which children should have when they are on the playground: For example, the area around the swings needs to be kept clear. If there is a railing, children need to stand outside of it.

The use of the slide presents a problem in cooperation. Going up the ladder requires consideration for the one ahead. Children can think through the way this may be done and evaluate their use of the equipment until the behavior patterns become automatic. Other activities such as hanging from the bars or swinging from the rings each present a challenge.

Another need of the child is to learn to come straight to school without loitering, and to go directly home after school unless he has special permission to do something else.

Classroom Responsibilities

Automatic behavior patterns related to reading experiences, science, numbers, writing, spelling, and social studies can be readily acquired as the need for them arises. There is the need for distributing books, keeping them in order when they are not in use, making other materials available, conserving time, going directly to work, going to another room or to the auditorium to work, working individually and in committees, speaking effectively before the group, securing and holding attention, working independently, organizing and preparing and delivering reports. Matters of this nature present themselves as problems repeatedly until they become automatic patterns.

You have the choice of introducing your own ideas concerning how such things shall be done, or of soliciting the children's thoughtfulness in assuming responsibilities for the room. When they realize these are their problems as well as yours, the children will help solve them by suggesting, demonstrating, and evaluating ways of carrying out routines until they become completely automatic.

Attitudes and Ways of Working

The establishment of automatic behavior patterns is by no means limited to physical responses. The manner in which work is undertaken, underlying attitudes, and viewpoints toward accomplishment are also included in this goal. Fundamental accuracy or carelessness, industry or laziness, order or disorder, can all become a consistent pattern of thought and action underlying the activities of a group or of an individual.

Setting Up Standards of Behavior

As children go through school their ability to achieve in any area of learning depends upon a number of factors which vary from one child to another. Therefore in evaluating a child's patterns of behavior at any time, a standard is needed in keeping with his own progress and ability.

Earl, whose situation is presented in an earlier chapter, was at the bottom of the behavior ladder. What could be expected from others in the group could not be expected from him. But he proved that when measured against his own standards he could grow. Suppose everyone were held to one standard of achievement in art or music! It could not be accomplished; yet many people think that one standard of achievement in behavior should exist for every individual.

Some teachers talk over with children the ways in which they can assist one another during group experiences and independent activities. They tabulate these suggestions for mutual helpfulness in chart form, and they are used as a reference by the children in evaluating their own behavior. In this way each child feels responsible for making the room a happier place to live.

Following is the chart one group developed which revealed school behavior patterns that were being established:

> **It makes us happy to be kind.**
> **Before we act, we think.**
> **When someone talks we listen.**
> **We take care of our hands and feet.**

Oral evaluation of the problems that arise are also helpful. In another group the children were learning to move with the rhythm of musical accompaniment. Rhythms were not satisfactory because of the confusion in stopping. The teacher called the group together and asked them:

"What can we do to improve our rhythms so we can really enjoy them?"
Frank said, "We need to listen."
"Tell us why, Frank."
"So we'll know when the music stops."
All tried walking and skipping. Everyone listened and followed the music. The teacher commended the children for being good listeners. It took several days to get the group to follow directions automatically, after which all could enjoy rhythms to the fullest. They established their behavior pattern so thoroughly and lent themselves so wholeheartedly to the rhythm that some of the children were able to play the accompaniment on the bells while the group responded. The automatic behavior pattern of starting and stopping together freed the children to be spontaneous in their interpretation of the music.

Automatic Patterns for the Teacher

Your own automatic behavior patterns can help or hinder you in teaching. Conscious attention to the development of certain ways of doing things may make them automatic, so that attention may be given to other matters. Continued effort toward a behavior pattern of reliability is essential.

You can set desirable standards for yourself which are capable of attainment. By thoughtful selection and concentrated effort you can develop a number of automatic behavior patterns so that you may do these things without giving special thought to them. This frees you for solving problems that may demand long-time planning or immediate attention. For example, it is highly desirable to form a behavior pattern of being on time or perhaps a few minutes early for appointments as well as with assignments. A habitual pattern of patience with interruptions, annoyances, and emergencies can also become an automatic behavior response. Only when a behavior becomes automatic is the individual truly secure in it.

QUESTIONS ON THE SIX GOALS:
II. AUTOMATIC BEHAVIOR PATTERNS

1. What behavior patterns need to be established to make democratic control possible in your classroom? Discuss some of the successful ways of developing these behaviors.

2. Mention several necessary or desirable procedures in a given classroom which could well become automatic patterns of behavior for the children? How would you help the children establish these?"

3. How do standards of behavior vary from one individual to another in the same classroom? Justify.

4. Suggest problems of making routines automatic, and explain how children can participate in planning ways to do this. What activities and responsibilities fall under this classification? Give examples.

5. Why should each child feel responsible for making the room an acceptable place to live? What bearing has this viewpoint on the development of behavior patterns?

THE SIX GOALS:
III. DEEP APPRECIATIONS

The English poet, Alfred Tennyson, voiced a universal longing when he wrote:

> And I would that my tongue could utter
> The thoughts that arise in me.

Most of humanity is silent in the presence of the eternal verities of life. Perhaps silence is the greatest tribute that can be paid to the splendor of beauty or magnanimous deeds or unutterable sorrow, but this silencing of speech need not extend to appreciation for the numerous small happenings that revolve the wheels of daily living. Unfortunately, there seems to be a blind spot in the mental make-up, an almost universal hesitancy to express this type of appreciation.

Negative Influences

One reason for a person's being inarticulate in expressing gratitude, or perhaps for not even feeling it, may be due to an early childhood influence of gushiness, insincerity, or hypocrisy. Mary Lou may hear her mother say, "Oh, come to see me again, Mrs. Smith. It has been so wonderful having this visit with you." Scarcely has Mrs. Smith reached the sidewalk before the mother remarks, "Why on earth did *she* come to see me? We have nothing in common. It was probably to see if I had new curtains." Examples of hypocrisy such as this may inhibit the child's expressiveness in later life.

Genuine Gratitude

A feeling of genuine gratitude is the keynote in teaching children to express appreciation. Parents and teachers sometimes attempt to force a child into artificial social graces. Unless expressions of appreciation spring from true feeling, they are but hollow words. A simple "Thank you" speaks volumes if it is spontaneous, but voiced from force of duty it is empty.

If Lyle's mother says, "Thank the lady for the nice time," and Lyle, parrot-like, says, "Thank you for the nice time," his mother may believe her child has fulfilled his obligation to their hostess. How much more meaning there is in a spontaneous statement! There needs to be a true expression of appreciation for what the hostess has done. Perhaps the child does *not* have a very good time, but still he may recognize the trouble the hostess has taken to try to entertain him. The parent can help by talking over with him in advance the things for which he can be appreciative. "It takes lots of Mrs. Smith's time to get ready for us. She has to go buy the food and cook it; she sets the table and puts flowers in the room, and gets the house ready for us to come. So when we go to eat at her house it is really very thoughtful of her to go to this trouble. The gracious thing is to tell her how lovely it was of her to do it."

Each day presents numerous possibilities both at school and at home for developing expressions of appreciation which are based on genuine feeling. The child may develop a life-long ability to find within his relationships with other people qualities for which he may sincerely express appreciation. This must begin in the everyday experiences which he meets.

Written Expressions of Appreciation

When children really feel appreciation, a written expression of it naturally follows, especially when parents and teachers have helped them realize that writing a note is the thoughtful thing to do.

Whether or not the parents have begun this training, you have a responsibility for helping children to feel and express sincere gratitude. Group "Thank you's" may be dictated or written by a committee and mailed or delivered personally by the children.

Adult Example

Half of appreciation is awareness and the other half consideration. Frequently in the home and school the amenities of life are forgotten or put aside in the pressures of daily living or academic learning. If the adults responsible for guiding children will develop an automatic behavior pattern of adhering to those standards desirable for children to follow, much can be done toward teaching them to observe these standards in their daily activities.

Teachers and parents so often do not realize what their thoughtless lack of common courtesies may mean to a child. Continual walking in front of individuals, grabbing books away from a child, or rudely interrupting him when he is speaking will only foster like actions. On the other hand, showing children the courtesies due them as persons will help to establish these courtesies as the order of the day in their thinking and in their actions.

Appreciation of Other People's Feelings

One of the important things about appreciation is developing sensitivity to other people's feelings. You can help the child recognize, for example, that someone may become anxious if he is unavoidably detained. If a committee is planning to work after school or if the child is staying at a friend's home, the considerate procedure is to call mother to explain, or better still, to let her know ahead of time that he will not be home at the usual hour. A child needs to learn to put himself in someone else's place and realize the anxiety he can spare the other person by showing consideration.

Particularly valuable for the child's own development are those offers of helpfulness which spring from within. Acts of thoughtfulness which the child initiates, rather than those originating from some outside influence or from requests that he "do" so and so, are indicative of this type of appreciation.

Awareness

The senses of touch, taste, smell, sound, and sight are all avenues through which appreciations are formed, and the more ways in which children can become aware of anything, the deeper will be their sensitivity toward it.

Miss E. was invited to the home of one of the children in her lower primary group. The child took her to view his case of treasures. She was startled to see the sign which he had placed in front of his display. It read, "You may touch any of the things in here."

In talking this over with a friend afterward, Miss E. remarked, "We tell children that we see with our eyes and keep our hands away from objects, but I never realized before how much I have overdone it with my children."

"We are all guilty of this," her friend replied.

It is often necessary to take children to stores and other people's homes where there are objects for them to see but which they may not touch. There are many other occasions when they can and should have the opportunity to touch and to explore. In order to develop concepts of things as they really are, children need sensory experiences much more than adults. There is much to be learned through touch; for example: the feel of textiles, the weight of objects, coldness and warmth, dampness and dryness, roughness and smoothness, size and shape. Children's appreciation of these qualities cannot develop when they are not permitted to touch. Older children who have had many sensory experiences learn to recall these to such an extent that they can look and imagine how something would feel or smell without actually touching or smelling it.

A museum developed especially for children with things which they may touch is an idea which has received encouragement from those who really know children. Only individuals who prove they know how to handle and take care of the objects they touch are permitted to progress through each room where items gradually become harder and harder to replace should accident befall them. There are hygienic considerations to be taken into account in such a venture, but these are not insurmountable. Facilities for washing hands may be made available, and children might be required to use these before entering the museum.

In many school systems three-dimensional materials may be loaned out to teachers for children to see. Some of these may be touched as well. While behavior patterns and attitudes need to be developed regarding the use of such materials, the gain in appreciation makes the expenditure of time and energy worthwhile.

The child appreciates the things around which he lives and works, for appreciations develop through experience. What he can do something with he appreciates more than what someone tells him about or does for him.

Incidental Observation

In a neighborhood school of early childhood a teacher has placed a bulletin board where pictures may be displayed at eye level for the children. On it one day she placed a picture of two children looking through a window out into the sky where a beautiful star shone.

Many of the children passed by without seeming to notice it, but David stopped, and cast his eyes over the picture for several minutes. Then Nancy came and said, "They are looking out the window and the boy is talking about the star. When they go to bed the star will still shine."

At the time, Peter seemed oblivious to all this, but later it was he who painted a picture at the easel "with a big bright star shining into the night."

Later when the children were talking with their teacher about their day, she mentioned Peter's painting. He brought it over and showed it to the boys and girls, and Nancy said, "Just like the star in the picture."

They decided to put Peter's art work on the wall. Instead of elaborating on the picture of the children and the star, this teacher had placed it without comment on the bulletin board where it had made its impression and penetrated its way into the children's consciousness. This group had had previous experiences in which they had learned to be aware of things in their environment. Their appreciation for the work of other children was evidenced by the above response. A group new to this type of approach needs guidance.

Harmony and Balance

Appreciation for harmony and balance in the physical arrangement of the room is acquired to a certain extent by exposing the child to these qualities in his surroundings. You will not try to balance a combination of colors and pictures merely to make an attractive room; you will want to keep in mind the influence of the room environment on the tastes of the children. At the beginning of the year you can make the room homelike and attractive, but you might leave some things to be added so the children can have a part in deciding what should be displayed, and why. The children can learn what is needed at any time, and where certain things are kept readily available. In discussing this, points about balance in color and form can be introduced in a practical way. There may be certain pictures, each desirable in itself, which are better appreciated if displayed at different times. As children see the reasons for this they become more able to make their own evaluations. They can learn to post material on the bulletin board with thought for balance and design, and remove items which no longer apply. If you yourself always do these things, you are depriving the children of opportunities to develop appreciation and judgment.

There are myriad ways in which you may foster incidental appreciation. One teacher placed a ceramic dog on the window ledge and watched to see which children noticed it. She said nothing about it until mid-morning when the children were gathered to compare ideas. Then she asked what new thing in the room they had discovered.

Billy mentioned the dog, and said it was just like his Aunt Linda's dog. A poem about the dog seemed appropriate, and the little white ceramic was brought over. The children noticed how smooth the finish was, and the teacher told about the man who had molded the animal from clay and baked it.

"He must be good to make a little dog like that," said Billy.

This simple statement meant more to the teacher than any smooth-sounding, memorized description of a work of art possibly could. It showed real appreciation of the ceramic.

In contrast to this is the method of the teacher who brings in a picture and immediately recites a description of the artist who painted it, talks about the artist's life, and then says to the children, "The name of this picture is 'The Horse Fair.' Now tell me what is the name of it," and they all recite it back to her. "And the name of the artist is Rosa Bonheur." They all repeat the name.

Many opportunities for incidental appreciation present themselves to you every day. When a child first brings flowers to school he is free to put them into the container of his choice and place them anywhere in the room, regardless of how they look. Later, you may have a beautiful bouquet and evaluate the flowers and the arrangement, saying nothing about the child's flowers. Gradually he will come to the point where he will seek a more suitable container and a more balanced arrangement. In other instances, you may talk with the child as he works, and later the two of you evaluate the bouquet together for the benefit of the other children. In this way children soon come to appreciate flowers that are well arranged.

Human Values in Art

Appreciation is not limited to intellectual knowledge of the arts—paintings, musical compositions, poems, and dances produced by the great artists. There are human values in art, music, and verbal expression which children should be led to appreciate. These include the experiences of the children themselves in using art materials, words, and other media of expression. Even with the youngest children, emphasis needs to be put on this aspect of the arts, and on the human elements in relation to other things and other people.

Appreciation of the art values in the child's work should certainly be on his level. "Dean does such good work cleaning paints. Thank you, Dean, we all appreciate it," was Warren's unsolicited comment. "That picture Mary made is lovely. The colors are smooth and she has done well," volunteered Dennis. For children to comment in these ways gives evidence that their teacher takes into account the things that matter *where the child is* in his development. This is carried one step further when the other children can say, spontaneously and sincerely, "Look how much Mary is improving today." It indicates that the third goal of childhood education, deep appreciations, is well on its way toward being realized.

Another human value in art is the individual's appreciation of his own efforts. When Ruth spoke somewhat slightingly of seven-year-old Cindy's painting, Cindy calmly replied, "This picture was hard to paint, Ruth, so you shouldn't say anything about it unless you could do better."

Another day, Sam and Paul were getting ready to paint their boat. Paul was rubbing a rough spot with sandpaper.

"Haven't you finished that yet?" asked Sam.

A growing respect for the work involved in producing something worthwhile was evident in Paul's reply. "This is no five-minute job," he said. "It's a big job and takes time."

Such are the foundations for genuine evaluation, which helps the person whose efforts are being evaluated.

A Basic Need: Commendation

Educators have come at last to recognize that commendation is as necessary to the life and happiness of an individual as food for his body and books for his mind. Appreciation is a basic human need.

One individual who was an administrator never commended any member of his family or professional staff, yet when any one of them had done praiseworthy work he was loud in telling everyone else about it. In turn, this administrator could not remember having ever been commended by his own family or his childhood teachers.

The bigger part of successful teaching is appreciating what a child is trying to do and the ways in which he may meet his problems. For example, Upton, who had for a time been too timid to climb at all, finally ventured to climb the lowest rungs on the jungle gym. His teacher saw him and remarked, "That's good, Upton." She was placing the stress on human values by recognizing the fact that Upton had conquered his hesitancy enough to climb a little. This encouragement helped him to venture farther the next time.

When children remember to do little considerate things, a word of appreciation from their teacher means much. Simple things which in themselves may seem insignificant nevertheless deserve recognition. The child picks up a chair and puts it in place or puts special effort into his cleaning or offers to help another child or is especially careful of a piece of equipment. These small observances provide you with countless opportunities to offer that child a word of well-deserved encouragement, a genuine rather than an artificial expression of appreciation for his thoughtfulness and effort. This helps to establish good rapport between you and him, and counterbalances other situations in which you must, for the good of the child, be firm.

The Child's Work

When time and energy are invested in a piece of work, why not enjoy what was done?

Sometimes you may tend to become so concerned about the time element that you do not encourage the children to enjoy what they have made. If a child has made something, such as an airplane, a train, a pin wheel, or a painting, time to enjoy it is justified and should be planned for in the total program. The total value of work lies not only in the product, but in appreciation of the accomplishment. The children may sit down beside what they have made, or stand and talk about it. What did John and Billy do? How was it accomplished? Mention what fun it was. Without prolonging the time unduly, there may be a spontaneous review of some of the things learned in the process. This is not for the sake of pedantics; it grows out of the enthusiasm of the children for the experience.

Leading children to decide in advance what they will do with their unfinished work is one way of helping individuals anticipate problems they will meet in working independently. A gentle reminder well enough in advance of the time to stop working will avoid interrupting a child when he is absorbed in his work. In anticipating his problem and helping him toward a solution you demonstrate to him your own appreciation of his working situation.

Interest in Other People

The young child responds to any genuine approach, and if he has constantly before him a consistent expression of sincere appreciation, it will become a natural part of him. Lois, who was ordinarily an extremely quiet child, was the one to notice the first really good day Paul had. Paul cleaned up his blocks and was sitting quietly on the rug with a book when Lois said to Miss Barrett, "Isn't it fine the way Paul has learned to help? He's really on our team now."

You need to be alert to capitalize upon the children's spontaneous expressions, even though the children may not realize you have made a special effort to do so. In the above example, realizing that Paul had heard what Lois said, Miss Barrett did not try to elaborate upon it, but she did register a look of understanding as she acknowledged Lois' observation with the quiet, reassuring comment, "He really is, isn't he?"

Appreciation of the rights of others is part of the development of self-control. Listening quietly while someone else is speaking can be a logical outgrowth of appreciation for that person and his right to speak. This spirit is expressed in the simple words of a song which contributes to the child's growing sense of values:

School and Teachers

Children who love and enjoy their friends are opening a pathway that leads to joys and satisfactions throughout life. Jimmy, age seven, not only voiced this appreciation of his friends, but also of his school, when he wrote:

"I like reading, writing, arithmetic, art, and music, but I just love the people big and little."

Appreciation of his own teacher and of teachers in general sometimes finds expression in spontaneous ways. More than one child has felt toward his teacher the warmth that he never found in his own home relationships. "I wish you were my mother" is a token of deep appreciation accepted by the understanding teacher in the spirit in which it is offered.

Sometimes evidences of appreciation come when least expected. The following story was told by a principal of a school in her talk to a group of teachers:

> A shiny new car was parked out in front of school one morning, and a number of the children and some of the teachers were out looking at it. It was really a big event for the school and for the teacher who had just acquired it. Right behind the new car was a very dilapidated one which belonged to Miss W., the middle primary teacher. While everyone was "ohing" and "ahing" over the beautiful new car, Juanita, a little Mexican girl who was in Miss W.'s room, came over and put her hand in her teacher's. "You mustn't feel bad," Juanita said. "We like your little 'put-put', too."

Indicative of genuine appreciation, also, are some of the letters which members of the family may write to the teacher. An eight-year-old who reflected a background of deep appreciation and the ability to express it, sat down at school and without help from anyone wrote the following letter to his younger brother's teacher, who had presented a puppet show to the children at school:

> I liked the puppet Fluffet very much. The part when Fluffet sat down on the turtle when he thought it was a rock was funny.
> I enjoyed your whole puppet show. Your Robin, Frog, and Polly-wog were nicely done. You are a very good artist.
> You make good scenery.
> That stage was hard to make, but you did it.
> Thank you for taking such good care of my brother all year. He doesn't want to leave you.
> Happy summer vacation.
>
> Love

Inspiration

In the early years, foundations are laid for appreciations of greatest significance. Some of these appreciations are for art, music, literature, beauty of color and form in Nature, and for appreciation of human values, including worthy effort, individuality, character, sensitivity toward others in the family, the neighborhood, the people of the world, and insight for their likenesses and differences. Such appreciations are the elements which help to make a full life. They are a stabilizing influence and offer a release for emotional disturbances. Whether or not they are acquired depends on the guidance a young child receives.

Each individual needs something deep and abiding that he can go to for inspiration at the low moments which are part of everyone's life. Some gain it from poetry, music, art, or dramatic arts. Others gain it from Nature. They may take a walk out in the open and come back renewed. Each must know where to go and what to do to "take the kinks out of his soul."

Inspiration may come from the natural resources of a home community, no matter how commonplace these may seem to the person who has traveled farther afield.

One cold evening, after a day that had been punctuated by intermittent rain and wind, a group of children were leaving a rural school. The sun was low in the sky and the clouds were touched with fiery gold turning into pinks. No one grumbled about the cold and the slush as they all walked along the country lane. Instead, they were watching and commenting on the beauty of the sunset, calling attention to the changing shapes of the clouds, and looking back to see the rose-colored hills behind them. Those children had a deep feeling for beauty that came from a teacher who had truly taught them to appreciate it.

Poetry

The same teacher found inspiration in poetry and was also able to impart this to the children. From her wide repertoire she drew verse with a simple statement, "You know, this reminds me of the poem about _____." The children learned to associate poems with their own experiences and interests and later, on their own, would search out poems in keeping with fresh interests and new experiences.

The child's appreciation of poetry is based on familiarity with lovely poems. In your classroom you may launch into the words of the poet without preamble. Your children's delight is reward in itself when they enthusiastically plead, "Say it again! Please say it again," and listen absorbed as you repeat it. Many poems are learned in this way and lend their inspiration to life situations when recalled by the children later. Appreciation of poetry for its own sake is cultivated as children become better acquainted with it and as it assumes a place of importance in their lives.

Broader Horizons

If you have a deep appreciation of childhood as the cornerstone of civilization, you will keep ever before you the vision of what each child will become, and lead him one step nearer his goal, which is the gradual full flowering of his personality. That your children are learning to feel appreciations deeply and to express them will be a major indication of their development.

The parents and teachers of one school district decided that their school should participate in a drive for clothing to send to a disaster relief area. Bundles of wearing apparel were brought by the children in the various rooms. Miss H. displayed in her upper primary room a picture of a young child, clad in tatters and seated on a curb. She waited for comments from her children. In the next few days several individuals mentioned the boy with the ragged clothes who would be glad to get something warm to wear. One of the children suggested what the boy might be saying.

Gradually it became clear that many of these children not only could appreciate the gratitude someone else might feel, but could also express this feeling in words the other person might use. The quiet influence of home and school is revealed in what was said during the discussion. Miss Holman wrote the children's exact words in large lettering beneath the picture. Their words read as follows:

New Shoes

My shoes are old.
My shoes are too small.
My toes are poking out
of my old shoes.
Someone sent me
new shoes.
Now my feet
will be dry and warm.
Thank you, God.
Thank you for the new shoes.
Now I can play
and run and jump.

Depth of Appreciation

In summary, the points stressed throughout this section on appreciation are concerned with the development of the child's appreciation of his personal worth; his appreciation of other people—their cultures, their philosophy, and their religion; and a deep appreciation of Nature and of natural forces. Your own patient sowing, as well as that of the parents, will make it possible for the child to reap in greater measure, not so much in materialistic gain, but in a philosophy and a way of life. His training will have produced in him an equanimity and a buoyancy of spirit that will help him to meet life with serenity, courage, and hope. The depth of his appreciations will keep him in harmony with the infinite. His foundations will not crumble in time of stress, nor will his life ever become "as sounding brass or a tinkling cymbal."

QUESTIONS ON THE SIX GOALS:
III. DEEP APPRECIATIONS

1. How can you let children know you understand how they feel regarding a difficult decision they have to make? What difference will your own attitude make? Illustrate.

2. What effect would your recognition of a child's efforts have upon his achievement? Illustrate.

3. How do children give evidence of their appreciations?

4. Why are deep appreciations included as one of the six goals of childhood education?

THE SIX GOALS:
IV. CREATIVE EXPRESSION

Response

I saw the richness of gold and blue,
Wheat ripe and tawny against the sky;

I heard the meadowlark call his mate;
I heard her answering cry;

I felt the beauty of earth and air,
Drank deep of life as I passed along;

My full heart welled through faltering lips,
And voiced an answering song.

Young children to whom the everyday world is yet new, are impressed with much which the adult takes for granted or overlooks. Surfeited by his immediate surroundings, the adult often removes his thoughts from them in meditative preoccupation. How different is their reaction from five-year-old Tom's, alert to all the phenomena of a new and absorbing world. Tom lifts his hand against the wind and observes:

"You can't see the wind,
But when you walk along
You can feel it."

An artist visitor to Crater Lake in southern Oregon had heard of the lake's rare quality of blue—visible only under certain atmospheric conditions. To her great delight when she arrived, the lake lay stretched out in all its breath-taking beauty, a perfect thing. As she spread out her easel and prepared to capture her joy on canvas, a group of tourists came by. Some of them were quiet when they saw the lake; others were loudly articulate. But one woman turned toward the blue water, gave it a glance, and when asked by an enthusiastic companion how she liked it, replied with no change of facial expression and no color in her voice, " 'S nice." Her complete lack of response to her surroundings was evident even to the most casual observer.

Avenues of Expression

What stifles creative expression? Fear of ridicule? A feeling that stoicism is commendable? Pride in being unemotional and inexpressive? Lack of ability?

For one reason or another, some individuals permit all the avenues of expression to be closed to them, or else limit themselves to one or two outlets without realizing it. Many people hesitate to attempt something in which they feel they are not gifted. Sometimes an individual finds no way of meeting his basic need to be expressive. Buffeted about and made to curtail inner drives in an effort to adjust to life's demands, some fail to give constructive release to their emotions.

An acceptable avenue of expression must be found if the individual is to remain able to continue his adjustment to the demands of society. Does this explain why Mrs. R. talks incessantly? Does she find release in recounting the minute details of an incident? Does it explain why Mr. F. boasts about every little experience he has had which may be over and above his neighbor's experience? Is that why he constantly mentions the "millions and millions" of this or that which he has seen or done?

Outlets are found by some along lines that are less demanding of their friends. Some individuals become creative in letter writing, others in gardening, flower arrangements, carpentry, cooking or even in the art of attractive grooming and dress. Individuals differ in native endowment, but abilities grow with experience.

Creative Forces in Every Individual

Although creativity is a characteristic of human nature, it is all too commonly overlooked. It often demands faith in individual resources that may have remained untapped for years.

A newcomer to a college course in early childhood procedures was told to be creative in her planning. "But I haven't a creative idea in me," she protested.

"You have if you will just let it come out," asserted the instructor.

Disbelieving, but challenged, the girl went home and started to think. She was amazed at the constructive ideas that came to her.

Spontaneity in Young Children

There are those who recognize creativity as basic to personal development, and know that if encouraged it wells and outpours from each individual. The way someone walks, looks, talks, and acts will reveal to what extent he has released the creative forces within him. Just as a flower will flourish and blossom when placed in an environment suited to its innate growth pattern, so creativity will develop within the individual who nurtures it.

Early childhood education, in making creative expression one of its goals, recognizes creativity as a basic characteristic of all human nature. It is by no means limited to childhood. Herein lies a challenge to the adult to unshackle the restrictions that keep him from being creative. Once this is consistently done, the outpouring of the self in response to impressions begins. Directing the course that creativity takes then becomes the chief concern; but young children possess the quality of nonselfconscious spontaneity that creativity demands.

Reflections of Impressions

Adults who desire to cultivate creativity within themselves should seek the quality of spontaneity which children possess. The premise, "There is no impression without expression," is more than a theory. It is a characteristic of growth. The young child can be outgoing and expressive with ease. He is constantly giving out what he has taken in. Through all of his five senses he receives impressions which he is impelled by nature to interpret. What the child says and does is an indication of what has impressed him. What he sees, hears, smells, tastes, and touches impresses him most, but more and more often, what comes forth is modified by his own interpretation of experiences.

David, age five, had watched the gold fish in his aquarium, but David had never had an opportunity to swim. When this experience finally came he told about it afterward in ecstasy. "A ripple came into my mouth, just like our gold fish."

Robert had seen palm trees in pictures and on television, but when he made a trip to a locality where he saw these trees in reality for the first time he remarked:

"Palm trees are people in skirts."

Greg came back from the duck pond with shining eyes, and said:

"I went over to those ducks and they were going

'Punk, punk, punk, punk, punk!' "

He made a series of rapid, explosive sounds as he spoke. His face lighted up and he seemed completely captivated by the repetition of the rhythmical pattern and said it over and over again.

Jackie used a combination of language and body motion to convey the impression he got of the ducks, in a chant he half sang, half said:

"The little ducklings are in the rain,
Quacking all around.
When their mother takes them to the pond
They swim round and round."

As he came to the last line he ran lightly in small circles, in and out.

Only in a relaxed atmosphere where children feel comfortable and free to express their true selves do they find the glow of satisfaction that comes in releasing their emotions through creative art, music, dance, language, and drama.

Gerald gave evidence of such an atmosphere when he said, "Hand painting twirls and whirls like music. It is fun to say 'twirls and whirls.' It feels good on my mouth."

In contrast to him was Jamie, who revealed the degree of restraint he was feeling in his indoor environment when he said, "I'm going outdoors to get all the wiggles out."

Ralph, six years, two months, in describing a piece of music, said, "It curls and swirls and twirls." He illustrated each word with a full body whirl.

These five- and six-year-olds found release, each in his own way. Their expression came through a variety of media.

What Happens from Within

If you are sensitive to the development of the children in your group, you will recognize that choice of art media and growth in their use are determined by the child himself, not by the curriculum. What each child does in the art forms is a matter of readiness and experience, as well as of native endowment.

Through creative expression, something happens to the individual from within. It may be through rhythmic body movement or songs or dance or simple instruments; through prose or poetry; through carpentry, clay, paint, or any one or all of the art media.

The child who uses colors, who puts his ideas and experiences into words or body rhythms, who enjoys dramatic expression in his own unique way because it brings satisfaction to him from within, will come forth with bits of loveliness from his own observations and experience, and will know the joy of creativity and the emotional release which it provides.

If the curriculum is to be governed by what is known about children, all who are ready to "begin where the child is" realize that what the young child produces is not the criterion by which his growth should be judged. What happens within him through producing it is the vital factor. His potentiality for further expression grows with each new satisfying experience in creativity.

While changing the water for her snail, Marjorie vocalized in singsong fashion:

Whether or not her song had a conventional rhythm is immaterial. For Marjorie the experience was the next step in her growth toward creative expression in music.

Sometimes a universal thought is re-expressed by an individual child. The words or the melody, unknown to him, may be very much as someone else has used them before, but in expressing them anew a child may be genuinely creative. In the following song Randy caught the spirit felt by the group. He sang it out as he felt it:

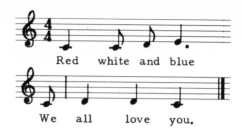

Delight in the Doing

The young child finds satisfaction in expression that does not require fine muscular or technical control.

Kathy revealed her delight in a simple, everyday experience when she said, "The sand tickles my hands."

Seven-year-old Patty said with genuine enthusiasm:

> "Music! Music! Music!
> Soft and loud,
> Fast and slow.
> What fun we have
> experimenting with the instruments!"

Patty's "instruments" were soft-toned drums and rattles providing extreme ease of manipulation.

Juanita, moving with nimble feet while she shook the tambourine, exclaimed, "I can dance in circles like the fiesta." Her body moved in a spontaneous pattern as she reconstructed in her own way the dancing that was a common experience in her home.

Arthur brushed a group of bright colors on his easel paper and said, "This rainbow makes me feel like singing."

Eleanor finished her work at the easel, using calcimine paint and a long-handled brush. It was a riot of color touched off with a bright yellow orb in the upper right corner. She expressed her mood with a simple statement: "The sun smiles on a happy picture."

Handpainting

In handpainting, more commonly known as finger painting, color and paints are used directly with hands outspread against the paper. Sometimes a quiet child will find this his first medium of creative expression.

Footpainting

Some children find keen satisfaction in painting with the bare feet. A piece of linoleum, oilcloth or plastic material serves to protect the floor.

Shoes and socks are removed and trouser legs rolled up or skirts pinned back. A waterproof apron protects the child's clothing.

To facilitate true creative expression, certain behavior patterns and attitudes must be established that insure effective use of the material. This is true of any art medium, but particularly of one which may be new to you or the children.

Parental approval is needed before a child ever paints with his feet for the first time, so that mother and father will not think Johnnie is turning into "something new and strange," should he come home with traces of green or some other color between his toes.

Individual towels are brought by each child and sanitary precautions are observed in changing the water used for washing the feet. Preparation for washing and drying the feet is made in advance of putting the feet on the paper where a small quantity of hand paint has been placed. As the child stands, he holds onto a table or other steadying support, but he has freedom of motion as he spreads the paint over the paper with his feet. The child's joy in discovering new effects produced by various motions of toes, ball of foot, heel and full print is heartening to observe. The experience is, of course, limited to one or two children at a time, but can be offered from day to day until eventually all who wish may try this medium of expression while the majority of the children work at various other activities. Many delightful pictures result, which the children can share with the group afterward if they wish.

Individuality Finds Expression

Each individual child, if he feels free to do so, is able to respond joyously and in his own way to the experiences life brings him.

Rosalie, in her sixth year, brought back an impression from a trip to the ocean. She ran in circles, arms outstretched, crying,

"Sea gulls are flying all around,
Up in the air and on the ground."

In a more restrained fashion, but nonetheless expressive, Arlene observed: "The seaweed makes jewelry for the beach."

Bernard, returning from the same trip, molded a large piece of pliable potter's clay to represent, "gliding, swooping, sea gulls."

Marie illustrated with musical tone blocks how "The ocean sounds swishy-swash."

Billy, with handpaint, showed how "The ocean grays away."

Denny, age eight, used the medium of written word as follows:

"Dredger, dredger, you go so slow.
　　You can't go fast because you're so big.
　　You push sand in round pipes,
　　　Then you go over to the pier."

Step by step, you will strive to lead each child to use whatever medium of expression makes him feel at ease and brings him a sense of accomplishment, be it paint, craft, rhythm, tone, drama, or words. Little by little he will find satisfaction in each of these forms. Through this approach you not only give him the freedom and joy of creativity, but also help him to recognize and cherish his own worth as an individual.

Charles went to the aviary and said very little at the time, but later at school, his eyes lighted up as he told the other children:

"There is a bird with a black tail
and striped red wings.
　　We saw him at the aviary.
　　He was all yellow underneath.
　　Oh, he was gorgeous!"

The Universal Appeal of Nature

Nature has universal appeal, and probably stimulates more creativity than any other influence.

Steve was going to take a vacation trip up the Redwood Highway in California. Knowing his deep sensitivity to beauty and grandeur, his teacher had encouraged his interest in reading on the subject. Steve's enthusiasm was caught by the others in the group, and parents and children alike joined in doing some intensive research on the significant characteristics of the "Sequoia Sempervirens."

Finally, Steve and his family arrived in the redwood groves, and the boy was completely captivated when he beheld the magnificence of these august giants of the forest. His background was so genuine that he approached these trees with depth of understanding, and to him they were living personages. This he expressed in spontaneous verse that shows his command of meter and rhyme:

King of the woods
So tall you stand;
You reach so high
Above the land.

I look at you,
You make me sing.
You are the largest
Living thing.

Your trunk is old,
Your green is new.
Oh, redwood trees,
I appreciate you.
                    Steve (9 years old)

Solitude

Many individuals catch the creative spirit through aloneness, thinking
and feeling in solitude. Every person needs some solitude, and children
can early learn to appreciate its beneficent effect. Far too frequently today, however, children race from one pressing demand to another and
are actively occupied or passively entertained hour after hour until they
almost drop from nervous exhaustion. Teachers as well as parents can do
much in encouraging individuals to have some solitude and to learn to
enjoy it.

Brian's parents owned an attractive trailer park for adults only. The
grounds were landscaped with trees and shrubs throughout. During his
growing years the son helped his father faithfully, keeping the grounds in
excellent condition. One day when Brian was ten years old he sat down in
the leaves to rest. Believing himself to be alone, he was heard to say:
"Oh, you beautiful Little Towhee! Thank you for coming to see me.
What do you eat, Little Towhee? Would you like me to find you a worm
among the leaves? Or do you like seeds? I'll have to read about you in my
bird book.
"I like your bright eyes and your soft feathers. Stay with me, Brown Bird,
while I rake leaves."

Fantasy

When children have maturity and background enough to discriminate
between the real and the imaginary, their command of the fanciful is reflected in their creative expression.
Bobby knows the basic scientific facts about the sun and moon, but his
poetic thought shows his joy in going beyond these facts into the realm of
imagination when he says:

"The sun sets the clouds on fire,
   and the moon puts them out."

Carl, another six-year-old, says:

> "Little tiny raindrops
> Fly down on their rocket ships.
> They hit my window sill,
> Bing, bing, bong!"

This child's delight at the moment is in discovering a certain similarity between the swift falling of the rain and his favorite mode of travel. This is the child artist's viewpoint—seeing the likenesses between unlike things, and expressing them in language, body rhythm, color, or sound. Confusion may result when the make-believe is forced on the child before he is able to make this distinction.

Personification is a stage of creative expression in which natural phenomena are endowed with human feelings and characteristics. Robert, five years, seven months, says: "The little baby cloud is trying to cry."

Joan, at ten, displays fine command of a delightful imagination through expressing an abstract idea in concrete terms.

> I am a butterfly,
> I light on the trees,
> You are the flowers
> That nod in the breeze.
>
> Buzz, buzz, buzz!
> I am a bumble bee;
> I am black and yellow,
> A funny old fellow.
>
> I am a spider,
> I am building a web;
> It hangs from a rose tree
> And looks like silk thread.
>
> I am Nature;
> I am in the sweet wild flowers
> And in the April showers.
> I am Nature.

With more maturity comes the ability to identify self with situations farther removed in time and place.

Time and Patience for Growth in Creative Expression

In guiding creative expression there needs to be much waiting and patient acceptance of the phenomenon of natural growth, whether it be individual or in group work. Days, weeks, or even months of quiet guidance are often needed. Much later can come discussion, evaluation, comment, re-evaluation, and sharing of thoughts and ideas that have to do with construction and form. Creative expression cannot be manufactured mechanically; it is the outpouring of an impression keenly felt.

A teacher had given her group many poems and songs all through the year. The children had delighted in and spontaneously learned a wide repertoire of poetry and song, but there had not been anything from them that seemed to indicate a desire to create in this medium. But one April morning when the teacher's discouragement was at its blackest point, Lois came skipping into the room saying:

> "Grass, grass, grass
> Grows all around.
> Trees are green,
> And canaries, jays and bluebirds
> sing all day long."

The response Lois elicited was like a chain reaction among her peers. Ray chanted:

> "Butterfly, butterfly,
> So black and yellow,
> So pretty.
> You fly high and drink nectar
> from the flowers."

Elsie said:

> "Birds fly in the air,
> They flutter and flap their wings,
> They fly to their nests.
> Then down they fly again to find
> Worms for their babies."

Patrick began to sing:

Then Patrick and several others moved in light, rhythmic steps as he hummed a spontaneous melody without words.

Lois, whose observation had inspired these outbursts of poetic thought, climaxed the experience by dancing joyfully about and singing:

From then on, the children almost thought poetically. The background the teacher had given them over a period of many months finally found expression when they were ready for it. Their growth was reward enough for their teacher's longtime guidance and understanding.

When you recognize the significance of creative expression, you will want to make it an integral part of your school curriculum. Teachers frequently fail to do this because of a false emphasis on the finished product, rather than on the creative experience itself.

A well-meaning teacher made much of the children "graduating" from her room. She insisted that there be a picture of each child in the last issue of the group's newspaper. Beneath the picture the child was expected to have an original poem. Some of the children created easily and spontaneously, but others were unable to make a rhyme. The teacher was not satisfied with anything but a rhymed verse under each child's name. Those who could not meet this requirement readily were kept after school until they had something, no matter how labored and with what rebellion of spirit it was "created."

Adults who are guiding children need to guard against the tendency to polish or work over what the children have done. Alice's verbal expression, simple though it may be, must stand because it is really her own:

> "What kind of music
> Does the gourd make?
> Rat——tle! Rat——tle!
> Rat——tle! Rat——tle! Rat——tle!"

Her teacher's recognition of this, which at the time was the best Alice could do, cleared the way for the child to try again. Not what she did, but the fact that she did it is the chief consideration here. This is no place for formal evaluation.

Rich experiences in doing, thinking, and expressing her happy, normal child interests gradually led Alice toward growth. Six months later she was making a whole series of questions and answers which reveal her progress in expressing herself:

> "What is sunshine for?
> To make it light so it can be morning.
> What is the moon for?
> To make it dark so it can be night.
> What is the night for?
> So you can sleep.
> What is a house for?
> To sleep in or else you'd get wet.
> What are clothes for?
> So you won't be cold when you go outside."

About this time Alice showed growth in her use of the rattle to express ideas. "The wind swishes the leaves," she said, making a whirring sound as she whirled the gourd at arm's length. This was not particularly unusual or difficult, but it was a truly creative experience for her.

Spontaneous Group Expression

In encouraging Alice in her earlier experiments with words and musical instrument, her teacher was freeing the child to make whatever use of the media she wished. This was essential, but it was not enough. Gradually, day by day, this teacher had led her group to become more aware of various things in their environment. Sounds, smells, colors, sizes; interesting observations about changes in weather, sunlight, clothing; details that interest children and sharpen their sensitivity; these and many other things were discovered by the group from day to day. Telling about those things, painting them, expressing them in bodily rhythmic activity, instrument, and song, all led to many experiences in creativity. There was joy in the doing and in the sharing of discoveries, rather than concern over the ways various art forms should be used. When new words were discovered, or interesting techniques arrived at in color combinations or sound effects, individuals shared their discoveries with the group. The result was a growing understanding of how various media could be used for creative expression.

As an example of the type of creativity that was typical before the end of the year, one spring day the children dictated the following lines to their teacher:

Rainy Day Noises

Pitter patter, pitter patter
   says the rain on the roof.
Trickle, trickle, trickle
   down the window pane.
Drip, drip, drip, as it falls
   off the roof.

By quiet guidance of the children's thinking, then waiting, watching, and encouraging creativity, another teacher was delighted when many composite verbal expressions came from her group, such as the following:

Fuzzy, wuzzy caterpillar
   is black and funny.
He creeps along quietly.
   Keep-a-keep-a-crawling,
Fuzzy little caterpillar,
   Spin a cocoon
   for a blanket.
When you wake up
   What will you be?

By providing many opportunities for experiences, by furnishing the children with an environment in which they may live in a democratic group, by developing the behavior patterns, attitudes, appreciations essential for growth, and by introducing the media for expression, creativity is nurtured. In such a school climate, expressions like the following will often come forth:

Our Sweet Potato Vine
(Poem Created by Group)

Our sweet potato grew so big,
It climbed right up the wall.
The little roots went down,
And the vine grew tall.

This poem was developed by lower primary children who dictated it as their teacher wrote it for them on the chalkboard. Later, she made several copies of the poem on standard sheets of paper, and individuals who wished to do so wrote their own copies from these at their seats, rather than from the chalkboard.

In the above environment, stories, songs, and poetry introduced by the teacher exert an immediate influence that appears in what is done by the children.

The story of an airplane journey, for example, was reflected in paintings, spontaneous songs, and dramatic expression, as well as in words. One of their first composite group expressions after hearing the story was:

An Airplane

The propellers go around.
The pilot pulls the throttle.
Roar go the motors.
The plane taxies, then takes off.
Fly, fly, fly.
Fly, airplane.
Fly away, away.

The first time Bobby worked at the easel after this composite story was made he had the following to say about his painting:

> "Flying o'er the ocean,
>   Out across the sea,
>   Watching the ships down below
>   Where the little
>   Toot-toot-tugs go."

Group Expression Through Conscious Effort

Older groups may produce with conscious effort what younger children, or those with more experience in creative expression, may do with spontaneity.

Ten-year-old Jack brought in a pet garter snake in his pocket. Instead of rejecting this threat to classroom equanimity, his teacher accepted the innovation in the spirit in which it was presented. Jack, as a result, gave a demonstration of his control over his pet by having the snake crawl over his hands and arms. An acceptable temporary pen was made for it, and the children, working through various sources, gained more knowledge of snakes in general and Jack's pet in particular. Then the group came together to compare their findings. Aside from the factual recounting of ideas, there was a desire to "make something really good" about Jack's pet.

"What words could we use to describe the way he goes when he crawls?" Ken asked.

"We could say 'Wiggle-waggle-wiggle,' " Billy suggested.

"The snake 'slithers' along," said Thelma, illustrating with her hand.

" 'Slithers' sounds good, but it isn't really a word," said Mary. "Let's think of something else."

"How about 'slides along'?" offered Jimmie.

" 'Slides' is all right, I know," said Jack, "but my Dad said the snake slithers along. I think that's a good word, too. Isn't it, Miss Bates?"

" 'Slither' has a special meaning," the teacher explained. "Where could you go to find out whether a word is good and what it means?"

"Let's look in the dictionary," said Billy.

"Thelma used the word first. It was her idea," said Miss Bates. "Mary challenged it. Which one of you would like to look it up?"

"I will," volunteered Mary. After finding the correct place she read aloud: "Slither: to slide or slip along, often in snakelike fashion." Then she added, "That's the very word we need."

"I think we should tell what kind of a snake he is," suggested Peter.

"It would be better to use some words of color, maybe," said William, thinking out loud.

After a discussion in this vein, the group elected Donald to be secretary and to write what they dictated about the fascinating intruder. The group's evaluation of their own ideas brought forth the following descriptive account:

Our Visitor

Wiggle-waggle-wiggle.
Jack's snake slithers along.
He is a black and orange ring-necked snake.
Sh! Sh! Sh!
He moves so quietly.

Encouraging Quality of Expression

Evaluation of creative effort requires a delicate balance between interest in growth of the individual personality and a desire to encourage greater command of the art media.

First must be built confidence that creative efforts, whether group or individual, will be acceptable, as long as they are "best efforts" done in good faith. The child's honest query must be, "Have I really tried to the best of my ability?"

The caution in this approach lies in the possibility that, if not balanced by certain other considerations, this attitude may lead to the type of reaction sometimes shown by the person who continually wants his work to be the center of attention and who, regardless of the merit of his artistic efforts, wants recognition merely because he has done something. The adult who "rides his hobby" in this way can be decidedly unpopular, and rightly so.

The child who can honestly say, "I have really tried, to the best of my ability," can feel a genuine sense of satisfaction in the sincerity of his efforts. But along with this must be the knowledge that personal growth can and will come through experience. Once established, these basic attitudes toward the child's own work and the work of his classmates, will generate growth in quality of expression. Then, and not until then, can thought be given to details of structure, content, and form in any of the art media.

When the child has sufficient maturity, evaluations of his work may include suggestions without stifling his creativity. He may be guided into further progress by calling his attention to a certain effect he has produced in the work he is doing or has just completed. "What makes it the way it is?" "What did you do to get it that way?" As he evaluates his work in this fashion, suggestions may come to his attention for improvements in his work or for different effects he might try. He may be helped to visualize what it would be like if he were to do it in a slightly different way next time. In such manner do standards change and grow. As the child develops, he reaches out toward new horizons of achievement, step by step, to accomplish certain desired purposes.

In any creative expression, the outward product is an index into the inner self, and as such is worthy of appreciation for what it represents. Because he is growing, what the child is producing will also grow with each new experience, little by little. Your faith in this type of growth brings better results in the child's mastery of media than too great concern over details of structure. An unhurried work atmosphere, free from stresses and anxieties, is reflected in greater control of art media.

Creativity acts like a generator in a powerhouse. Once in operation it continues to convert the child's inner resources into constructive channels of expression.

QUESTIONS ON THE SIX GOALS:
IV. CREATIVE EXPRESSION

1. How does the reaction of the five- or six-year-old to his immediate environment often differ sharply from that of the adult? Why? Discuss the educational implications of the child's response.

2. Through what media other than words do children express their impressions of life? How? Give illustrations from your own observation of children.

3. How is the child's individuality expressed through various creative media? Illustrate and discuss.

4. Explain why no two paintings are ever the same when children work creatively. What is the educational significance of this fact?

5. Discuss the premise that creativity is a universal characteristic of all human beings.

6. a. Why is it important that the child be able to discriminate between what is real and what is imaginary?

b. How does the child's creative expression reveal his "command" of the fanciful?

7. When you are not as much concerned with what children do as with the fact that they do it, how will you guide them toward creative uses of materials? Discuss the educational significance.

8. Why are days, weeks or even months of quiet guidance often needed before children will express their impressions creatively? Illustrate.

9. How can you encourage and guide group experiences in creativity? Give concrete suggestions. Discuss.

10. Discuss the viewpoint that something keenly felt will lead to creative expression. What guidance from the teacher is needed for this to happen?

11. How can you recognize and encourage growth in quality of expression without stifling the child's creativity?

12. What is implied by the term "creative teaching"? Give examples.

THE SIX GOALS: V. INDEPENDENT
THINKING AND PROBLEM SOLVING

America needs a literate population; even more, she needs people who are willing to cooperate with others, while still thinking independently and solving their own problems; a people who approach each new task with enthusiasm, imagination, and vision.

Problem Solving Is Universal

One of the objectives of the school is to develop thinking, purposeful individuals who first review all the facets of a question and then consciously choose the way that is most beneficial to the group—not the way that would further their own selfish interests. Such individuals are educated, not only intellectually, but socially and emotionally as well, and each is ready to become a constructive member of society.

Many people think of problem solving only in relation to arithmetic, but in reality this ability concerns whatever problem the individual meets. Whether they relate to a child at school or an adult in the home, there are problems in human relationships; problems in how to do things the best way; problems in planning; and problems in the use of equipment and supplies. Creativeness evidences itself in the way the individual attacks a problem to be solved. Problem solving cuts across all fields of study and every phase of life.

It takes time and patience and much guidance for the child to learn to think independently and still recognize his responsibility toward other people. Together with his ability to solve problems, he needs a strong social consciousness to help him set up standards for himself in his relationships with other people. Unless this social consciousness is built up with his problem solving ability, he may become anti-social, self-centered and bossy, or even criminal.

Developing Individual Responsibility for Problems

Children learn to think by thinking. All through the day there are problems that require thought. The child's zone of action may encompass reading, writing, arithmetic, dramatization, or painting. It may include a story or a poem, rhythm and song, block building, carpentry, or assembling a puzzle. Whatever the child does, it should create the need for thinking.

When the child meets a problem, you can say to him: "Do this, and this, and this," but unless he has a share in thinking through how it is to be solved, he will need your help for the next problem, too, and the next and the next. Instead of telling the child just how to solve each problem he meets, you may ask, "How would it be if _____?" "What could happen if _____?" "Is this a different problem from the one you had when you _____ _____ _____?" "How is it different?"

You can employ many stories to illustrate the problem solving principle you are trying to impart, and then use the discussion period to direct the children's thoughts to it. "Why did you do it that way, John? What problems did you solve?"

"How could Arthur have avoided getting into this difficulty? What is his problem?"

"Ralph, what would you do?"

"Betty, what do you think about _____? Why?"

If your children are constantly to be challenged to think, you must bring them into zones of action which compel them to reason. If a child's problem is one he is capable of solving, he needs the experience of doing the thinking himself.

In formulating questions for children it is important to make them challenging and direct. Questions that can be answered by a "yes" or "no" are seldom as thought-provoking as those which require further thinking.

"Does the sky look as if it might rain?" is not as challenging a question as "What makes us think it might rain today?"

Your Help May Be Needed

In developing his ability to solve problems, the child may need an adult to assist in the performance of some manual skills which he may not yet have acquired the physical coordination to accomplish. If you would lead him toward independent problem solving, make sure the child feels free to ask for help whenever it is really justified.

> Five-year-old Glenn came to the teacher with two toy cars and asked, "Please tie these together for me."
>
> Teacher: "What could we use to tie them?"
>
> Glenn: "We could use string."
>
> Teacher: "Where could we find some string?"
>
> Glenn: "Maybe in the drawer."
>
> Teacher: "You can go get the string."
>
> Glenn went to the drawer, and returning with string said, "Now you can tie up my cars."
>
> Teacher: "How shall we tie them?"
>
> Glenn: "Tie the string around here."
>
> Teacher: "You show just where it could go."
>
> (Glenn indicates with his hands.)
>
> Teacher: "Like this?"
>
> (Glenn nods.)
>
> Teacher: "Now what shall we do to make it stay."
>
> Glenn: "Tie a knot."
>
> (The teacher ties a knot.) "There! Now the cars will stay together."
>
> Glenn: (Off with cars.) "Toot! Toot!"
>
> Glenn participated in thinking through how to accomplish what he wanted to do, even though he had to call upon an adult's assistance in accomplishing it. This is far different from simply turning the problem over to the teacher for solution.

When You Are Not Needed

When Billy comes to you to have his apron tied, you might say to him, "What would you do if I were not here?"

Billy's answer: "I would go and ask Judy to do it."

Your smile reassures him and Billy will go over to seek Judy's help. Judy will undoubtedly be delighted to help Billy, and the problem is solved without the need for adult assistance.

Independence in solving problems is achieved through the type of guidance that is aware of children's actions but does not dominate them.

> Ernest, at the music corner, was working with drums and other instruments. Mary, who was feeding the rabbits, said, "Someone is playing the drums too loud. It will startle the rabbits if we play the drums so loud." She went over to the music table and explained the problem to Ernest who was willing to cooperate in solving it.
>
> In another group the following was overheard as the children caught the significance between one situation and another: "If the kids walk on the plants we can do the same thing we do with blocks—you know—just sit down and talk it over." Here, a means of meeting one problem carried over into another.

Requests That Stimulate Thinking

Through skillfully questioning children you can do much to stimulate mental activity. Sometimes, however, a statement is better than a question, if it demands that the children think and use judgment.

"Can you read what Sally did?" may put doubt in the child's mind as to whether he can really read it. A more effective way is to say, "Read the sentence that tells what Sally did."

Later, the child who has learned that to read is to find out something, would readily respond to the request, "Find out what made Sally go to the park." By reading and thinking independently the child would be able to comply with this request.

The "would you like to" type of question is justifiable only when an answer either way is acceptable. It implies an independent choice. If you ask a question of this kind when the child's compliance is expected, you raise the issue of whether or not he wants to do what is requested without offering him a genuine opportunity to decide. When the child really answers the "would you like" question truthfully, a negative reply should be just as acceptable as a positive one. Such a question is best avoided in matters where the child can have no choice.

Another type of question to be avoided is one that can be answered by an untruth, as "Did you spill the paint, Alfred?" The wrong kind of thinking is invited here, and falsehood is more likely. An alternative might be: "Somebody had an accident, didn't he? Accidents do happen sometimes. Whoever it was can help by wiping it up. You know where we keep the floor sponge."

Such a statement will offer the child who did it an opportunity to solve the problem he has created.

Toward Self-Direction

You must take the child's mental maturity into consideration when you give directions. Many adults tend to overlay idea upon idea. "Clean up your work, wipe up the paint, get a book from the library table, and then come to the rug," is not the kind of direction that the majority of children can follow. The last thought, being the most recent one, will probably be followed. The children will forget about the clean-up.

Directions may be given in such a way that they stimulate children to think. "Look around where you are and see how you can clean up your work, now." A few minutes later this might need to be followed with, "You know what to do when you have cleaned up."

Many times a child fails to stop doing what he is engaged in when a change of activity is in order. First, you should give him questions such as, "Why is it important to put these things away now?" "What else needs to be done next?" "How can we get ready to do that?"

The foundation must be laid for such thinking through many discussions of how things are done, why, and what children who have finished their work might do while waiting for others to finish. Instead of telling the children just what to do time after time, you should encourage them to think through with you what needs to be done and how to do it. Each day brings greater independence in accomplishment. Growth takes place not only in doing, but in thinking and planning.

Choices

Making choices and decisions is a form of independent thinking. Instead of being merely a matter of preference, a choice may involve deciding which of two alternatives would be better.

Although there are certain things, such as: rest, going to the toilet, waiting turns and sharing, which every child must do, there are many opportunities for free choice, as,

"Choose a picture from the file and make a story from it."

"Are you going to work with clay or at the easel today?"

"Would you rather water the plants, or would you prefer to care for the bird this week?"

Children usually select the thing in which they are interested and can learn to choose what is within the range of their ability. Even young children may choose the equipment they will use for the time being, the colors with which they will paint, the vase for the flowers they have brought, the songs they will sing, the stories for you to tell. True, the vase or the book selected is one of several already placed on the shelf; the songs and stories are from those previously presented by you. Nevertheless, the decision is the child's, as far as he is concerned.

A child may not only choose some of the activities in which he will participate, but he may make his own plans before he begins work. It takes a certain amount of maturity for Jack to say: "I am going to build with blocks today. I am going to make a boat. It will be a long boat, and I will put three people in it. One will be my Daddy, and one will be Fred, and one will be me."

A less mature child works such things out as he goes along. Either way, there is independent thinking in accordance with the child's stage of development.

Making Decisions Important to the Child

Six-year-old Ricky had eight wooden doll people huddled in a group next to a wooden train. The teacher inquired what the "people" were doing, and the answer was, "Well, they all want to be the engineer of the train, so they're talking it over."

After several minutes of this, Ricky looked up and said, "They decided that all of them would be sleeping on the train while this blue man is the engineer."

To Ricky it was really important to think things over, even in the manipulation of his toys.

Thinking in Concrete Terms

In an effort to encourage choices, you may be tempted to try to have the child think in the abstract before he is ready to do so. With younger children, thinking is closely related to action. Three-dimensional materials are needed for his problem solving.

Which dress fits best on this doll?

Which ladder will reach to the top of the block house?

How many children can work comfortably at this table?

Where may the easels be placed so those who paint may have the best light for working on this cloudy day?

These choices involve reasoning rather than preference.

Older children may select the committees on which they will work; the ideas they would like to develop in a chart; the research they will undertake; the roles they are to portray in the dramatization; the way they word their diary accounts of experiences.

These are only a few of the many opportunities children may be given to make choices each day. The more choices and decisions they make, based on sound reasoning, the more they grow in ability to make wise judgments.

Responsibilities Mean Thinking Independently

Even in primary, a child can judge his own progress in learning the number combinations, by means of a graph on which he plots his daily score. He can keep a record of the words and phrases which he has difficulty reading, and be responsible for mastering them independently. He can have the care of certain centers in the room and report to the group his recommendations for the management of the centers. All of these duties involve not only responsibility, but independent thinking.

Children who run to you with every problem are not learning how to take care of things for themselves. They need guidance in standing up for their own rights and in settling difficulties among themselves. One example of this is in the use of equipment and supplies. The mere problem of several children using the slide at the same time presents an opportunity for independent thinking. One solution would be for you to make a rule autocratically that one person slide at a time. "We don't go backwards, We don't push and shove, We don't crowd," and other negative admonitions stifle independent thinking.

A better approach when the children start crowding is to draw the group together and say, "Here is a problem. Let's talk it over. What are we trying to do? Ben, what do you want to do?"

Ben: I want to slide.

Elaine: I want to slide, too.

Teacher: When two people want to use the slide, what can we do?

Elaine: We can take turns.

Teacher: If we have more than two people, what can we do?

They decide how they can work it out together. You watch to make sure they abide by their decisions, and guide them as necessary.

Your Thoughtful Guidance

When children are led to become increasingly independent of you in resolving their own social difficulties satisfactorily, they are learning to substitute reason for physical might, and they are being encouraged to think. You talk to them, person to person, and help them see how they can solve many of their own problems. A child will rise to the occasion when given to understand that you have confidence in what he can do and expect him to take responsibility. Opportunities of this type present themselves to you frequently if you are primarily concerned with your children's development.

When Mike called his plane a "baby plane," his teacher might have responded, "No, Mike, it is not a baby plane; it is a sea plane." But instead of telling him outright she led him to want to know what kind of plane he really had, and how he might find out. She taught him how, with a little research, he could uncover the facts for himself.

Similarly, when Kathy pounded a nail through a piece of wood, and the nail went into the bench, the teacher did not remove it for her, but helped her solve her own problem, thus leading her toward independent thinking.

When two children both want to sharpen a pencil, one may rush in ahead of the other. The second child may attempt to shove the first one out. You might say, "Roger, take your seat," or you might send both to their seats, but if you are attuned to the problem solving philosophy you will say, "Roger and Billy, what is your problem?" and help them to solve it for themselves.

You may guide the children so deftly they are scarcely aware of it. You encourage them to suggest, to choose, to think through, and then to carry out their ideas, but you demand only what the child is able to give. Your guidance depends on the basic attitude in the group of children. If a child has been told over and over again what to do, and is trying to do it merely because someone says so, how is he going to learn to take the responsibility for his own actions, and to think things out for himself? On the contrary, complete abandonment without any guidance will result in confusion. Each experience that offers consistent help for independent thinking makes the child more able to meet his next problem. The particular way you work with your children will, of course, depend upon their degree of maturity.

Responsible Thinking Within the Sphere of Growth

This philosophy of problem solving is opposed to the viewpoint which some hold, that children require the domination of wiser, more experienced adults until they reach an age where they can make decisions for themselves. This viewpoint overlooks the fact that in order to reach the age of discretion the child needs opportunities to make decisions in matters which are within his ability to handle. Children do need guidance and close supervision, but observation, study, and experience show that the young child is capable of thinking independently within his developmental limits. The problem is to discover ways of guiding him within that wide world of activities where he has the capacity and freedom to exercise control. Responsibilities within this sphere will mean growth to the child if he thinks them through independently. There are some matters, of course, for which he will need help in making his decisions; while in some still more weighty matters, decisions will need to be made for him.

It is sometimes difficult to differentiate between what a child is able to do alone and what he needs guidance to do. You can help alleviate this difficulty if you observe and listen to the children and discover how they really think. Through the general trend of their behaviors they reveal themselves and their backgrounds.

Too Soon Forgotten

An experience which affords numerous opportunities to think things through is the field trip as it is planned in the modern school—in contrast to the teacher-controlled excursion. In the traditional "book way," before her children went to the depot, one authoritarian teacher said, "We are going to take a trip to see the train station. No one will run ahead or shout. You will listen to everything the man tells you, and won't interrupt him to ask any questions. Then when we come back again, we will see how much of it you can tell me about."

Then the children were bundled into cars or transported by bus to the depot. They heard a man give a long talk and they walked through the station. They got back in the bus and returned to school. Then their teacher started questioning them. "How many trains did the man say went through the depot every day? How much steam pressure do they have? How fast did the man say the trains go?"

And the trip was soon forgotten.

Laboratory for Learning

A similar group of children took a trip to the depot and came back better able to reason, plan, and learn from observation.

Before going to the station *these six-year-olds had exhibited a marked interest in trains.* They asked many questions, some of which could be answered through books and pictures of trains. For days they were concerned with what they could find out by going to the depot. The teacher guided their work and jotted down questions as they arose. One of their purposes in going on the field trip was to discover more from personal

observation and inquiry. Some of the questions this group suggested are
here recorded *in their own words*. Differences in maturity are evident:

> How big are the trains?
> What kind of tickets do they sell at the depot?
> What kind of trains do people sleep on?
> Do they have tables to eat on?
> Is there a kitchen on the trains?
> What makes the trains go?
> How do the wheels work?
> What makes the train hang together?
> Who makes the train whistle?
> How does the train stop?
> How do people get on and off the train?
> Where do they put their suitcases?
> How do the people know when to get off?

Instead of correcting a child's question when it was poorly phrased, or
restating it herself, this teacher would ask, "How could you say this in a
different way so that it will mean more to us?"

The questions became more thought-provoking as she and the children
continued these discussions. The teacher was always careful not to inhibit
the children's thinking by putting words in their mouths. In situations of
this kind it is important that children have the opportunity to deliberate
about their problems until they reach satisfying conclusions. A certain
quality of patience is of paramount importance.

On the way to the depot the children looked for things they wanted to
know more about. They even noticed a new stop light on the street
corner, and they went through a new underpass in which they became
deeply interested. This led to more questions and further study at a later
time.

Planning and Following Through

One of the problems these children solved with their teacher before
going on the trip was, "How will good citizens conduct themselves on a
field trip?" There are other ways this question might be stated: "What
are the things we need to remember about how to go and come?" or,
"What rules will help make this a good trip?"

Such thought-provoking questions helped these children realize the
need for self-control. They insisted that all should stay together and
walk slowly. "There are other places to run and play at school and at
home," they concluded, "but the depot is a place where people go to

board the trains, or to meet people getting off of trains, or to see the trains come in."

Children who habitually conduct themselves in a democratic manner as a group will be able to do so on a field trip as well as in their school environment. Other groups will find a field trip a practical way to learn how to plan together democratically and follow their plan. Orderly coming and going is an important phase of this planning. The challenge of wanting to find out about things they have listed before going makes it highly desirable for each individual to watch and listen and learn all he can by observation. Boisterousness and foolishness are seen to be in opposition to the best interests of the group and contrary to the purpose of a successful trip as evaluated by the children.

Independent Thinking After the Field Trip

The children's independent thinking was guided during the days following the trip. Comments were made at various times:

> "We found a trip can be fun, and we can learn many things at the same time."
> "Good planning made our trip successful. We should plan our next trip carefully, too."
> "We learned how trains run. We saw how people can live on trains while they are going places."
> "A blind girl was allowed to take her dog with her into the train because he is trained to guide her. There is a rule that most dogs have to ride in the baggage cars where they will not bother people."
> "It costs something to ride on a train. The fare depends upon what kind of accommodations people get, and how far they want to go. You can get a round trip to _____ for _____."

When discussing "Why our trip was successful," the children brought out the following points:

> "Talking it over before we went helped us know how to act. We knew why we were going and what we wanted to find out."
> "Each one watched his own self and thought what was best to do."
> "Everyone stayed together."
> "We looked and listened, mostly, and learned all we could. When we talked we really had something important to say."
> "We helped each other remember what to do."
> "It was fun to go together."
> "When can we take another trip?"

Many ideas found expression in paintings that revealed the impressions the trip made on various individuals. Certain children also demonstrated in bodily rhythmic activities some of the problems that arise in moving trains in and out of the sidings when there are other trains and signals. They compared this with the flow of traffic along the streets and highways and at intersections, where each driver has to follow laws and solve problems to get where he wants to go.

Growth in Ability to Solve Problems Independently

Children who are consistently guided into thinking out a means of solving their own problems grow in their ability to meet them and learn to proceed on their own power. They cease to come back continually to ask for direction, and when the task is completed, they are ready for the next thing, and will have the feeling that the accomplishment is their own. This is the finest type of leadership you can give.

The pertinent factor in the development of independent thinking is that a person is truly educated only when he knows how to undertake problems and bring them to a successful conclusion. He may not know all the answers or the solutions in advance, but he does know how to arrive at many of them.

The Ultimate Outcome

Instead of its being your burden to attempt to fill the child with information, much of which he would promptly forget, it is your responsibility to guide him into finding the facts, working out solutions to his problems, and discovering what needs to be done. What he learns in this way, at his own maturation level, will long be remembered because it becomes an integral part of him. Furthermore, he will know where to go to find other information when he needs it. Graduate schools often employ this approach to teaching, and some colleges and high school departments recognize its merit. It is, however, a *must* for the early childhood years if the schools are to assume their rightful responsibility and develop true leadership. While some men and women in various communities who are recognized leaders claim to be "self-made," many of them feel that their leadership potentialities were fostered by teachers, parents, and community organizations that encouraged self-expression, independent thinking, and problem solving.

QUESTIONS ON THE SIX GOALS:
V. INDEPENDENT THINKING AND PROBLEM SOLVING

1. What type of independence is demanded of the child in the democratic classroom? How can this be developed?

2. Cite an example of a situation in which you would make sure that a child solves his own problem without the help of others.

3. How can children effectively help each other solve problems? Cite an example of a classroom situation of this nature. Evaluate it from the standpoint of: a. the child who was helped; b. those who did the helping.

4. Give examples of questions that cause a child to think independently. Discuss.

5. How can you give the child directions in a way that will stimulate independent thinking as well as cooperation? Give examples.

6. What are some of the problems a five-year-old can solve for himself? Give illustrations. With what problems does he need your assistance? How can you help a child and still lead him toward independence? Cite examples.

7. How can you give your children more experience in thinking independently by offering them choices? Illustrate.

8. When does a decision need to be made for the child? Illustrate.

9. If a decision is to be the child's own, what guidance is needed from others? Who? Discuss classroom situations.

10. Why is a child's thinking largely in the concrete rather than the abstract? Give examples.

11. What are the implications of No. 10 for academic learning?

12. How do children reveal their thinking? Give examples.

13. Why is it imperative that fact finding, problem solving and independence in thinking be well established as a policy of action in the early years of childhood? Why are these important also in later childhood and adolescence? Illustrate.

14. If you have confidence in a child's ability to take responsibility for his own actions, how can you apply this effectively in the classroom? What are some of the ways you would proceed early in the year? Later in the year? Why?

15. Following the procedures you recommend in No. 14, in what ways would you expect to see growth in self-direction and problem solving in the children in your group throughout the school year? Give illustrations.

THE SIX GOALS:
VI. UNDERSTANDING,
KNOWLEDGE, AND SKILLS

Understanding, knowledge, and skills are listed last in the goals of early childhood, not because they are any less important than the others, but because if the other five goals are really functioning, the sixth goal becomes alive. In perhaps no other phase in life is the Biblical saying, "To him that hath shall be given," more true than in this field.

When the major emphasis of administrators and teachers is on this sixth goal, to the exclusion of the other five, the result is that knowledge and skills are often demanded before the children are ready for them. In this type of program the teacher is usually a dictator in absolute command of the children; they do what she says when she says it, and as she wants it done.

All Six Goals at Work

In groups where *wholesome attitudes, automatic behavior patterns, deep appreciations, creative expression,* and *independent thinking* are stressed, experiences continually arise which are rich in learning possibilities for the widening of *understanding, knowledge, and skills.*

For example, the children in Miss Holman's primary group had had many meaningful experiences which had culminated in creative expression. The group had reached the point where everything had a creative approach. One day as these buoyant children were together, they started to discuss what time of year their various birthdays came. They decided to group themselves according to the calendar months in which they were born, and then they made an interesting observation: those with the same birthdays were the same age, but were different sizes. "Oh, look!" they said. "Some of us are tall and some are short."

A lively discussion followed. Miss Holman sensed the value of this experience for developing understanding, knowledge, and skills in the academic fields. As the children made their contributions she jotted down in manuscript writing on the chalk board what was said. As the children read back different comments they had made, they said, "We could make a poem out of it, if we would change it just a little bit. 'Tall' could rhyme with 'small.' If we put it all together that way it would make a real verse."

The result was rewarding:

People in Our Group

Some are short,
Some are tall.
Some are big,
Some are small.

Some are thin,
Some are fat.
Some are this,
Some are that.

The next day the teacher had the rhyme ready as a reading chart. It was written in large clear manuscript writing on a sheet of 24″ x 30″ tagboard so that all could see it.

As the children were reading the chart and discussing it, they clapped out the rhythm of the poem, then played it on one of the drums. They thought of ways their feet, arms, and body could move to this rhythmic pattern: short, short, long. The children had had these same words before, but now they had a different meaning. "Why, we made a dance," they said, delighted.

After they danced the rhythm they made the poem into a song with an original tune. Some of the children later painted illustrations to show different things they had done with the poem. One picture showed a group of children dancing the rhythm; another, a child playing the pattern on a drum; and still another, someone painting the illustrations. Others made clay figures to represent the children with birthdays alike, showing how they differed in size and weight. Altogether, the experience drew upon all phases of the curriculum, including manuscript writing. Some of the children wrote out the sentences from the poem that the various illustrations represented. One child made a chart showing the rhythmic pattern with long and short dashes. Others in the group went to the marimba, played the song tune, and then wrote it out in numbers. Another group made a chart giving the months of the year and the names of the children whose birthdays came then, together with the dates of the individual birthdays.

Understanding? Certainly. Knowledge? Assuredly. Skills? Most definitely.

Early Beginnings

The development of understanding, knowledge, and skills is by no means confined to the older years. The child is not, in his earliest years, merely marking time until he reaches an age in which he may learn. Understanding and knowledge, in primitive stages, develop from infancy onward. Rudimentary skills are also budding as the child learns to control his responses and redirect his unacceptable actions into acceptable channels.

By the time he reaches the toddler stage, the baby is grappling with life that is real. He is already wise in many of the ways of his world.

> At eighteen months Bobby had been having difficulty learning to indicate his need to go to the toilet, and there had been many lapses. Bobby was making every effort to cooperate. One day his mother accidentally spilled a small amount of water on the kitchen floor. Bobby came in, saw the puddle, and looked at it in a puzzled way. Then he felt of his own clothing. "Bobby dry," he announced, and repeated it for emphasis, "Bobby dry."

His *understanding* of the situation was clearly shown. It was his *skill* in controlling himself which was questioned, and he wanted it clearly shown that he carried no evidence of guilt on his person. In his own baby way he was using his *knowledge* of vocabulary to prove his innocence.

Your Responsibility for the Child's Learning

A whole world of learning waits at the threshold for the child who enters any new stage of his development. There are many facts the child needs to learn, and much knowledge you can help him acquire. How is all this going to be achieved? The keynote is that knowledge is mastered when there is need, when there is understanding, when there is a wholesome attitude and good rapport between you and the children. Understanding comes from problem solving related to experience and need, rather than through the memorization of a body of facts.

Ability to learn is a natural characteristic of all children. It is your responsibility, as well as that of his parents, to discover what understanding, knowledge, and skills the child is capable of acquiring on his own maturation level. You must find ways to help him develop them in terms of how children learn. Home and school share in this responsibility.

The Child Sets the Pace

The child is not made to have knowledge showered upon him. Nor is he ready at any age to have the skills and understandings taught to him which he will only later be prepared to grasp. Adults must gear their demands to what the child is able to learn at the time. Here the motto, "Begin where the child is," has particular significance. Concrete experience and observation come first, supplemented by facts from other people and from books.

Sometimes a young child's knowledge and understanding in a given field is astonishing. His wide background in most instances can be traced to an unusual opportunity to learn from life itself.

> For example, there was Adelaide, a five-year-old from the lower economic brackets, who attended a semi-rural school. One day her teacher said to her, "Adelaide, while I am bandaging Edna's cut, it would be a great help if you would, tell the children a story from the pictures in this book on the farm." It was a story about bringing in the cows from the pasture.
>
> Adelaide took the book and appeared to be reading from it. She made her story far more interesting than the original version.
>
> Afterwards, the children said, "Adelaide can read even better than you, Mrs. Seger."
>
> Adelaide said, "I really don't know how to read, but I tell the story because I love it so much, and I know when to turn the pages. When I get home," Adelaide continued, "I have to bring the cows back to be milked."
>
> "Whose cows are they?" asked the teacher.
>
> "They are our neighbor's cows."
>
> Mrs. Seger said, "Is that a really true story, Adelaide, or is it just a pretend story?"
>
> "It is really true," Adelaide replied. "I get ten cents a day for bringing the cows in."
>
> Because her statement had been questioned, Adelaide gave considerably more background, displaying unusual knowledge of cows.
>
> Upon investigation, Mrs. Seger found that Adelaide spent a full hour every afternoon going after the cows. What she told, she knew from experience. She had background on this subject far beyond her years.

Recognizing the Child's Background of Knowledge

A child with a wide background of experience may have much to contribute to a teacher who is willing to recognize this source of knowledge and has insight and skill enough to draw on it. On the other hand, a child such as Doris may out-distance a teacher who is unwilling or unprepared to accept the contribution she is able to make.

> Doris, who was in the upper elementary school, had spent several months in Norway. The children in her room were studying the Scandinavian countries. When they came to Norway, Doris was eager to tell all about her first-hand experience there. The teacher had never been abroad, and overlooked

some of the most colorful details. When Doris tried to clarify some of her statements the teacher refused to let her speak. The teacher did not feel secure; she resented the fact that Doris knew more about the subject than she did. On the other hand, Doris, with her background of firsthand experience, could weigh the teacher's statements.

Because of the teacher's attitude the child lost all faith in her and would not accept any statement until it was verified. She even questioned the teacher's spelling of a common word. To this day, Doris, now grown, recalls how surprised she was to discover that the "e" in "does" really comes before the "s," just as that teacher had said.

Guiding Understanding, Knowledge, and Skills Through Group Experiences

Nothing can more clearly present an illustration of the relationship of understanding, knowledge, and skills to attitudes, behavior patterns, appreciation, creative expression, and independent thinking than can children and teachers at work in the classroom. The following description is given without benefit of parenthetical remarks in order to show the series of learning experiences that naturally grew out of a bona fide interest in Kim's sugar beet.

About the middle of October Kim brought a large sugar beet to school that his father had given him to share with the other children.

The seven-year-olds in Mrs. Pauline Sander's group had been studying plants. As they talked, Miss Marshall, the student teacher, painted pictures of the sugar beet's roots, stem, and leaves.

Susan asked, "Is it real sugar in the beet?"

"How can we find out?" Miss Marshall asked.

Tim suggested that they taste the beet. Wayne said, "Let's cook it and taste the juice."

Launching the Experiment

All of the children were interested, and Wanda, Beth, and Kim first washed their hands and then scrubbed the beet with a brush to get it clean. Then every child washed his hands and took a paper plate, a paper towel, and a wooden tongue depresser to use for a taster. Pieces of the beet were cut off for each to taste. Some of the raw beet was kept so that its flavor could be compared with the liquid solution later when it would be ready. The remainder of the raw beet was diced, put into a pan and covered with water. The children watched the beet cook as they went about their normal activities.

Miss Marshall recalled the suggestion of the dental hygienist and asked the children to tell how to take care of teeth when eating sweets.

"You should rinse your mouth after you eat something sweet," said Peter.

"Brush your teeth if you can," said Ed.

They discussed the effect of sugar upon teeth, and the children decided that they would rinse their mouths well after they tasted the juice from the beet.

In all tasting experiences that followed, this was done. A note of explanation was dictated by the children and taken home to the parents.

Comparing and Making Distinctions

The next morning the children compared the sugar beet solution with brown sugar. "How are they alike?" asked Miss Marshall.

Barbara said, "They are both brown, but the brown sugar would have to cook with water in it to be liquid."

The children decided the brown sugar tasted "like syrup we put on hot cakes."

Miss Marshall poured molasses into a pitcher. Randy thought it was honey, "because it is creamy like honey," and Wendy thought it was chocolate. Debbie said, "We could find out whether it is honey or chocolate if we tasted it."

After tasting the molasses, Elaine was convinced it was "what they make cracker jack from."

Kelvin thought it tasted "like cough syrup," but the children were unanimous in their reaction that the molasses was sweeter than the sugar beet solution.

Miss Marshall explained that this molasses had come from sugar cane, not from sugar beet. This led into a discussion of the difference between sugar cane and sugar beets: where they grow, how they grow, what they each need in order to grow, and why. Miss Marshall showed the children pictures of growing sugar cane.

Understanding and Describing

The sugar beet solution continued to cook and Bob suddenly noticed the bubbles on the top and the steam coming from the top of the pan.

"There is lots less of the liquid now," said Craig, "than there was yesterday."

"There is a word that describes what is making it less," said Miss Marshall. "Ann, come and hold your hand over the pan. How does it feel?" (Miss Marshall saw that Ann held her hand over the pan, but not close enough to burn her.)

"It feels hot and steamy," observed Ann.

"Take your hand away and look at it. How does it feel?"

"It feels wet. The steam made it wet," was Ann's reply.

"The steam is the water boiling up from the pan. When water gets hot enough to boil it changes to a gas," continued Miss Marshall. She digressed a moment to explain the difference between this type of gas as opposed to gasoline. Then she explained condensation by holding a mirror over the steam. "The water changes to steam and comes out in the air. Because the air is cooler outside than it was in the pan the steam changes back into water when it is stopped by some object like the mirror. See, the water is dripping off the mirror."

Then Freddie announced, "Water doesn't make smoke; it just makes steam."

The teakettle began to whistle, and Miss Marshall said, "Listen to the teakettle. Its song is going up higher and higher."

Laura sang a spontaneous little song:

Miss Marshall repeated it after her, and all the children sang it several times.

Miss Marshall said, "Now, when I 'disconnect' the cord from the 'socket'—when I pull out the plug—what happens to the whistling?"

Burt: "It stops."

Miss Marshall: "Why did the kettle stop whistling?"

Kathy: "The electricity is off and the water isn't as hot as it was."

Miss Marshall went one step beyond this and explained how the water in the lakes and rivers goes up in the air and helps form clouds that sometimes meet cool air up in the sky. "The cool air acts just like the mirror did: it *condenses* the vapor of the clouds and turns them back to water. Then we have rain."

Genevieve remarked, "I am glad I know now. I used to think it was smoke that went up in the sky and made the clouds. Now I know it is water gas."

"Yes, clouds are water vapor," replied Miss Marshall.

Explaining Meanings

The children were eager to experiment further on evaporation. They filled two jars that were just alike with the same amount of water. They left one jar open and screwed a lid on the other. They left these jars for a number of days and observed how the jar with the closed top remained full, while the water level of the open jar grew lower and lower. The children took turns painting a red ring where the water level was each day.

In explaining the process to a visitor Wendy said, "The water evaporated out of the open jar."

"What does that mean?" asked the visitor.

"Evaporation is what happens when the water is taken up into the air," said Wendy.

"When water spills on the floor," explained Patricia, "we can wipe part of it up with a sponge, but there is still a little water left. We have to wait for it to evaporate before the floor is dry."

These explanations gave evidence that the experiment represented a meaningful experience which the children were able to recall vividly.

Miss Marshall explained that the molasses they had tasted had once been a very thin solution and had been boiled down; water had evaporated just as it had evaporated from the beet water.

Discussion of Terms Continued

The sugar beet experiment continued to hold the interest of the children. They compared white granulated sugar and brown sugar. Two of the children had seen the large sugar refineries where brown sugar is made white or refined in the Imperial Valley of California, and they looked at pictures of plants where sugar is refined. The children felt both brown sugar and white granulated sugar. They decided that the brown sugar felt crumbly and the white sugar grainy. When powdered sugar was added Danny said, "The powdered sugar is the softest, the white sugar is sticky, and the brown sugar is bumpy."

From time to time the children discussed what they had learned:

"What do we have when we boil down the water from the sugar beets?"

"We have molasses syrup."

"When the syrup is very thick and we set it aside it *crystallizes*. What do we have then?"

"Sugar comes."

The children liked to say the word "granulated." They felt the granulated sugar with their hands. "How does it feel?"

Timmy: "It feels like sand."

Kathy: "It feels crunchy."

Wendy: "It feels like salt."

As the children tasted the beet solution from time to time, they found that as it boiled and more water evaporated it became sweeter. "Why?"

Susan: "Because the water goes away and leaves more sugar in the pan. The sugar doesn't go away in vapor."

Knowledge from Shared Experiences

Miss Marshall put some sugar in a test tube and melted it over the fire. It turned brown. The sugar was caramelized. She poured the sugar out on a greased paper and the children felt it. "How does it feel?"

"It is hard," said Elaine.

"This is like the caramel on cracker jack," said Kelvin.

They also tasted the caramelized sugar. Some liked it; others did not.

"How do we get sugar from cane?"

Timmy (who had lived in the Hawaiian Islands): "We grind it and squeeze out the juice and boil it down till the water evaporates. That makes brown sugar."

Kathy: "The beets are crushed, and the juice is boiled."

Purposeful Reading

The children were so interested in their sugar and evaporation experiments that they wanted to keep talking about them. There were four reading groups and each developed a story about the experiment. The less mature group dictated:

Our Sweet Day

Today we had a sugar experiment.
We tasted four kinds of sugar.
Molasses tastes like coffee caramel.
Sweet brown sugar is good.
Powdered sugar is good, and feels soft to us.
Grains of sugar taste sweet.
Yum! Yum! Yum!

The more advanced group dictated:

Our Sugar Experiment

What we learned:
1. White sugar melts to make brown caramel.
2. Powdered sugar feels soft as snow.
3. Brown sugar feels like crumbs.
4. Sugar comes from beets and from sugar cane.
5. Water evaporates to make steam.
6. Molasses comes from sugar cane.
7. Sweet sugar makes us smile.
8. Experiments are fun.

Knowledge Extended Through More Experiments

The following day Miss Marshall said:

"We have found out that sugar beets and sugar cane both contain sugar. There is a way to find out whether or not other vegetables contain sugar. We call it the iodine test. When you cut the vegetable and put iodine on a piece of it, there will be a darker spot on the place where there is sugar."

The children cut the vegetables, and Miss Marshall applied the iodine. She was careful to explain that one should not taste or drink iodine. Like the bitter rind of grapefruit or an unripe persimmon, it isn't good to eat or good for us, but it *is* useful in testing for sugar content.

The children tried the experiment with an Irish potato, a sweet potato, a carrot, and a radish—all vegetables that grow under the ground, and saw how the vegetables that contained more sugar took a darker stain than the others.

At the culmination of the sugar experiments the children made candy. A few weeks earlier they had experimented with a candy thermometer and had watched how the blue line of the thermometer rose when the instrument was placed in hot water and how rapidly it dropped when thrust in ice water.

Skill in Measuring

"We will use our thermometer in making candy," Miss Marshall told the children. "We will also use the big measuring pitcher we have used before." There were lines to measure the contents. "How much does this big pitcher hold, Elaine, when it is filled to the top line?"

"It holds two cups," said Elaine.

Miss Marshall: "How many cups does the measuring cup hold, Beth?"

"It holds one cup."

"If we fill the measuring cup and pour it into the larger pitcher, how many times will we have to do this to fill the big pitcher?"

"We will have to fill the measuring cup two times," said Esther.

"Two times is twice," volunteered Warren.

Miss Marshall: "My recipe says to use two and one-half cups of sugar. How will we measure that much?"

"If we fill the large pitcher we will have two cups," said Judy.

"How much more sugar will we still need?" asked Miss M.

"We will need half a cup more," said Karen.

"How can we measure half a cup?" asked Miss M.

"We will have to fill the measuring cup up to the line that says half full," said Buster.

"You come and do this, Buster," said Miss M.

Buster stood with the cup in his hand.

"Where is the half-way mark?" asked Miss M.

Buster found the mark and the children watched closely as he put in the sugar.

At Miss M.'s suggestion, Barbara helped Buster to see when the sugar reached the half-way mark on the cup.

"Thank you, Buster and Barbara. That was well done."

"Do we have half a cup of sugar in the measuring cup now?" she asked.

"Yes, the cup is half full," said Buster.

"How much sugar have we measured altogether?" asked Miss M.

"Two cups and half a cup make two and a half cups," said Peter.

"Now I will measure half a cup of Karo syrup," Miss M. said.. "You tell me when the cup is half full. Wendy, you take the cup after I am through and measure one cup of water. Our recipe calls for these ingredients. What do we mean by ingredients?"

"Ingredients are what you put in it," volunteered Elaine.

Further Understanding

When the ingredients were measured, different children stirred and stirred until the sugar was partially "dissolved." Then Miss Marshall set the candy on the electric hot plate to cook. No one stirred the candy after it began to boil.

All the sugar "disappeared," and the children watched the candy begin to boil. All these points were discussed as the group watched.

"What are some other things you know that will dissolve in water?"

"Salt will dissolve."

"You can dissolve jello."

"Soap dissolves."

Miss Marshall had some water boiling next to the candy. She asked the children to look at the boiling candy in one pan and the boiling water in the other.

"Do they look the same when they are boiling?" she asked.

Laura said, "The sugar makes rolling waves like a boat going fast. The water looks like it does when you go up and down in the bathtub."

Miss Marshall: "The water with the sugar is thicker because it has the sugar in it. Would a jar of water and a jar of the sugar and water weigh just the same?"

"No," said Tim, "the sugar and water would be heavier."

"That is good thinking," said Miss M.

As they waited Miss Marshall said a poem to the children:

> The water is here on the stove in the pot;
> The heat is turned on, and it's getting so hot.
> "A-bubble, A-bubble" the hot water goes—
> Stay back from the kettle and don't burn your nose.
> And watch how the steam rises up, up so high
> Almost like white clouds way up there in the sky.

The children joined with her in spontaneous actions as they said the poem, using the full body movements of an action play.

Active Minds

Miss Marshall showed the children where the thermometer should register when the candy was ready to take off the stove (238 degrees). She also showed how to test for the "soft ball stage" in cold water.

When the candy was done it was removed from the stove and set aside to cool while the children tried some experiments with plain water and a sugar solution. Miss Marshall put a string in the sugar solution. It did not sink at once, but slowly drifted to the bottom of the glass. "Why do you think it sank?" she asked the children.

"Because the string got wet; it absorbed the water and that made it heavier, so then it sank."

They tried other things in the room to see if they were "absorbent." A piece of cotton floated on top of the water for a time; then it sank to the bottom. The cotton "absorbed" the water.

They tried a milk carton next, which of course did not absorb the water.

"The milk carton is covered with wax," said Craig. The children had learned from a former experiment that wax will not absorb water.

"If it was raining and you went out in the rain dressed as you are now, why would you get wet?"

"Because our clothes are absorbent. They absorb water."

"How could you keep from getting wet?"

"Put on a rain coat and rain shoes," said Lyla.

"Why would a rain coat keep you dry?" asked Miss Marshall.

"The water can't get through the coat. It repels the water. It sheds it," said Tim.

Skill with Language

Miss Marshall put her hand on the kettle in which the candy had cooked. It was now cool. The children, too, felt the pot and found it was warm but no longer hot. They poured the candy onto a large tray.

They took turns stirring the candy and talked about how it looked as they stirred.

"It looks like combed hair," said Timmy. "What did it say then?"

"Pop! Pop!"

"It looks like vapor rub."—Elaine

"Sounds like rice crispies."—Kelvin

"It looks like apple sauce."—Mark

"It's getting whiter all the time."—Katherine

"I've just got to try this stuff."—Bob

"It's getting shiny."—Tom

"It looks like paste."—Wanda

"You are making drip castles. I like to make them at the beach."—Elaine

"Now it looks like soft butter."—Susan

"It looks to me like mashed potatoes."—Beth

The children were each given a piece of the candy to taste.

"How does it taste to you?"

"It tastes like snow with sugar in it."—Elaine

"Yummy."

"Soft and sweet like marshmallows."—Debbie

"It feels a little like sand in my mouth."—Genevieve

"Is the candy as sweet as the sugar?"

"No."

"Which is creamier?"

"The candy."

"We had fun today. Experiments are fun to do."—Craig

Values of This Experiment

This experiment not only helped the children gain considerable scientific knowledge; there was also much opportunity for learning practical arithmetic, for growth in the arts, and for using language as closely related to experience.

"Making the candy from sugar, and relating it to processes that the children understand, was the perfect culmination of a thrilling experience," explained Mrs. Sanders to the parent group afterward.

"When you are teaching children to understand and remember what they learn, you are not just interested in presenting facts to them; you are interested in what is happening to the child and the quality of thinking ability which is being developed."

There is a basic difference between teaching subject matter and teaching children to use subject matter for various purposes, through knowing and understanding.

QUESTIONS ON THE SIX GOALS:
VI. UNDERSTANDING, KNOWLEDGE, AND SKILLS

1. Why should those concerned with curriculum first discuss the classroom implications of democracy and the six goals?

2. Why is it essential for you to evaluate the learning experiences of children in terms of the individuals within the group?

3. Why is understanding as well as knowledge important in the democratic classroom? What skills are demanded of the children? Of the teacher?

4. How does attitude enter into the development of skill? Illustrate.

5. How can you provide opportunities for more intellectually endowed children and children with richer backgrounds of experience, to work to

capacity without jeopardizing the growth of the others in your room? How can these better-equipped individuals retain their identity with the group at the same time that the others are given the opportunity to learn at their own rates? Describe some of the contributions that can be made to the democratic classroom by each type of child.

6. What is wrong with the idea that all the children in your group will be ready to undertake the same learning at the same time? What bearing does this have on so-called "directed-lessons" in a given area of learning? Discuss.

7. Suggest another classroom illustration such as the sugar beet experiment and describe ways in which the first five goals are of major concern to the teacher.

8. a. Show how understandings, knowledge and skills are promoted simultaneously with the other five goals. b. Illustrate how academic learning is evidenced. c. Justify the use of classroom time for the experiment from the standpoint of the growth of the children.

9. Discuss the understanding which a young child of your acquaintance has within a particular field of interest. How did he acquire his knowledge?

10. When children seem to have a similar opportunity to learn from a given situation, why do some acquire more knowledge and understanding than others? Discuss.

SELECTED REFERENCES

Armstrong, Martin, THE PAINTBOX, New York, The Macmillan Co., 1931.

Carrier, Blanche, INTEGRITY FOR TOMORROW'S ADULTS, New York, Thomas Y. Crowell Co., 1959.

Hartman, Gertrude and Ann Shumaker, Editors, American Educ. Fellowship, CREATIVE EXPRESSION; DEVELOPMENT OF CHILDREN IN ART, MUSIC, LITERATURE, DRAMA, 2nd Ed., Milwaukee, E. M. Hale, 1939.

Lowenfeld, Viktor, CREATIVE AND MENTAL GROWTH, 3rd Ed., New York, Macmillan, 1957.

Mayer, Frederick, A HISTORY OF EDUCATIONAL THOUGHT, Columbus, Ohio, Charles E. Merrill Books, Inc., 1960.

Piaget, Jean, THE MORAL JUDGMENT OF THE CHILD, Glencoe, Illinois, The Free Press, 1948.

Russell, David H., CHILDREN'S THINKING, Boston, Ginn & Co., 1956.

Verbeck, Blanche, CHILDREN SPEAK THROUGH BEHAVIOR, Assoc. For Childhood Education International, Reprint Service Bulletin No. 25, Guiding Children in School and Out, Washington, D. C., Association Childhood Education International, 1952-53.

Von Fange, Eugene, PROFESSIONAL CREATIVITY, Englewood Cliffs, New Jersey, Prentice-Hall Inc., 1959.

Zirbes, Laura, SPURS TO CREATIVE TEACHING, The Putnam Series in Education, New York, G. P. Putnam's Sons, 1959.

VII. EVALUATION, AN INDICATION OF THE SIX GOALS IN THE CLASSROOM

No discussion of the six goals is complete without taking into account the role of evaluation in the continuous learning of children. It is in this area that the interrelationship of the goals evidences itself particularly.

As the child grows in constructive attitudes and behavior patterns, in the ability to appreciate, to solve problems, to think independently, and to express himself creatively, he becomes better prepared to evaluate his own progress and that of others.

Definition of Evaluation

The term *evaluation* has been so misused that it needs clarification. Evaluation covers such a broad field that it can be applied to practically everything, but its purpose is *not* to examine critically, to find fault, or to censure. These only serve to make the child feel the crushing blow of continual disapproval and failure.

There are various shades of meaning in everything; nothing is ever all strong or all weak, but only relatively so. Children, in learning to evaluate, need to recognize this. They should learn to weigh values, see both sides of the picture, act in the light of their best knowledge at the time, and realize that there may be several viewpoints.

True evaluation is just what the word implies: to find the real value. It is to give recognition and appreciation; to talk things over and share ideas; to show interest in what someone else has done; to look at one's own work as others see it; to think constructively; to discover and solve problems; to develop ideas of what is expected and to try to do better the next time; and to establish values and focus attention on points that need to be stressed or remembered. These are all done in a positive approach and with the idea of improvement for the future.

You will want first to interpret the results of the work done, then try to find how the result was attained.

The Role of Evaluation in Learning

Objective evaluation demands a quality of thinking which is valuable in all walks of life and in all levels of experience. It is the ability to project oneself out of oneself. It is the type of mental activity which occurs when, for example, an individual attempts to play the piano and imagine himself in the far corner of the room listening at the same time. Frequent evaluation is one of the best ways to stimulate thinking and to develop action in the right direction, according to accepted standards. When viewed in its broadest sense, evaluation is an essential phase of any learning situation. There is perhaps no facet of the education program which offers as much real learning as thorough and consistent evaluation, the ability to *guide* as well as *measure* the integrated growth and development of children.

For the child, evaluation may mean the ability to see the worth in what he has accomplished as well as in the achievements of his associates; to determine where he and they are going; to share his discoveries with them; and to recognize the problems he and his friends and neighbors are facing in their daily activities. In any case, evaluation is of no avail unless it be fully realized that through it growth is taking place.

In making valid evaluation, of yourself or of the child, this point must always be remembered: you cannot afford to evaluate a situation at a particular moment only, apart from what has gone before and what is to come; you must view it in relation to the growth that is occurring in the individual.

Guidance Toward Thoughtful Evaluation

Children need guidance in formulating standards by which they can judge their own thinking and actions. Incidental opportunities for this continually present themselves. In a beginning group, Lyle was running through the room. When asked, "What is the right thing to do, and why?" he replied, "I should walk because it is safe." He adjusted his actions accordingly.

Sometimes guiding a child is simply a matter of turning his thinking in one direction or another by a wisely chosen question. Matthew, in lower primary, said, "When I went on a train we went to the ticket station." His teacher immediately queried, "Where did you go?"

It would have been far better if she had asked something about the station, so that this child's experience there could contribute to the discussion. "Tell us more about it, Matthew. How did you happen to go to the ticket station and what did you see there?" A few well directed questions will help the child to evaluate his experience in the light of its true worth to his peers.

Criticism of himself or of his peers arbitrarily imposed upon the child from someone else's viewpoint is not true evaluation. When the children in one six-year-old group were trying to evaluate their work the teacher said, "How did the committee work at the easel painting?"

The chairman said, "All worked but Linda."

Then the teacher asked the group, "How did the people at the clay table work?"

The chairman said, "They were a little bit noisy."

The teacher replied, "Next time we will work more quietly."

Then the teacher asked, "How did the handpainting group work? How did they clean up?" Without waiting for an answer she said, "You worked very well today. Most of you cleaned up nicely."

That was her evaluation of the children's work time.

In sharp contrast to this is the opportunity you give the children to think through to conclusion. You need to state questions specifically enough that you bring out the children's constructive answers. Compare the child's response in such questions as "Are you going to put posts on the fence?" or "Why would it be a good idea to put posts here?" with the way he would answer the following: "What will you do to make the fence stand up?" "What does the fence need to make it stronger?" "Where will you put the posts? Why?" and "How are you going to fasten the tank on the frame?"

If questions such as these fail to bring a response, you may find the child will be led to think for himself if you offer him alternatives, such as these: "Would it be better to tie the tank on with something or to drive a nail through it? Why? What would you use to tie it? Would wire or string be stronger?"

Evaluation of working procedures verges on planning when the children recall a previous evaluation in solving a problem at hand. They are not necessarily aware of the source of their ideas, but offer them as their own suggestions.

Miss Thompson said, "We have become careless in our painting lately. What do we need to do?"

Fred: "Plan before we paint. Think first."

May: "And wipe our brushes on the edge of the jars."

Ralph: "Work hard on one painting instead of doing two or three in a hurry without planning."

Larry: "Put newspapers down under the easels."

The Selfless Teacher

You, as a teacher of young children, must be able to evaluate yourself objectively, impersonally, honestly, and constructively. Also, you must accept an equally objective evaluation from those who know you best, whether they are superiors, peers, or subordinates. Then, and only then, will you be qualified to guide young children in the evaluation of things important to them. The art of "seeing ourselves as others see us" is perhaps the greatest accomplishment of the "truly educated person," even though it was first presented in a now famous poem by one of the most unschooled poets, "Bobbie" Burns.

A teacher who did not quite understand evaluation herself had been working very hard to explain what it meant to the children. In the midst of her effort to have them be objective and impersonal in the process, the bell rang and the children were excused for recess.

When they returned to the classroom the teacher said, "What were we discussing before you went out?"

One child said "arithmetic."

The teacher said "No."

"Reading," said another child.

"Not reading," said the teacher.

"I know," said Johnny. "We were discussing 'evaporation.'"

When you stop to analyze it, Johnny was not so far off, because to be truly objective in an evaluation it is necessary to "evaporate" from the scene, so that your personal preferences are not allowed to color your thinking.

Your Procedure in Oral Evaluation

By your example and your recognition of individual contributions the children can see demonstrations of democracy at work.

Two points you will want to keep before you: first, guard against your talking for the child; refrain from asking and answering the questions and explaining what he has said. Encourage him to clarify his own statements. Second, help the children to see the importance of making suggestions directly to the child whose work is being evaluated rather than to you.

Look for interesting elements in the child's work and try to discover and recognize what his idea was rather than point out the things he neglected. Always remember Abraham Lincoln's admonition, "He has a right to criticize who has a heart to help."

You can say, "Let's talk it over and see how you really feel about it now. What happened? Why? What is the problem you are trying to solve? What are you going to do about it to make it come out right?"

All of these questions give the child a share in determining his objectives and in interpreting accomplishments, and they bring a glow of self-worth.

These are discussed "on the spot" with the child or children who are working together and, perhaps later, when the group has gathered for discussion, Burt will tell something of what he has been doing, what he is trying to do, and what he has to do next to accomplish his purpose.

Through your positive, consistent culling of the children's suggestions and trend of thought you will help them as a group to formulate a common, wholesome mind-set or attitude toward an ever better way to reach higher goals.

You can not only evaluate all activities, but you can summarize the morning, afternoon, or the entire day. "What made this a happy, successful day? How did we accomplish our purpose? What were we doing? Why? What will we want to remember about this so we can do it this well again?" Or, if the day did not go well or the work needs improvement, you may ask, "What happened today and what can we learn from this so it will be better next time? What would be a better way?" Suggestions are given, based on experience and thinking, and evaluation becomes a means of profiting by experiences. In this way you help the children recall the strong things about the day, and recognize their own needs, thereby strengthening their ability to evaluate.

> Bobby could read almost anything he wanted to soon after he started in beginning primary. He would frequently refer to the encyclopedia to find out what he wanted to know. He didn't like to paint, model with clay, or do other things requiring dexterity, and he often annoyed the other children with his infantile behavior.
>
> The children were talking with the teacher. Various comments were made: "Some of us can do one thing and some another. Bobby can read well." "Yes, but he can't walk very well. He crawls on the floor a lot."
>
> Bobby looked surprised. He seemed to sense the note of sincerity in their voices. For the first time in his life he saw himself through the eyes of his peers. After the conversation his behavior matured considerably.

Occasionally a child tends to ridicule work done by another. One day Wendell said: "Gloria's painting doesn't look like what she says it is."

Miss Roger replied: "Gloria painted the part that is important to her. She is improving in her painting every day, and remember how well Gloria sings. All of us do some things well and other things that need much improvement."

Each day Miss Rogers dwelt briefly on individual strengths and needs. She was deeply gratified some days later when Wendell said,

> "Look, look,
> See Gloria's good work.
> Pretty, pretty work, Gloria!"

Group Evaluations

The individual will discuss his work with you, or with a small group, more readily than before the entire class. Later, if he does present the results of his work to a greater number of listeners, what he may say is partly a recall of his previous conversation with you. As a teacher at the early childhood level you will have a definite purpose in calling the group's attention to what various children are accomplishing.

Group evaluations help children to be objective, and accustom the child whose work is being evaluated to accept the suggestions that have been offered and to profit by them. These discussions give children opportunity to organize their thoughts and present them to others. No matter how young the group may be, many worthwhile recommendations will be made. For example, the size of the paper used may result in a helpful evaluation. Tommy plans to paint a picture. He describes what he is going to paint. You ask, "What size paper will you use for your picture, Tommy?"

With his hands Tommy indicates a piece of paper about 6″ x 8″.

"That won't be large enough," says Freddie.

"We couldn't all see it," says Helen. "Make it about this size, (indicating paper about 15″ x 18″) and then everyone can see it."

Others agree, and as a result of their suggestion, Tommy paints a picture that everyone can see. When his picture is finished and he shows it to his group he is pleased and encouraged by their commendation.

You should notice particularly problems that individual children are facing when these problems can be diminished by suggestions from the group. Through these brief but carefully directed "evaluations," the thinking of the group will be stimulated and directed. Evaluation then takes on a new significance and is far more than the mere sharing of experiences with the group.

Opportunities to Follow Through

Always guide the children to comment upon the strong features of the individual's work, and then suggest places where improvement can be made. No child should get in the habit of saying "Mine is the best," even if it is true. There is always some further skill to think about and to work toward.

From the evaluation of six-year-old Joseph's "boat on a river," as he described his first block construction, came the idea that next day he might build a big boat. Over a period of five weeks, this led to his building a big ocean liner, the harbor, a dock, a freighter, a ferry boat, a tanker, an aircraft carrier, an airplane, and a fire boat. By evaluating and stimulating his thinking along the way, his teacher helped him to see a task through and to develop new interests.

To carry out new ideas, children need to do research. Sometimes observing things more closely helps. By experimenting with the length of his clay man's legs, Bill discovered that when they were short and fat, his man would stand. Picture books gave Michael the clue to how he could make a lumber car, and gave Joseph the idea for his fireboat. When Bill couldn't get the pontoons on his hydroplane, he took it home so that he could talk his problem over with his father. These boys were learning to think about and get at the facts in a situation.

Growth Through Evaluation

Evaluation is in itself a skill that is strengthened through exercise. Children who participate in the democratic classroom grow in this area especially. It is the child's right to have a part in whatever evaluation is made of his own efforts and his work. It is his obligation to be objective in that evaluation.

Evaluations made by your children in the classroom help you to know how well they understand what they are learning, what attitudes and appreciations they have, and what standards they hold for themselves and for each other.

By the same token, evaluations are your opportunity to help children develop standards of work and to guide them toward better understanding, knowledge, and skills.

QUESTIONS ON EVALUATION

1. Why do children who participate in the democratic classroom grow in the area of evaluation? Illustrate.

2. What do your children's evaluations reveal to you about: (a) their attitudes, and appreciations? (b) their standards of work? (c) their growth?

3. Why is it important to follow an evaluation with opportunities to act upon it? Illustrate.

4. Give a classroom example of an evaluation which leads to a constructive experience for a given child. What evidence might there be of the learning which would take place?

5. Why is it essential that evaluations be made during the experience rather than afterward, for the young child? Discuss "on the spot" evaluations in the classroom. How will you guide these?

6. In evaluating a day's experiences, what are some of the points to be considered: (a) by the children? (b) by you, the teacher? Illustrate.

7. How will you keep your own evaluations positive and constructive?

8. Mention the relationship between evaluation and planning in the classroom. How does tomorrow's plan grow out of today's evaluation? Illustrate.

9. Cite an incident in a classroom that illustrates the following statement: "The evaluation becomes effective when it leads to a constructive experience that shows evidence of the learning which is taking place within the child."

10. How would you clarify the true values of evaluation for the parent or other interested person who considers it as a classroom situation where one child sits in judgment of another?

11. How can parents be informed of their child's work at school and of the standards by which it is to be evaluated?

12. Suggest a certain piece of work which a child in a given classroom might undertake. List some of the problems he would encounter. What suggestions might be offered by the group? (a) How would this prove helpful to the child? (b) In what ways would the others profit by participating in an evaluation of this nature?

SELECTED REFERENCES

Green, Mary McBurney, IS IT HARD? IS IT EASY?, New York, Young, Scott Books, 1958.

Herrick, Virgil E., John L. Goodlad, Paul W. Eberman, Frank J. Estvan, I LIKE SCHOOL BECAUSE . . ., Englewood Cliffs, New York, Prentice-Hall, Inc., 1959.

Shane, Harold G., and E. T. McSwain, EVALUATION AND THE ELEMENTARY CURRICULUM, New York, Holt, Rinehart, and Winston, 1951.

Vander Werf, Lester S., HOW TO EVALUATE TEACHERS AND TEACHING, New York, Holt, Rinehart and Winston, 1958.

MAJOR INFLUENCES
ON LEARNING

Part Three

IN THE CLASSROOM

I. ENVIRONMENTAL INFLUENCES

Room Climate

A good room climate is the end product of an arranged environment, so planned and organized as to produce a happy, childlike, inspirational atmosphere where each child is an important part of the whole, and where there is no doubt in anyone's mind that each and all belong. Thus, the individual child unquestionably recognizes his own worth and feels at home. Here, wholesome attitudes, constructive behavior patterns, deep appreciations, independent thinking, creative effort, together with understanding, knowledge, and skills all thrive and operate toward the child's growth.

Such an environment is conducive both to group and individual pursuance of varied ideas through diverse experiences. It fosters integrated development, so that each member of the group learns within his limits to accept responsibility for his own actions after careful independent deliberation. In brief, it is life itself, lived under a happy leadership which permits a democratic choice of acceptable behaviors in an atmosphere that inspires thoughtful work. Here cumulative learning is bound to occur.

An Environment for Learning

A child needs *space* for freedom of movement and activity, well selected *equipment, materials and facilities,* and *aesthetic harmony;* but most of all he needs *understanding adults* to guide him, and *time* to respond and participate without pressures. In such a climate he will grow and develop naturally, act and talk with spontaneity, and learn thoughtfulness and consideration about things that are vital to him and his associates. This is the environment in which the democratic group flourishes and learning is continuous for the individual child.

Space

Even one child needs room to move about, in order to grow and learn. Children in a group learn from one another as well as from their teacher when there is *space* to work in together. Not only is the size of the area important, but also your every effort to utilize space constructively.

The physical plant, housing, indoor and outdoor environment are often rather fixed, but you can do remarkable things in rearranging the facilities you have. The placement of various pieces of equipment and centers will influence the effectiveness with which children will use them.

The Immediate Environment

It is your problem to create a room environment which is interesting and alive for each child. How will you do this and what will be its characteristics?

First, you must see the room through the children's eyes. You must ever keep in mind that the school is primarily for the education of the child, and the classroom is the Children's Center, the place where they work and live. It must have a child-like orderliness. There should be enough quiet for reading or other concentration of attention (according to the maturity of the group), and for speaking and listening as needed, yet the children should be free to communicate with each other as long as growth is taking place in the individual and no child is interfering with the growth of another.

The atmosphere should be free from pressures and other confusions and frustrations. It should reflect what the children are thinking and doing each day.

A well-organized room with simple aesthetic arrangement, all in scale with the room itself, free from clutter and with enough free walking space, shelves, and cupboard tops will give a tranquil work atmosphere. What is left out is probably just as important, if not more so, than what is brought in.

With thoughtful planning, available space can be adapted to freedom of movement.

The Child's Own Workroom

A glimpse into the classroom will reveal the kind of learning that is taking place, and the attitudes of the teacher and the school toward children. Does the room show that you know how the child learns and what he is capable of accomplishing? Is it a place where he feels at home? Is it indeed his room or is it for the most part the teacher's room? If the individual child is to feel it is his school, you will recognize his need to take part in the planning of the room.

Displays on the library table and near the science center, and elsewhere at various times, afford the children opportunity to express their ideas. When possible, you will want flowers in the room with one arrangement made by you, and others by various children. Leaves or dried plants may be arranged and attractive books and objects of interest effectively utilized if no blossoms are available.

The early childhood classroom can be a living, learning laboratory that presents joy, adventure, and challenge. To achieve this, adequate space is necessary so that the entire class can gather on a rug or other central location for group discussions, music, dramatic and literary activities; room should also be provided in which small groups can frequently engage in active and passive endeavors without having to move furniture and equipment to clear a space.

About the room you may place artistic pictures as well as examples of the children's own work to interest and challenge them. Of course you will have some wall and shelf space on the level of the child's eye, and within his reach, where he can post pictures and prepare other materials for exhibit. Other parts of the room may be devoted to aesthetic, scientific, and other displays.

New examples of the children's paintings or other work attractively arranged on bulletin board or walls every day or two gives the children pride and respect for themselves and their room. Be alert to the length of time displays are up and keep them flexible and current. It is important to have representative work from every child at one time or another.

You will need to provide a space for finished and unfinished work. When feasible it is advisable to have a place where some of the work that is in progress can be left out; too often so much time is spent in preparing and clearing up that there is little time for actual accomplishment.

The child can learn to rehabilitate the place where he has been working so that it will be ready either for his own use again, or for someone else who may plan to work there.

Every child needs some location to call his very own, such as a drawer, a shelf, or a box.

Basic Principles in Room Arrangement

The principles underlying the room arrangement are comfort, attention to health, beauty, friendliness in familiar things, curiosity, and challenge in what is new and unfamiliar. There will be many things which suggest action which the children are privileged to use and manipulate; there will be a few things, such as loaned exhibits, which they do not touch unless under special supervision—things to see and talk about, and when there is sufficient maturity, to write about.

You will also need space that can be utilized for block building, hand-painting, foot painting, and much shelf space for things of all sizes and proportions.

The fixed "centers," such as storage and construction areas provide stability in the room. There are special shelves and cupboards for paints, clay, books, blocks and tools for construction. The children share in keeping these in their proper places.

It makes for efficiency when work centers are near the supply cupboards and when the library center is near a bulletin or chalkboard, or where a portable one may be used.

A rhythmic arrangement of decor and furniture will allow for utilization of space, and equipment and materials can be added, substituted, or eliminated as the need arises. The addition of gliders or casters will make it possible to adapt the room to various needs.

Open-minded Attitude

You need to be open-minded toward changes from time to time in the arrangement of the room. Even such familiar objects as your desk may prove far from indispensable. You may find yourself in a classroom where you could use the space better if the desk were moved to another part of the room or eliminated entirely.

Imagination and ingenuity in planning can do many things with environment, both indoors and outside.

Flexibility

Intellectual curiosity can be stimulated by an environment that is flexible rather than static. The attitude of discovery with which display material, books, and pictures are approached makes for long-life learning.

The positive, happy, inquiring thread of wonderment must run through all activities. Great as is the need for physical space, there is even greater need for intangible areas in which the child's spirit can free itself and fly with unclipped wings. An effective environment not only helps the young child to learn to think, and to master the academic learning up to his maturation level, but also to see, to feel, to hear, and to imagine. Body, brain, heart, and spirit should all be given opportunities to grow.

In short, the classroom is a place of beauty where living and growing things are nurtured with love and tenderness, and where there is active participation by everyone present. Frances said enthusiastically, as she entered the room on a Monday morning, "Our room looks like a fine museum, there are so many stuffed animals and growing things around. It is good to get back to our school home."

Equipment and Materials

Children grow through their ability to explore, to think, to experiment, and to engage in physical activity. In order to provide this development the school needs to furnish certain basic equipment in the classroom which will be used day after day. You yourself will provide many materials that you will modify and augment from time to time in order to challenge the children's interest and increase learning possibilities.

"Where There's a Will There's a Way"

There is a growing tendency to recognize the fact that certain kinds of classroom equipment are needed for growth, not only in the earliest years, but all through the years in school.

A growing number of school systems have centers where individual teachers may requisition items on long period loans for use with the children.

If, however, you find yourself in a situation where you must take the initiative on requisitions, you will need to make a careful survey and then compile a list of your most urgent needs, indicating the price and where each item may be procured, and then present this list to your principal. A business-like presentation with reasons for the need will often bring surprising results. For example, many school boards and even school administrators might question the need for a punching bag, but when it is explained as a means by which children find release from tensions in a legitimate way, the request takes on new significance.

Even if supplies are greatly curtailed, discard materials and ingenuity bring satisfying results. If you have mechanical aptitude it will serve you well in devising teaching materials. If you do not possess this aptitude but know what you want, some obliging person who is endowed in this respect may be glad to assist and will take pleasure in seeing how the children enjoy and profit from the things he has helped to provide. Often the parents will be happy to cooperate in this venture and prepare some of the necessary articles at a workshop type meeting, or in their own homes.

The goal in setting up a room for primary children is to provide an area that is clean and safe, with equipment that is sturdy and simple in design. Whatever is procured should contribute to a functional, challenging environment where children can live and explore constructively.

Work tables, chalkboards, displays, and other teaching aids can be judiciously placed so as to take full advantage of proper lighting.

Appearance and Use

Through evaluation, children learn to consider both attractiveness and function as they help decide where things belong and assume responsibility for keeping them in place.

Although children need to be taught to care for equipment, it is essential that they have freedom to work constructively without undue restraint. The area where painting and clay work take place should have smooth, washable floors. You are fortunate if tops are washable, too, but if they are not you may need to have plastic or waterproof covers for them. Sponges are desirable for clean-up, which children can be guided to do for themselves. Where installations are not accessible, water pails may be drafted into use on a temporary basis until proper facilities can be made available.

Aesthetic Harmony

From the earliest days man has responded with delight to what he considered beautiful in his surroundings. If a child is to know the full joy in living, he, too, must find aesthetic beauty in the life around him, and come to appreciate it in its myriad forms. This is a gradual process and one in which you, his teacher, can play a major role.

The Influence of Everyday Surroundings

Each person learns to appreciate what appeals to him as lovely in his everyday life. The child is no exception. If you would guide him toward appreciation of aesthetic harmony you must first learn to see beauty from the standpoint of each child.

Look around you and find the beauty that is a part of each child's life. Here is his starting point. Here, in truth, is his own garden of beauty to discover. This is the gate through which he will eventually learn to see the beauty in other gardens not his own and appreciate what appears there, different perhaps from what he had first learned to think of as beautiful. As his teacher, you are in a unique position to help him select what is harmonious and aesthetic in his own surroundings. This is largely a selective process in most instances.

Ugliness and Beauty

The camera makes an all-inclusive replica of the ugly along with the attractive. The photographer must calculate carefully to exclude from the line of vision what he wishes to suppress. One artist sees the morning-glory vine climbing up the old building and disregards the electric wires, the clothesline and pole, the faded wall. Another school of thought includes all these and considers them art.

In your search for the beautiful in the child's environment, there is no dearth of aesthetic beauty to be found, no matter how drab the locality. Look for color, texture, balance, contrast, design, repetition of pattern. All these may be noted in nature, in pictures, in the use of word sounds and word meanings, in music, drama, art. All these you will want to keep ever before your group of children in an intricate variety of ways.

Rhythm and Musical Sound

Perhaps the love of rhythm and musical sound comes first. The infant is soothed by swaying, rhythmic motion and laughs with glee at an abrupt halt or change in rhythmic pace. He never loses this appreciation, although his taste changes with increasing maturity. The young school child rejoices in the beauty of rhythm and song, and he delights in the simple songs which he himself composes. Release from tensions may come through rhythmic expression and listening to and making music.

There are many other sounds which will lead the child to this appreciation of beauty, depending of course, upon where he is. There may perhaps be the sound of water rippling in a brook; the gentle patter of rain; wind in the tree tops; bird calls, especially those of evening, while a few scattered stars spill their twinkling light in the gathering dusk; the low moo of the mother cow, the rumble of trucks and traffic; or the mellow call of church bells.

Color, Line, and Form

The beauty of color, line, and form are found in countless ways, depending upon the geographical location. You may find it in the thousand glowing lights of a city; in white clouds floating in sunset skies and far blue horizons; in the endlessly stretching treeless plains; in a sliver of a moon, or a fat yellow one; in the soft green of new leaves; in tree forms and the varied texture and color of tree trunks; in the loveliness of flowers; in the color and shape of fruits and vegetables. Wherever you are it is yours for the asking. You and the children together may find it in bridges, ships, and highways, in landscaping and architectural structures, in the orbits of planets, in the precision of space flight, and in the movement of the stars in their courses. High and low, far and near, here, there, and everywhere, in animal, plant, and mineral is the essence of design, yours without reservation.

Aroma

You may have known the spring smells of flowers and wet earth; the summer smells of ripened vegetables and fruits; the smell of campfires and burning wood; the smell of soaps and perfumes, and the rich aroma of soup; the feel of keen cold wind and the comfort of warmth. The children you teach may often encounter these same types of stimuli; however, you may find yourself among entirely different surroundings where it is necessary to search diligently for the aesthetic or learn to find it in strange, new forms which to the child are entirely familiar.

Human Values and the Wonders of Nature

There is forever the beauty of friendships and family relationships, of which some children are deprived; the exchange of ideas one with another; the happy communion of laughter; of learning that people everywhere have the common problems of food, clothing, and shelter. These again are exemplified in endless variety.

There is the wonder of the human body and the function of its many parts; of Nature's adaptation of animal life to climatic conditions. This also applies to plant life—the desert plants and shrubs that have a root system which garners every drop of water that falls; the polished leaves and stems that seal in the moisture; even the ability of the saguaro cactus to expand its accordion-like body to take in more moisture when the rare opportunity comes to do so; the lush greens of rainy climates and the rich autumn tweeds of hillsides and valleys.

Rich Sources of Beauty

There is the joy of storytelling beginning with the here and now expressed in words that bring life to the child's own experiences. There is the beauty of poetic expression. From here it is but one step further, when the child is ready for it, to begin to explore the storehouse of literature, both contemporary and traditional. There are both the folk tales, dear to the hearts of children, and the thoughts of the philosophers.

The list of possibilities could be expanded indefinitely. It is your responsibility to help the children to appreciate their birthright of marvels that surround them; to find delight in touching, tasting, seeing, smelling, hearing; and to take just pride in developing their own creative potentialities.

There is a constant source of joy to be found in discovering beauty within the child's own range of experiences, related to his growing interests and widening horizons of learning. For example, in helping a child recognize likenesses and differences you are not only strengthening his background for reading, but you may also lead him to appreciate the interplay of repetition and contrast in everyday things within his environment, which is in itself one of the basic structural principles of all art form.

Inner Resources

Not to be overlooked are the qualities within the individual which respond to the beautiful in life, and the power of silence in the presence of beauty. Influential, also, is that inner communion with spiritual forces which becomes more treasured when shared afterward through an exchange of thoughts and impressions.

One who learns to appreciate beauty in all its various manifestations has inner resources which will help him all through life to combat boredom, loneliness, and disappointment, and because of this depth of appreciation, he will make the world a finer, better place in which to live.

QUESTIONS ON ENVIRONMENTAL INFLUENCES

1. What is room climate and how does it influence the child's learning in school?

2. Contrast the room climate in a democratic classroom with that in an autocratic one.

3. How can you tell when you see a classroom what type of teaching and learning is going on there? Illustrate.

4. Describe a classroom you visited recently and show how it reflects the thoughts and activities of: (a) the children; (b) the teacher; (c) the community.

5. Show how you would rearrange an old classroom to adapt it to the needs of your children through utilizing the space and the permanent facilities to the best advantage for learning. Be specific.

6. What points will you discuss with your children when they help decide where materials and equipment belong in your classroom? How will you dramatize, and in other ways make sure, that children learn to put things in the agreed places?

7. Discuss what it means to have a flexible rather than a static room environment and give examples.

8. Justify the inclusion of aesthetic harmony in your list of the major environmental influences of your children.

9. Analyze the sounds to be heard on a stormy autumn day in a given locality, and compare them with those of a bright spring morning or some other time of year.

10. How do inner resources fortify a child against disappointments, boredom, and unforeseen tragedies? Illustrate with concrete examples from your own experience.

SELECTED REFERENCES

Ambrose, Edna and Alice Miel, CREATING A GOOD ENVIRONMENT FOR LEARNING, 1954 Yearbook of the Association for Supervision and Curriculum Development, N.E.A., Washington, D.C., The Association, 1954.

Association for Childhood Education International, EQUIPMENT AND SUPPLIES, General Service Bulletin No. 39, Washington, D.C., Association for Childhood Education International, 1959 Revision.

Association for Childhood Education International, SPACE, ARRANGEMENT, BEAUTY IN SCHOOL, Bulletin No. 102, Washington, D.C., Association for Childhood Education International, 1958.

Brogan, Peggy, and Lorene K. Fox, HELPING CHILDREN LEARN, A Concept of Elementary-School Method, New York, World Book Company, 1955.

Caldwell, Edson, CREATING A BETTER SOCIAL ENVIRONMENT THROUGH SOCIOMETRIC TECHNIQUES, San Francisco, California, Fearon Press, 1959.

Kinney, Lucien, and Katherine Dresden, BETTER LEARNING THROUGH CURRENT MATERIALS, Stanford: Stanford University Press, 1952.

Thomas, M. M. and others, CLIMATE FOR LEARNING, Pittsburgh, University of Pittsburgh Press, 1953.

II. THE SCHOOL ADMINISTRATION

The farseeing administrator can do much to safeguard the interests of children and the individuals employed to teach them. The leadership of the superintendent can permeate a whole school system and encourage creativity in teaching. The supervisors and consultants can lend vision and insight and give helpful, concrete suggestions.

The Principal's Role in Opening School

Other than the classroom teacher herself there is no one individual in the school system who is in a position to do more to aid the physical and emotional climate of the early childhood classroom than the principal. Take, for example, Mr. Thornton, an alert, dedicated young principal of an elementary school in California. His philosophy of education is in accord with the foremost planners in the field. Being a practical man, Mr. Thornton realizes that the changes he advocates cannot be effected immediately, but must be a gradual process of public education that will bring about provision for and justified use of school funds. However, if he is unable to do everything he believes would be for the good of the school he administers, there is much he can do. He holds with Robert Browning's philosophy that:

> The common problem,
>   yours, mine, everyone's
> Is—not to fancy what
>   were fair in life
> Provided it could be,—but
>   finding first
> What may be, then find how
>   to make it fair,
> Up to our means.[1]

Since the school system is one in which the principal participates with other administrators in the selection of needed personnel for his own school, Mr. Thornton spares no pains in his effort to secure well-trained, alert, enthusiastic teachers who are first of all well integrated personalities. In his school system teachers are required to report for duty some days before the formal opening of school. This time is spent in orienting new teachers and in preparing for the current school year.

---

[1] From "Bishop Blougram's Apology."

Let us say you are a teacher in this system who has been selected to teach five-year-olds in Mr. Thornton's school. During the orientation period he will do everything possible to help you get ready for your work. He will supply you with all the data he has at hand to aid your adjustment to your new situation. This will include the names of your children and something of their backgrounds.

Previously he will have arranged a time prior to the opening of school when parents and children may come to meet their new teacher. At this time each five-year-old will be given a picture tag of identification which is his admission ticket. This pre-school meeting with parents and children avoids the confusion and strain of numbers of children and parents clamoring for simultaneous attention on the opening day of school. It gives you an opportunity to establish rapport with each child so that on the first day of school he will be coming back to a known and happy place. The child's feelings of loneliness and homesickness, which are too often prevalent, are thus alleviated, and you are free to work with all of the children during the first days of school.

Safeguarding Opportunities for Teaching

In a manner of speaking, Mr. Thornton is in a unique position to run interference for you who are delegated to carry the ball in teaching the children. For example, he consults with you about the room arrangement and sees that shifts which you deem desirable and practical are made. A portion of his budget is reserved so that additional purchases may be made.

Having convinced himself through a study of your school records and his personal observation of your work that you know what you are about, he gives you freedom to use your own discretion in ordering your school day. He frees his school from bells that traditionally announce recess periods at stated intervals. You do not have to adhere to a rigid schedule, but within reasonable limits may take your children for an outdoor intermission when the time seems opportune. This avoids breaking the continuity of some worthwhile classroom experience that would be difficult to duplicate.

Only in a real emergency does Mr. Thornton intrude upon the teaching day with notes about matters that are to be cared for. These communications are ordinarily reserved until the children have gone.

Mr. Thornton realizes that each teacher has the heavy responsibility of learning to know her children and their parents, and that she will be interested in what happens to them around the clock, rather than just during the part of the day spent at school.

You will make frequent reports to parents on the progress of their children and will put forth every effort to secure parent cooperation and support in providing the children with the best possible guidance. These things require time and thoughtful effort, and Mr. Thornton tries to see that you are not burdened with extraneous responsibilities that will interfere with your major duties to each individual child. He will not ask you to collect cafeteria money or teach a class in remedial reading, take charge of the library, or do extra playground duty, just because your actual teaching day may happen to be shorter than that of the upper grade teachers. He knows that you will accept responsibility for the supervision of your own group in the outdoor environment because it will help you to know more about your children than you could learn in any other way.

Adjusting the Teaching Load

This administrator believes, and insofar as he is able, puts his belief into practice, that the classroom teacher's skills and professional training should be utilized as completely as possible and should not be dissipated in a mass of trivia that could be handled as effectively by a less highly trained person. He looks forward to the practice, which is already being followed in some school systems, of employing a teaching assistant, other than the principal's secretary, to perform time-consuming clerical duties, such as duplicating teaching materials, keeping the register, attending to milk and lunch money, and when time permits, assisting with mounting pictures for bulletin boards, and other independent activities. He makes sure the per room enrollment is not increased because of this assistance.

Mr. Thornton shares the viewpoint of many other educators that in the long run it would be national economy if the size of the classroom could be reduced so that no teacher would have more than 20 or 25 children. He believes that the greater amount of time the teacher would have to devote to the individual needs of children and to seeking the cooperation of parents by consulting with them regarding their child's development and progress would pay dividends in the form of better adjusted children and more effective adult citizens. He believes less money would need to be spent for remedial teachers, for prisons and other corrective institutions, which are more expensive to operate than the public schools.

The Greater Part of Administration

In short, Mr. Thornton is a principal who believes that administration fulfills its responsibility on a high plane when it provides conditions necessary for the individual teacher and child to live effectively in the classroom.

QUESTIONS ON THE SCHOOL ADMINISTRATION

1. What questions about your classroom would you appreciate the opportunity to discuss with a consultant or supervisor who can lend insight and give you concrete suggestions for your teaching? Be specific.

2. If you were a consultant or supervisor what kinds of help would you offer a teacher and how would you proceed? Give examples.

3. If you were a principal, what kind of meeting would you call for the teachers as a group, and what matters would you discuss? How would you plan to help individual teachers with classroom problems?

4. Discuss the school assembly in terms of the six goals of childhood education. Give specific examples of the contribution your group of children might make without exploiting individual members of your class.

5. What can the administration do to protect teachers from interruptions in the classroom?

6. Justify the idea that secretarial help be available for the preparation of classroom materials and school reports. What responsibilities could be better carried out by you if such help were available?

SELECTED REFERENCES

American Association of School Administrators, Hollis A. Moore, Jr., Chairman, PROFESSIONAL ADMINISTRATORS FOR AMERICAN SCHOOLS, A.A.S.A. Yearbook in 1923.

Association of School Administrators, Thirty-third Yearbook of the American Association of School Administrators, STAFF RELATIONS IN SCHOOL ADMINISTRATION, National Education Association, Washington, D.C., The Association, 1955.

National Education Association of the United States, Department of Classroom Teachers, CONDITIONS OF WORK FOR QUALITY TEACHING, Washington, D.C., National Education Association, 1959.

Yauch, Wilbur A., IMPROVING HUMAN RELATIONS IN SCHOOL ADMINISTRATION, New York, Harper and Brothers, 1949.

III. THE INFLUENCE OF THE TEACHER

In the education of the child such factors as the physical properties of the school, together with a curriculum which provides opportunities to develop and grow and provision for aesthetic satisfactions and pleasures are all highly influential. However, the number one environmental influence is YOU, the teacher, whether you teach the five, six, seven, ten, fifteen, or twenty-year-olds. You can do much to help these children *be* whatever age they are and to find their own self-realization rather than a realization of an artificial pattern set up by you. This means that you will not expect more of them than they can do, as did Miss G. Earl, age seven, was working with her, and his performance was poor. Miss G. was urging him to do better. Finally Earl burst forth in complete frustration, "Golly, gee whiz, heck, Miss G.! What do you expect of me? I'm only seven years old!"

If you are to achieve the hallmark of superior teaching you will always remember, too, that each day is a chain of minutes and that every minute contributes to learning in some way, either constructively or negatively.

Major Attributes

Many attributes are essential if you are to make a contribution to your profession, but there are two that are basic. If you possess them you will have a bulwark against discouragement and disappointment that will make you equal to any emergency or situation.

Do you have a basic belief in the ability of children to learn and grow under your guidance, and do you delight in the individual child's all-round development? If you have these essentials, other things will be added unto you, because you will be eager to acquire the technical skills and the personality traits that will bring you success. You will learn to evaluate yourself candidly while you guide children toward an attitude of objectivity. Your abilities will increase as you evaluate your own strengths and needs for improvement at the end of each school day.

Emotional Climate

The emotional climate of your room reflects your personality. Because you live in close proximity to the children during a large proportion of your waking hours, you, yourself, have a tremendous effect upon their spirits. You must be worthwhile as a person and have a zest for living before you can be a successful teacher. What you think and the way you think; what you enjoy and the way you enjoy it; how well you know yourself and can be yourself are all a vital part of your work.

You will strive to be natural and spontaneous, yet will maintain a quiet dignity and honesty of purpose that will be exhibited in your teaching. You will be a part of the throbbing universe and of humanity, not a set of rules, routines, schedules, and theories. You will create an emotional climate in your room that will be made up of your attitudes, your example, your reactions, your courage, the standards you uphold, the guidance you give the individual, your confidence and your faith and trust, and children will reflect your example.

Your Principles and Practices

Thinking of and doing for others will become so much a part of your being that nothing will interrupt your good deeds. You will strive to overcome negative influences and help bridge the bewildering gap between childhood and adulthood. As a wise and true mentor you will hold to the intangibles, the things that you feel, that you believe, that you know to be true, rather than only to something you can see.

Let there be no gulf between your ideals or principles and your practices. When such a conflict exists the children tend to doubt the integrity of the adult. To the child your resources are meaningful and valuable only when they meet live learning situations. Let there be no question of values, but let the ideas you accept and stand for theoretically be your practice in daily life. Among other things you will guard against making promises that you may forget or that circumstances will not permit your keeping.

Your Relationship with Your Children

Some relationship must necessarily exist between you and your children. The question is only the kind and degree. Will it be the warm, enthusiastic, joyful sharing of friends, or will it be hostile, resistant, rebellious? The relationship between you and the child is of inestimable significance in effecting growth in the child. You can "pour in facts" and turn eager learners into rebellious, antagonistic rebels, or you can make learning a joyous shared experience long to be remembered.

If you are gracious and radiate warmth and friendliness, there is usually a contagious friendliness among the group. If you are autocratic, domineering, and rigid in your relationships with the children, it tends to build tensions that they will take out on each other.

Your influence is felt not only directly in what you think, say, and do, but indirectly through your attitudes and expectations. Children are sensitive barometers of your every mood, and respond to the warmth of a gracious, physically buoyant personality. You should not be childish, but you *can* strive for a *child-like* spontaneity and a whole-hearted delight in living in the child's world. Knowing that democratic attitudes are formed more rapidly through action than through verbal explanation, you will share in the children's experiences and capitalize upon their spirit of play for genuine learning; also upon their interests and questions. A child's simple question can be the self-starter to tremendous learnings.

Creative and Expressive Energies

You must always endeavor to become even more expressive and creative. Learning will become an adventure you are eager to experience with your children. It is your task to release the energies and creative forces of the learners, forces which are conditioned by the classroom climate. You will continually search beyond the obvious for the best results. Creativity is hindered by a lack of understanding and group rapport, just as it is fostered by friendly encouragement and recognition.

You must love learning and have the same inner drive for intellectual curiosity you want the child to have. "You cannot kindle a fire in any other heart until it is burning within your own."

You will need to spend almost as much time in learning as in teaching and preparation, but you will want to make sure your knowledge is not sealed off in specialized cells and lost in relation to the feelings and inner drives of the individual child. You will want to continue personal growth with new challenges, new insights, and new avenues of adventure.

Inner Joy

You will recognize the place of a positive, happy smile that radiates throughout the entire room because it springs from the heart, rather than a surface grimace like an artificially plastered façade.

A sparkling sense of humor, merriment, laughter, exuberance will brighten your day and the children's, and a happy outlook and freedom from moodiness and periodic depression are reflected in the attitudes of your children.

Such a teacher is Miss Holman. One day, as usual, she had joined the children's play at recess. Later, she said, "I must go and get to work now because you will be coming back into the room right away."

Seven-year-old Mark asked in dead earnest, "Get to *work!* What do you mean? Do *you* work?"

"Yes," said Miss Holman, "of course I work. I teach school. I teach all you boys and girls."

"Why," said Mark, "I though you just had fun with us. I didn't know you worked. Do you really get money for having such a good time every day?"

Children Reach Out to You

Your approach—the tone of your voice, how you listen to a child—speaks louder of your love and friendship than any words. If you will but listen, children will tell you their needs, their interests, their hopes, what they think and why. David expressed this need for understanding friendship one day. He was possessed of a high potential of achievement but was not being kept constructively busy. Therefore he was finding other outlets for his energy. When reproved by his teacher and sent away from the group he muttered, "If I only had a real friend when I am feeling this way!"

There are heart hungry children who reach out frantically for something that will bring security, love, and a sense of belonging. If you are to succeed in teaching you must have a deep affection for children as individuals and in groups, and you must have faith and trust in them. You must care deeply about each child as a person and let him know that you do. Children seem intuitively to recognize the sincerity in which the adult holds them. They sense insincerity and artificiality. If adults knew as much about children as children know about the adults in their environment, it would be an entirely different world.

As seven-year-old Larry said with deep perception when he was talking confidentially to an adult friend, "Today we had student teacher observers. We like having them with us, but when they get to be teachers they'll learn a lot. You know children hide their wiseness from grown people. We usually know a lot about things we don't tell."

Your Relationships with Parents and the Larger Community

Among the long list of attributes which you will seek to acquire, you need to learn to enjoy people, if you do not already, and to be a good mixer. You will need to make every effort to develop a sensitivity toward the way others feel. This quality makes for good relationships with associates and with the parents of your group, as well as with the children.

You need to know the local community, the activities of the people, their hopes and goals. It is a valuable means of getting more background.

In this world of today where the man on the other side of the world has become a close neighbor, you need depth of understanding of world problems. The quality of what you need to know is changing, and it is imperative that through your knowledge of wider areas you can make them real to children.

Of course, the most important phase of your community relationships is with the parents of the children. This is true with any age group, but particularly so if you are teaching the youngest. Because the young child is still so close to his own family, you are drawn more naturally into the orbit of his home than the teacher of older children. You will find, too, that parents can help you in many ways. Not only will their moral support be of inestimable value; your association may help them to see and understand their own children a little better. A father or mother may come to your classroom and play an instrument, or share an experience or a talent. It is an excellent way to stimulate interest in the school and in the way children learn.

The Child's Concept of Teachers

The demands of teaching require tremendous physical vitality, buoyant health, and a strong vigorous personality. Six-year-old Billy said to his teacher after she had been absent with an illness, "I'm so glad you're back, Mrs. Cardona. I didn't like that other girl."

"Girl? What do you mean, Billy? Is she smaller than I?" Mrs. Cardona visualized the pretty but somewhat buxom teacher who had substituted in her absence.

"No," said Billy, "she's much larger, but she had to order people around all the time. Nobody who has to order people around is grown up."

However, as children gain in maturity and experience, it is surprising how their concept of teaching widens. For example, a visitor asked a group of middle primary children how they always knew to do the right thing at the right time.

Linda answered without a moment's hesitation: "Because we are all teachers. There are thirty-two teachers in this room, plus Miss Holman, who makes thirty-three. We help each other solve our personal problems, do arithmetic, learn words in reading, make charts, find words in the dictionary, and work on reports."

Attitude of Evaluation

Remembering that learning blossoms in an atmosphere of warm friendliness, you will want to guide your children to an appreciation of the worth of others. Help them to see true value in each other's work, which is an excellent way of encouraging each one to achieve status in the eyes of his peers.

Self-appraisal must necessarily take place, so that each teacher may avoid an abrupt, "This is wrong—fix it," and will instead guide the child himself to say, "I can see a better way of doing this. Another time I would do so and so." In this way the child moves from a defensive position to the attitude expressed in, "I'm learning so much; I'd like to do it over again."

The self-appraisal which you guide the children to make, should apply to your own work in even greater measure. Always you should strive to improve your teaching ability by engaging in a process of constant evaluations to keep doing better today what you did yesterday.

A Secondary Teacher's Viewpoint Toward Early Childhood Teaching:

Mrs. Irene Lansing, English teacher at West Seattle High School, Seattle, Washington, wrote after she had taken courses in Early Childhood Education one summer:

> Perhaps the greatest return from this summer is my amazement at how *much* Early Childhood teachers have to do, and know. They have to be, apparently, philosophers, artists, musicians, carpenters, weavers, dancers, librarians. They have to cut and sew, and paste and paint. Most of all, they have to *plan*. Apparently breaking down a year's plan for literature takes no more time and effort than does a year's plan for five-year-olds, and I'd honestly have supposed differently! My mind whirls when I consider the number of songs, stories, charts, books that must be a part of their repertoire, and the instruments, toys, and countless other things to be taken care of. Worse than that, they apparently have to provide everything—they often make it, and pay for it. And, then,—my blood boils at this—they are given extra jobs like cafeteria and playground, because they GET OUT EARLIER! From now on there will always be one voice raised in the high school section to prevent this.
>
> "Undoubtedly, parent-counseling is a wonderfully forward move—highly desirable,—but *how* is this paragon, already mother, psychologist, psychoanalyst, sociologist, scientist, angel, law giver, and expert in group dynamics, going to fit herself to be also an expert in adult education, which is what this amounts to! Perhaps in the long run, though, it will make things easier!"

Your Own Viewpoint

One highly successful teacher states:

> "I don't do all things according to the book, but I can truthfully say I have a fine relationship with my children and parents in the community.

The children are happy and are usually quite well prepared for the level ahead. And the rewards? When Madelyn looks up and says, 'I just love teachers, and you're the bestest teacher in the whole world,' that is ample reward for the time and thought and effort that goes into my teaching."

This teacher knows that she is constantly dealing with some of the most frustrating and at the same time most soul-satisfying problems in life. Not every effort on her part is a success, but she works earnestly and sincerely, and because of her fidelity to her profession she rates high as a teacher.

She speaks to her children through poem and story, through music and art, but the best language of all is the love and sympathy she gives them. Treating each one with individual attention and affection, she grows in her ability to give every child what he needs to make life good for him. And he in turn, will remember her always as a teacher who made him feel safe when he was forlorn, neglected, and staggering under perplexities and confusions.

If each child throughout his school career could have this type of teacher; if teacher, consultant, and administrator could work together with understanding of the child, and with his interest the keynote, there would be a new and better civilization.

Henry Adams spoke as a seer and a prophet when he said, "A teacher affects eternity. He can never tell where his influence stops."

QUESTIONS ON THE INFLUENCE OF THE TEACHER

1. Justify the viewpoint that you as the teacher are one of the environmental influences in your classroom.

2. Discuss the difference between being child-like and childish. How does this apply to teaching?

3. What personal growth is desirable in a teacher? Be specific.

4. What do your children gain through your own self-appraisal of your teaching from day to day? Describe.

5. From your knowledge of the goals of childhood education and democracy in the classroom, list the characteristics of a successful teacher of children. Evaluate yourself in terms of these characteristics. List your strengths and needs and suggest ways of strengthening your own qualifications for teaching.

SELECTED REFERENCES

Alexander, William M., ARE YOU A GOOD TEACHER?, New York, Rinehart & Co., 1959.

Association for Supervision and Curriculum Development, LEARNING AND THE TEACHER, 1959 Yearbook, N.E.A., Washington, D.C., The Association, 1959.

Bruce, William F. and A. John Holden, Jr., THE TEACHER'S PERSONAL DEVELOPMENT; AN INTRODUCTION TO SELF-AWARENESS AND INTER-PERSONAL RELATIONS, New York, Henry Holt, 1957.

Douglass, Paul, TEACHING FOR SELF EDUCATION: AS A LIFE GOAL, New York, Harper Bros., 1960.

Eye, Glen G. and Willard R. Lane, THE NEW TEACHER COMES TO SCHOOL, New York, Harper & Bros., 1956.

Harrison, Raymond and Lawrence E. Gowin, THE ELEMENTARY TEACHER IN ACTION, San Francisco, Wadsworth Publishing Co., 1958.

Highet, Gilbert, THE ART OF TEACHING, New York, Vintage Books, 1955.

Jersild, Arthur T., WHEN TEACHERS FACE THEMSELVES, New York, Bureau of Publications, Teachers College, Columbia University, 1955.

Keliher, Alice, TALKS WITH TEACHERS, Darien, Conn., The Educational Publishing Co., 1958.

Kyte, George C., THE ELEMENTARY SCHOOL TEACHER AT WORK, New York, Dryden Press, 1957.

Lane, Howard and Mary Beauchamp, HUMAN RELATIONS IN TEACHING, Englewood Cliffs, New Jersey, Prentice-Hall, 1955.

Leonard, Edith M., Dorothy D. VanDeman and Lillian E. Miles, COUNSELING WITH PARENTS, New York, The Macmillan Co., 1954.

Liebermann, Myron, EDUCATION AS A PROFESSION, Englewood Cliffs, N. J., Prentice-Hall, 1956.

Menninger, William C., SELF-UNDERSTANDING: A FIRST STEP IN UNDERSTANDING CHILDREN, Chicago, Science Research Associates, 1951.

Moustakas, C. E., THE ALIVE AND GROWING TEACHER, New York, Philosophical Library, 1959.

Sharpe, D. Louise, Ed., WHY TEACH?, New York, Henry Holt, 1957.

Stiles, Lindley, THE TEACHER'S ROLE IN AMERICAN SOCIETY, 14th Yearbook John Dewey Society, New York, Harper Bros., 1957.

Wilson, Charles H., A TEACHER IS A PERSON, New York, Henry Holt, 1956.

Yauch, Wilbur A., HELPING TEACHERS UNDERSTAND PRINCIPALS, New York, Appleton-Century Crofts, 1957.

IV. UNDERSTANDING THE CHILD

Background of Experience

Starting school is an event in a child's life second only in importance to his birth. He enters, bringing with him the background he has acquired at home, including his reactions to people, animals, and things in his immediate neighborhood; his likes and dislikes; his interests, his secret hopes and ambitions; his church; television; the parks and other recreational facilities; the varied and powerful influences of his outside world from which he has formulated his own set of personal values; his social background; and his own unique history.

Through visitors from other places, through books, radio and television, one child may have had the entire world brought into his home. Another may have traveled the world over. But for many children school represents the first step away from the family. Some may previously have been supervised by one person or many; some are from homes where servants come and go; others from situations where the mother works and takes her children to a child care center or to an individual "baby sitter"; while still another may have been sent to camp merely because his parents are too busy to supervise him personally. All too frequently children are taken to a movie, or put before a television set and permitted to view unselected programs, or told to go out and play so mother can be uninterrupted in her personal pursuits or duties. Whether or not you are aware of what they are receiving, children bring to school with them the impressions gained from all these influences.

Extremes Within the Group

As is true throughout the entire educational program, the early childhood teacher has children in varying degrees of maturity and experience. Even the beginning group contains wide extremes, from the shy, timorous, regressive child who has barely graduated to toilet independence, to the aggressive extrovert who is familiar with the environment, converses with people without hesitation or embarrassment, and is eager and outwardly ready to live his school day to the fullest.

You have to take all these children, with their multiple reactions, and work with them until they blossom into their potential personalities.

Each child sees the world as it is portrayed to him through his own experiences and understandings, and his empathy to human needs is vitalized or destroyed accordingly. Hence the family into which a child is born affects his development at school through direct and indirect expectations, pressures, and support.

Diversified Family Backgrounds

Some children come to school from large families, having had much "give and take" from their earliest days. How different are their problems from those of the only child, of whom there are several varieties. There is the child who actually has no brothers or sisters. This fact does not in itself set him apart, but the way his family meets the situation may do so. Billy, for instance, lives in a world of adults, is treated like a grown up, and really knows no childhood, while Arthur, another only child, has friends his own age, and his household recognizes his active growing childhood interests.

But there is also Martha who has two brothers, ages nineteen and twenty-one. She is virtually "the only child" in her family at the present time. Martha has the equivalent of four devoted parents, since the entire home revolves around her slightest whims. There is also Milton who has been delicate and ill for a long period. This has made him much like an only child in the household because of the whole family's catering to his constant demands. There is, too, the child who is most beloved or who for some special reason is considered superior to the other children in his home.

Older Parents

Children raised by grandparents or by parents the age of grandparents will naturally respond in a different way from those who are brought up by younger parents. The old cliché, "Children are for the young," has some element of truth, since a child is a serious responsibility and, although there are exceptions, older people cannot always be expected to have the patience or energy to undertake all the duties of parenthood.

Conflicting Demands

Adults react in a variety of ways and set up widely diversified standards and demands. It is almost disastrous to any child to have a number of adults in the environment who confuse him with wrangling, hurry, over-expectation, clash of ideas between adults or adult and child, and make him a victim of too many requests and often continual nagging.

One adult may try to keep the child a baby, another may try to make a man of him and frown on all normal childhood activities, and yet another may treat him as a friend. Tenseness and rebellion are a natural by-product of such an environment. Some children, however, have learned to play their parents against each other and early become clever strategists in getting their wishes gratified.

Physical and Mental Health

To assure the child's satisfactory progress in school he needs to be in good mental and physical health. There are many factors that could cause serious difficulty, such as malnutrition or lack of eye or ear acuity. Rejection and neglect are apt to affect a child in a physical way. Many children do not get enough time during the twenty-four hours for resting, relaxing, and sleeping, and their difficulties in school can be traced to this fact.

The fives and sixes have an earlier point of exhaustion than the older child, which builds up to a frustration point or over-stimulation where release is found through unrestrained, obstreperous behavior. You must be aware of the manifestations of fatigue, and of poor mental as well as physical health. Some of the symptoms are irritability, flightiness, nervous tics, crying, nailbiting, thumb sucking, hair twisting, chewing corners of clothing or other possessions, and masturbation and enuresis.

Security

Teachers, as well as parents, sometimes fail to realize the importance of the emotional development of the young child, yet it is a known fact that emotional tension is a robber of happiness at any age and a saboteur of efficiency. An individual's emotional resourcefulness in later life is often made or lost in the early years of his existence.

Insecure children have different ways of evidencing their lack of confidence. A child may resort to bravado and boast, swagger, and attempt courageous pretenses, or his instability may take expression in trying to exploit himself by showing off, which is an unconscious way of covering up what he really feels. When you encounter the more humble insecure child, of which there are a large number, you must help him build faith in his own value and give him a feeling that he belongs. Children are keenly sensitive to the "all's well" attitude, and are sometimes quicker than are you to know when this is in jeopardy.

Spontaneity and Emotional Security

The well-adjusted child has a happy balance between emotional security and spontaneity. Some indication of the balance between these two factors is reflected in his response to his immediate environment. While most children climb easily and joyously to the top of the jungle gym, the slide, or the ladder, perhaps calling to you or to a friend to watch, occasionally a child will avoid climbing at all. The child with muscular ability who hesitates to climb is evidently held back by some emotional inhibition. Withdrawal from the environment is a problem which is not necessarily remedied by putting the child to playing with some toy. His reaction may be indicative of insecurity, which should be watched carefully by you. A certain amount of withdrawal when a child first enters a new situation may be expected. If this disappears within a reasonable span of time and the child soon works wholeheartedly and spontaneously with other children and equipment, you may feel assured that he is attaining a balance between stability and spontaneity.

In a psychology class seven-year-old Marilyn was being given an intelligence test. She passed the linguistic and mathematical phases with the ability expected of a fourteen-year-old, but was adamant in her refusal to do any of the manipulative parts: "I'm just no good in using my hands and legs. I can't paint or use clay or even climb as well as my little four-year-old sister." Part of this was, of course, a reflection of the attitude of the adults in her environment, but Marilyn had a sincere feeling of inadequacy when it came to motor activities and was unwilling to even attempt to gain experience in this field. This presented a serious problem for Marilyn, herself, as well as her family and her teachers.

This child needed to be encouraged to experiment with hand painting, easel painting, clay, and balancing equipment in order to find out how they feel and what can be done with them. This would shift attention away from her own lack of skill to a delight in manipulation and discovery of possibilities.

Regardless of background a child will evidence his degree of security by his attitude and responses toward new environments, new things, new adults, new children, and new experiences.

Peer and Group Experiences

The beginning school child needs a sense of security through group experiences. He must be accepted by his group if he is to be happy. In fact, this need exists throughout the life of the individual, although many develop their inner resources to a far greater degree than others and are therefore less dependent.

Sometimes it is difficult for the child to get along with his peers, although in some cases good child-to-child relationships may come more easily than teacher-child relationships.

Often a more intelligent child will be found failing to achieve academically. Sometimes such a child is preoccupied in his struggle to be acceptable in the eyes of his peers and therefore has little time or interest in meeting academic expectations. If he continues in this direction he will be among those who place popularity beyond scholastic achievement, and will be satisfied with average or lower academic standards. Although capable of achieving an outstanding quality of work, he feels that to do so might set him apart from his peers.

Gail and Pam are striking examples of rare individuals who possess child-to-child rapport even when they enter school.

Gail, five years, seven months, suddenly burst forth one day with, "What good is it, Miss Meredith, to have David leave the group so much! How can he learn when he is away?"

Pam followed this statement with, "It takes all kinds of people to make a group and we need to help David to belong to our group."

Evidences of Need for Your Guidance

The child entering school craves response from adults and needs the companionship of those who do not become excited or upset over his actions, but are calm, steady, and consistent.

The child with emotional problems is often seeking basic security and success, a sense of belonging, and constructive avenues of responsibility on his own maturation level.

The destructive child, the child who has tantrums or who cries at the slightest provocation, the one who continually is mean to other children, these and many others reveal symptoms of maladjustment that need careful diagnosis and guidance.

Whatever his background, the child in the beginning group is entering a new environment, a new world of people, situations, experiences, and problems. It is of vital importance that his feeling of emotional security (if he has it) remain intact, and (if he lacks it) be given every opportunity for development. While he explores a new field and adjusts to living with others who have interests and ambitions that parallel his own, it is essential that he recognize you, his teacher, as an understanding friend who has a profound sympathy for him and his problems.

This presupposes you are a sensitive, patient, courageous individual, able to conceal a shock reaction to anything the child says or does, a teacher-friend with whom he feels secure in pouring out his heart. Affection, friendliness, recognition, an opportunity, encouragement, and wise guidance will help to assure him that he is a much needed member of the group.

Tattling

The child who has difficulty in adjusting to school sometimes finds a certain satisfaction in tattling and being critical of his peers. This is irritating to those guiding him, but it may be a transitory stage of development and hence a sign of growth and the beginning of evaluation. He needs help in winning his way into constructive group living. There is also the child who finds emotional satisfaction in getting into trouble and running to you with his woes.

The Accident Prone

The accident-prone child whose hurts are numerous can frequently be soothed by something as simple as a word of encouragement, the meeting of eyes, a special squeeze of the arm in passing, a sympathetic nod of understanding over a bruised knee, or sometimes by a ligature for a psychosomatic sore finger.

Love and Hate

The child's body is the instrument on which his emotions play. At this age he loves intensely and hates equally as much, and there may be a very short span between these two extremes of expression. Freddie and Joe may be the best of friends and may have played happily together throughout the afternoon. However, in their building activity Freddie may want to place the blocks in one way and Joe in another. They each grasp the block and glare at each other. "Go home!" says Freddie, "and stay there, and don't come back again. I hate you." And for the moment he does hate Joe.

Joe returns the hate and goes home in anger. Five minutes later Freddie goes in the house and finds that Mother has made cookies. He takes one for himself and asks, "May I take one over to Joe?"

His mother consents and he runs happily over to Joe's house waving the cookie, anger completely forgotten. Comradeship is resumed with no remembered rancor and no thought of apology.

Emotional Outlets

In the course of the child's activities and social relationships he expresses the changes and fluctuations in his inner consciousness through laughter, tears, shouting, and singing. He may use clay to express his interest, or painting, or block building, or he may find an emotional outlet through language, body rhythms, music, dramatic play, or a combination of all these activities.

Drives to Action

It is your responsibility to know each child so well that you can recognize and interpret his feelings, which are his drives to action. They influence his attitudes and behavior patterns as well as his appreciations. They also affect the interaction of his past environment and his day by day environment in and out of school. If you find an emptiness in his life you may help him compensate for what he lacks if you have learned to live in the child's world and see things from his vantage point.

The Child's Viewpoint

Each child has a unique view of the world by which he interprets the learning to which he is exposed. How his parents feel about discipline he receives; social customs, traditions, and the way the family feels about the child himself—all of these influences affect his adjustment to school. If he has been coerced, pressured, and unjustly punished, he tends to become inimical to the whole spirit of learning, hostile toward adults, and generally belligerent and ready to attack anyone, anywhere.

Adults frequently forget the way a child looks at things. The five- or six-year-old has not yet felt the importance of conformity to group patterns, and still has a tendency toward *negativism*; he often says "no" to everything, due largely to his search for independence from babyhood. He is still a child of conflicts. At one time he seems a mere infant; soon after he may evidence surprising maturity. He may go from one extreme to another within a few minutes, changing from the overly-compliant or withdrawn child to one who is defiant and stubborn.

He has to learn to give and take, to *communicate* his needs, desires, anxieties, and inter-actions to all the new people in his environment through the channel of the spoken word. This is how he learns to live within the standards of his group. He has to build within himself the fortitude to meet the demands, the pressures, and the conflicts of his new environment. Frequently his whole stability suddenly collapses, and he sometimes finds that throwing a tantrum is the weapon he can use against the powerful adults in his environment, to gain their attention and get what he wants when he wants it.

Futility of Labeling a Child

There are dangers in the superficial labeling of a child with an apparent problem or maladjustment, such as describing him as an "emotionally unstable" child, an "aggressive" or "withdrawn" child, "a deviate," a "slow learner," or an "exceptional child," or indeed by problem behavior of any kind. Even the term "gifted" can lead to awkward situations when applied to a definite individual or group. Close, unbiased, impersonal observation may reveal the fallacy of such terminology. Anecdotal records, intelligently taken, can be of inestimable value in helping you understand individual children, but indiscriminate labeling may encourage undesirable behavior.

Acceptance and Recognition

When parents are harrassed, frustrated, or distraught, their conflicts react unfavorably on the young impressionable child. The reactions of teachers also have their influence. When you accept the child for the individual that he really is and help him to know himself better, to appreciate himself for his own qualities, to know his own strengths and needs, and to look upon himself as a growing person capable of great changes, it will go far toward creating the type of class-room climate essential for good basic learning foundations.

The child who feels himself a functioning part in the daily activities goes home with the attitude that school is a good place to be, and that he is an important person there. He has no reason to feel he is important unless those in his environment treat him as if he is.

When there is basic security within the group and in each child, difficulties of all varieties will be replaced with happy, buoyant living.

Your Own Perspective

Perspective is an important means of viewing the child, over and above the adult's emotions. Children need reassurance, as do all human beings, but teachers sometimes get to the place where they withhold this reassurance, since it frequently takes the patience of Job to accept the child's expression of tumultuous feelings. There must, however, be an empathy toward his blustery behavior. This does not mean countenancing it in any way, but working with it, starting where the child is at the moment, and guiding him into a modification of his behavior until he achieves the desired standard.

Not only must he recognize you as an understanding friend who has profound sympathy for him and his problem; it is equally important for him to know that you represent law and authority and are present to help him help himself to do the right thing at all times.

A Child's Reason

Children need a reason they can understand and accept rather than an adult explanation of things. For example, six-year-old Clarence was a polio convalescent and had to wear heavy braces on both legs. He complained vehemently over his handicap and the fact that he could not be an active participant in his group. His parents patiently explained that the braces were necessary to strengthen his legs and make it possible for him to walk later on, like other boys. Clarence could not accept this reasoning until his teacher talked the problem over with him and helped him understand it was because his parents loved him especially much that they wanted him to have strong legs so he could walk with his friends. This explanation gave Clarence the security he needed and he wore the braces with understanding because he had been given a child's reason.

A Mind-Set Toward Uniformity of Instruction

Instead of attempting to learn what the children in her group were ready to undertake, Miss R. made out work papers which she expected every child to do. The children who did neat, attractive, correct coloring had a star on their papers. If their work was correct in every other way, but the coloring was not "prettily done," they were given an "S," and otherwise an "X."

It is evident that Miss R. had a mind-set toward uniformity of instruction. She thought each child should do the same thing at the same time in the same way. She did not recognize that within her group there were differences in maturity and that some of the children could not be expected to do what she asked them to do at that time, no matter how hard they tried. She either would not, or could not, adapt her thinking to the point at which she could try to provide various learning experiences at the same time for individual children. To her, "first grade is first grade," and the child who could do first grade work was honored above the others who could not.

An Immature Child in Miss R.'s Classroom

When Jerry, who just barely met the age requirement (birthday December first), entered Miss R.'s room, he was put right into coloring small balls and other tiny figures. Jerry tried valiantly, but he just wasn't able to do neat coloring within the lines, as his muscular coordination had not developed to that extent. He was the youngest in the class, but day after day when he brought home papers marked "X" he kept saying, "I'm not doing good work. I can't color right."

Jerry's mother was an understanding, cultured person. She went to talk with Miss R. about her son. The mother was not upholding Jerry unreasonably, she merely wanted him to have a little appreciation for his efforts. The teacher said, "The children's work has to fairly take my breath away to have a star."

She showed the mother some of the better work of the class. The children had traced over the letters and numbers. "You can't even tell it was gone

over, they got it so exact," the teacher said. "The only way you can tell is
that one is in purple and the other in pencil."

This, of course, did not console Jerry's mother, but she *did* feel, perhaps,
that she had gotten the teacher to give Jerry a kind word now and then. "I
don't expect him to do wonders," his mother said, "but I *do* want Jerry to
be happy in school."

Parental Confidence

"It's going to take more than a daily paper with an 'X' on it to get our
Jerry down," his father said, but, even so, Jerry was far from happy that
year and was rapidly developing a deep insecurity and inferiority. "I just
am no good. I can't do anything right," he would say as he burst into tears
day after day upon his return from school.

Jerry was penalized for his immaturity, but he felt it was because of his
"dumbness." He could have developed a deep and lasting sense of inadequacy and defeat.

Home Influence

However, Jerry's parents gave him so many experiences in large muscle
activities and such a sense of success in his achievements at home that he
went into upper primary with a joy in school. When he brought home his
first report card from upper primary with an "O" in writing, he said to his
parents, "And that doesn't stand for 'Awful' either. It means 'Outstanding.'
I used to have difficulty with my work, but not anymore."

Competition and Achievement in the Early Years

Competition in the early years of life needs to be in terms of self-
improvement rather than by comparison with the achievement of others.
The timid, slow, insecure child needs all the encouragement he can be
given. Under the stress of competition he may refuse to make even an
effort. It may also result in attempts to deceive. Cheating often stems
from a lack of self-confidence, or from social pressure, over-emphasis on
grades from home or teacher, too high standards of accomplishment, or
a great, unrealized longing for approbation.

On the other hand, the gifted child may develop habits of idleness as
he waits for the slow learners; he may come to consider himself much
better than the others, not because of his own efforts to achieve, but
because of his native endowments. He needs guidance on his own maturation level, enlivening challenge, and continuous learning situations
through a variety of valuable experiences that will satisfy, encourage and
enhance his personal interests and give a feeling of satisfaction through
independence. "I did it all by myself," brings a glow of triumph to any

child. This demands that he compete with himself only, rather than with someone else.

The pressure of competition too often leads the immature child to inhibitions, emotional blocks, tensions, frustrations, and the danger of a sense of defeat even to the point of futility. While he is in this flexible state of development he needs time to grow, to become strong, stable, and fortified for experiences in which he will learn to meet the competition he must face in adult life.

Inner Motivation

Competition with himself may be a powerful inner motivating force for the slow as well as the accelerated child. Success is imperative for this inner motivation and it cannot be threatened by demands that are beyond the achievement level of the learner. Each individual needs commendation for every evidence of growth, no matter how meager. It must always be remembered that the rate of progress varies with each individual and the adult cannot motivate the child. It is you who create the conditions, encourage, guide, and help the child to develop and set up his own purpose. Once he has an inner driving purpose nothing can stand in the way of his learning. He will go far beyond any goal which the adult could ever impose upon him.

Recognition of Consequences

Along with this inner motivation the child must learn to develop purposes that include recognition of consequences. This demands that he be given opportunities for choices for which he is equal to accepting the results and abiding by them. This needs to be done with discretion, as he must be protected from having too many decisions thrust upon him before he is ready to assume the burden of the responsibility for the results of his choice.

> Nine-year-old Marian had been ill and out of school for six weeks. The day she returned the children were having an examination of the work covered during the entire semester. Marian was completely lost until she asked the child sitting next to her to give her quietly a few key words on each question. Doris was devoted to Marian and consented to the scheme.
>
> Marian was highly endowed and with the gist of the topic was able to write a dramatic, colorful, and interesting series of answers to the geography questions.
>
> When the papers were returned Marian had a big "A plus" on her efforts, while the plodding Doris received a "C minus."
>
> Marian's basic integrity came to the fore and she went to the teacher and

said, "I don't deserve this grade. Doris told me the answers to all the questions." The wise teacher replied, "I knew that, Marian, and I was positive you would evidence the true stuff of which you are made and admit your temptation. It really wasn't fair for you to take the examination, anyway, when you had been out for so long. We'll throw this paper away and I'll prepare another test for you."

The important concern is the child's *total* learning, rather than how quickly he learns a given subject.

Individual Progress

As the child moves forward, he needs to learn to evaluate and compare what he did yesterday with what he has done today. This comparison should never be made in terms of what others are doing but in what he himself is accomplishing. The child who says, "Yesterday I forgot and ran into the room; today I remembered and came in quietly," or who says, "Last week I couldn't read this chart, but today I can read all of it," is learning to evaluate his progress.

In contrast to this, some teachers exhibit lists displaying how many books the various children have read. Perhaps a few will have twenty or thirty while others have only one or two, or even none.

In a similar way, other teachers ostentatiously place "Our Best Work" on the bulletin board, displaying only the work of the superior children, or the name of "Our Best Reader Today." How different is the children's attitude in groups where work that shows progressive growth is placed for everyone to enjoy and admire.

Each child may have a graph of his own growth, but a class graph is unwise. The individual needs to feel that his own progress is the important factor involved, not whether he is better or poorer than someone else.

Cooperative Games

In cooperative games there is a goal that is common to all players. There is no team against team, nor player against player. All play together in an attempt to attain their goal. There is no winning or losing. The players compete against non-human elements—a ball or numbers, or cards or time—rather than against other players.

In a cooperative game the players do not necessarily play identically but rather unitedly in an effort to reach the common goal.

The rules in such games are agreed upon by the group before they begin, and can be more flexible than in other types of games because there is no other side or team to play against. This flexibility stimulates more creativity; hence new games or variations result. More planning also takes place while the game goes on. More suggestions are made. There seems to be less resentment toward an individual bungling a play. The group as a whole attempts to correct individual errors and to teach those who need help.

Cooperative games are structured on the assumptions that play is one of the channels whereby learning takes place and that cooperative attitudes are desirable and can be fostered. Attitudes are readily built through activities. Play is an activity and games are one type of play.

Unwholesome Competition

A revealing example of unwholesome competition is found in the case of Randy, who was accelerated intellectually and socially but slightly retarded in motor development. Randy was popular with the children, but had never been able to make the junior football or baseball team at school. One afternoon he came rushing back home and said, "Mom, Mom! I need my mitt and bat. Our room is going to play in the all-school game and I've been asked to play on the team. You'll just have to come over and see us play."

As Randy hurried out the door, his mother bundled her three younger children in coats, scarfs, and blankets, and started out, pushing one child in a buggy, pulling one in a cart, and instructing the third to stay close beside her. The mother was almost as excited as Randy, because she was so eager for her child to be an all-round American boy.

When she reached the school she saw a group of nine boys from Randy's room playing the game with an enthusiastic audience of most of the other class members. She looked everywhere for her son but could not find him. At last she asked one of the children, "Where is Randy?"

"Oh, he's inside with the teacher."

When the mother reached Randy's room she found six boys working at the table. She asked the teacher if she might speak to her son. Upon questioning, Randy said, "I have to do arithmetic. Just the best players get to be on the team. I am one of the best in arithmetic so I have to work these problems for our open house program."

The mother spoke to the teacher who said, "You see, we are having an all fifth grade game, so we have this period for the children who are to take part in the competition to practice. Randy excels in arithmetic and he will help bring glory to our school in that field. You know yourself athletics is certainly not Randy's strong point."

Randy needed opportunity for physical activity free from competition with others who might show him to disadvantage by comparison. Emphasis on achieving the most advanced level of accomplishment rather than upon growth in arithmetic ability gave this child a false standard upon which to offer his cooperation.

It cannot be over-emphasized that every child develops best in a climate built by experiences resulting from his being a happy, cooperative member of the group. Such rapport begets complete security because he knows he is loved and appreciated for what he is—not for how he compares with others or for how advanced his work is.

Humor

Teachers everywhere can attest to the fact that a constructive sense of humor has saved many a situation. Fun, joy, and laughter are great teachers and have a therapeutic value in themselves.

A child's sense of humor often differs from an adult's. Among all the other things you need to do in order to understand a child fully is to learn what he considers humorous. When the adult learns to laugh with, but not at, the child and is wise enough to avoid taking everything on the same plane of seriousness, there will be a wholesome relief from tensions and insecurity, release from tired taut muscles, and the sundering breach in child-teacher relationships will be greatly eased. It is good to laugh together.

A dragon fly flew into Mrs. Jones' room during the discussion of a chart. Gordon said, "The dragon fly saw the word *Look* on our chart and came in to look and see." The children thought this was almost the funniest thing they had ever heard. They and Mrs. Jones had a hearty laugh together.

During a Likeness and Difference experience with a group of six-year-olds, Mrs. Jones took three shoes walking that she had borrowed from three of the children. She returned the first shoe to the wrong person, saying in a low exaggerated voice, "Put me on your foot, please." The child answered in the same kind of voice, "But it isn't my shoe." After two other "intended mistakes," the shoe finally reached the owner. The children thought this extremely funny, but even more so when she did the same thing with another set of shoes using a high squeeky voice. The humor of the situation brought home her point about likenesses and differences.

The reason behind the lusty laugh is really unimportant, but the fact that children and adults have wholesome fun, and laugh together, is highly significant.

In primary groups, collections of jokes, cartoons, funny stories, riddles, rhymes, and other humorous pictures and writings can be placed on the bulletin board or made into interesting scrapbooks, subject, of course, to the fundamental principles of selecting materials for young children.

Children of sufficient maturity can write creative humorous anecdotes, poems, rhymes, and stories.

Teachers need to take Walter Winchell's apt quotation to heart in guiding their children into joyous living: "If you are too busy to laugh, you are too busy."

Understanding the Child's Curiosity

Why?

I ask my parents questions
I ask my teacher too;
"Why do waves come rolling in;
What makes the whole sky blue?"
They sometimes try to help me
Or say, "Go read your book,"
I often find no answer
Though I look and look and look.
"Why do worms just creepy crawl?"
"Can angels really fly?"
"Why can whales and fishes swim
Better than you or I?"
I keep on asking why it is
And just what makes it so;
I haven't found the answer,
And I really want to know.

An endless round of questions will come forth from the mouths of your children from the earliest years of their lives. Their questions are frequently as revealing as they are overpowering and baffling. This intellectual curiosity is healthy and needs to be nurtured and guided because it is the essence of much of the child's search for knowledge as he learns from, and responds to, his surroundings. It is this natural curiosity that leads to understandings, insights, mental vision, and a background of information which helps the child eventually to distinguish between facts and opinions.

Curiosity continues progressively to dominate the young child's course until he becomes almost a living question mark, not only through his spoken questions but as he picks up things, pulls, punches, tastes, and smells, and finds out for himself. He observes, investigates, explores, experiments, and learns to combine all these experiences into facts. Finding the answers to many things that adults take for granted is the child's natural way of learning.

Evidence of Critical Thinking

You have but to listen to some of the young child's questions to realize that he is, perhaps, doing more critical thinking than are the adults in his environment. Of a spiritual nature, there are questions such as these:

> Gale, 3-6, asks earnestly, "Who made God?" while Tommy, 5-0, wants to know, "Why can't I see God?" and Philip, 4-2, asks, "Does God look like Daddy or like Uncle Bill?" Sally, 6-2, inquires, "Does God have to use the same people over and over again to be born?"
>
> After hearing the rumble of thunder George, 5-6, asks, "Is God cleaning His house in Heaven and moving the furniture?" and Mary Ann, 5-8, wants to know, "Is God punishing some one when it lightnings and thunders?"

Equally bewildering are the philosophical questions such as those of:

> Esther, 5-4, who asks solicitiously, "Why can't I see myself grow?" and Doris, 5-5, "What makes some people white and some people black?" Roger, 6-3, wants to know, "Why can't we buy time?" and Patrick, 6-1, asks, "What is a city father?"
>
> In the realm of the physiological, Patty, 5-0, is concerned about, "What happens when we sleep?" and Clara, 6-0, is anxious to know, "Why is 98.6 called a normal temperature?"

There are innumerable other questions of this nature, equally as revealing of what is going on in the mind of the child. You will find it a source of understanding if you will keep a record (and encourage parents to do likewise) of some of the more profound questions that the individual child asks.

You may be disconcerted, also, by the natural science questions, such as those of:

> Steven, 3-3, "Does it hurt the grass when Daddy cuts it?" and Bob, 3-9, "What makes the white flower smell good?" Peter, 4-9, wants to know, "What makes it get dark?" and Brian, just five, asks, "What makes a clock tick?" Tommy, 5-6, is concerned with "Where does the sun go at night?" and Billy, 5-7, with "What makes the ocean taste salty?" and Jane, 5-9, with "What makes the red go up in the thermometer?" while six-year-old Jimmy is disturbed in his search to know, "Do the bees sting the flowers?" Dennis, 6-6, asks, "Why are the waves on the ocean and not on our lake?" and Ronald, 6-6, wants to know, "How do mountains grow?" and Edna, 6-7, "Why isn't it the same time in New York as it is in California?"

Knowing How to Meet Questions

The important thing for you, as the teacher of these children who are searching for explanations, is to keep their intellectual curiosity alive, to give them confidence that any question is acceptable, to leave the way open for further questioning by avoiding too lengthy explanations, while at the same time answering all questions frankly. The amount of detail given will of course depend upon the age and maturity of the child asking the question. You will avoid nonsense answers or those that puzzle, tease, or annoy the child. It is difficult at best for the young child to understand this complex world, and you do not want to add to his confusion in any way. Frequently you will reverse the process and turn back to him those questions that he is capable of solving himself. Also, you will ask questions of the child that will give evidence of his growth, start him thinking creatively and independently, and help him develop an informed, critical, and confident mind. Sometimes this can be done by helping him solve his own questions through organizing and clinching his past learnings.

There will be times when you feel you cannot answer the child's questions, but rather than give inaccurate information or put him off, go with him to someone in your community who is a specialist in the field or lead him to adequately selected pictures and books for his answers. Oftentimes the question can be answered through your combined thoughtful observation and exploration. The answer to a question can often be found by thinking carefully how to go about it. Sometimes it is largely a matter of knowing how and where to search for the answer.

Six Questions to Guide You

To be ever-ready for this bombardment of questions, you as a teacher of early childhood need to take for your own living motto:

> I listen to six friends of mine
> And wiser now am I
> Their names are *how* and *what*
> and *when*
> And *where* and *who* and *why*.

These six are not idle questions. Together they hold the keys to their own answers.

Curiosity is the child's own active response to the world around him. When he is alert, his surroundings impress him. He learns through these impressions. To investigate just to satisfy curiosity may be to get hurt, but curiosity directed into constructive channels of investigation becomes the basis for educational research, and brings stature to the learner.

QUESTIONS ON UNDERSTANDING THE CHILD

1. Describe the extremes within one group of children with which you are acquainted.

2. What are some of the things you can tell about a child's family through observing him away from home? What family influences affect his development at school? Give examples.

3. What are the manifestations of fatigue in children, and what significance does your discovery of them have in your classroom?

4. What is desirable about attaining a balance between stability and spontaneity in the children in your classroom? In what ways will the children give evidence that such a balance is being maintained? Give examples and discuss.

5. Why is it essential that the child recognize his teacher, as an understanding friend? Discuss. Why is it equally important, for his own good, that you represent law and authority? What has this to do with your helping the child to help himself do the right thing at all times? Illustrate.

6. What difference will the child's reason for what he is doing make in your guidance of a situation? Discuss and illustrate.

7. How can security within a child's home and understanding parents help him through a difficult period at school? Illustrate.

8. What are the perils of competition for young children? Why would you compare a child's achievement with his own past and future record rather than with that of other children? Illustrate.

9. How can you help children grow in the area of accepting responsibility for the results of their own decisions? Why is this essential if the child is to follow his own inner driving purpose?

10. What is your part in helping the child develop and set up his own purpose? What is to be gained when a child is spurred on by an inner drive? Discuss.

11. Give an example of a cooperative game and the creative planning that may accompany it. What are the educational implications?

12. What is your policy in regard to displaying children's finished work in the classroom? What objection is there to posting "Our Best Work"? How can recognition be given to superior achievement without discouraging other children?

13. Illustrate the fact that everything should not be considered with the same degree of seriousness in childhood education. Discuss the value of humor in your classroom.

14. How do a child's questions often reveal what is going on in his mind?

15. Why should older children and adults refrain from the temptation to tease or puzzle a young child? Why should nonsense answers to his questions be avoided?

16. Give examples to show how you would turn back a question to a child in such a way that he will discover his own answer. When is this desirable? Illustrate.

17. How can you help children learn how and where to search for the answers to their own questions? Discuss the educational implications of this.

18. How can you as a teacher keep children's intellectual curiosity alive? Why is this essential? Give examples.

19. Give examples of children's questions which you have recorded verbatim. In each instance state the child's age, the circumstances under which the question arose, and the trend of thought. How can this procedure help you better understand the child? Discuss.

20. Discuss how a question can hold the key to its own answer. What are the implications of this in childhood education?

21. Discuss the learning possibilities of the following: (a) who; (b) what; (c) where; (d) when; (e) how; and (f) why.

SELECTED REFERENCES

Almy, Millie, WAYS OF STUDYING CHILDREN, New York Bureau of Publications, Teachers College, Columbia University, 1959.

American Council on Education, Commission on Teacher Education, HELPING TEACHERS UNDERSTAND CHILDREN, by the staff of the Division on Child Development and Teacher Personnel, Washington, D.C., Commission of Teacher Education, American Council on Education, 1945.

Association for Childhood Education International, DEALING WITH FEARS AND TENSIONS, Bulletin No. 24, Washington, D.C., Association for Childhood Education, International, 1952.

Association for Supervision and Curriculum Development, GROWING UP IN AN ANXIOUS AGE, National Education Association, 1952.

Axline, Virginia, PLAY THERAPY, Boston, Houghton Mifflin, 1947.

Bro, Marguerite H., WHEN CHILDREN ASK, Chicago, Willett, Clark & Co., 1940.

Buhler, C., Faith Smitter, Sybil Richardson, and Franklin Bradshaw, CHILDHOOD PROBLEMS AND THE TEACHER, New York, Henry Holt, 1952.

Carroll, Gladys, CHRISTMAS WITHOUT JOHNNY, New York, Macmillan, 1950.

Cohen, Dorothy and Virginia Stern, OBSERVING AND RECORDING THE BEHAVIOR OF YOUNG CHILDREN, New York Bureau of Publications, Teachers College, Columbia Univ., 1959.

Department of Elementary School Principals, GUIDANCE FOR TODAY'S CHILDREN, Thirty-third Yearbook of the Department of Elementary School Principals, Washington, D.C., National Education Association, 1954.

D'Evelyn, Katherine E., MEETING CHILDREN'S EMOTIONAL NEEDS, New York, Prentice-Hall, 1959.

Elting, Mary, THE ANSWER BOOK; COMPLETE ANSWERS TO 300 QUESTIONS CHILDREN ASK MOST OFTEN, New York, Grossett & Dunlap, 1959.

Gesell, Arnold, Frances L. Ilg and others, CHILD DEVELOPMENT: AN INTRODUCTION TO THE STUDY OF HUMAN GROWTH, New York, Harper and Brothers, 1959.

Gruenberg, Sidonie, and Staff of Child Study Association, Ed., OUR CHILDREN TODAY, New York, Viking Press, 1952.

Hartley, Frank and Robert Goldenson, UNDERSTANDING CHILDREN'S PLAY, New York, Columbia University Press, 1952.

Horace-Mann-Lincoln Institute of School Experimentation, HOW TO CONSTRUCT A SOCIOGRAM, New York Teachers' College, Columbia University, 1947.

Humphreys, Alice L., ANGELS IN PINAFORES, Richmond, Va., John Knox Press, 1954.

Humphreys, Alice L., HEAVEN IN MY HAND, Richmond, Va., John Knox Press, 1950.

Jenkins, Gladys Gardner, HELPING CHILDREN REACH THEIR POTENTIAL, Chicago, Scott, Foresman and Company, 1961.

Jenkins, Gladys G., Helene Shacter and William M. Baurer, THESE ARE YOUR CHILDREN, Chicago, Scott, Foresman and Co., 1953.

Josselyn, Irene, THE HAPPY CHILD, New York, Random House, Inc., 1955.

Kauffman, Carolyn, and Patricia Farrell, IF YOU LIVE WITH LITTLE CHILDREN, New York, G. P. Putnam's Sons, 1957.

Landreth, Catherine, PSYCHOLOGY OF EARLY CHILDHOOD, New York, Alfred A. Knopf, 1958.

Langdon, Grace and Irving W. Stout, THESE WELL ADJUSTED CHILDREN, New York, John Day Co., 1951.

Langford, Louise, GUIDANCE OF THE YOUNG CHILD, New York, John Wiley & Sons, 1960.

Lee, Jonathan M., THE CHILD AND HIS DEVELOPMENT by J. Murray Lee and Dorris May Lee, New York, Appleton Century Crofts, 1958.

Leonard, Edith M., Dorothy VanDeman, and Lillian E. Miles, COUNSELING WITH PARENTS, New York, The Macmillan Co., 1954.

Meeker, Alice M., I LIKE CHILDREN, Evanston, Ill., Row Peterson, 1954.

Mitchell, Lucy S., Ed., KNOW YOUR CHILDREN IN SCHOOL, New York, Macmillan, 1960.

Moustakas, Clark, THE YOUNG CHILD IN SCHOOL, New York, William Morrow, 1956.

Murphy, Lois, PERSONALITY IN YOUNG CHILDREN, Vol. II Colin; A NORMAL CHILD, New York, Basic Books, 1956.

Prescott, Daniel, THE CHILD IN THE EDUCATIVE PROCESS, PART II "ON UNDERSTANDING CHILDREN," New York, McGraw Hill, 1957.

Rasey, Marie I. and J. W. Menge, WHAT WE LEARN FROM CHILDREN, New York, Harper & Brothers, 1956.

Redl, F., CHILDREN WHO HATE, Glencoe, Ill., Free Press, 1951.

Runbeck, Margaret Lee, OUR LITTLE MISS BOO, New York, Appleton Century, 1942.

Runbeck, Margaret L., TIME FOR EACH OTHER, New York, Appleton-Century Crofts, 1944.

Sarason, Seymour B., Kenneth S. Davidson, Frederick K. Lighthall, Richard R. Waite, and Britton K. Ruebush, ANXIETY IN ELEMENTARY SCHOOL CHILDREN, New York, John Wiley & Sons, 1960.

Savery, Constance, ENEMY BROTHERS, New York, Longmans Green & Co., 1943.

Scone, A. and G. Onque, LONGITUDINAL STUDIES OF CHILD PERSONALITY, Commonwealth Fund, Harvard Univ. Press, 1959.

Slavson, S. R., CHILD-CENTERED GROUP GUIDANCE OF PARENTS, New York, International Universities Press, 1958.

Stem, Catherine and Tonis Bould, THE EARLY YEARS OF CHILDHOOD EDUCATION THROUGH INSIGHT, New York, Harper and Brothers, 1955.

Strang, Ruth, AN INTRODUCTION TO CHILD STUDY, 4th Ed., New York, The Macmillan Co., 1959.

Ward, Muriel, YOUNG MINDS NEED SOMETHING TO GROW ON, Evanston, Ill., Row Peterson, 1957.

Washburn, Ruth W., CHILDREN KNOW THEIR FRIENDS, New York, William Morrow and Co., 1949.

Watson, Robert I., PSYCHOLOGY OF THE CHILD; PERSONAL, SOCIAL AND DISTURBED CHILD DEVELOPMENT, New York, John Wiley & Sons, 1959.

V. THE INFLUENCE OF TIME

Time to Grow

The chrysalis changes slowly
Into a butterfly,
But in an alien climate
The pupal life may die.

A tiny acorn bravely sends
Out tender root and leaf,
In time achieves a majesty
And strength beyond belief.

A child needs time to ponder things
To know life's sun and rain,
To learn to hear, to see, to touch,
His stature to attain.

For Nature in her wisdom has
Set up the way to grow.
She richly feeds and nourishes
But her cycle may be slow.

Time Is Priceless

It is your responsibility as teacher to give each child under your guidance, time to find his own unique place in life, time to think, to admire, to appreciate. Give him time to assume leadership as well as followship, to give and take directions, to work independently, to participate in joint enterprises, to make choices, to accept responsibility, to carry out plans, to unravel the tangled skeins of life for which even a young child sometimes finds himself responsible. Every child needs time to react to experiences unhurriedly, and time to grow and develop normally at his own speed and through his own inherent potential.

To paraphrase a well known quotation,

"Give children time to drink deeply of life
and let them splash around in it."

If you are to achieve all this you will recognize that time for each phase of the curriculum will vary. Your day's activities will be well-planned, but experiences will be lived through to their natural culmination rather than being held to a strict schedule by the calendar or by the clock. In the ideal situation there are no bells or buzzers to interrupt some bit of loveliness of the moment. You will keep your eyes more on the children than on the clock, but you will help them learn to conserve that priceless personal commodity, TIME.

Appreciation of Time Values

The child's consciousness of time develops gradually, and as he becomes more aware of it he can be led to appreciate other people's time. Keeping an appointment can in like manner become a challenge based on consideration for the other person who is striving to meet the same exigency of time and place.

Plans for work or play need to take into account the time necessary to accomplish what is to be done and how this fits into a total plan for the day or week. All this demands an ability to estimate and appreciate the problems that may be encountered, and to anticipate what time may be needed to work them out. This comes gradually as the child develops the ability to appreciate the value of time.

To quote Goethe, "Time is infinitely long and each day is a vessel into which a great deal may be poured, if one will actually fill it up."

And to John Ruskin's, "There is no wealth but life," might well be added, "And time is the essence of it."

QUESTIONS ON THE INFLUENCE OF TIME

1. What can you do to help your children make effective use of their time? By what standards will you evaluate this?

2. How will your day's program be influenced by the fact that each of your children needs time to grow at his own pace? Discuss.

3. How can you arrange your environment so you will provide for a diversification of activities that will allow your children to work in small independent groups, or individually, according to needs and abilities? How does this release you to work with a few at a time? Discuss how the six goals and democratic living contribute to this.

4. Discuss the effects of time pressures on the young child made by the demands of family and community life. Why is dawdling a problem to parents? How can you provide a school climate free from the hurry and frustrations of crowded time schedules?

5. If your children need varying amounts of time to complete their activities, how will you arrange it so that each child may finish his work without wasting the time of some or hurrying others?

6. Why is it best to reserve the introduction of historical characters, scenes, and stories until after the child gains some concept of the present day world and can organize his knowledge accordingly and project his thinking into the past? Discuss the implications of this in your own classroom.

7. Discuss the child's growing sense of time values. What can you do to help clarify his understanding of the passage of time? Be specific.

VI. THE ORGANIZATION OF THE SCHOOL FOR CONTINUOUS LEARNING

Providing for the Child Who Needs More Time to Grow

In some school systems the child begins his educational career in the Kindergarten (followed by junior first, or junior primary if he needs more time to mature), and then enters the primary grades. In some rare instances nursery education centers are an integral part of the program.

Special Grouping for the More Immature Child

Groups of pre-reading children have been designated by many names, "Junior First," "Pre-Primary," "Transition First," "Foundation Group," but the plan back of these various classifications to which parents tend to react emotionally and antagonistically, is an effort to break down the first grade program and to separate those who are not able to measure up to standard. It still dodges the basic issue, which is the need for a program for this age child based on his growth characteristics, rather than on pressure to push him through at a given pace. This is one of the critical problems in education today.

No less a threat in the Junior Primary organization is that in many systems there is open competition between the regular first grade teachers and the Junior Primary teachers, and the latter feel pressured into keeping the same standards of accomplishment as those of the regular first grade.

Advanced First Grade

Burbank, California, meets the issue squarely by having every child go from kindergarten to the first grade; then, at the end of his second year in school he goes either into second grade or advanced first. Any child who has missed school on account of illness, or who for any other reason needs more time to acquire a strong foundation, is placed in advanced first. This is not a year of repetition of first grade but one full of continued development, while the child lives joyously with pressures removed, doing work he can do successfully and gaining an appreciation of his own worth rather than meeting defeat and frustration. As rapidly as the individual child achieves the standards set up for him, he moves on to more advanced experiences. After a year of rich experience each member of the advanced first is able to start second grade with joy and enthusiasm and a readiness for the work ahead. This seems to bring far greater rapport, understanding, and cooperative support between the home and the school than other plans which have thus far been developed.

Recognizing Individual Patterns of Growth

Teachers, as well as parents, must realize that even though all children have an inborn capacity to learn and often seem to go through the same process of learning, still, because of divergence in gene patterns, they do not all have the same degree of potential learning power. Learning is an individual process. Reluctant as some parents and some teachers are to accept the fact, it still remains that all children are not capable of learning the same things, to the same degree, at the same time, in the same manner. Each one learns at his own rate and in his own way and there can be no uniformity.

Some children are ready for the great adventure into the academic program earlier than others. Some, though later in getting started, advance at a more rapid pace, while still others are naturally slow to learn. It is no reflection on the slower child's character or personality, but is often just a delayed maturity which most individuals have in one respect or another from lack of experience in a particular field.

A rhyme or a pleasing and easily remembered message shared with the group of parents to whom this applies, or sent home for their own reading, is helpful.

A Continuous Laboratory for Learning in the Early Years

Continuity of Experience

Some educational leaders throughout the country recognize in a functional way that learning is a continuous process and that it is the school's responsibility to organize its facilities in such a way that "all of the children of all of the people," with their various unique abilities, personalities, and potentials can develop to optimum capacity.

To do this the emphasis in learning has to be placed on continuity of experience rather than on organization of isolated subject matter. This means organization of the curriculum in terms of the continuous growth of the individual children, and thinking in terms of experiences rather than lessons. The teacher, instead of covering so much subject matter with her group in a given time, must work toward classroom progress in respect to development of various members of the class. The teacher who merely "hears lessons" is considering subject matter rather than growth.

A teacher who thinks of the children as individual human beings, not as a single class group, plans her work with the constructive development of each child as her objective. She is well aware of the fact that within the unselected group of six-year-olds (for example), there are children who run the gamut—some as slow as four-year-olds, and others as advanced as those nine years of age in physical, mental, social, or emotional maturity. The teacher of such a group is faced with the problem of trying to squeeze into an already excessively crowded schedule, as much personal time to both extremes as she can manage. It is impossible, however, to keep any of the children working at maximum capacity unless those of high ability are challenged, while at the same time the particularly slow are given time and recognition for their accomplishments.

The Primary School

Advocates of the continuous learning program are attempting to inform the public in general and their patrons in particular about the value of the Early Childhood Education Center, or the Primary School, as it is more popularly called. Here the educating of children from three to eight years of age is administered as an Early Childhood Unit. (The age span varies in different localities, some from five to nine, others from two to eight.)

The purpose of the School of Early Childhood is to give equality of opportunity to each child, by being cognizant of the vast differences in native endowment. It strives to maintain the integrity and dignity of human life by developing the child's four-fold nature: spirit, emotions, reason, and senses, to the point where each individual may be in his own right a fortress of strength commensurate with his own potentials and able to cope with the problems and pressures of the greater world outside the school.

Organizing the school into working groups is aimed at bringing every individual to full maturity, helping him find his level as a group member without losing his identity and individuality, and encouraging him to live with inner peace and faith in himself. Grouping of this nature tends to free teachers and parents from thinking of the grade level as something static by which children can be compared one against another, and thereby releases the children for creative action and self-fulfillment. In this type of organization the deadly lock step of passing a child along from grade to grade and from teacher to teacher no longer exists and the tendency to think in terms of grade levels and of the curriculum as isolated subject-fields is eliminated.

Safeguarding Children Against One-Sided Development

If the child is to be free to develop according to his own unique rhythm or cycle of growth, he must be encouraged to speak and to understand verbal communication.[1] This draws attention to the futility of trying to pressure any child into "giving an expression to an impression" and attempting to force him into language.

In a democratic environment where the six goals of early childhood are in operation, every healthy, developing child will be enthusiastic over mathematical relationships, the world of science, literature, music, and art when he himself is ready and finds a pertinent need for each of them, and is then led to *discover* them, not *coerced* to master them, or to memorize isolated information for its own sake.

The child in this school organization has a genuine need to learn to speak, to command language, to read, to write, to spell, in that order, and in due time. When he is ready for a learning experience and feels the inner compulsion for it he will, with guidance, acquire these abilities and make them a part of his personal equipment because he is facing life and meeting its demands as a participating member of society.

In the continuous environment for learning the child must be familiar with the world around him. There is an impelling force to get along with

---

[1] Verbal Expression is discussed in Parts Six and Seven.

people, to be creative in literature, music, and art. These powers all come in their own time sequence gradually as the individual child's potentialities unfold and he gradually acquires more background and more abilities.

Children need to be safeguarded against one-sided development, especially in the early years. This is the period when they learn to see, to feel, to think, and to imagine constructively.

Close Correlation Between Early and Secondary Education

A seven-year-old, asked to define a circle said, "A circle is a straight line that runs clear around and meets itself."

This definition is a pertinent example of the cycle of continuous learning in the school program. It can be clarified further by quoting again Mrs. Irene Lansing. The courses to which she refers include observation of children ages five through nine in a continuous learning program.

> Knowing that young children usually go to school happily, and pondering the fact that a very small percentage really "like" school by the time they reach us in high school, and that far too large a percentage actually resent it, I decided to do some personal research of my own as to what takes place in the schools in which the eager primary child too often becomes the far-from-eager secondary school pupil. So I enrolled in the Early Childhood Education Procedures, Music Education and Parent Counseling Classes at the University of California, Santa Barbara, really expecting, as probably most high school teachers do, to find that the trouble started in the primary school in an atmosphere of play and fun with which later teachers had to cope when they began to teach subject matter to young people.
>
> I've never had a greater surprise and a more therapeutically humbling one! We have read many times, and believed, that the best teaching is done in high school. One reason for this belief on my part was that the Seattle High School as an experimental school has set a high level of instruction. I'll confess I expected to find very little at Santa Barbara that would be of direct use to me.
>
> Wrong again! From the very first day I began to keep notes on the close correlation between early and secondary education. That list has grown so long I can only touch on part of it here. I am returning to my work with a new point of view and a better understanding of the youth I teach. Also, a deep appreciation of the teachers who have preceded me—all with thanks for the work I have had this summer.

Continuity of Early Childhood Principles in Secondary Schools

To be exact about some of the direct application of early childhood to high school, these are some of the notes I made:

During our observations in the early childhood school itself, I keep seeing my students. Peter reminds me of Roger and Bill—both as full of charm as he, and both as babyish, and I wish *they'd* had a Mrs. Bishel (the teacher of the five-year-old group) in *their* first years. I see how imagination is fostered, but also how the children are directed away from their "fantasy proneness." One of my problems as a teacher of literature is to start with my folks' interests but to get them as soon as possible out of escape reading and beyond their specialized fields. The first days of the block building reminded me of the beginning of my public speaking course, where we try to find the interests and possibilities of the youngsters, to set them at ease, to create a laboratory atmosphere of working at their own problems, but also of helping others. I realized that in the early childhood school as in the secondary school the technique and personality of the teacher are the final factor.

Principles of Guidance Carry Through

After years of successful teaching and an almost total absence of disciplinary troubles, I have learned much from a teacher of young children as to how to guide and understand the people who get side-tracked on detail, the ones who interrupt (maddeningly) at the time one feels the whole point of the experience is going over, and the non-conformists. The five-year-olds who didn't care to join the group in the creative use of instruments, but scornfully said to each other, "All that silly noise!" and drew aside in a "men's club" to discuss the family pets reminded me of the first days we concentrate on poetry in Senior Literature. These three (since successfully absorbed into the group) seemed quite babyish in other activities, and have helped me to realize that most of my poor reading students, and the non-conformists also, lack maturity. In my music education course, too, I have learned techniques that will be useful with these people in introducing poetry. This observation in the school of early childhood has also made clear how vital it is to all human beings to feel satisfaction. I've seen the children's first attempts guided to progressive accomplishment. The young child develops his boat or airplane in much the same way my student writes a paper. Now I'm aware, too, how important it is at any level not to make things too hard, and not to put on too much pressure. Our folks complain loudly that every teacher forgets they have other courses, and probably we do push them too hard.

Very impressive, too, are the efforts made to have the children desire to finish what they start, and to take care of the equipment and clean up after their work. Unfortunately, this doesn't hold through life—high school students are lamentably untidy. Nothing but constant struggle makes them neat. If all the grades gave this problem the same care the early ones do, we surely would be a neater nation.

Recognizing Home Influences

I was amazed to find how effectively the school of early childhood has pioneered in recognizing the mutual responsibility of school and home. The fine home background which some children have is reflected in their ability to adjust to all types of situations at school, whether in the early years, or later. Parents have a definite place in the life of the school of early childhood, and as secondary teachers we must open up ways for parents to contribute toward a better understanding of the problems of their teen-agers.

It has been interesting to see how young children in a group are as really individual as they are in high school, and that as early as five and six years of age they have developed such distinct mannerisms and personalities. It was refreshing to hear that Mrs. Bishel's "Raymond" irritated her as greatly as "Bill H." did me. (Her patience was unlimited.) She did far better than I did, since Bill held out for months.

Awareness of Values

I have noted a great deal of concern on the part of early childhood education teachers and specialists regarding the fear-element in books and stories for the very young. The point for us in secondary education seems to be that we become more aware of the emotions which are nurtured or presented through the literature and drama our young people are encountering. I was delighted to find interest expressed on the part of early childhood teachers in being sure that children's books do not tolerate or foster any of the stereotypes of racial, religious, or economic prejudices. Our concern in high school must be to encourage open-minded evaluation by our students. The young child is capable of planning and evaluating his day's work. Why shouldn't our high school students be given more opportunities for this?

Continuity in Behavior Patterns and Attitudes

The emphasis on behavior patterns in the early years suggests that the problem of how to preserve the habits that the early childhood school builds should be a major concern of all teachers; consideration for others in walking through the corridors, being quiet in passing other rooms, and being careful about causing interruptions are things one might justifiably assume many high school people have never heard of. The stress on listening while someone else talks, and the successful elimination of hand raising from discussion groups of young children suggest that listening ability and consideration for others are often what need to be developed before a satisfactory discussion situation can be built up at any age.

If the respect for possessions and the attention to small deceits were as carefully watched at all levels as at the early childhood stage, our secondary students would conduct themselves far more honorably than is sometimes the case.

Learning from Life

The most thrilling part of this experience has been to see the problem-solving method used so consistently. It's been wonderful to find, too, how daily and familiar things are used as the basis for learning experience. The dramatic element in learning at the early childhood level reminds me of trying to help my students toward the writing of better compositions by having them notice details.

I was impressed by the relation of music to life in the early childhood years. We try in high school, also, to make school a living thing, not a separate thing of "book learning." The young child makes the sounds he hears in his environment, using simple musical instruments. He dramatizes the life around him in rhythmic pantomime to musical accompaniment. My high school students recreate impressions of life situations in written and spoken words. The young child makes a sound like a vacuum cleaner, or builds an automobile of blocks; the high school boy in my classes gives a clear talk or writes a paper on "Why the Vacuum Picks Up the Dirt," or "What Happens When You Step on the Starter."

Resources Within the Learner

We've decided that most people don't really learn grammar unless the need or use for knowing it is apparent to the learner, and now I realize that younger children, too, are learning by doing, and are capable of research at their own level.

The young child's spontaneity and freedom of expression is a natural resource he brings with him to school. Strangely enough, we often attempt to teach him to acquire in high school the very qualities of expression that he can readily attain through encouragement and recognition of what expressiveness he has to offer on his own. If verbalization were developed generally throughout the elementary school as intelligently as I have seen it done in the rooms we observed, my students would not show such distressing poverty of vocabulary as they do (and I base that remark on experience in four states).

Continuous Growth Throughout the Years

To plan for continuous learning, then, is to think in terms of growth in language, growth in music, growth in manipulative experiences, growth in art, growth in number concepts and scientific facts of all kinds, and as the child reaches the maturity for it, gradual growth in reading, writing, and spelling, with strong foundations of experience all along the way. This is the philosophy behind the Early Childhood Education Center or the Primary School. Children advance through experiences as they are ready for them, rather than by being assigned to specific grade levels.

The center of gravity for the entire program, the point from which its true balance is measured in all directions is *the child,* not alone, but in his relationship to life, as he has already lived it, as he is living it at the moment, and as he will live it as he takes his place in the universe of tomorrow to make his contribution to his own growth, as well as to his family, his community, his country, the world, society, and humanity.

QUESTIONS ON THE ORGANIZATION OF THE SCHOOL FOR CONTINUOUS LEARNING

1. Explain and evaluate various plans for adapting the school program for children of varying degrees of maturity in the first two or three years of the elementary school.

2. Discuss the differences in achievement of individuals in a given age group. What bearing has this on assigning children to given classrooms for the year?

3. Discuss some of the types of guidance your children may need during the year in your classroom. Which of these may carry over into the next year? What advantage would there be if you were assigned to the same group for more than one year?

4. What problems may arise from transfers and new assignments of children to your group during the second year in No. 3, above? Discuss what you might do to provide continuous learning for the group. How will the goals of childhood education enter here? What bearing will democratic living have on continuity?

5. What can be gained by a teacher in secondary education's coming to know and understand the curriculum and the guidance offered children in the early elementary years?

6. What opportunities are there for the child who has participated in evaluating his own program of work to continue to do so in the secondary school? How can the student who has not had this experience in the early childhood years be introduced to democratic procedures in planning, initiating, and following through on ideas?

7. Discuss the unique opportunities the early childhood teacher has by virtue of the fact that her influence is extended throughout the entire school day with the same group, as compared to the somewhat briefer shift of classes throughout the departmentalized school.

8. Discuss the teacher-student relationships encountered by a given individual as he makes his daily round of classes in a departmentalized program.

9. Discuss the contrast between determining the curriculum for children on the basis of (a) grade placement or (b) the pattern of continuous growth in accordance with readiness of individual children for the next step in learning.

SELECTED REFERENCES

Christianson, Helen M., Mary M. Rogers, and Blanche A. Ludlum, THE NURSERY SCHOOL: ADVENTURES IN LIVING AND LEARNING, New York, Houghton Mifflin, 1961.

Department of Elementary School Principals, CREATIVE SCHOOLS, Twenty-third Yearbook, Washington, D.C., National Education Association, 1944.

Goslin, Willard E. (Chairman), ORGANIZING THE ELEMENTARY SCHOOL FOR LIVING AND LEARNING, Washington, D.C., Association for Supervision and Curriculum Development, 1947.

McKean, Robert C., PRINCIPLES AND METHODS IN SECONDARY EDUCATION, Columbus, Ohio, Charles E. Merrill Books, Inc., 1962.

Nesbitt, Marion, A PUBLIC SCHOOL FOR TOMORROW, New York, Harper and Brothers, 1953.

SENSORY IMPRESSIONS IN

Part Four

CHILDHOOD EDUCATION

I. SENSORY IMPRESSIONS AS AVENUES
OF LEARNING

Ruskin would have gone on record as a keen observer
of human nature had he made only the one statement: "A
hundred men can think for one who can see." Frequently,
this ability is not acquired through formal education, as
is illustrated over and over again by many self-made individuals.

Academic Foundations

For example, Joel took paper that was too porous for
successful hand paint work. Mrs. Brouhard had him feel
the two kinds of paper to tell the difference. He found the
paper he had first chosen was rougher and heavier than
what was best for the use he intended to make of it. How
many teachers might thoughtlessly have corrected Joel's
mistake by saying, "Joel, you have the wrong paper. Get
your paper from this stack," rather than showing him
how to learn from his own five senses.

So natural is it for the child to smell, touch, taste, feel, as well as look and hear, that adults too often overlook the urgency of his doing so, not only at an early age, but as he grows.

The "Grass Roots" of Each Area of Academic Learning

The arts are based on expression, representation, and organization of impressions. Each area of academic learning has its grass roots in sensations arising from environmental stimuli, and as such has meaning for the young child. Science consists in observing, comparing, controlling, organizing, and evaluating observations. Within the field of his viewing, hearing, tasting, smelling, and touching, scientific thinking begins for the child.

Mathematics, fundamentally, consists in identifying like things, enumerating and grouping them, increasing or decreasing, multiplying or dividing, in terms of numerical relationships. When even the simplest of such relationships becomes familiar to the child through direct experience, their nature is known thereafter and remembered, and he uses this knowledge to solve problems as they arise.

Language is the communication of ideas through words which are, first of all, auditory sounds that have meaning to the child because he associates them with his own wealth of impressions. Language for him represents the world as he personally experiences and interprets it. The child's earliest language is directly associated with action and sensations, but as he grows, words come to represent for him basic understandings and descriptive ideas, and he learns to appreciate ways of sharing and communicating his impressions. In recalling and interpreting what impresses him, the child slowly develops ability to command words.

The Child's Response

Some statements made by children are unusually fresh and poignant, as when four-year-old Blyth, walking with utmost consideration for the other resters, was astonished when someone noticed her approach. She asked, "How could you tell I was coming when my stepvoices were so quiet?"

Impressions of his surroundings increase the child's comprehension of his environment, and hence of the world in which he lives. Identification and naming things call for awareness of similarities. Recognition of what is the same and what is different means comparison not only of immediate impressions, but of those retained and remembered. Seven-year-old Barbara, on a field trip, heard the meat saw, and with the assurance of having experienced deeply, said, "That sounds like when the dentist drills my teeth. Grrr! It tickles and hurts at the same time."

Selectivity

Guidance is needed not only in providing opportunities for immediate sensory impressions, but in helping the child recognize and select out of the maze of stimuli that come to him in the modern complexities of living, those which are most worthy of his attention.

Selectivity is of utmost importance to the young child who is by nature deeply impressed by immediate surroundings. In the midst of lights and colors, people talking, moving objects, and a multitude of unrelated sounds, smells, and opportunities to taste, the growing child is continually bombarded by stimuli to which, but for their multiplicity, he could respond with eagerness and profit.

Nine-year-old Wallace philosophized on the situation when he said, "There are some things I just don't pay attention to anymore. Sometimes it is just like I'm way out there in outer space somewhere. You have to tune me in when you want me to listen."

The democratic classroom is a place where first-hand impressions are gained without the confusions and pressures that often confront the child in the adult community. You, the teacher, can provide a classroom where learning is assured by your guidance of the child's opportunities to respond to concrete illustrations, demonstrations, and experiments. Much incidental learning can arise from observations derived from one or more of the five senses as you plan and evaluate with the children.

First-Hand Experiences and Concrete Illustrations

Many teachers do not let a day go by when there is not some type of science taking place through experiment, observation, study films, field trips, or the sharing of some idea or object by one of the children. The deepest impressions, of course, are those based on first-hand experience and colorful concrete illustrations that simulate life.

The thinking child draws his own conclusions, and with but a little guidance, goes from one basic learning to another. Gregory, age five years, eight months, following an experiment in calling across open spaces and against walls and shrubbery, sagely remarked: "It won't echo where soft things are."

When a problem or question arises, the children may find many of their own solutions and answers from observations and experiments, supplemented by picture references, consultation, interviews, and reading, after you discuss where some of these sources of information may be located. When the children have presented all the data they can find, you may add additional material through your own background, reading excerpts from certain books, and, when warranted, inviting a scientist who understands children, to come in and discuss the question with them.

In this type of environment scientific experiments and discussions become an almost automatic activity with the children. This is evidenced in such spontaneous comments as occurred early one fall morning in a primary group:

> Chris (age six years, nine months) : "I have an experiment. See this piece of paper? When I drop it, it goes down. If it were not for gravity, it would float."
>
> David, 7/1: "If we didn't have gravity we would all float in mid-air."
>
> Larry, 6/5: "In space there isn't any gravity, and we'd go flying off and have to eat up there and drink up there."
>
> Tommy, 6/6: "Gravity means everything has to come down."
>
> Gregory, 6/6: "It's what makes people stay on earth."

Shared Discoveries

The child's responses are an index to his thinking, and as you recognize this, you can follow through on many of them. Recorded in stick figure pictures for the younger children, and charts or written notes for the older ones, the individual's own comments and questions will lead into further investigations.

You will find your children are eager to share discoveries verbally and to listen carefully to each other. As they share, they gradually acquire the ability to recall and to express their reactions through words. There is also growth in appreciation of the feelings and responses of their peers. From these verbally shared experiences your children reconstruct the sensory impressions and the mental images which the words represent. In pictures, songs, poetry, and stories you and they together discover similar ideas expressed in colorful and effective ways.

Viewed in the light of the above considerations, sensory experiences are an essential foundation for all academic learning.

Presentation and Discussion Herein

The relationship between the five senses is so close that an experience involving one of them usually includes others, and sometimes embraces the entire gamut of sensory functions. People see and hear; see and touch; smell and taste; touch and smell; touch and hear, *ad infinitum*.

Integrated activities comprising a number of the sensory experiences are possible for most of the schools throughout the country to supply. Where an experience as described seems impractical, something of a similar nature within the school environment may readily be substituted.

No matter where the location, there is a wealth of material awaiting you. It is your job to find it and adapt it to a wide-eyed and eager group at their level of understanding. Fortunately, you are not alone in your search. Your children will discover many things, and their responses will suggest much.

Significant Types of Sensory Impressions

Viewed from the standpoint of their educational significance as well as their importance to the child himself, the following types of sensory experiences are essential:

1. Visual (demanding clarity of vision).
2. Auditory (depending upon accuracy of hearing).
3. Tactile (based upon the sense of touch).
4. Olfactory (related to the sense of smell).
5. Gustatory (concerning taste discrimination).
6. Thermal (sensitivity to coldness or warmth).
7. Kinesthetic (referred to as the muscle sense and significant in learning to write) .
8. Equilibrial (sense of balance; stability; state of equipoise, as between weights, different elements, or opposing forces). (See Balance; Blocks in Index)

QUESTIONS ON SENSORY IMPRESSIONS AS AVENUES OF LEARNING

1. Discuss the value of learning through keenness of observation in contrast to having everything pointed out. What guidance is needed to avoid going to the extreme in either direction? Discuss.

2. Cite incidental opportunities to make careful observation habitual for your children.

3. Why is selectivity a major problem in the education of the young child today? Explain.

4. (a) Discuss the multitude of sensory impressions that may confront the young child in the adult community, keeping in mind a given locality with which you are familiar. (b) What guidance will aid a child in learning to discriminate among these? (Discuss in specific rather than general terms, keeping in mind such factors as age, personality, experience, economic position of the family, et cetera.)

5. In what ways is so-called "higher education" of an individual dependent upon a broad foundation of learning through sensory impressions in childhood? Discuss.

6. Discuss the place of sensory experiences as a foundation for academic learning in early childhood.

II. LEARNING THROUGH VISUAL IMPRESSIONS

Looking and Seeing

Capacity for observation and awareness is essential to the growth of the young child, and it is your concern to guide him to acquire visual powers.

To look and really see is to become aware of many possibilities that are completely unappreciated by the non-observing eye. In your efforts to develop the child's ability to observe, you will need to make sure that the object is within his view, that he has the visual acuity to see it, and also that he is a participant in an experience long enough and deeply enough to react intelligently to it.

The Seeing Eye

Identical twins present a problem in identification for most people. Dick and Randy were constantly attempting to clarify this matter for their confused friends. "I'm Randy" was always said with a patient smile, but "I'm Richard" was said with disgust.

While differences in personality give helpful clues, the problem of distinguishing between one person and another is primarily a matter of visual awareness. It may mean selecting from a maze of impressions the one detail which is different. In this case it was a question of discovering something that could be depended upon to remain different.

The boys' mother tried to lend her support by dressing them in different colors, but it was always hard to remember what each was wearing on a particular day.

During all this confusion, Miss M. began to notice that there was one child who always called each of the twins by his correct name. Finally, she asked, "How do you know which is which, Billy?"

"That's easy," came the reply. "Randy has a little brown hole on the side of his head!"

The "hole" to which Billy referred turned out to be a minute mole, overlooked by everyone else, which Billy's sharp eyes had spotted. It was the size of a pin point.

Children's powers of observation can be strengthened by calling attention to lines and color and identifying differences in objects in the environment which are similar. Instead of referring to the book with the brown cover, call it the book with the white spot on the front cover. Speak of the chair with the bent corner, or the kitten with the necktie under his chin. The child has to look closely to observe these things. In everyday experiences there are constant opportunities to observe more closely than ordinarily, until careful observation becomes habitual.

An interesting experiment is to place something different in an inconspicuous place in the room without calling attention to it, and then wait to see which children notice it. Later it may be mentioned casually, and a clue given, and others will look for it until it is found. This can be done incidentally, while the children go about the day's work. Later a discussion of the object may arise. It may be a small flag placed on a ledge, or a snapshot or clipping pinned on a board. Perhaps it is a new mobile, or a colorful jacket on a new book. It may be anything that will lead to further learning, and it can be planted anywhere at varying eye levels, perhaps near the floor, or even high on the wall somewhere.

Observing for a Definite Purpose

You and the children may walk around the school grounds or the block. As you go out the door you can ask them to tell what they can see close at hand. Some typical answers may be: each other, the steps, an ant walking across the path, a butterfly, a flower in a flower pot. Then you may ask them to tell about something they can see over on the far side beyond the school yard. It may be a boy walking, a man driving a big truck, a bird on a fence, a tree in bloom.

An interesting variation is to describe the object and talk further about it, without naming it. If someone knows what it is from the comments that are made, he tells something more about it without using its name. Finally it is identified by everyone.

Children become adept at describing what they see at different distances, and enjoy talking about things to look for.

This observing for a definite purpose is important. In addition to being an excellent readiness for reading experience in giving evidence of the child's comprehension and interpretation of what he sees, it is a splendid means of checking on his eye acuity without calling attention to it.

> The power of observation of the child is often revealed in his verbalizations. Bob, age five years and five months, said, "The pollywog looks like a lizard to me, because he has a long tail, only he is smaller."
>
> Martha, 5/6, said, "If it's sunny and rainy at the same time, there are rainbows."
>
> David, 6/2, observed, "When the red traffic light tells the cars to stop, the green light tells the other people to go."

Seeing at a Glance and Recalling

Your children may observe closely while someone opens a book of wall-paper samples or a favorite picture book and holds up one page, then closes the book. Someone describes what he saw, then the book is opened and the description compared with the original. The procedure is varied when one of the children opens the book and finds the page which was shown, or when the one who first showed the page holds up five or six more, including the first page shown, which the others try to identify.

You may encourage your children to recount exactly what they saw happen at a program, in a film, or in a recent experience. A short scene may be dramatized in which characters move in pantomime, and then some of the observers take the parts and reenact what they saw from memory. The same may be done with puppets or shadows, in which the pose of one of the characters is observed and then described or reproduced.

Upper primary children often become intrigued by the idea of looking at something and then deliberately turning away from it and recalling from memory what was seen.

More mature children who are ready to do so may experiment with increasing observational span by working in small groups independently, preparing spontaneous arrangements of objects and displaying them for a few seconds, then covering them and naming accurately the objects, their location, and description.

The word "look" is one of the first words in the child's earliest reading vocabulary. It has infinite possibilities for depth of meaning and carry-over into the child's interests and experiences. Long before he meets this word in written form he can learn to experience the power of keen observation, retention of what he sees, and organization of his thinking accordingly.

If forced upon a child who has difficulty with it, this can bring a sense of defeat. On the other hand, it may bring much satisfaction to the child who is ready for it and can lead to unusual alertness.

QUESTIONS ON LEARNING THROUGH VISUAL IMPRESSIONS

1. Discuss the incidental opportunities that present themselves throughout the day whereby you may strengthen the visual perception of your children. Give specific examples.

2. a. What values can come to sighted children in having a sightless child enrolled in your classroom? b. How can the other children help him without hindering his development? c. Discuss the guidance that may be

necessary to safeguard the sightless child's growth in all six goals of child-hood. d. What home school cooperation will be necessary?

3. Compare the impressions gained by the child through sight with those of hearing and feeling.

4. How does a young child endowed with all of his senses explore his surroundings? Compare this with the way a child deprived of one of his senses explores. As you consider the resourcefulness of the child who is denied the use of sight, or hearing, what conclusions can you draw re-garding the untapped resources of all children regarding sensory impres-sions? What application has this to your own classroom procedures? Give examples.

5. Consider the words in the everyday vocabulary of the young child which describe some of his visual impressions. How can you provide ex-periences which call forth descriptive comments, in which many of these words can be used? Illustrate.

6. What can you do to help your children develop the ability to observe changes and retain details observed in the immediate environment?

III. LEARNING THROUGH AUDITORY IMPRESSIONS

The World of Sound

The young child's world is a cacophony of sounds—dishes clattering; the sound of the washing machine, the electric refrigerator, the vacuum cleaner, road machinery at work; the sounds of walking and running, tri-cycles on gravel, skates on sidewalk; the teakettle boiling; the fire crack-ling in the grate; human voices talking, laughing, singing; babies cooing, gurgling, crying; animal calls, musical instruments; clocks, door-bells, schoolbells, chimes, bees humming, birds singing, frogs croaking, crickets chirping; the wind blowing, the rustling of leaves, raindrops splashing—a great medley of sounds, discordant and euphonious. And all of these sounds may be translated into terms that make a child's life richer and more meaningful.

Learning to Listen

In many locations where children live, silence calls attention to itself because it is different. A noisy road machine had been roaring near the school since early morning, when suddenly it stopped. Patty Jean commented on it immediately: "It sure sounds still as quiet in here, doesn't it? Only the sprinkler makes noise now."

It is a well-known fact that a person who lives where the roar of an elevated train, or the whistle of locomotives dins continually in his ears, becomes immune to those sounds. He sleeps through their uproar and goes about the business of daily living without apparently noticing them. To him a momentary silence is more penetrating than the noise. If he goes to some remote place where such sounds are not heard, for a time, at least, he is disturbed by the silence. To a degree the same condition obtains with children today. They hear the radio, the programs on television, and all the myriad noises of complex social living which continually bombard their ears. But it is doubtful whether this increased use of the ears has made either adults or children more efficient listeners. Both groups tend to listen only to those things which are of immediate interest and to close their faculties to other things that are happening about them.

There is perhaps as great need for a certain natural silence and quiet as for control of unnecessary sound in everyday living. Opportunities to get away from sounds are few for many families, and the individual's ability to disregard irrelevant noise is important to mental health; but there are instances where in his effort to exclude unwanted auditory stimuli, the individual disregards all sound. Cases of psychological deafness sometimes occur in young children and are indicative of special needs. Overdemands, nagging, or some other situation to which the child is not able to adjust may be causing him to withdraw from external stimuli in self-defense. The child in this condition needs understanding and thoughtful guidance. The problem is really one of discovering the cause and either helping the child make an adjustment to it, alleviating it, or removing him from the pressures he feels. Fortunately he is the exception rather than the rule. Usually the growing child is responsive to immediate environmental stimuli, and the problem of guidance is one of developing discrimination and selectivity.

A child's learning to listen should not be left to chance any more than should his learning to read. Listening awareness is an art; and art in its broadest sense is expressed awareness. You will want to provide your children with many opportunities daily for revitalizing their listening sense to the many things that are interesting to them, keeping in mind that a child often will listen more intently to one of his peers than to his teacher.

The child who is deeply interested will give undivided, not surface, attention to what is transpiring, and minor happenings in the room will not distract him, but he will be interested only if he understands the meaning of the discussion. You, as teacher, are responsible for choosing subject matter within the limits of his experience and comprehension, and for bringing it to his attention in concrete ways. When new expressions and new concepts are gradually introduced they challenge the child's interest and encourage listening; when administered in too large a dosage, both interest and attention wane.

When a child has found the delight of harkening to the sounds within his environment he will be like Soren, who announced happily, when he saw his teacher was about to tell a story without opening a book: "Oh, good! This is a listen story with no pictures."

Impressions of Rain

Much emphasis is placed throughout this text on guiding children into an appreciation of nature.

The brilliant colors of autumn suggest to the adult the delight he may have felt as a young child scuffling and rustling through a carpet of fallen leaves. Sensitivity to beauty can either be encouraged or stifled in the formative years. It can be extended to an appreciation of phases of inclement weather about which many adults complain bitterly. If you, as a teacher of young children, really appreciate the rhythm and beauty of rain, snow, and wind, it will do much toward helping your group to catch their true spirit of exhilaration.

Wind that stings the cheek, winds that soothe and lull, winds that brace and invigorate, all these the child can learn to enjoy and appreciate.

One rainy afternoon Miss Holman started a discussion on "wet" sounds with her middle primary group of children, repeating from memory several lovely poems. The children rapidly began giving their own impressions of these sounds. Miss Holman realized that remembering sounds and likening them to other known sounds help children acquire both vocabulary and fluency of expression. Accordingly, at the children's request they spent some time that afternoon reciting rain poems, recalling personal experiences of rainy days, and finally writing a composite poem entitled:

Listen!

Listen to the rain on the roof.
"Tap-a-tap! Tap-a-tap!"
It sounds like woodpeckers tapping.
"Tap-a-tap! Tap-a-tap!"
Thumping, thumping, goes the rain,
like falling wood.
Beating, beating
like a noisy drum is the rain on our roof.
Noisy, quiet! Noisy, quiet!
It is raining hard
on the roof!
Listen!

Later, this same group composed and wrote a book of individual responses to a happy afternoon when the rain was coming down in torrents. Each child contributed and all thirty-two were different and interesting. One of these follows:

Bill

Hello. My name is Bill. I am a little raindrop. I like to splash-patter, drip-drop, all over houses, hotels, and many other places. It's fun, but sometimes people don't like me. Some children like rain. Others don't like me, but I give the flowers a good drink as I patter down on their cheeks. I clean streets and wash roofs as I swish down on them in a gusty hullabaloo.

The animals that like me most are ducks and fish. Trees like me, too.

The farmers like me especially. I give their crops water so they will grow. A farmer is happy when I come, but not all the time because he must get outside sometimes. He needs time when it is dry to plant his crops and feed the animals.

I, Bill, like to fall down and play with my friends. We splash and play in the puddles that other raindrops make. We play tag and swim.

When my friend, the wind, blows, leaves dance and jump and leap across the sky with their feet high over the sky, and trees rock back and forth with their branches moving back and forth like they were keeping time with music.

When the rain dies out and the sun starts to come up, I will say, "Goodby. Goodby, friends, one and all."

The End

Ann

Associating Sounds with Their Objects

Children need to listen to many types of sounds and to experiment with a large variety of things to make other new sounds.

Mrs. Vigus gave her five- and six-year-olds a "homework assignment." They were each to bring in something to make a sound.

Next day Mrs. Vigus invited each child to go behind a screen and demonstrate the sound made by the object he had brought to school. The other children were to listen and tell, "What does this sound remind you of?" Then they would compare the sound for pitch, loudness, softness, and estimate whether it was made of wood, metal, plastic, or glass.

The children brought many types of objects. For example, Brian brought a paper bag which he blew up and popped; Soren a package which he unwrapped so the children could hear the crackling of the paper; Beth brought a clarinet to blow into; Harvey, two wooden discs to clap together.

Comparing Sounds

Many teachers establish a "sound" table in the school room. It contains a wide selection of objects which the children may handle and whose sounds they may control. One such table contained a can of fruit, a metal cellulose tape box with a roll of tape, some waxed paper, a large sheet of metal, poster paper, a package of dried soup (aluminum foil), a box of cereal (cardboard), some plastic bottles of cake decorations, and a box partly filled with boullion cubes.

Terry shook the can of mixed fruit and remarked, "It's a sloshing machine."

Martha had the plastic bottle of cake decorations and George the boullion cubes. Martha shook the cake decorations and George occasionally shook the boullion cubes. "It sounds like jumping beans popping," said Sammy.

The children began shaking the two objects in a rhythm and said they were making a noise like water boiling hard.

When they waved the sheet metal and the poster paper they said it made "thunder" or the "roar of the ocean."

The box of cereal was "real hard rain" or "sprinkles," depending on how vigorously it was shaken.

From time to time objects may be removed from the table and others substituted. They constitute a never-failing source of interest to the children who like to relate the sounds they produce to sounds heard elsewhere.

Listening Becomes Habitual

One fall morning Dick came into the room. "Crunch, crunchity, crunch go the leaves under our feet," he said.

A few mornings later when the wind was blowing hard, Dale remarked, "The wind is crying in the trees."

Miss M. made notes of many things the children said that revealed their new awareness of sound. Chris, listening to the steam whistling from the tea kettle, exclimed, "It sounds like an ambulance!"

The following is an example of how listening to sounds may become a part of the child's pattern of behavior.

Judy and Johnny were bathing the doll in the bathinette in the patio. "This is fun," said Judy. "We're listening for sounds so we can make a chart story."

"How does it sound?" asked Miss T.

"Splitter, splatter," said Judy.

"Splash, splash," Johnny said.

Other six-year-olds joined Judy and Johnny to help develop the chart:

Splish, splash!
Splash, splish!
In goes the baby,
out goes the dirt.
"Ziggle, zaggle, ziggle,"
says the drain as the water
goes down into the bucket.

Following this, the children began to hunt for various sounds in their environment. From time to time a child would remark, "There's a dog barking. Someone must have left him in the car. I can tell he's not happy there."

In stories, an upper primary teacher and her children described various sounds and what they mean. This group also started a list of the kinds of sounds for which to listen. The list grew, as each day they compared their reactions:

Squeaky sounds	Voices of people
Hollow sounds	Animal sounds
Harsh sounds	Bird sounds
Soft sounds	Insect sounds
High sounds	Far-away sounds
Low sounds	Home sounds
Foot sounds	Quiet sounds
Clock sounds	Machine sounds

There were also sounds near the ground, in the sky, wind, rain, and fog, night sounds, empty sounds, laughter.

The above interest in sound started early in the school year. It was gratifying to note by spring, the way these children used colorful expressions in their everyday conversation both at home and school. It was not unusual for one or another individual to make a remark including a reference to sound such as the following, "That old mower is as noisy as an outboard motor."

On one occasion in this same group a committee was laying out and measuring a strip of wrapping paper several feet long, from which they intended to make a frieze. One of the children remarked, "Moving this great big piece of paper sounds like a crackling fire."

Listening and Responding

Adults as well as children are intrigued by any new means of conveying ideas without words. This can be done by sound. The children may close their eyes while someone goes to the window and opens it, or sharpens a pencil, or performs some other commonplace activity. A child who listens, tells what he thinks happened, basing it upon what he could hear. Details can be conveyed to a surprising degree by sound alone, as the children will discover as they learn to listen and really hear.

For example, Mary may go to the cupboard, open the door, reach in and get a can, close the door, take the can to the faucet and fill it with water. Then she goes over to the window and waters the plant in a certain container. It is interesting when the children who heard but did not look, tell everything that happened and how they knew what Mary was doing. Such details as, "How full did she fill the can?" and "Which plant did she water?" are not too difficult for the attentive listener.

Listening to and Interpreting Music

In another room, Miss Hartlett said to her five- and six-year-olds, "Instead of a story today, we are going to have music you will enjoy. Peter brought us this record." Miss Hartlett played "The Chugging Freight Engine." The children listened attentively and Miss Hartlett noted that they dramatized the engine as they went out on the playground to wait for their mothers.

Another day she played Respigi's "Pines and Fountains of Rome," and asked the children to talk about how it made them feel. Lee said, "It sounds like a man walking in the back yard that has gravel on the walk— and the birds are singing."

Barbara said, "Maybe it was spring."

Science Discoveries, Too

Sometimes the child's interest carries over into discovery of a scientific fact as well as in the identification of the sound with something familiar, as when Sally brought a large seashell to show the children. One child put the shell to his ear and discovered its loud roaring. This phenomenon was discussed and as the children talked they realized they needed more information than they had to answer their question: "What makes it sound like the ocean?" Lindy said, "It must be because the shell came from the ocean and the sound was recorded."

After following up on several good references the children discovered that the shape of the shell made it pick up and amplify the noises in the environment. "The air in the shell carries the sounds to our ear, and the roar reminds us of the ocean," Lindy explained.

Children can tell by the sound why large blocks are called Hollow Blocks. A child may knock on a large hollow block with a rhythm stick while all the children may listen and be ready to respond. Stephen said, "It sounds like someone knocking at our door."

Jeanne remarked, "I think it sounds like a hollow tree, a hole that a squirrel made."

"The block is empty inside. All it has in it is air. That's why it sounds hollow," said Burt, and he proceeded to draw an illustration on the chalkboard explaining the structure of the block.

After a number of the children had commented on the sound, another child knocked on a wooden block made of 2″ x 4″ material. "*It* is different. Not hollow at all. It is *solid*," he commented. (This experiment offers a good lead for the science of density of air, water, and floating things, as well as the more obvious experience of listening to the sounds of instruments which are hollow, like the drum, gourds, and rattles.)

One "hollow" block and one "solid" block each cut in half may show the children what is inside and verify what the sound of the blocks suggests about their internal structure.

Working with Sounds

Begin Wherever You Are

"The drum can talk. Listen to it." Miss V. tapped it in time with the spoken words: "Good *morn*ing boys and girls. How *are* you?"

This idea was followed through as Miss V. and various boys and girls made the drum say other things.

As they were working with the drum, Vivian came in very quietly. Miss V. played the drum the way Vivian's feet sounded.

Douglas walked. The teacher accompanied him on the drum.

Judy took the drum, and played it while Doug walked, but she had difficulty following his feet. Then Judy set the rhythm for Doug to follow.

Another time, Betty asked, "What makes the drum louder?"

Bob demonstrated with the drum.

"Bob put more *pressure* on the drum head. His hand was heavier when he played it," explained Miss V. "Show us on the piano, Stephen."

Stephen played a loud note, then a very soft note. "Sound has *volume*," explained Miss V. "When the drum sounds loud, it has more volume. Which note that Stephen played had the most volume?"

Various children illustrated this on the drum, and with other musical instruments.

Experiences such as these are spontaneous, and learning is incidental. Each day presents many opportunities to work with sounds extemporaneously.

A Series of Experiences with Sound by One Group of Children

Many learnings are incidental throughout the year, as in the foregoing illustrations, but groups often reach a stage of development where concentrated attention on sounds seems justified.

Miss Una Wyatt, a primary teacher at the Abraham Lincoln School in Burbank, California, had a fascinating experience with her group. It all began after a quiet rest when Tom said, "We were so quiet that I could hear the cars go by." (The street was some distance away from the classroom windows.)

"Yes, we could," replied Miss Wyatt. "Let's listen as we go about our work for sounds we hear from our room."

As the sounds were mentioned Miss Wyatt wrote what was said on the chalkboard:

Sounds We Hear from Our Room

Clock ticking
Scratching chalk
Bells ringing from the church tower
Tree boughs blowing against the roof
Blinds rattling in the wind
Birds twittering and singing
Whistling from out of doors
Musical instruments
Voices—some happy, some sad
Feet moving—some light, some heavy
Chairs scraping
Carpenters hammering
Airplanes zooming
Bicycles skidding
Street sweeper "swirling"
Cars whizzing by
Car horns honking
Fire trucks, ambulances, and police sirens
Dogs barking
Policeman's whistle

For permanency, the above list was made into a series of charts by Miss Wyatt and illustrated with easel paintings by the children.

Listen at Home, Too

The homework for the next day was to listen for all the sounds in the home they could hear and plan to make a matching sound of one or more of these.

The next morning the findings were recorded by Miss Wyatt and illustrated by the children with their hands or mouths, which was an excellent phonics readiness:

Home Sounds

Alarm clock
A tea kettle whistling
Baby crying
Toast popping out of the toaster
Door bell chiming
Running feet
Tinkling of Ice Cream Man's bell
Door opening and closing
Buzzing of Daddy's electric shaver
Splashing of water
Object falling on floor
Whirling of washing machine and dryer
Clanking of garbage pails
Radio announcer
Television
Humming vacuum cleaner
Electric mixer
Egg beater
Balls bouncing
Toy train puffing, whistling
Croaking frogs
Pet bird pecking

Gerry, Jane, Frances, Dick, and Fred found magazine pictures of things that make sound. These were classified as to the type of sound and where it was made.

Experiment with Musical Instruments

All of these sounds afforded opportunity to experiment with various instruments. The Music Center had several types, such as drums, xylophone, bells, cymbals, coconut shells, moracas, cabacas, giras, and glasses filled with varying depths of water.

The children explored the possibilities of each instrument. Coconut shells, for example, were found to be best for reproducing the sound of the leaky faucet and of horses' hoofs.

A further development was making a sound on an instrument and then thinking what it sounded like; then matching this sound.

The instruments were classified according to the way the sounds were made: hitting, shaking, plucking, blowing. The children discovered for themselves that the various size drums have different sounds. "Listen," said Glen as he struck the largest drum made with sheep skin, then the next in size, and finally the smallest goat skin drum.

The sound of coconut shells was compared with the moraca and the cabaca, and the construction of each was explained. The different sizes of woodblocks were played and compared.

The sand blocks were explored and three sizes of rhythm sticks were found to show tone and velocity.

These children also discussed which instruments would be best to play the rhythm of the songs they sang. Debbie remarked as she interpreted a song with a rattle and body rhythm, "The music goes up and down. Sometimes we skip a step because it is broken."

Arriving at Scientific Conclusions

The interest of Miss Wyatt's children in sounds had by no means waned. Mark greeted the group one morning with an announcement that he had just heard that there were no sounds on the moon. A lively challenging discussion followed, and Scott wanted to know "Why is this so?" Many ideas were given, including the one that there is no air on the moon.

Miss Wyatt then asked, "Why do we hear all of the sounds that we have been talking about?" Many of the children were interested in contributing their own theory on this question, and gave such ideas as, "We hear because we have ears and brains."

Kenneth came forth with "We hear the vibrations." This led to a discussion on vibration. The children, under Miss Wyatt's leadership, felt their throats move as they talked and experimented with tones as deep and low as they could command as well as with high squeaky ones. They felt their own and each other's throats as they made the sounds. Another experiment was done by stretching rubber bands around nails driven into a piece of wood. The children watched the rubber bands move back and forth and whirr as they plucked them. They also tapped lids of pans as well as a triangle in various ways, felt the movement, and learned that this also is vibration. Still the question of why they hear sounds had not been solved.

Roger said, "The sounds are carried by air." This remark called for more experimentation. First the group used a small alarm clock for several experiments. The clock was held up and the children listened to it tick. Then it was placed on the table and each child took turns putting his head on the table about the same distance as when the clock was just held up. The children discovered that now the sound was clearer and more distinct. The clock was then placed at one end of a metal curtain rod and a child put his ear at the other end of it. This intensified the sound even more. The children arrived at the following conclusions:

> Sound is just vibrations that go into the ears.
> Air carries sound and makes it resound.
> Sound coming from metal is clearer and more resounding than when it comes from wood.

Echoes were discussed and the children discovered that air comes out of the mouth in vibrations. If it comes into contact with a wall or other physical obstruction it is reflected back to the one who sent it forth. A mirror was used to help clarify this concept, and Miss Wyatt also painted illustrations on the easel to make lucid the reasons for the returning vibrations being smaller.

The children, intrigued by their discoveries and experiments, asked to make a telephone. This request was made after experimentation with talking through the garden hose.

Experiment in the Transmission of Sound

After reading and discussing possibilities, the children dictated the following instructions:

To Make a Telephone

We Need:

1. Strong string.
2. Bees wax.
3. Two pieces of paper.
4. Some tape.
5. Two tin cans.
6. Two small sticks.

Each member of the class had a turn in making the telephone. A nail hole was driven into the bottoms of the two number ten size tin cans. Then bees wax was rubbed on approximately twenty feet of strong string, one end of which was put through each tin can hole and a knot tied in each end. By keeping the string tight the children could talk and hear through their homemade telephone.

Interest was at such a height that Miss Wyatt appealed to the telephone company to give the children a guided tour through the mysteries of the inner working of the telephone exchange. The children were captivated, asked such intelligent questions, and made so many sapient remarks that the people responsible for the field trip felt well rewarded for their efforts. When the children left they were given a long time loan of two unattached, but real telephones which are vital items on the list of equipment of any early childhood teacher.

The conclusions drawn from the telephone experiment were that:

> There are several different kinds of telephones but they all have a mouth piece and a receiver.
>
> Voices travel to far off, as well as close places via the telephone. It is even possible to talk to people clear across the water by telephone.
>
> Voice vibrations are changed to electric vibrations which go down the wire. When they reach the other end the electric vibrations are changed back to sound vibrations.
>
> Some automobiles are equipped with telephones.
>
> People can tell what kind of persons we are by the way we talk over the telephone. We always need to be courteous and thoughtful when we use the telephone.

That this group gained a genuine appreciation of sound and how it is produced is evidenced by Larry's remark, "Sound makes the air waves ripple to its rhythm," and by Pat, who said, "You could feel the sound vibrate even if you couldn't see it."

QUESTIONS ON LEARNING THROUGH AUDITORY IMPRESSIONS

1. Discuss the value of sharing ideas conveyed through the medium of sound without words. Illustrate from classroom situations.

2. What types of impressions may be conveyed to children through music? How? Discuss.

3. What interesting comparisons are readily suggested by your children in associating simple instrumental sounds with those of familiar activities in home, school, and neighborhood?

4. Select a neighborhood of your acquaintance and list the sounds which children would recognize. Suggest ways some of these might be reproduced in your classroom, and words your children might use in describing the activities and situations with which the sounds are associated.

5. Discuss the importance of clear auditory impressions: a. in speech development; b. in learning a new language; c. in recognizing people's names when introduced; d. in learning to associate spoken words with their written forms; e. in working with musical and other sound producing instruments.

6. Discuss some of the problems which are likely to arise in classrooms with: a. a dearth of challenging and interesting sensory stimuli; b. an overabundance of challenging materials and sounds.

7. How can working with sounds contribute to the child's growth in the six goals? In academic fields? Discuss.

8. How can a tape recorder be used to advantage as a recording device in a democratic classroom?

IV. LEARNING THROUGH TACTILE IMPRESSIONS

The possibilities of learning through the sense of touch are often minimized or overlooked.

Starting with a Poem

One hot day in early fall Miss C. introduced touch by quoting a poem from her memorized repertoire:

Barefoot Fun

I took off my shoes
One summer day
And ran right out
On the grass to play.

I found some mud
In a dried up pool,
It felt just like
The clay at school.

I "squished" my feet
In a big sand heap
And sifted it on me
Heavy and deep.

I felt round pebbles
Under my toes,
And the prick of a thorn
From the yellow rose.

I had great fun
All that summer day
When I went barefoot
Out to play.

At the end of the poem Martha said, "Why can't we take our shoes and socks off and feel things with our feet?"

Much fun was experienced feeling the smooth floor, the rug, the grass, the concrete, the sand, pebbles, and so on. In the next few days Miss C. and the children made up the following rhymes:

When I walk on the rug
It feels soft and snug.

When I run on the grass I try to be fleet,
Because the grass whiskers tickle my feet.

I pat a wee frog house with my hand,
And push my foot into damp cool sand,

Sand slows my feet when I try to run
But to dig in it is lots of fun.

I'll step in the mud and print with my toes
To show which way the 'Possum' goes.

My dog walked through and left a track,
And the mud will tell when he comes back.

Concrete is hard and slick and cool
When I walk on it in the morning to school,
But by noon time it's the other way,
It feels hot to my feet when I run and play.

The children also enjoyed remembering previous experiences and later verifying them. They began bringing in things they found that felt rough or smooth, slick or soft or hard, and calling attention to things in the environment that felt alike or different.

Bringing Objects to Feel

Another teacher, Miss K., set up a table of things to feel, and invited the children to bring objects for it. John found some gravel and put it in a box. Miss K. placed a small can of water on the table. Margaret brought an acorn and Betty a piece of newspaper. Other things on the table were pumpkin pulp, clay, mud, sand, soil, a plastic bottle top, a sponge.

The children felt and compared various objects in the environment. When a question arose about the tree bark on which the acorn grew, Billy volunteered to go and feel the bark of that tree. It was rough. They learned what oak leaves feel like, too. The next day the children brought various pieces of bark from wood that was cut. Some of the bark felt rough and some was smooth. Miss K. asked three children to find something on the science table that felt rough. Ellen found a piece of sandpaper and Joe found a grater and Meredith a handful of gravel.

Miss K. asked three other children to go to the table and find something smooth. Beth found a piece of satin, Arch a piece of wax paper, and Jane a stainless steel lid. Then Davey said, "I saw something on the science table that is soft like a kitten." He had touched a piece of cotton. Miss K. asked Davey to find something else that was soft and he held up a piece of velvet. Gerald felt the pumpkin pulp and remarked, "It is gooshy, muddy, squishy, and rocky. It feels like wet cement."

Impressions Gained Through Feeling

Interest in touch is by no means limited to the younger groups. Other children are challenged by the fact that things sometimes have a different feel than one might expect, and are intrigued by the idea of finding out all they can about an object without looking at it until afterward.

One upper primary teacher had an interesting Tactile Center set up in her upper primary room one morning. On it were a piece of linen, a piece of corduroy, a piece of cotton roving, thin plastic, cotton rope (hard), and ropy yarn (soft), wrinkled aluminum, a crinkly plastic doily, a fuzzy pipe cleaner, and a string of paper clips. The children clustered around it, touching it and asking, "What's this for?"

To stimulate their curiosity was exactly the purpose of the exhibit.

Later Tom said, speaking of the pipe cleaners, "This feels like wet horse's hair."

The board was labeled, "Feel first, then look." Additions and suggestions from the children were welcomed and much interest centered around this table. The children brought in new tactiles frequently and this activity never seemed to grow old.

One of the joys in these experiences came in inviting parents, relatives, and friends to come in, stand with eyes shut, feel the objects without looking and tell what they were, then look.

Endless Variations

The experience of "Feel and Find Out" is capable of many variations. Some teachers have a good-sized paper bag in which are a number of objects such as fur, cotton, a paint brush, a comb, an eraser, a sponge, a shell, a bottle stopper, a ball, a marble, and a rubber band. Sometimes the bag is passed around and each child closes his eyes, reaches in, and finds one object. He feels it and describes it, then either he or another child tells what it must be, according to his description of it. Questions may be asked as a guide to intelligent thought and inquiry: "Is the object hard? soft? dry? wet? smooth? bumpy? big? little?"

After the discussion the child pulls out the object he has touched and everyone verifies or corrects his impressions.

QUESTIONS ON LEARNING THROUGH TACTILE IMPRESSIONS

1. (a) Describe a bulletin display featuring tactile impressions which you might plan to have in your classroom. (b) Suggest how your children might participate in planning and evaluating it. (c) How will you teach your children to distinguish between situations such as this where they are encouraged to feel and learn, and other situations where "hands off" is the policy?

2. What balance between sensory impressions and language expression needs to be maintained in your classroom? What bearing has this on your guidance of experiences involving the sense of touch?

3. (a) List the words which might be used to describe incidental impressions gained through touching and working with various equipment and materials throughout the day in your classroom. Be specific. (b) Suggest other objects you might make available to your children to strengthen their tactile perception. How might these be used, and how would you introduce them and locate them in your environment? (c) Evaluate the activities in (a) and (b) from the standpoint of effective use of time and equal opportunity for participation by various children, as well as of individual differences within your group.

V. LEARNING THROUGH OLFACTORY IMPRESSIONS

New avenues of appreciation and learning may be continually opened up to the child through his sense of smell. You may provide many opportunities to help him in acquiring this discrimination and knowledge. Experience in smelling may be significant for the type of mental processes demanded in good reading. It is also an important medium for expanding the child's vocabulary.

Teacher and Children Explore Together

Rodney brought a lovely bouquet from his mother's garden and arranged it in a vase which he placed on a table near the bulletin board. Laurie was standing near the vase. Mrs. Moulton saw Laurie put her hands over her eyes and stoop to smell one flower after another. Then Laurie announced happily: "You know what! I can tell which is the rose and which is the carnation, not by seeing it or hearing anyone say, or feeling!"

"How do you do it?" asked Mrs. Moulton.

"By the smell!" said Laurie.

The other children were interested in Laurie's discovery and wanted to find things which they, too, could identify by smell. One by one a child was blindfolded, and other children brought everyday things for him to smell and identify: the jar of paste, some grass, an apple, a banana, a small handful of alfalfa hay which the children fed the rabbit they had been given for a few days' observation; a carrot, a piece of soap, a jar of mentholatum; a sprig of cedar, an orange, some grapejuice, a peach.

After each child had tried his skill in identifying these objects by smell, the children dictated a chart about their experiment which Mrs. Moulton wrote for them. "When we are able to tell what a thing is by its smell," she said, "we *identify* it by its smell."

A variation of this activity was smelling an object and telling what the smell reminded them of. Following are some of the children's observations:

"Violets smell like soap."

"This powder smells like sweetness."

"Carrots smell like something you want to eat."

"Yes, and when we smell something we want to eat our mouth gets juicy."

After their experiments the children were much more conscious of how different things smell. After washing his hands for a snack, John remarked, "My hands are clean already. I can still smell the soap."

Mrs. Moulton recalls also how a group of upper primary children she had were rehearsing a creative play in the cafetorium where the aroma of cooking food wafted in from the kitchen. As the children were leaving the area, Terry said, "It smells so good in here, I'd like to go back for second smellings!"

Field Trip and Homework

Another group of children went on a field trip to gather seeds, weeds, rocks, pebbles, and wild flowers. When they returned to the room Mrs. Vigus painted two pictures for the children to use as a guide in separating their collection by smell or feel. The first picture was of a child smelling a flower, the second of a child feeling a rock. When the children were ready to go home they asked for their homework. "What would be a good idea for homework about smelling?" Mrs. Vigus asked.

"We could bring something to smell," suggested Billy.

This idea was discussed. There were some things that just couldn't be brought. Why not remember the different smells noticed in or about the home or on the way to and from school.

The next day Agnes told of the smell of wet woolen cloth. Her mother had been washing her father's woolen hunting shirt.

Many of the children described the smell of food in the kitchen when Mother was getting dinner. Gerry had helped bring in the washing from the clothesline and remembered the smell of the freshly laundered clothes; Lois noted the smell of the catnip growing in her grandmother's herb garden. Glenn, who lived on a dairy farm, reported on a medley of smells; the smell of the earth after a shower that fell during the night; the smell of the sweet alfalfa hay; the smell of new milk going into the container. Chris brought a small bottle of nail polish remover and remarked, "It smells a little like ether." (This child's father was a doctor.) Beth remembered the smell of her new shoes. Tommy brought two cakes of soap. "They are both carnation soap," he announced. "They smell just alike."

Susan remarked, "We had ambrosia for dessert last night. I like to smell ambrosia."

"What is ambrosia?" asked Herbert.

"It's oranges, coconut, and powdered sugar," replied Susan. "I watched Mother make it. The oranges smelled most, but I could smell the coconut, too."

"Ambrosia is a word people use to describe a delightful taste," remarked Mrs. Vigus. "Anything that tastes or smells especially delicious could be called ambrosia."

"Susan's recipe must be called Ambrosia because it tastes so wonderfully good," remarked Billy.

For mid-morning snack the next day Mrs. Vigus and some of the children prepared a bowl of Susan's recipe, and each child was served a small portion. All of the children enjoyed it, and several remarked that it had an "ambrosial" taste.

Three days later Billy was telling about a weekend trip he took with his family. "And the food tasted just like ambrosia," he said.

Identification and Association

Identifying many different kinds of food by smell made another group of children much more discriminating in their ability to distinguish between scents. One day it was decided each child would bring an object from home and ask the others to tell by smelling whether it came from the yard or from indoors, and if the latter, from what part of the house. The children identified the kitchen or dining room, (food) ; living room (fireplace wood) ; bedroom (leather slipper) ; bathroom (tooth paste) ; yard or porch (newspaper, when boy first delivers it) ; garden (leaf of mint) .

In the weeks that followed the children verbalized their awareness of various fragrances in the environment. Their reading charts also included more exact description of smells.

One day Mrs. West told her children about a blind girl of her acquaintance. "This girl goes everywhere," said Mrs. West, "and never seems to be lost. On the street she identifies most of the shops by their smell. There is a very special smell that comes from a service station, a smell that comes from a restaurant or cafeteria, a smell that comes from a shoe repair shop, the special smell of a vegetable stand, the smell of a freshly painted house, of roses in bloom as a yard is passed, and the earth smell from a vacant lot."

The children were glad they could see, but they thought it would be fun to be blindfolded and have someone lead them past the shops to see which places of business they could identify by the smell. Some of them admitted that the sound also helped.

Later when these children painted pictures of various places they visited, they planned to display their paintings together with a chart explaining the principal purpose of the business. "It would help if we could make it smell something like it, too," said Charles. After a discussion the children decided to place something beneath the picture that would remind them of the odor. A small rag saturated in shoe polish was placed in a tightly closed tin box beneath the shoe repair shop chart. "When someone wants to smell it he can open the box," said Lou. "That way we won't get the smell mixed up with the others." A branch of a pine tree was enclosed in a plastic jar and placed beneath the chart telling about the city park where pine trees grew.

Describing New Smells

The children decided it was a good idea to describe smells in words and see if the group could identify each one. They enjoyed this activity.

Their conclusion was that if you were trying to describe the smell of something that another person had never smelled, you should compare the new smell to something familiar.

QUESTIONS ON LEARNING THROUGH OLFACTORY IMPRESSIONS

1. Suggest how a certain familiar smell might be brought to the classroom and identified by your children, without the aid of the other senses. Then describe the associations it might suggest to the children and how they might present in words, or through painting or dramatization, the location where the smell could be found and their own experiences connected with it. What values would be derived from this classroom activity? By what criteria would you select the odors to be employed in this experiment?

2. List words associated with various odor characteristics and discuss their connotation as related to the education of the child.

3. How can olfactory experiences have a significant place in laying a foundation for the type of mental processes demanded in reading for meaning? Illustrate.

4. a. List various locations in your community, or in an area familiar to you, and the impressions to be gained of these by a child through the sense of smell. b. Discuss each from the standpoint of such factors as selectivity, experiential background of the children and association of ideas.

VI. LEARNING THROUGH GUSTATORY IMPRESSIONS

Experiences in Taste Discrimination

It is surprising that so many people today are unable to classify a distinctive taste. *Bitter* and *sour* seem to be the two terms most commonly confused. Young children should have opportunity to taste different foods in order to learn and appreciate their likenesses and differences, as well as those that are pleasing to the palate. There are possibilities for a wide variety of experiences in this field.

Mrs. Vigus introduced the subject to her group at mid-morning snack time one day by painting an apple and a pineapple. "This is an experience in tasting," she said. Into tiny paper cups she poured a small amount of one or the other of the juices for each child to taste. He then went to the painting and showed which fruit juice he had tasted.

For a beginning experience it is better if the child tastes only two things, and the quantity served need be only enough to taste. Some suggested combinations are: peach-plum; orange-lemon; Irish potato (raw), Irish potato (cooked); sweet potato (raw), sweet potato (cooked); Irish potato-sweet potato (either raw or cooked); cabbage-turnips (either raw or cooked); rice-oatmeal (cooked); rice with salt in it or without salt; celery-radish; oil (as soy bean or peanut oil) or butter; peanut-pecan; pecan-walnut; soda-salt; nutmeg-cinnamon; chocolate-vanilla.

There is literally no end to the taste experiences that a young child may be afforded. The choice should be made from foods which he will be likely to encounter in his environment.

Classification

He should learn to classify a food as sweet, sour, bitter, salty, oily or neutral; as bread, milk, and meat. Much of this is done orally, but you may make it an independent activity by pasting pictures on cards for children in primary grades to place in slots under the appropriate title as suggested above.

Tasting and smelling are closely associated, and many experiments can be done relating one to the other.

In the beginning the child will make little discrimination in taste. He will say, "That's good!" or "I don't like it!" The attention may be shifted from preference to a more acceptable view, as "I can eat" or "I cannot eat" with pictures of a mountain, a car, a sandwich, a piano, a glass of milk, a telephone, an apple to be placed under the appropriate caption. The children may also paint a picture of something that tastes a certain way, as cold or hot, wet or dry, slippery, crunchy, or sticky. These latter, though largely a matter of texture, are associated with the experience of tasting and require feeling with tongue, teeth, and mouth. Other things that may be detected in the mouth are burned food, raw, strong, and weak flavors.

Safety Precautions

Those responsible for children must acquaint themselves with the items in the child's environment which are dangerous if taken internally. There are certain plants and other common things which seem harmless enough, but which will cause discomfort, to say the least, and in some cases, if taken in sufficient quantities, may prove fatal. Certain bulbs, for example, among them the tulip, the bark and berries of some shrubs, eyes of potatoes and, of course, the lowly toadstool, not to mention various microscopic organisms on blades or stems of grass are undesirable if not entirely lethal matter. All known poisonous chemicals and other such household products should be clearly labeled for identification and kept out of the child's reach. His cooperation may be secured in this, but caution rather than fear should be sought. One family made it a rule to mark all dangerous substances with something red about the lid or neck of the container. Such things need to be done without drawing undue attention to them so that they will not have the opposite effect and intrigue the child to explore. Attitude is the ruling force here.

Because of the many things which are harmful if taken by mouth, a child must learn at an early age to distinguish between food and other things. He must learn to put only what is good for him into his mouth. Some things are harmless, others dangerous, but if he keeps all things away from his face and mouth except at meals or snack time, he can be sure he is safe. All tasting must be done with this safeguard in mind.

QUESTIONS ON LEARNING THROUGH GUSTATORY IMPRESSIONS

1. Discuss ways children might work with you in planning and completing a display employing many gustatory impressions. Evaluate from the standpoint of the child's education and growth.

2. Compare the values of stressing likenesses and differences in foods in contrast to emphasizing individual preferences for various tastes and flavors. In view of this, what questions would you ask your children in regard to foods? Why?

3. How can the sense of taste be used for educational purposes during snack time when the children are eating a variety of fresh fruits? Other food? Describe.

4. Justify and describe an experience you plan for your children, centered in gustatory impressions. List words especially associated with the sense of taste and show how they might be used by the children during or following the experience.

VII. EXAMPLES OF CLASSROOM EXPERIENCES BASED ON ALL FIVE SENSES

Simple experiments lend themselves to development of many sensory experiences involving all of the senses.

Experiences with Popcorn

Mrs. Brouhard, primary teacher at West Covina, California, planned a series of rewarding incidents with her children which integrated many constructive sensory experiences. The idea came about in a natural way as the children were discussing "fun things" to do at Halloween. When Arthur suggested popping corn, Mrs. Brouhard seized upon the thought, realizing this could be a delightful learning situation.

Jimmy asked, "But how would we pop it? We don't have any stove in the room."

So a list was made on the chalkboard as follows:

Things We Will Need:

Hot plate—Mrs. Brouhard

Wire popper—Mrs. Brouhard

Popcorn: Cindy
          Michelle
          Roger
          Ronnie
          Charles
          Susan

Butter—Mary Ann
       Helen

Napkins—Kathleen

To borrow from Cafetorium—

Large bowl—Linda

Soup Dipper—Ryan

Next a chart was developed of:

Things to Think About

1. What popcorn looks like before we pop it.
2. How popcorn sounds when we pop it.
3. How it looks *after* it is popped.
4. What the popcorn feels like before we pop it and after we pop it.
5. How long it takes to pop the corn.
6. How the popcorn smells when we pop it.
7. What the popcorn tastes like.

When the list was completed Ronnie said, "Will you write me a note to bring the popcorn so I won't forget it?" Each child responsible for a contribution felt the same so Mrs. Brouhard wrote the list of "Things We Will Need" on paper and cut it into strips for each child to take home as a "remember note." The next day, a similar list of things was made on the chalkboard. It was found that everything needed had been brought. This provided more purposeful experience with visual reading.

Next Mrs. Brouhard gathered data that would prepare her for the many questions that might arise concerning this popcorn experience. She had books available for her own use and also "planted" source reference books and pictures about the room for the children's use. The next day the inevitable questions followed in a guided discussion:

"What did the popcorn look like before it got into the can?"

"Is it like the corn we eat for dinner?"

"How is it different?"

"How does popcorn grow?"

"Where does it grow?"

"What is inside an unpopped grain of corn?"

Experiences in Visual Learning

Many rich visual concepts were built up from the popcorn experiment. However, emphasis was placed on other sensory experiences, so only a few of the significant visual observations are listed here.

Kathleen remarked: "The popcorn kernels swell up like cream when my mother whips it."

Kenny said: "They look like flowers breaking open for spring."

The charts and the children's verbalizations were made into a book which afforded numerous opportunities to see the printed word. Lists of questions were made as they arose from discussions. These incorporated some of the more difficult sight words the children would soon have in their basic reading vocabulary, such as *how, what, where,* and *why.* New words were also introduced, as *popcorn, heat, experiment.*

The children discussed the color of the corn before it was popped and afterward. This brought up the need for research in answer to "What makes the popcorn white?" Mrs. Brouhard said they could probably find the answer to this question in the dictionary. How does the word popcorn start?

Dean said, "Like pumpkin!"

Then Mrs. Brouhard looked under "P" in the dictionary, found *popcorn,* and read aloud: "A type of Indian corn having kernels which on exposure to dry heat are burst open by the explosion of the contained moisture, forming a white, starchy mass." The children opened an unpopped kernel with the pliers and found it had a small bit of white substance in the middle of it. They decided this must expand when heated. A magnifying glass was used in examining the popcorn at all stages.

Opportunities to Develop Thermal Reading

"The popped corn does not look anything like the unpopped corn."

"The kernels are lots bigger than they were before."

"What made the corn change so much?" asked Mrs. Brouhard.

The children reasoned that the only thing different about the popcorn that made it pop was that it got very hot. They checked the temperature with a thermometer. Then they developed a chart which they read:

What Heat Does to Popcorn

We popped corn: (using empty can from which popcorn came)

1. First our corn looked like this: (package of corn unpopped)
2. Then we heated it. (picture of flame and popper containing corn)
3. See our popcorn now. (large white kernels of popped corn in bag)

Auditory Impressions

Most of the children's verbalizations were of likenesses to sound, as Eileen said enthusiastically, "The popping corn sounds like rocket ships blasting off."

Mrs. Brouhard commented afterward, "Of course, Eileen knew the sounds weren't really like rocket ships, but she felt the joy of experiencing poetic license."

Other comments were made from time to time:

Roger—"The popcorn sounds like when we clap."

Gregory—"Listen! It sounds like thousands of snapping fingers."
Ray—"To me it sounds like clouds bumping together."
Cindy—"They sound like a cat with hiccoughs."
Troy—"They crash like when you bend a twig."
Dean—"They sound like millions of flat tires, or cars on the freeway backfiring."
Susan—"They sound as if they are just bursting with joy."
The group dictated the following and Mrs. Brouhard made it into a chart:

Popping Corn

Sh-sh-sh! The popcorn falls
into the popper.
Scrape, scrape, scrape,
goes the popper on the hot plate.
Snap! Crackle! Pop!
Pop! Poppity! Pop!
The kernels break open
into white fluffy balls.
What fun it is
to make popcorn!

Need to Develop More Olfactory Discrimination

Then Mrs. Brouhard quoted for the children the poem, "Smells," by Christopher Morley[1], and recited the verse, "Pop Corn Man."[2]

A discussion followed in which the children related the popcorn smell to theaters, variety stores, and a circus, but they did not make the comparisons Mrs. Brouhard had thought they would—the ones she, herself, associates with popcorn, such as a campfire, a cold night in front of the hearth, Halloween, Christmas, something cozy and warm. When she asked the children how the smell of popping corn made them feel, the most universal answer was "hun-

[1] From FOR A CHILD, Wilma McFarland, editor, Junior Literary Guild, Westminster Press, 1947.
[2] From TALKING TIME, by Louise Binder Scott and J. J. Thompson, Webster Publishing Company, St. Louis, 1951.

gry." It made her realize the need for further helping them develop sensitivity to variations in smell.

With this in mind, Mrs. Brouhard encouraged a game of "Smell and Think." The children closed their eyes and she passed various things for them to smell such as a lemon, an onion, perfumes, soap, an apple, an orange, and other things with which they were familiar. They described the smell of each one and how it made them feel.

Sense of Touch

The children were impressed with the difference between the hard cold unpopped seeds and the soft white kernels of warm, freshly popped corn. Descriptions were given based on the sense of touch. Remarks included:
"The popped corn feels like sponge."
"It is hard and soft, squashy, like rubber."
"It makes me think of a ball my dog chewed up."
"It is like the sponge rubber Mother used to fill the sofa pillows."

Concept of Time

Words such as "first," "second," third" were used as the children compared the batches of corn they popped. They used their wooden clock face with the movable hands and showed how many minutes were employed each time. They developed the following chart:

> **Time**
>
> **How long did it take?**
> **First batch 10 minutes**
> **Second batch 2 minutes**
> **Third batch 5 minutes**

The children decided after some discussion that the longer length of the first popping could probably be attributed to the "warm up" time for the hot plate.

Kinetic Reading

There were many opportunities for "discharge of kinetic energy." When Michelle said, "The popcorn kernels shake for joy," all the children joined in popping corn body rhythms. They also demonstrated the other verbalizations by shaking, jumping, and chattering teeth.

The children decided to create an action play with lines that would "rhyme." They began by thinking how it would feel if each of them were a little grain of popcorn. They would not have arms and legs and would have to crouch like seeds in the ground. Susan said, "It is like chicks hatching out of eggs, and that is like being born." The children thought how the words "corn" and "born" sound alike; also, "hop" and "pop." "Words that sound alike 'rhyme,' don't they?" volunteered Betsy.

The children felt the hard, unpopped kernels and thought seriously about what happened to make the corn "explode" and become like the soft, white kernels that are so much bigger and bumpier. Each child curled up with arms wrapped around his own knees, then flung his arms and head and legs out as he jumped up for the "pop."

Their own action play follows:

Popcorn Popping

I'm a little grain of corn
Waiting, waiting, to be born.
(Crouch in a ball)
Sizzle, shake, jump, hop
(Still in crouching position, shake
body, jump and hop.)
6, 5, 4, 3, 2, 1. POP!
(Throw hands and feet out
on the word "pop" and rise to
standing position.)

There was no imitation of somebody else's motions here. Each child "was" the corn popping. The concept, when expressed in body rhythm, became more meaningful. Ideas were being communicated based on sensory impressions, and foundations laid for language development.

Following the action-play, the children continued their experience by "popping" to rhythmic accompaniment, in full body motion. For this they used drums, and also the wood block, castanets, and rattles.

Further Experiments with Heat and Cold

The experiences with popping corn led into further experiments with hot, warm, cold, and freezing temperatures in the making of jello, freezing and melting ice cubes, and making sherbet. Interesting reports were brought from home by various children of butter melting on hot cornbread, of what happened to batter on the hot stove, of chocolate melting in the sunlight, and of milk rising in the bottle when it was too close to the freezing compartment.

Collecting Rocks

You will find that rocks have a general appeal for your children and they will delight in bringing and talking about them. They are thrilled with any rock which catches their eye, and will temporarily adopt it as their own. Much learning through many fine sensory experiences takes place when rocks are compared one with another, from the standpoint of size, weight, color, hardness, and composition. Your children will enjoy the feel of individual rocks, and it will interest them to know why some rocks are smooth and others rough or jagged. The appearance of rocks under water, in bright sunlight, or shadow may also be observed.

Rocks lend themselves to listening experience, as well as to seeing and feeling. A few pebbles in an empty paper box or even held in the cupped palms of the two hands closed upon each other will provide a challenge if your children listen closely and estimate "how many" separate pieces they hear being shaken together at different times. The comparative size of the pebbles can also be ascertained in this way. With more experience, your children will detect other differences by listening, such as sharp edges or round corners, heavy or light material, one smaller rock rattling against another heavier one.

Actual identification of the rocks brought in may sometimes be difficult. Children may, however, when they pick up a rock, notice whether it was dug up out of the ground at the spot where it was found, or brought there by water, by people, or whether it may have rolled or fallen from some place else, and how it differs from or is like other rocks nearby. More advanced children may also study the structure of the rock in terms of three broad classifications: igneous, sedimentary, or metamorphic.

The size and shape of specimens will of course vary from one locality to another, but it is possible for almost any schoolroom to have a creditable rock collection. Smaller rocks may be glued onto charts or into box lids according to a given plan. However meager it may be, a collection of rocks begun in childhood may develop into an interest that will remain throughout life.

QUESTIONS ON THE SIGNIFICANCE OF CLASSROOM EXPERIENCES INVOLVING THE FIVE SENSES

1. Evaluate the classroom experience in popping corn from the standpoint of academic learning and justify the use of school time for a project of this type. Suggest another concrete experiment in which all the senses would be employed for constructive learning in the classroom. Evaluate.

2. What do children gain from collecting rocks? How will you guide their learning in this activity? Illustrate.

3. Discuss No. 2 from the standpoint of each of the following: a. discrimination; b. association of ideas; c. recall of experiences; d. classification; e. organization of effort; f. observation; g. power of concentration.

4. Consider the ways a sightless child may employ various types of sensory impressions to compensate for the absence of direct visual images of the life around him. What conclusions can be drawn regarding the untapped resources for learning available for all children through avenues other than sight?

5. Consider the keenness of visual observation developed by children who suffer a loss of hearing. What are the educational implications for all children?

VIII. FURTHER SIGNIFICANCE OF SENSORY IMPRESSIONS IN THE CLASSROOM

Direct Experiences

Children who are in the foundation stages of learning think chiefly in terms of direct experiences. In some respects the process of "growing up" consists of learning to enjoy and appreciate *remotely* as well as *directly*; to profit from *vicarious* as well as *immediate* experience. As the young child grows he learns to use words as a substitute for experiences and to represent sensory impressions through the process of linguistic association.

Learning Through Participation

A healthy, eager child wants to be a participant. He cannot be passive; it is normal that he be restless and bored when he must undergo physical inactivity for overlong.

> A three-year-old went with his aunt to visit a neighborhood school. He had anticipated the event with enthusiasm. When he returned home his mother asked, "Well, Jimmie, what did you and Auntie Sarah do at school?" With a deep sigh the boy replied, "Oh, just sitted."

Unfortunately, many school programs are so organized that a child is expected to listen almost sixty percent of his time, although what transpires in the room often may not arouse his active interest or make him feel there is a reason for listening. When children are asked to listen, they should not only recognize the purpose behind the request, but in many instances should themselves have some voice in deciding to what they shall give attention.

It follows, then, that the learning program must be one of active participation guided into constructive channels, rather than passive listening. It is personal knowledge that counts with the child, and participation is his inalienable right. The modern school builds the program on what a child can do to become an active learner in the group, in terms of what he is intellectually and physically ready to achieve.

Interpreting Impressions

The child's inherent aptitude for learning challenges you as a teacher to become aware of the myriad environmental impressions clamoring to be recognized. You strive to help the child interpret what comes to him through his senses in terms of his own experiences and discoveries, and his own previous learnings. As he shares his thoughts with interested friends language becomes more meaningful to him, and whether he is listening to others or communicating ideas, his interpretation of sensory impressions becomes a reservoir of experience for his own future development.

GENERAL QUESTIONS ON THE SIGNIFICANCE OF SENSORY IMPRESSIONS IN CHILDHOOD EDUCATION

1. What is the role of the democratic classroom in providing selected sensory impressions for the child? Describe some of these.

2. Illustrate No. 1 above for a certain group of children with whom you are familiar.

3. Be on the alert for children's comments that reveal power of observation through each of the five senses. Make verbatim notes on these and suggest possibilities for further learnings which you, as teacher, might guide the children to make. (Indicate the age of the child and the circumstances under which each comment was made.)

4. How can you make the child's casual comments lead to constructive investigations? Give examples.

5. Where does scientific thinking begin for the child? Discuss.

6. Discuss the guidance you may give the classroom whereby your children may find their own solutions to problems and experiments.

7. Present some of the conclusions a child may draw from his own thoughtful observations. Be specific.

8. Which of the conclusions in No. 7 above need clarification? Explain.

9. Discuss ways you can have an environment in your classroom whereby educational experiments and discussions based on sensory impressions become a daily occurrence. Illustrate and evaluate.

10. How can a balance be achieved between the young child's need to investigate and explore in order to learn, and his need to restrict and redirect this tendency? Give illustrations.

11. a. What impact has No. 10 on your classroom environment? b. How does your understanding of children help you regarding your own classroom procedure as it relates to No. 10, above? Give examples.

SELECTED REFERENCES

Borten, Helen, DO YOU HEAR WHAT I HEAR? New York, Abelard-Schuman, 1960.

Nelson, Mrs. Lee, ALL THE SOUNDS WE HEAR, Austin 6, Texas, The Steck Co., 1960.

Zim, Herbert S., OUR SENSES AND HOW THEY WORK, New York, William Morrow & Co., 1956.

THE QUEST FOR

Part Five

SCIENTIFIC KNOWLEDGE

I. THE CHILD'S GROWING HORIZONS

Science is concerned with observing, comprehending, being aware of structure and function within the natural world. The young child is also concerned with these same things as he seeks to make his own discoveries about the world.

Your responsibility is two-fold in regard to the child's growing horizons in science.

First is his need to learn to think in a scientific manner—to be observant in terms of cause and effect—to verify his own observations, to solve problems. You can help him learn to see likenesses and differences in common everyday things, to notice trends, and to discover the basis for functional as well as structural classification. You can help him learn to plan and execute experiments which will provide him with data on which to base his conclusions. You can teach him to suggest hypotheses and then go about establishing their validity.

Second, you have a responsibility in a world of scientific knowledge to bring to the child the findings—the facts known to man today—in such a meaningful way that the child is eager to continue his own quest for scientific knowledge, and to learn all he can of what others have discovered.

This must be done in terms of the child's own pattern of growth, according to his developing abilities to do and to understand.

The child's natural tendency to hear, smell, touch, taste, see, remember, and compare leads him to his first scientific deductions. Classifying is more than naming things. It is being observant of how they move, how living things grow, breathe, eat, sleep; how inanimate things are constructed; how they work and move; what their purposes are. Also, there are forces at work in the world of science which cannot be seen or otherwise sensed, but can be recognized in terms of their influence on something else. Electricity is comprehended as a reality by the young child because he can control it at the turn of the switch, and can see the results of its force in his daily life. The thought that unseen rays and vibrations travel great distances with lightning speed is in keeping with an age in which the magic carpet of the fairy tales of countless generations is becoming almost a reality.

Children must accept the realities of the life to which they belong and seek to understand them. The degree to which a child understands any scientific fact depends upon how well he grasps the basic concept underlying it, and this, in turn, is taught him by relating it in some way to his own life experience.

The child's first understanding about his world is specific. When he compares one specific with another and makes a scientific discovery in each, he may begin to make a generalization. Growth in this direction is gradual.

In your effort to bring to your children a wealth of scientific knowledge, make sure you are not overlooking what is within their immediate sphere. The familiar, accessible, tangible is more filled with possibilities for learning than the remote and abstract. Start with whatever is at hand and bring to it the spirit of discovery.

Science Is Everywhere

Even the toddler is concerned with problems in the realm of science—problems of balance when he is learning to walk; of volume and inflection in coordinating the sound and rhythm of his own repetitive babble as he learns to talk; problems of taking things apart and putting them together again; interest in his own body functions.

By the time any healthy child is ready for school, whether he comes from a farm home or the tenth story of an apartment house, he has already acquired considerable rudimentary scientific knowledge. One child knows the strength of the wind blowing because he remembers when it almost capsized him as he ran. Another feels the power of the push button elevator through the pull of its upward thrust. One child may know the wonder of new life on the farm: baby calves, baby chicks coming out of the shell, blind kittens or puppies. Another may be familiar with hoists and levers. Most children have seen lightning in the sky and experienced the violence of a thunder storm. Many children will have known hail or snow. Some may have discovered tiny plants coming up out of the earth, or they may have planted a bulb in a flower pot and seen the pointed leaves push themselves up into air and light. To another the planets and their orbits are as well-known as the labyrinth of streets he transverses daily.

The scientific knowledge a child has acquired depends upon his environment, his mental acumen, and the type of persons with whom he has been associated. Yet the miracles of technical science are to many children as familiar as the day—automatic home appliances, television, telephone, electronic devices, airplanes. There are many simple experiments throughout the school of early childhood which bring children some understanding of the basic scientific principles which made these and other inventions possible. Experiments in science are a part of the child's day to day experience, integrated with the language arts, arithmetic, and other learnings.

Help for the Teacher

Many teachers are reluctant to guide the child's advancement in the science field, feeling their background to be inadequate. For this reason some few school systems employ science specialists to aid teachers who need their help. The specialist is also the custodian of a wide variety of science materials available to teachers upon request.

Other boards of education are purchasing science kits which are designed by experienced persons. They are sturdily built and equipped, and will permit a maximum number of experiments. They also afford a place for storing science materials. Much can be said in favor of these kits.

However, availability of aids is not the deciding factor in making science available to your children. Much of your most effective teaching will come out of the unforeseen circumstance upon which you capitalize—crystallization on the sides of a bowl, refracted light from a dish, the spider that has invaded the classroom and is busily weaving her web; seeds with wings of down blowing through the air on a windy day; a butterfly that balances on a shrub—these and a thousand other incidental happenings afford you opportunity to help the child in his uncharted quest for scientific knowledge.

Your Own Attitude

If you are unable to answer his ever-recurring "why?" you need feel no embarrassment. The true scientist never pretends to knowledge he does not have. He is always questioning and seeking, and your attitude of "Let's find out together" will not only keep interest alive, but will help a child acquire the attitude of the scientist who seeks to unlock the unknown.

First Hand Inquiring

The scientific point of view calls for careful observation of details, ability to describe what is seen, and to discover cause and effect, likeness and difference, trends and tendencies, and physical laws which can be depended upon in nature.

Much of the child's early education is drawn from his ability to respond to the world around him, and he can readily be led to make discoveries and to explore and investigate in such a way as to find the answers to many of his natural questions.

When the quest for scientific knowledge is followed, its trail leads through the center of every day. Knowledge gleaned by others is valuable, but normally follows, rather than precedes first hand observations, which the children can make for themselves. These observations you will learn to capitalize on at the psychological moment.

If a significant local or national news event is uppermost in the children's minds, enlarge upon its constructive scientific aspects in your classroom. Take advantage of publicity given to scientific discoveries within the ability of your children to understand.

If there is a sudden change in the weather, take immediate notice, so that learnings may occur when phenomena are at hand.

If Mrs. J. brings in some baby chicks, take time out to watch how they drink, how they walk, what their wings look like. Compare their appearance with Mary's half grown pet that she brought for the children to see.

Note likenesses and differences. When questions are asked, answer them by looking and watching.

Help the children plan ways of finding how they can discover the facts they need. With your encouragement they will think:

"What do we want to know?"

"How could we find out?"

Fresh live interests are in the making, and as they are followed they provide impetus and ideas that lead into all the academic learnings. Thus the scientific approach in acquiring knowledge will be inherent in each discussion.

What you hope to do is to teach children to observe and compare; to weigh, measure, organize thoughts, and evaluate. If a child learns to do these things he has acquired the first requisite of a scientist—an open mind, an interest in discovery, and an ability to direct his own line of questioning toward a consistent course of action.

Young Scientists in the Making

Starting with whatever is at hand, the child finds something to notice, to compare, to remember.

For example, when Barbara asked if she might bring her duck, Perky, to school, Miss D. gladly gave her permission to do so. Perky was an invited guest, and knowing that ducks like water, the children prepared a small pond for him. Perky saw the pond, waddled to it, and dived in. When he stepped out, big drops of water rolled off his neck and back.

"They don't even make his feathers a bit wet," observed Andy. "Why doesn't he get wet?"

This question led to inquiries and consultation from other people and books. The information that the feathers contain a kind of oil that makes them waterproof brought with it a whole gamut of new interests. Pictures were painted explaining how Perky could swim. Other waterproof things were discovered. What made the raincoats shed water?

Perky's native ability as a navigator was challenged. "How well do baby ducks swim? Why can a duck stay up in the water, and what makes him go?" These and other questions gave rise to further observations. "The big webs on Perky's feet look as if he could paddle himself along," said Ben, "and he can."

The children also observed that Martin's hen, Penny, could outdig Perky with her scrawny claws. "She scratches for her food. But when it comes to swimming, you can count Penny out," Martin said.

Likenesses and differences in the two pets led to other discoveries. "Just to look at Penny's sharp bill you would know she would peck in the ground the way she does. Did you see how she caught that worm and pulled him right out of the grass?" Raymond exclaimed.

"Perky's bill is much broader and longer. You can see how he can scoop things out of the water with it. and poke around in the mud in the bottom of the pond. Can he see under water when he ducks like that?" asked Bertha.

Again the friends and the books were consulted, and so facts were discovered first hand from available evidence, and because of this, authorities were respected for the observations and experiments upon which
their greater knowledge was based.

From experiences such as the foregoing, children acquire ways of looking at things in their environment. When natural curiosity is guided into
channels of independent thinking, they learn how to formulate questions
and make comparisons in situations similar to ones they have previously
investigated.

The above group was delighted one morning when they went for a
walk to notice Wilbur's dog digging frantically beside a high wooden
fence. "Just look at the dirt fly," was Betty's reaction.

"He sure must have sharp claws," said Pete.

"A lot sharper than Penny's claws," said Ann.

"Dogs do have sharp claws, but not nearly as sharp as cats," observed
Ellen. As if to prove her point a dark, short-haired, furry animal darted
up the fence and disappeared on the other side. "See! What did I tell
you!"

"Aw, everyone knows cats can climb like that," exclaimed Albert.

"But does everyone know why cats can climb?" asked Miss D.

"Why do they?" asked Ann. "Why can cats climb so well, and dogs
not?"

This discussion led the group to arrange for Wilbur to bring his dog,
Tanner, for a brief visit. The children observed his padded feet and toe-
nails. "I see now why they are just right for digging," remarked Billy.

The following day Bertha's mother came by with a half-grown kitten.
The children immediately noticed the structure of the feet.

"If it wasn't for his sharp claws he couldn't hang on like that," observed Pete.

"Could he hang on to the side of a concrete fence?" asked Miss D.

"No," said Billy thoughtfully, "his claws wouldn't stick into cement
like they do wood."

"That is right, Billy," said Miss D. "Your answer shows you have done
some good thinking."

One of the pictures painted that day showed a cat going up the side
of a wooden fence and a dog digging in the ground.

In their discussion the children compared not only the cat's fur and
the dog's hair; they also compared the eyes of the two animals and many
other characteristics.

Thus the budding scientific mind puts down its roots and flourishes
under teacher guidance.

Diversification of Home Resources

The child's normal exploration leads him to discoveries within his home environment, whether it be hovel or mansion. The location of his home and the times in which he lives influence his learning.

Many adults who had their beginnings on farms or in villages remember their delight in digging in earth, in making "frog" houses, forts, robber caves, a "bed for bears to sleep in," a great row of mud pie cookies. Sometimes they modeled large families or other crude clay figures that sat in the sun to dry. It brought a pang of regret when the figures crumbled, and of triumph when they emerged from their sunbath hard and unbroken. The figures that held together and did not "die" in the sun, later attended church, cultivated the garden, tended the baby in his leaf cradle, reprimanded the older children, and generally lent themselves to re-creating in dramatic expression the entire gamut of family living. Unconsciously the child who engaged in this play acquired a body of knowledge through his experiences which integrated his learnings. Through modeling his figures, his cattle, his houses, and his stockades he engaged in primitive art and knew joy in the manipulative processes; when his clay people "sang" in church he enjoyed music; from the numbers of figures he modeled he learned rudimentary addition, and from those that crumbled he learned subtraction.

In this era of rapid living, great numbers of children have little opportunity for this close contact with earth. The school must now supply this type of life laboratory which children in a more primitive culture automatically acquired in the home.

On the other hand, the modern child may be given the opportunity for scientific experiments in his own home laboratory. Guidance and careful selection of materials are needed in order that he may appreciate and interpret the basic concepts involved and learn to plan for himself and direct his own thinking. Valuable, also, is the opportunity to work with the raw materials and natural resources provided by the area in which he resides, according to his own growing ability. Many of today's children are filled with scientific facts acquired incidentally from their association with adults. Jet propulsion and super-market doors that open automatically, processed food, automatic air-conditioning, and sub-zero freezing temperatures for the preservation of food are taken for granted as part of his heritage by the child whose family and community provide him with such advantages. Many fathers and mothers have vocational skills that are concerned with scientific discoveries or the mechanics of operation of modern inventions. The child hears the vocabulary of these vocations at home and assimilates much of their meaning.

Take inventory of what your children know, listen to them and get your cues as to what they are prepared to learn next. The old adage, "Start where that child is" applies here, especially.

Mrs. B. says, "My six-year-olds are way out in outer space and I have to go out there and get them and bring them back to earth before I can expect them to be interested in other things."

The child's knowledge is often amazing to the adult who may not have followed the current newscasts and some of the better programs on television. In some instances the misconceptions that need to be cleared up for the child are also astounding. You can help him discriminate between the fantastic and the actual, remembering always that today's science fiction often becomes tomorrow's facts.

Planned Experiences

You will not only capitalize on incidental occurrences which lead to the building of scientific knowledge; you can also plan experiences and make definite preparation for them, even though you may wait for an opportune time to introduce them in your classroom. Science learnings are continually interrelated with other facets of the day's program. (See *Science* in Index.)

By providing simple, first-hand science experiences you can help children answer for themselves many of their perpetually uttered "whys."

In the "Earth and Water" study (See Section on Language Through Science) note the additional learnings inherent in the experiments which the child performs under teacher guidance, and how his added learnings enrich his joy in them. Many of these things were once bug-a-boos of high school science, but in the early elementary years they are acquired naturally and joyously as part of the child's growing understanding of his environment.

In the experiment with shadows (See Science Through Language) he learns more of the "processes of the suns" as they relate to our own sun in a galaxy of suns—and his appreciation grows for the sun about which the earth moves, and from which is derived the light and heat that are necessary to all life.

Progressing to "Weather," he learns that this same sun is responsible for the constantly moving tides and the ever-changing atmosphere, and that these great phenomena affect our climate and our way of life.

During early childhood such learnings are accepted with enthusiasm. They come within the scope of the child's daily interest, and help orient him to life. You as teacher inspire, suggest, watch for receptiveness, and subtly guide his experiments into a realization of the deep spiritual significance of the forces of nature and the complexity of the universal plan.

You plan experiences such as these not as science *per se* but as a rightful part of the child's eager interest in living. He talks about what he has done and his vocabulary increases along with his fluency of expression; he paints and draws pictures to illustrate what he has learned and to depict how he feels about it.

Through his music experiences he learns many of the scientific principles of sound and how sound waves are carried by the crude telephone he constructs. He becomes aware of rhythm all around him: the rhythm of raindrops, of a bubbling stream; of man-made machines; of wind in the swaying trees; of walking feet. He makes his own rhythms with sand or pebbles in a can, with rhythm sticks or drums; and listens with interest to stories of how other people in a different land use drums as the telephones of the jungles.

Coupled with these are the vast possibilities of dramatic interpretation, appreciation, and the poetic aspects of the association of sounds.

Your Motto Regarding Science

You, as an early childhood teacher, will plan for science experiences and make provision for experiments, but you will never shun the opportunities for learning that are continually arising incidentally in the life of your children. Your motto as an early childhood teacher might well be to listen to each child's questions, then encourage him:

> To search, to find, to see,
> To explore the great wide wonder
> Of his world's immensity.

This, indeed, is *science* in the school of early childhood.

QUESTIONS ON THE QUEST FOR SCIENTIFIC KNOWLEDGE

1. Discuss the scientific implication of the children's growing ability to discover likenesses and differences.

2. How can the child's curiosity and keen awareness of sensory impressions be guided into channels of scientific investigation? Describe.

3. In what ways will you develop your children's ability to observe closely and describe accurately? How will you teach them to set up experiments, make observations, and think through the results to a logical, objective conclusion? Give illustrations on the maturation level of your children.

4. How can you have the scientific and the aesthetic combined in the classroom experiences of your children? Describe a classroom experience that combines both of these.

5. Why is the major portion of the examples of science experiences included in various sections of this book rather than under the general heading "Science"? (See Index)

6. Think of some logical, but unforeseen occurrence in the classroom and show how, with your guidance, it might lead to opportunities for the children first to observe, verify, make discoveries, and then seek further scientific knowledge through pictures, films, other people, and books. Be specific. (Sugar Beet Experiment See Index)

7. A museum of natural history provided mounted stuffed specimens of animals in cases showing them in their natural habitat. These were available to schools where they were shown in classrooms for a period of several days.

The museum, wanting to provide live animals for children to observe, established a "zoozeum" open to visitors. Discuss the possibilities of farming these live animals out to families and classrooms on a loan basis.

Contrast the value of the mounted specimen and the live animal in the classroom. Discuss.

8. Discuss other ways live animals might be brought into the classrooms, or children taken to see them. Evaluate.

9. In science experiments you teach the child to ask:
    What would happen if—?
    What can we do so we can see it happen?
    Now let's watch how it turns out.
In time he learns to record his findings in this manner:
    We wanted to find out_____.
    We decided to _____.
    What happened was _____.
    This is what we discovered_____.
Select an area of science, describe an experiment the children might conduct in the classroom and state their procedure in terms of the above.

10. What place have pictures, books, and films in children's quest for scientific knowledge? Discuss and give examples for various age groups in the early childhood years. Describe the background of the children in each case.

11. Select a film presenting information in some phase of science and evaluate the experience that it might bring to children in the classroom.

SELECTED REFERENCES

Adler, Irving, and Ruth Adler, THINGS THAT SPIN: FROM TOPS TO ATOMS, New York, The John Day Company, 1960.

Bendick, Jeanne, THE FIRST BOOK OF SPACE TRAVEL (Revised Ed.) New York, Franklin Watts, Inc., 1960. (Ages 8 and up).

Blough, Glenn O., MAKING AND USING CLASSROOM SCIENCE MATERIALS, New York, Dryden Press, 1954.

Blough, Glenn O., Julius Schwartz, and Albert J. Huggett, ELEMENTARY SCHOOL SCIENCE AND HOW TO TEACH IT, (Revised Ed.) New York, Holt, Rinehart and Winston, Inc., 1958.

Bruce, Guy V., EXPERIENCES WITH HEAT, Science Teaching Today, Volume IV, Washington 6, D.C., The National Science Teachers Assn., 1951.

Bruce, Guy V., EXPERIENCES WITH LIGHT AND COLOR, Science Teaching Today, Vol. VII, Washington 6, D.C., The National Science Teachers Assn., 1951.

Bruce, Guy V., Washington 6, D.C., The National Science Teachers Assn., EXPERIENCES WITH SOUND, Science Teaching Today, Volume VI, 1951; EXPERIMENTS WITH WATER, 1950.

Burt, Olive, SPACE MONKEY—THE STORY OF MISS BAKER, New York, John Day, 1960.

Clemons, Elizabeth, ROCKS AND THE WORLD AROUND YOU, New York, Coward-McCann Inc., 1960.

Craig, Gerald S., SCIENCE FOR THE ELEMENTARY SCHOOL TEACHER, New Ed., Boston, Ginn & Co., 1958.

Department of Elementary School Principals, SCIENCE FOR TODAY'S CHILDREN: THIRTY-SECOND YEARBOOK OF THE DEPARTMENT OF ELEMENTARY SCHOOL PRINCIPALS, Washington, D.C., National Education Assn., 1954.

DeRegniers, Beatrice (Schenk), THE SHADOW BOOK, New York, Harcourt Brace, 1960.

DeVries, Leonard, THE BOOK OF EXPERIMENTS, New York, Macmillan, 1959.

Elting, Mary (Mrs. Franklin Folsom), HELICOPTER MYSTERY, Irvington-on-Hudson, New York, Z. E. Harvey, Inc., 1958.

Foster, Willene Kay, and Pearl Querse, SEEDS ARE WONDERFUL, Chicago 7, Illinois, Melmont Publishers, Inc., 1960.

Freeman, Mae, and Ira Freeman, FUN WITH SCIENTIFIC EXPERIMENTS, New York, Random House, Inc., 1960.

Gibson, Gertrude Hevener, OUR WEATHER, Chicago 7, Illinois, Melmont Publishers, 1960.

Gold, Ruth Elizabeth, NATURAL SCIENCE IN 3-D, N. Y. Pageant Press, Inc., 1960.

Gottlieb, William P., JETS AND ROCKETS AND HOW THEY WORK, Garden City, New York, Doubleday, 1959.

Greenlee, Julian, TEACHING SCIENCE TO CHILDREN, Dubuque, Iowa, William C. Brown Co., 1958.

Guilcher, J. M. and R. H. Noailles, A TREE IS BORN, New York, Sterling Publishing Co., Inc., 1960.

Hapgood, Charles H., GREAT MYSTERIES OF THE EARTH, New York, G. P. Putnam's Sons, 1960.

Hochman, Vivienne, and M. Greenwald, SCIENCE EXPERIENCES IN EARLY CHILDHOOD EDUCATION, New York, Bank Street Publications, 1954.

Houston, W. Robert and M. Vere DeVault, SIR ISAAC NEWTON, Austin, Texas, The Steck Company, Box 16, 1960. (Ages 8 up).

Hubler, Clark, WORKING WITH CHILDREN IN SCIENCE, Boston, Houghton Mifflin, 1957.

Hunnicutt, C. W., ANSWERING CHILDREN'S QUESTIONS, New York, Bureau of Publications, T. C., Columbia University, 1949.

Larrick, Nancy (Editor), Junior Science Books, Champaign, Illinois: The Garrard Press, 1960—BEAVERS by Alexander L. Crosby; ELECTRICITY by Rocco V. Feravolo; FLYING by Rocco V. Feravolo; STARS by Phoebe Crosby; TREES by Robert S. Lemmon.

Leeming, Joseph, THE REAL BOOK OF SCIENCE EXPERIMENTS, New York, Garden City Books, 1954.

Lewellen, John, THE TRUE BOOK OF MOON, SUN AND STARS, Chicago, Illinois, Children's Press, 1954.

Ley, Willy, SPACE STATIONS, Poughkeepsie, New York, Guild Press, 1958.

Ley, Willy, SPACE TRAVEL, Poughkeepsie, New York, Guild Press, 1958.

Mandelbaum, Arnold, ELECTRICITY, THE STORY OF POWER, New York, G. P. Putnam's Sons, 1960.

Mayall, Newton, and Margaret W. Mayall, A BEGINNER'S GUIDE TO THE SKIES, New York, G. P. Putnam's Sons, 1960.

Navarra, John O., THE DEVELOPMENT OF SCIENTIFIC CONCEPTS IN A YOUNG CHILD, New York, Bureau of Publications, Teachers College, Columbia University, 1955.

Pine, Tillie S. and Joseph Levine, AIR ALL AROUND, New York, Whittlesey House, McGraw-Hill, 1960.

Platt, Rutherford and the staff of the Walt Disney Studio, SECRETS OF LIFE, New York, Simon and Schuster, 1957.

Podendorf, Illa, THE TRUE BOOK OF ANIMAL HOMES, Children's Press, Chicago, Illinois, 1960. (Age 7 and up).

Podendorf, Illa, THE TRUE BOOK OF PLANT EXPERIMENTS, Children's Press, Chicago, Ill., 1960.

Podendorf, Illa, THE TRUE BOOK OF SCIENCE EXPERIMENTS, Chicago, Ill., The Children's Press, 1954. (Excellent science filmstrips also available).

Redlauer, Edward, and Ruth Shaw, ATOMIC POWER FOR PEOPLE, Chicago 7, Illinois, Melmont Publishers, Inc., 1960.

Ross, Edward S., INSECTS CLOSE UP, Berkeley & Los Angeles, University of California Press, 1953.

Ruchlis, Hy., THE WONDER OF LIGHT, New York, Harper Brothers, 1960.

Schneider, Herman, EVERYDAY MACHINES AND HOW THEY WORK, New York, Whittlesey House, McGraw-Hill, 1950.

Schussler, Eileen, and Raymond Schussler, STARBOUND, New York, G. P. Putnam's Sons, 1960.

Tannebaum, Harold E., SCIENCE EDUCATION FOR ELEMENTARY SCHOOL TEACHERS, Boston, Allyn & Bacon, 1960.

Waring, Margaret, SMALL PETS FROM WOODS AND FIELDS, Nashville, Tenn., Abingdon Press, 1960.

Wyler, Rose, THE GOLDEN PICTURE BOOK OF SCIENCE, New York, Simon & Schuster, 1957.

Zim, Herbert S., HOW THINGS GROW, New York 16, New York, William Morrow and Co., Inc., 1960.

Zim, Herbert S., LIGHTNING AND THUNDER, New York 16, New York, William Morrow & Co., Inc., 1952.

Zim, Herbert S., REPTILES AND AMPHIBIANS; A GUIDE TO FAMILIAR AMERICAN SPECIES (Golden Nature Guide), New York, Simon and Schuster, 1953.

Zim, Herbert S., SCIENCE FOR CHILDREN AND TEACHERS, Association for Childhood Education International Pamphlet, 1953.

Zim, Herbert S., SHOOTING STARS, New York, William Morrow & Co., 1958.

Zim, Herbert S., Numerous other books on Science that are excellent.

Ziner, Feenie and Elizabeth Thompson, MY EASY-TO-READ TRUE BOOK OF TIME, New York, Grosset and Dunlap, 1956.

FOUNDATIONS IN

Part Six

VERBAL EXPRESSION

I. INCIDENTAL OPPORTUNITIES FOR CONTINUOUS LEARNING IN LANGUAGE

The six goals of childhood education, when realized, serve in every way to develop language expression. Language is a tremendous medium for continuous learning. Your own classroom can be rich in opportunities for your children to advance in the art of communication. Through your guidance the individuals in your group gain power in their use of words day by day.

Influence of the Home

If all the children had harmonious family relationships with many shared experiences and opportunities to talk about them, your work in developing the language arts would be comparatively simple.

Language Through Association

The child is already well on his way to mastery of his native tongue before he comes under the influence of the

257

school. What he knows about language he has learned through close association with other people. His environment, over which he has had no
choice, has played a major role in making him the type of child he is.

Without help from you he has acquired knowledge of life, people, and
how they communicate. If the language he has heard was well spoken; if
he has lived an active life as a family member; if he has joined in conversations as an individual in his own right, and has had listeners who
were interested in what he had to say, he will usually have a command
of speech, vocabulary, and grammar that will give him a great advantage
over the child less fortunate in these respects.

But regardless of home and neighborhood environment, the child's
greatest personal asset is his phenomenal ability to learn from the situations in which he participates.

Diversified Backgrounds in Language

You are of course aware of the children from homes where there is a
high degree of wrangling, discontent, strain, or other forms of tension
and strife. Such conflicts influence speech both directly and indirectly.
Then there are children from families, whether congenial or not, in
which grammatical errors are part of the accepted form of speech. Other
children come from non-English speaking families, or families where
broken English is spoken.

Children who come to school using poor English need security and a
sense of being contributing members of the group. With patience on your
part and that of the other children, as these newcomers gain in confidence, so will their enunciation and pronunciation improve. However,
children from homes where meticulous language is spoken by adults,
often have had little opportunity to talk themselves. Much of what they
have heard has been "over their heads," or about things that don't concern them directly. These children may have become inhibited, are
usually immature in their speech, and need special help.

Many immature children who enter school have to learn to substitute
words for physical contact. They want to touch, hug, kiss; they hit, bite,
pummel, and push. When Johnny snatches a toy, you teach him to ask for
it; you provide situations in which he will learn to share. Instead of
pushing others out of the way to get to the slide, Gregory learns to wait
his turn. He is learning, too, the distinction between "yours" and "mine"
and gradually replaces his earlier weapon of physical contact, force, or
vociferous crying with social graces which will help him live harmoni-
ously with others in an ever widening environment.

At the opposite extreme is the child who has been treated as an adult.
This child is inclined to have an appreciation for academic background

far beyond his years and is not satisfied with the level of conversation, discussions, and literature of the group. He, too, needs your consideration.

Meeting the Individual Child's Language Needs

Conditioned, then, by influences, some wholesome and others of a negative nature, the child comes to school with certain individual needs which have to be met if he is to develop in his use of language beyond what the home has taught him. It is your responsibility to guide each child into ever more effective ways of speaking and listening. At school, as well as at home, he needs help in associating language with meanings. He must continue to discover the infinite variety of ways in which words can represent concepts and ideas. Each child must have countless opportunities to interpret experience through his own use of language.

To accomplish this you must build upon each individual's unique background, which will demand diversified language patterns. You will be able to recognize a variance in language growth as in other phases of child development and to know that the ability to learn depends upon intelligence and mental age as well as experience.

The child with intellectual interests beyond his years needs to work and play with his peers so that he may benefit from the social give-and-take of those of his own age.

There may also be a child with such a meager background that he has little to contribute, and a very limited vocabulary to express the ideas he does have. School will bore him and he may be a problem to control.

Children, with their wide diversity in home background, need an environment that will insure growth in language power for each child. Each presents a real challenge to you. Marshall may comment:

"If I mix sand and water together and wait a while, the sand settles to the bottom of the can. Why does it do that?"

Mart may ask, "Where big blocks?"

Marshall may say, "Our Siamese cat has three kittens. A Siamese cat is different from other cats. A Siamese cat has blue eyes."

He may also tell how Siamese cats differ in color and disposition, information he has acquired from the adults at home.

Mart may say, "Me dot twain. Daddy buy twain."

Each is imparting information and sharing a home experience or observation, and each is advancing in his use of language at his own particular stage of development.

You should not allow these differences to discourage you, nor should any child be made to feel conscious of them. The Marshalls of the school, because of greater natural endowment, a richer background of experience, and present opportunity will always be in advance of the Marts. Each child, according to his ability, will have opportunity to build and manipulate, to observe, to listen and reflect, and those experiences will help give him freedom in the use of words.

Clear Auditory Impressions

Your chief concern in helping a young child speak correctly is to give him a clear auditory impression of the sounds of words by using them in natural ways. By speaking slowly and distinctly you help him to hear with more accuracy. This is done by communicating ideas to him rather than by drawing his attention directly to the speech sounds.

The young child readily imitates what he hears in his own environment. The buzzing of a bee may be reproduced, or the hum of a motor. Attention is focused on the idea he is dramatizing rather than on himself, while he gains facility in producing the sound.

The tendency of individual children to substitute one sound for another in ordinary conversation may be determined by controlled observation of his speech. Where you have no professional assistance you may listen as a child tells you about what he sees in a series of pictures, while you note his ability to pronounce various sounds independently in the words he uses. With a little thought, your picture book may be assembled so that each sound in the language is represented. If the experience is to serve you for diagnostic purposes, care should be taken that the child does not hear the word spoken just before he gives it. You may help him at a later time, after you have made your diagnosis. Your help will be incidental, and he may not be aware that you are assisting him. As you talk together you will use words which happen to contain the sounds which he needs to learn to say correctly, and he will, of his own accord, take unto himself the pronunciation he has heard you give. Pictures may suggest many of these words which will be casually drawn into the discussion. No special attention will be paid to them other than for you to pronounce them slowly and distinctly whenever they occur in your own speech.

A child first entering school may need special guidance in just a few sounds. Once these are determined, you may find ways to use them incidentally in everyday language while speaking to all the children, or to him individually.

To give the most effective auditory impressions of sounds you can use words that begin with a single consonant sound preceding the vowel. As you note Burt's substitution of "th" for "s" you may consider, for example, experiences in various centers of interest and analyze them according to the speech sounds that would naturally occur as you discuss them. The words you plan to use with Burt in conversations and discussions regarding the home center might be, for instance, *soup, sieve, sink, soak, silk*. There are other, more general words, such as *see, sit, sand, soft, sun, song, sudden, sound, size, save, so, such, send, Sunday, summer, soon*.

Effectiveness in the use of words such as the above depends upon the attention and interest of the child. Usually one who hears the correct pronunciation of a sound in ordinary conversation will later use it correctly in his own speaking. Occasionally you may find a child with whom you have to make special effort to be sure he is listening carefully to you. It is particularly helpful if you seat yourself in a chair or on your heels as you talk to him so that you appear to be the same height as he and can look directly into his face as you speak.

Other Speech Difficulties

Sometimes speech difficulties may be due to immaturity, or a tendency to be tongue-tied. Some children have a decided speech impediment. When a child has had opportunity to hear different sounds used in meaningful situations and continues to mispronounce them, or if he cannot repeat the word or sound correctly after hearing it, then it may be necessary to look further into the emotional background, or perhaps the physical. A child will not necessarily overcome his speech defect in a few days; it may take several days or weeks for him to master it. Professional help may be needed. Many school districts have a speech correctionist who works with individuals.

Children with a speech handicap may experience a feeling of failure and inadequacy. They need many types of activities in which they can be successful. They grow through being allowed to express themselves without interruption. Some are helped by receiving hearty commendation for even minor improvement; others gain more confidence if no undue attention is directed toward their speech.

Infantile Speech

Baby talk at school can cause a child much embarrassment. People who consider infantile speech entertaining show little consideration for their child. When he grows to the point where he feels different from the other children, he is apt to suffer severely. Incorrect pronunciation can lead to trouble in reading and later in spelling and word analysis.

If nothing is organically wrong, the child with such a handicap will quickly overcome this problem when he consistently hears words correctly spoken and is given special help by you. It is usually only a matter of time until all traces of baby talk disappear from his speech.

Refusal to Speak

Sometimes a child refuses to talk, which gives him a weapon against the adults within his environment. Attempting to coerce him may only give emphasis to negative behavior.

In many instances when there is no malformation of the speech organs, the cure for refusal to talk lies in ignoring tantrums or unspoken demands. When the child finds it is necessary for him to talk, he talks. On the other hand, a child from a foreign culture may find the language barrier too great, and be unable to speak, or refuse to make the effort:

> Juanita, born in Mexico, entered an overcrowded five-year-old group, one among several varying nationalities. Her teacher had no time, thought, or energy for the individual child. When Juanita went into beginning primary she was shy, insecure, and rejected, and because of her language barrier, was considered stupid and a failure. However, her new teacher saw Juanita's potentialities and under wise guidance and special attention the child became a bright eyed, eager, and enthusiastic member of her class. Within a few weeks she was talking, laughing, and carrying on interesting conversations with her peers as well as with her beloved teacher.

The Challenge to You

As a participating member of a peer group under guidance, and, where possible, with the cooperation of favorable home influences, each child must build his own skill in communication and acquire deeper shades of meaning in spoken language, because he shares in more and more meaningful experiences in which communication is needed.

Some children require much time and experience before talking; others seem to learn almost independently. However unfavorable the situation, you must have the vision and the courage to devise ways to inspire each individual to listen, to talk, to grow, and to be his true self.

II. EXPRESSION BEYOND WORDS

Barriers to Communication

The need to communicate is universal. The world is shrinking as neighbor is brought closer to neighbor, community to community, and nation to nation through faster travel, advanced postal service, newspapers and periodicals, telephone, radio and television. Translators are constantly at work when international groups meet to make what is said intelligible to those who speak other tongues. Being understood, however, is more than having words brought to the attention of someone in the language he knows. Barriers exist even between acquaintances and associates. Those in positions of authority and prestige seldom have the opportunity to know how their words and actions impress those with whom they communicate. Even when friends express themselves freely, minor or major misunderstandings often spring into being. It is difficult to get people to understand what is said or even to listen to anything they do not want to hear.

Even though the young child is frank and outspoken, there are barriers in many groups in which he must participate as he takes his place in the family, the neighborhood, the community, and the world at large. All too soon he begins to realize that he must learn to communicate in a cultural atmosphere in which people seldom dare say everything they really think, and in which what they *do* say means far more than appears on the surface. Children are quick to realize, too, that what remains unexpressed often has more significance than what is said.

The Essence of Communication

Guidance in communication is more than merely providing children with opportunities to listen, to talk, to read, to write, to paint, to model with clay, to sing, to participate in rhythmic activities, or even to create. It demands an individual interest in things the children do, things they say, things that bring special joy or grief or enthusiasm or passive acceptance or rejection or revolt or antagonism or any other emotion.

In a climate where children are free to burst forth in uninhibited ideas, creative stories, rhymes, dramatizations, poems, songs, and body rhythms they portray the depth of their thoughts, attitudes, feelings, and perceptions concerning their environment and the people in it. In the broadest sense creative expression is anything in which the individual

puts a part of himself; and every time he participates in any such enterprise he is enriching his own life and is also giving the adults in his environment a glimpse into his innermost thoughts. This is also true of art,
graphic expression, and block building. If the child's wings are not
clipped and he is unfettered from emphasis on form, variety, or adult
standards, he will naturally explore his environment through the gamut
of sound, rhythm, song, color, form, and design. Through these media
he will truly communicate his relationships with his own world and continue to take unto himself, through listening and reading, the ideas of
others. He will then impart to others what he has acquired through
verbal language. In this way he will retain his wonder, his spontaneity,
and his sense of the sublime, and will remain attuned to his own faculties
of perception. He will extend his horizon until he will continually hear
sounds he has never heard before, see colors he would otherwise have
been oblivious to, and take rhythm and song everywhere he goes.

The Role of Confidence

Many a child feels that there is a tremendous difference between him
and his elders, and that he and they are oceans apart in thought and
experience. However, if you show love and sensitivity toward the individual child's viewpoints, accord him unfailing interest, give him opportunity to talk himself out, and help his parents understand the necessity
for so doing, channels of communication may be opened and kept alive
in spite of the gulf which the child believes exists.

When the child's confidence is established and he knows that what he
has to offer will be acceptable to you and his peers, he may convey a
whole new discovery to the group without needing a comment or question to draw him out. Seven-year-old Gregory, who didn't talk for several
weeks, suddenly exclaimed, "I did an experiment. You know what? The
sugar all disappears when you sprinkle it into hot water. You can't see it
at all. That's because it dissolves. If you put it in cold water it takes it
longer to become invisible, but it does finally dissolve."

If you yourself are a good listener, who refrains from censure, you will
find as you listen to children that they will pour out their confidences to
you, and through them you will learn their expectations, dreams, and
fears. Even in creative rhymes, poems, songs, and stories children will
sometimes reveal their attitude toward a condition or circumstance. One
seven-year-old wrote:

> My dolly hates to go to bed,
> Her face is washed, her prayers are said,
> And still she hates to go to bed.
> She wants to sit and watch t.v.,
> A cowboy play she wants to see.
> "No, my dear, you cannot stay,
> "You'd be sleepy all next day,"
> But if she could stay a little while,
> She'd go to bed with a happy smile.

Wanda, six years, nine months, portrayed a sublety of feeling when she dictated out of the blue to her teacher:

"If I were a kitten I'd run to the one who really and truly loves me."

And Wendy, just six, gave evidence of her appreciation of the aesthetic when she closed her eyes and imagined what she would see if she were a moth just coming out of a cocoon:

"I see the beautiful golden sunbeams and the lovely tall trees and all the bright flowers."

Helping children understand language means listening to them and watching for responses not only in words but also in behavior.

The Language of Inner Thought and Emotion

Language is a powerful medium to convey thoughts, ideas, and feelings, and the child who has opportunities to grow normally in language expression feels satisfaction in using words to gain the respect and goodwill of his associates.

It is your privilege, as an early childhood teacher, to cultivate the language of emotions, feelings, and reactions as well as the language of ideas. Words alone are not enough. A combination of the media of communication is essential for the child's control and understanding of his part in the world. It is for you to guide each child into communicating in as many media as possible by being sensitive to his thoughts, interpretations, hopes, and needs.

Numerous times no words need be spoken between you and the child, but meanings are communicated one to another through gestures and facial expression, a genuine smile, an occasional pat on the shoulder, a nod of approbation, the art of stopping to listen to what the child has to say or to look at what he has brought—all these may be a way of communicating with him.

Through this understanding of the individuals in your group, you will help them to develop an ability to read all of these things in their peers and other associates, as well as to learn to experience another's feelings through words.

Successful communication of ideas then, implies not only that the individual can express how he himself feels, but also that he is sensitive to how the other person feels. This empathy toward other people is the basis of social graciousness and is developed much earlier in the life of the child than is often supposed.

Inflection

Tone of voice conveys far more than words alone. Oral communication needs to be vitalized by clear, fluent inflection that gives the correct idea to the listener, but inflection is more than artificial voice pitch. It must spring from a need to convey something deeper than the words alone can say.

This was brought home forcefully to the children in Mrs. Gerry Jones' beginning primary group one day:

> Six-year-old David had forgotten day after day to bring his painting apron. One morning he remembered and Mrs. Jones wrote on the chalkboard, "Oh, David!" which he read with an expression of joy, inner satisfaction, and achievement.
>
> Then Mrs. Jones said, "How would David have read this before he brought the apron?" and Ruby read, "Oh, David!" with exaggerated dejection.

Communication of the Intangibles

A child appropriates to himself his listening experiences. He approaches them without the mental blocks and hedges that grownups acquire, and is therefore more ready to receive new impressions and new understanding.

In today's cataclysmic civilization it is more and more essential for every child to become competent in listening, in discerning and independent thinking, in succinct and precise expression, and in sensitive understanding and appreciation. Only then can he be fortified for any communication experience in which he may participate. As the child listens to the mother cat call her kittens or hears the short warning note in her cry when one of her over-playful babies bites her tail, he may learn to translate some of the meanings that lie beyond the complete understanding of humans. He may by observation and listening find, too, that other animals have a means of communicating the basic needs of hunger, fear or warning, mating, or parental love through their cries.

Fostering interest and love of animals widens a child's background for verbal communication, just as does encouraging a friendly interest in people of different cultures and national backgrounds. Children are sensitive to atmosphere. A sense of brotherhood, not only with mankind, but with all living things can be either nurtured or destroyed during the growing years of childhood.

Growth in language brings the increasing ability to use words effectively, but first of all it means using language to convey meanings that are interpreted by someone who in turn responds with his reactions and ideas. Thus, growth in language expression is fostered by verbally sharing feelings and reactions with a sympathetic listener who appreciates the intangible meanings behind the spoken words.

Listening to Children

As you listen to your children you learn from them. You realize that you are the gainer in all the experiences in which a child recognizes you as a true friend whom he can trust to appreciate and understand what he says.

When you provide opportunities for children to communicate with each other in acceptable ways while they work together, you are richly rewarded. You hear many remarks through which you become aware of the individuals in your group and you are able to plan classroom experiences that will follow through on developmental needs as well as expressed ideas.

Making Use of Children's Verbalizations

With experience you gain in your ability to recognize what is valuable in the verbal expression of your children. Some of this you will record verbatim. As you do so you gain skill in making note of what your children say.

A few well selected notes provide material which you may read back to your children at a later time. As they hear you telling what they said in their exact words they are delighted. They will recognize and recall the experience.

You can become proficient in writing down key words and filling in the remainder of the sentences soon afterward, as time permits. Make note of the name of the child who spoke, and learn to date all verbalizations so that you can refer to them as evidence of individual growth in language expression.

III. GROWTH IN VOCABULARY

Influence of Your Own Enunciation

Your own enunciation and pleasantly modulated tone influence the children's speech. You should speak slowly enough for each word to be heard and recognized by the children. This helps to correct their tendency to run words together and to substitute coined words. You say, "What are you going to _____" instead of "Wattcher gonna _____" and "want to" instead of "wanna." Endings are important, too, and you should voice the full sounds of words: "coming" instead of "comin" and "smallest" instead of "smalles," to mention only two out of legion.

Careless enunciation, and failure to explain the meaning of a word, confuses and embarrasses a child on many occasions that the adult finds humorous. To laugh openly at a child may prevent him from attempting to enlarge his vocabulary.

Margery returned home early in her first year in school chanting lustily:

> "Little Miss Muffet,
> Sat on a tuffet
> Eating her curls away."

"Curds and whey" meant nothing to this five-year-old who interpreted the sound of words according to her own experiences.

Background in Meaning of Words

English is recognized as a complex language, and there are fine shades of meaning which are sometimes difficult for a child to grasp. For example, Aaron was describing his father's stature, "He is kind of—you know—high," he said.

Through conversation, questions, and examples his teacher helped the children realize the difference in the way "high" and "tall" are used. "We may speak of a high shelf, but of a tall person," she said.

The exact meaning of words is often confusing even to adults who are learning a language other than their native tongue. The ability of persons to acquire a working vocabulary in a foreign language is surprising and deserves the utmost commendation, but occasionally a humorous situation may result from the use of a word in an entirely different setting from which it was learned.

> A family newly arrived on American shores was struggling valiantly with the language. The young son was fascinated with some of the longer words. When he asked about the word *procrastinate* his father told him it meant "to put off." When the school bus was nearing his home the boy said to the driver, "Will you please procrastinate me at the next corner?"

Difficulty in interpretation of words may also be due to the association which is so strongly in the child's mind that he does not see any other meaning.

When Marilyn heard that her beloved aunt was not able to see anyone because she was in such acute pain, Marilyn said, "But mother, how can a pain be cute if it's so bad we can't even see her?"

> One morning Dennis, age five years, four months, announced to the class, "My grandmother's head came off." The teacher passed it over lightly and went on to another topic, but the child seemed disturbed.
>
> Two days later Dennis said, "My mother's gone away. She had to go help my grandmother find her head."
>
> The puzzled teacher did a little investigating on her own and found that Dennis' mother had remarked to his father, "It's a big problem and mother has lost her head. I'll have to go to her or there will be no end of trouble."

Mention of any known word may suggest something different to each member of the group, and words a child already knows may have for him either a pleasant or an unpleasant connotation, depending upon the philosophy, the point of view, and the circumstances under which he learned them. For example, if a child has been painfully scratched by a cat, the word "cat" for him will have an unpleasant association, but if he has delighted in a pet kitten of his own, enjoyed cuddling it, caring for it, and watching it lap milk, the word will create a pleasant aura.

An activity that calls forth much enthusiasm is to give each member of the group a noun, such as *brook, ocean, mountain, house,* or any other word for which there is a concrete concept, and then ask the children to write or paint a picture employing adjectives that describe the noun.

Building an Enriched Vocabulary

In laying a foundation for the language arts, much emphasis needs to be devoted to helping the children develop and enrich their vocabularies.

The child garners new vocabulary through hearing words in use.

In teaching children it is of utmost importance that their concepts of words be meaningful and true. Longer, more difficult words, if used with purpose, often become a part of the child's vocabulary more readily than seemingly simple ones. These concepts are formed in many ways. The impressiveness of the occasion seems to have a direct bearing here through association with the word and the person, or animal. Outdoors, the teacher commended John for his *intelligent thinking* on solving a problem. Later she heard two other children talking. One was saying in all earnestness, "Are you using your intelligent thinking?"

In discussing standards for work, this teacher used such expressions as:

"We complete our work."
"When we work efficiently
things are well done."
"There is a logical place
to put things. Think what it is."
"Our problems can usually
be solved when we discuss them."

Each statement was then carefully explained in terms the children could understand:

Randy sat at the library table, scattered the books, and left them. The children then discussed whether or not Randy had *completed* his task. Since standards for care of the room had already been set up, the children were quick to note that Randy had left the table without *completing* his work. Randy then returned to the table and put things in proper order. He had *completed* his job.

Debbie put on her apron without buttoning it. She had not *completed* her preparation for work. Then she buttoned her apron and her preparation was *complete*. Every child in the room understood the statement, "We do things completely."

Children also have words firmly imprinted on their minds through story, poem, song, and dramatization, as well as through seeing, touching, hearing, smelling, and sometimes tasting.

That children are impressed by words they hear when used in meaningful ways is beyond dispute. However, evidence of this may be delayed. The adult may not know whether the child remembered the word until later when he suddenly employs it in something he is saying:

Kenneth, with several other five-year-olds, was watching the sun play hide-and-seek with the clouds. First, it would be shadowy and then bright. "Look, Mrs. Vigus," said Ken to his teacher, "the sun shines and then it doesn't."

"Yes," said Mrs. Vigus, "The weather man said there would be intermittent showers today." She went on to say the same thing in a different way to make sure the children understood the meaning of *intermittent*.

A day or two later *intermittent* came up again. "That's something that starts and stops, like rain," Joe said. Mrs. Vigus gave a careful explanation of how other things might be intermittent, too.

Nearly three weeks later Ken went home with a pain in his side. His mother tried to remain calm, but he sensed her concern. "Don't worry, Mom," Ken said. "The pains are only intermittent."

In many instances a word can be understood because the rest of the sentence sheds light on it. This is particularly true of a word that has some bearing on an experience in which the child has participated. He knows what is intended to be said so he knows what the word means even though he may not have heard it before. Sometimes when the word is used as a result of an experience it does not really become the child's own, for while he may use it correctly he may have gained only one rather unusual meaning through the way the word happened to be used.

Children can learn to express ideas in different ways when meanings of words are discussed. Even five-year-old children can take part creditably in a discussion of words whose meanings are within their experience.

When Mrs. Vigus' five- and six-year-olds were discussing the word *sturdy* they decided it meant "nice and strong." Robert added, "Strong as father." His comment not only revealed his idea of "strong," but also his idea of "fathers."

After a walk, this same group gave evidence of the influence of their discussions about how to stay together when, as they were returning to the room, Mark said, "A group means nobody is too far behind."

Soren added, "It means nobody is too far ahead either."

These comments brought forcefully to Mrs. Vigus the fact that children take to themselves the concrete application of words rather than the generalization. To these children "group" did mean "stay together." She said to the children, "When we stay together, we stay in the group. Each of us is part of the group."

The children were interested and spent some time discussing the word "group." Becky said, "When some of us are working with blocks, that's a group, too." The children discovered other groups, like those at the easels, and still others in the home area and those working with clay.

They placed their chairs into one big group. Then they re-arranged them in two smaller groups, then three, and finally four different groups. This brought up a new word, "arrange." "We can arrange the furniture in different ways. We place it where we want it to be. We arrange it," said Mrs. Vigus.

Small wonder that "out of the mouths of these babes" came such words as "crustaceous," as they displayed their extensive shell collection, and "propeller," "stabilizer," "fuselage," "strutz," "wind sock," and "hangar," in connection with their block building of airplanes, and discussions of planes they had observed or flown in.

You can help the parents to realize that if there is cooperation in the home, the family can help a child greatly in expanding his vocabulary. A family not alert to this possibility laughed when Timmy remarked, "I certainly cherish my new book," and Carl, his older brother, teased, "What's cherish? Is it something good to eat? If it's not, then don't use it here."

In contrast, in her home ten-year-old Susan used the word *rapport* and was thrilled to learn it was really a new word to the family and that not even Mother or Daddy had heard it.

Acquiring Word Meanings Incidentally

You, as teacher, become almost like a living glossary to young children because you increase their repertoire of words for creative expression through your own use of meaningful and appropriate vocabulary. You introduce these new words in context and follow them by saying the same thing in words that are familiar to the children. In this way you give them an example of clear, simple, and colorful expressions which encourages them to enjoy language and develop a larger vocabulary. This gives your children a background, so that when they are ready to use the picture dictionary and later the real dictionary, they experience the activity with delight and are eager and interested in words as a means of communication.

Hearing expressions that are not "watered down" gives the children opportunity to reach up for new words.

For the past week the days had been gloomy, but during the course of the morning Miss Maxwell's children noticed how the wind scurried the clouds across the skies until the whiteness disappeared over the horizon. The sun shone warm and bright, and a bird came and sang from the top of a telephone pole. Plainly the group of eight-year-olds had their thoughts on the out of doors, and so did their teacher.

"Let's go outside and enjoy all the loveliness of the morning and look for signs of spring," Miss Maxwell suggested, and the children eagerly assented.

Kirk said, "Look! The trees are beginning to turn green."

Miss Maxwell thought this would give a splendid opportunity to use correctly the word *delicate,* which had been misused previously.

"Yes," she said, "I love that delicate green of the budding trees. The leaves are soft and tender and delicate, too. They are exquisite."

Later in the day the children wrote their impression of the morning's experience:

> Spring is all around us.
> Everything outside is soft and tender and delicate.
> Everywhere we look we see exquisite new life.
> The birds are singing about it.
> Soft tender leaves are opening,
> and the trees look as if they are singing, too.
> Bowing and bending in the delicate breeze
> the trees are laughing at the warm sun.

Opportunities for individuality to find expression are continually provided in the democratic classroom. Miss Maxwell's room was of this calibre. As is often true, a more protracted learning developed out of the above shared experience. One interesting phase of this is that each child will use the new descriptive words which hitherto were foreign to his vocabulary. Sometimes the carry-over is direct. Miss Maxwell was not surprised when, the next morning, Wayne brought a bee into the classroom, and when the group about him were examining it, he remarked, "It has such delicate wings."

"His buzz is soft and delicate, too," said Leslie.

Miss Maxwell realized that this interest was genuine, and would be well worth capitalizing upon at this time. She suggested books in which more information could be found, told stories about bees and how they live and work; and eventually there were many follow-up experiences, among them a visit to an estate where there was a "live museum" that enabled the children to see through glass the bees at work in their hive.

The day after this visit, when the children were writing a "true" story, several of them centered around bees. Among these were the following:

Bees

Bees have two eyes just like we do.
They are very smart insects.
Bees are very delicate.
Their legs are skinny.
The buckets on their legs are often so heavy
        they cannot fly.
A bee will not sting you unless you annoy him.
The stinger feels like a hot prick.
When you touch it the stinger burns like fire.

The ultimate in vocabulary carry-over presented itself in the scrawly handwriting of another child:

"Tommy lives in the country.
He is gathering honey the bees collected.
The worker bee is so smart that it is hard to catch him.
When he works he goes buzz, buzz, buzz, buzz.
The worker bee is small, but the queen is much larger.
She is busy all the time because she lays two thousand eggs a day
My mother would be very delicate if she had that many babies a day."

Capitalizing on the child's immediate interests creates a wonderful environment for learning. Children discover it is fun to find the word that will best express what they feel about an experience or a sensation. If encouraged they will ask questions, toy with and even coin acceptable words.

After you have given your children many examples, and they have had happy times experimenting with lovely words, they will enjoy thinking of different ways they can say something that needs to be said. "Beth was laughing to herself." "Beth was chuckling softly." "Beth smiled and her eyes were dancing": three delightful ways of expressing the same thing.

Such experiences enable a child to build word pictures that accurately present the images he wishes to evoke in the minds of his listeners. He not only gets but gives enjoyment to others through his increasing power in the use of words.

A challenging experience for upper primary children is a dictionary activity. You may put words on one set of cards and the meaning of words on another set, and then shuffle them. Each child may draw a card from the box. If he draws a card with a meaning he tells what the word is; if he draws a word he explains its meaning.

Homonyms

The young child is confronted with an oral language which attaches meaning to only a few separate sounds in an infinite variety of combinations. The vocabulary he can command in his own speaking lags somewhat behind that which he understands but his rate of acquisition of new words is rapid. Among them are found many homonyms: "words having the same pronunciation but different in meaning and often in spelling, as *bear* and *bare*." Even a five-year-old speaks fluently about the "board" he needs for his work, and the hole he "bored" in it, imitates the conductor's call "all aboard," understands what his uncle means when he tells how he works for his "room and board," knows his grandfather is a member of the "school board," and that Aunt Ellen is "bored" listening to Uncle Ben's fish stories. Each of these words fills a separate need in communication of ideas.

Adults with years of experience with language and its shades of meaning can shift rapidly from one connotation to another. Sometimes they fail to realize what a problem a word with more than one meaning may present to the young child.

Jimmy's teacher thought her six- and seven-year-olds would enjoy doing some art work centered around Halloween. She gave each child a large sheet of manila paper with a short verse printed at the bottom. Each child was to create a picture about his verse. The verse Jimmy received was:

Bats are flying in the air,
One flew down and sat on a chair!

Jimmy thought the verse was rather strange, but he was anxious to please Miss B. So he proceeded to paint his picture of the bats—baseball bats—which were the only kind he had ever heard of. He painted baseball bats that were flying, sitting, and standing. The teacher had assumed that he knew that bats were associated with owls and black cats at Halloween, but he did not.

Realizing the children's need to feel at ease in shifting from one meaning of a word to another, you may suggest that your upper primary children choose some word that has more than one meaning and write a creative story, using that word in as many ways as possible.

Nine-year-old Danny was gaining security in shifting readily from one connotation to another when he wrote the following story on "Spring":

One spring day Jack said to Peter, "Can you stay over-night at my house so we can get up early and go fishing down by the nice cool spring?"

"No," said Peter, "Father has gone to the city to buy a new chair. A spring popped out of our old one."

"Do you have an old pair of shoes," said Jack.

"Yes," answered Peter.

"Then let's make some spring shoes," said Jack.

"All right, Jack, that will be good spring fun."

So the two boys made spring shoes.

They were hopping in their spring shoes one day when a man came up and said, "Boys, that's a good idea to have spring shoes. I am going to make spring shoes a toy."

And he did, and from that day on people have been buying spring shoes.

Similes Appeal to Children, Too

A simile (a figure of speech in which one thing, action, or relation is likened or compared to something of a different kind or quality) is a natural form of expression for a young child. David, age 5/5, says:

"That drumbeat goes just like my heart beat."

Whatever the child observes that is new he tends to associate with some impression from his own experience. Children's vivid imaginations run riot when they have an opportunity to express their individual interpretation of life experiences in words.

The simple and delightful originality and depth of feeling of children's similes is a welcome relief from the age-old clichés of the adult world.

Five-year-olds spontaneously said:

"As cold as my puppy's nose."

"As rainy as our shower bath."

"As little as an ant."

This interest in expressing ideas in terms of previous experiences means that similes become more useful to the child as he grows in his ability to express himself through words.

Middle primary children originated the following:

"As hot as the pavement on my bare feet."

"As clean as Mom's washing."

"Soft like smoke curling through the air."

"As tall as our morning glory vines."

"As wide as fluffy clouds."

Your appreciation of such expressions when the children use them in talking will encourage other similar ones. You may wish to discuss what a simile is.

Upper primary children may become adept at suggesting new comparisons in describing things that impress them in the life around them.

"As loud as a jet crashing the sound barrier."

"As still as a shadow."

"As quiet as a snail crawling."
"As silent as the light from a star."

SELECTED REFERENCES

Brown, Roger W., WORDS AND THINGS, Glencoe, Ill., The Free Press, 1958.

Krauss, Ruth, A HOLE IS TO DIG; A FIRST BOOK OF FIRST DEFINITIONS, New York, Harper, 1952.

McFarland, Wilma, Ed., Junior Literary Guild, FOR A CHILD, Philadelphia, Westminster Press, 1947.

Minteer, Catherine, WORDS AND WHAT THEY DO TO YOU, Evanston, Ill., Row, Peterson, & Co., 1953.

Rand, Ann, SPARKLE AND SPIN, A BOOK ABOUT WORDS, New York, Harcourt Brace & Co., 1960.

IV. CONVERSATION

The Value of the Spoken Word

In spite of the barriers that often have to be overcome before there can be a free and candid conversation between people, there is, perhaps, nothing more intellectually refreshing than a lively exchange of constructive thoughts between congenial friends. To quote the old Chinese maxim, which is as good philosophy today as when it was first written:

A single conversation
across the table
with a wise man
is better than ten years'
mere study of books.

Words for words' sake lack vitality. Language grows when it is a part of life; when it meets a real need of conveying ideas from person to person.

Children need a background of rich oral experience in which words are immediately associated with activities, with concepts, and with natural everyday symbols that represent ideas.

Your Own Objectives in Oral Expression

When young children talk, discuss, or tell stories, you, as teacher, should have several objectives in mind. You want the child to be able to speak before the group without embarrassment and with confidence and self-assurance. You want to help him to have clear ideas and to express himself in sentences in a distinct well-modulated voice, with clear enunciation, correct pronunciation, and concise expression. Young children who are as yet unacquainted with the hackneyed and the trite, have a unique, child-like quality of expression, and tell things exactly as they feel or see them.

To think through what he has to say and to express it clearly and briefly is more of a problem for one individual than for another. Some children speak readily, others too freely, while still others need to be drawn out. As the children talk things over together, under your guidance they learn to recognize these differences in themselves and to assist each other in this respect.

As your children have opportunity to listen and to talk with sympathetic friends in a democratic classroom, each according to his own abilities, the art of conversation thrives and grows.

Greetings on Arrival at School

An opportunity for language expression that is frequently overlooked is the spontaneous exchange of ideas, which is such a genuine part of arriving at school each day. In order to make this natural and informal, you give your individual attention to it, greeting each child warmly and sincerely with some special, personal message. After a few words with you the child may go directly to his work, instead of being sent outside to await the summons of a bell.

In some instances administrative policy may demand that all children be outside until time to come in *en masse*. If this policy obtains in your school, you may be able to arrange for your children to come in and talk briefly with you as they arrive, then go out to the yard until called inside. The personal greeting sets the tone for the entire day and through it you become better acquainted with your group, can plan with their needs and interests in mind, and can adapt what you have to say to individual backgrounds and experiences.

Bob, 6/6, said as he greeted his teacher one morning:
"I'm not going to be here very long. My Mom's going to get a new baby. My brother and sister and I are going to my grandmother's for a few days."

Miss L. asked, "Will you go to school while you are at your grand-mother's?"

"No," said Bob, "I'll have to help my grandmother and grandfather."

"I hope our new baby will be a girl because I've got a sister and a brother and Carol needs a sister."

Later . . . "Our baby came, and I'm glad it's a girl because I have a sister and a brother, and now my sister has a sister and two brothers."

Dismissal

In a similar manner, the dismissal at the end of the day can make or mar the attitude with which the child goes home.

If there have been individual control problems the child involved needs to be assured that "all's well," and that it was the thing that he did that was unpopular with you and his peers, and not he, himself. Satisfy him that you are still his friend, that you hold no grudge or ani-mosity toward him, and that your feeling or the feeling of his associates has not changed.

The best public relations envoy, as well as the finest teacher-child rap-port the school can ever have is to send each child home happy and eager to share the day's activities with his family and friends and enthusiastic for tomorrow to come so he can go back to it all again.

This demands a planned dismissal with time for a summary of the day's learnings, sharing thoughts and ideas, some quiet conversation, perhaps, a song or two, and an individual "good-by" to each child, with some brief but vital personalized message.

Telling What Happens

Talking over what has happened, making plans together, and evalu-ating experiences is a natural way to teach language. As children work in a democratic environment, ideas are communicated. Here, conversation is a medium of exchange related to what has just happened and what is about to take place. Thoughts can change what might happen, particu-larly when suggestions are compared. Action can be guided by words. This leads to further thinking and further exchange of ideas.

There is much valuable language expression through the child's relat-ing of current happenings. At first these are of value because they are of interest to the child who is speaking. The fact that he stands before the group and relates something may be enough to justify his doing so. First attempts may be brief homely statements such as: "I raced my Daddy to the corner, and I won," or "My tooth came out," or "My baby sister cried all night. She's sick," or "I played with my dog when I got home from school." A number of unrelated accounts will have varying degrees of value to other children in the group. Through skillful guidance you may accept each for its worth as a sincere expression of what the child who is speaking has to offer, and you may blend these into an experience of general interest through introducing appropriate songs, action plays, and poems. A very brief story from your own experience gives recognition to the others who have had similar experiences.

Gradually the first efforts give way to attempts to relate what fits in with the general trend of thinking. One group of lower primary children referred to this as "matching." The question they asked themselves was, "Does what I want to say match what we are talking about?"

Billy might tell the others, "I went with my dad and we drove a long way. We went to see a new house."

His statement may have no particular bearing on what the children in the room are doing. The children may learn to discriminate between related and unrelated ideas by your asking where Billy's story would fit. "It would be helpful when we are talking about ways of going to different places, or doing things with daddy, or kinds of houses. If this is something Billy really wants to tell us about, when would be a good time for us to hear it?"

This brings up the necessity of spontaneous expression, such as that provided for at snack time.

Lunch or Snack Time Brings Language Opportunities

Children may be taught to regard "snack time" as an opportunity for happy, spontaneous, constructive sharing of ideas. At first you will need to guide the conversation into topics of interest to all the children, and help them remember to listen while someone else is talking. The group soon accepts the attitude that lunch is an opportunity to discuss current happenings and interests of individuals. Earlier in the day topics may be brought up which could well have more time given to them. You say, "This is something we can talk more about at snack time, today," and encourage the children to recall such things for discussion at the lunch table.

What Mary tells about may remind Billy of a similar experience he has had, and as he talks others may have something further to say on the same matter. Taking turns, waiting while another person finishes talking, presenting topics of interest to others in a way to command the attention and respect of the group—these are abilities that are developed during snack time, whether it be mid-day, mid-morning, or mid-afternoon. Your questions and comments will help the children think, and will teach them to direct their conversation along constructive lines. To be a participating member of a conversational group of this type is an experience which the individual will remember all his life, not necessarily because of what was discussed, but because being able to listen and to speak under these conditions is a highly desirable asset.

Controlling Participation

The ability to say what needs to be said in a few effective statements can be acquired even by the five-year-old. The necessity of this became very clear to Penny during the course of her first few weeks of school. Penny was the type who had something to say on every occasion and on all topics, and to help her the teacher made it especially emphatic that what anybody said should really be important and should match what others were saying. "Think carefully to yourself and be sure you have something to contribute to the conversation," Mrs. Williams said to Penny. Then Mrs. Williams explained what this meant.

Penny visibly restrained herself for some minutes. After what seemed like several rather boring statements from other children, Penny said earnestly, "But, Mrs. Williams, I *really* have something to contribute."

Ability to talk to a point of interest is an art that develops through verbal conversation. The happy balance between listening and speaking is an important aspect of this.

Oral language is controlled not by permission or restriction from you. Under your guidance the children learn not only to listen, but also to communicate their ideas in order to accomplish common purposes. There is much need for talking and for giving close attention while someone else is speaking. Learning takes place through many experiences of thinking things through, illustrating ideas with concrete examples, discussing and exchanging viewpoints, and evaluating in terms of goals set up. Under these conditions language flourishes.

You will want to commend, but to avoid excessive praise of the efforts of all, especially of the shy, reticent child; guide over-aggressive children from monopolizing the conversation; help each child to think for himself, to listen critically, to ask questions courteously, to say what he means, and to defend statements if challenged. You will avoid interruptions. There are times when children need help in solving problems, and it is important to know when this need exists or when each child should be encouraged to work alone. In the beginning your help in clarifying and summarizing is essential.

Conversations will sometimes be carried on at length when the interest is high, but you must be alert to terminate them before the children tire.

Sharing Things Brought from Home

The process of presenting objects brought from home may be merely routine unless you help draw the children out. It can be an opportunity for the individual child to put ideas into words in an interesting way. Other children may help, not only by listening, but by asking intelligent questions that will serve to clarify what the child is recounting.

Personalizing the presentation by direct questions and answers, if gradually developed in a natural way, can bring good results. With individuals who hesitate, "What else would you like to know?" calls forth more language expression from the group, as well as from the child who has the floor. Some of the questions may stem from a personal acquaintance between one child and another as when Bob asks Jane, "Is it as big as your brother?"

As long as there is genuine thinking going on, and the interest is of vital concern to the children, and along constructive lines, this procedure offers splendid possibilities for improving language fluency.

When children first bring objects to show, attention may center on the novelty of each. To avoid having the process of sharing become a mechanical one, the children may think:

"What would we like to know about Ethel's first aid kit?" (or whatever it may be that a particular child has to share.)

They may ask:

"How did you get the kit, Ethel?"

"Show us what you can do with it."

"What is the box made of?"

With the help of these queries and a few suggested by you, Ethel presents enough about her treasured possession to hold the attention of her group, not only by showing her kit, but by what she has to tell.

The group may discuss what individuals need to keep in mind as they talk. For instance, "How do I take good care of it?" and "Where do I keep it?" or "How large is it as compared with some other object?"

Even the beginning groups can learn to keep certain points in mind when they present something they have discovered at home, school, or elsewhere. You and the children together may keep bringing up questions until the group is ready to formulate a list of those most commonly asked, which will, of course, be varied from time to time.

Incidental Sharing Can Contribute to Group Learning

Under adroit teacher guidance, incidental sharing of individual interests can provide recognition for first one child and then another, and yet be a series of worthwhile learning experiences for relatively immature children. Observing the inter-action between teacher, group, and individuals during a given block of time furnishes opportunity to study the continuity of language expression which guided sharing of this type affords. The teacher's steering can safeguard individual initiative and make the children better able to participate as a group.

During one twenty-minute interval early in the year a group of six-year-olds "shared" an odd assortment of objects. The responses of the children as their teacher spontaneously followed through on "leads" illustrates how individuality can be respected while shared interests become meaningful to all.

Carol was a child who shrank from talking, yet she volunteered to show her toys. She set the doll on the table and opened her suitcase while she mumbled her words.

Complaints came from the others, "I can't hear."

Miss Rose saw that Carol was absorbed in handling the toys, and knew it was a big step forward for this child to go before the group at all.

"Carol," said Miss Rose, "what you say is interesting. Tell Bertha and Ann and Robert how you got your doll. When you talk to someone in the group, then all of us can hear."

Her teacher's encouragement seemed to help Carol. "My big sister gave her to me, and she gave me the suitcase, too."

Miss Rose saw that the children's attention was centered on the doll. She started to sing one of the group's favorite songs, "My Doll," and Carol went back to her place in the group, smiling.

The difference in development and personality between one child and another, though evident, was never mentioned by Miss Rose.

Kathleen came forward with a doll that wore skates. "Her name is Roberta," she said, as she stood the doll on the table for all to see.

"Do the skates really roll?" Robert asked.

Apparently this question had never occurred to Kathleen, who thought about it seriously before giving her answer, "They really don't roll, but I like to pretend they do."

"You have to use your imagination," said Miss Rose, "whenever you plan something. You have to be able to see things the way you would like to have them. The man who built the big bridge had to plan it before he could build it. That means he had to have imagination to see it in his head, first. He had to imagine how it would look in order to build it that way."

"Kathleen sees how the skates would work if they were real skates. She has imagination," added Miss Rose.

Kathleen made her doll skate on the table and said, "See how I make her skate. Like this."

"That reminds me of a song," Jack said. "Take your roller skates and come along with me." It was a short song. Jack sang it, then Miss Rose picked up his tune, and the group sang it with him the second time.

Tommy had brought a box of commercial paints suitable for handpainting. He held up each bottle and named the colors. As he did so, he mentioned something else in the room of the same color. Miss Rose made mental note of the readiness being exhibited for color words. "There is a book on our library shelf, Tommy, that has pictures of different colored jars of paint. When you find it you may show it to us.'

While Tommy was looking for the book, Eugene brought his yellow and red truck and rolled it on the table. "It can go pretty fast," he explained. "It has ball bearing wheels." He held the wheels up for all to see as he rolled each one with his fingers. "See how they keep rolling for a long time."

"Tell us something more about ball bearing wheels, Eugene," said Miss Rose. "What are ball bearings?"

Eugene's father was a mechanic and Miss Rose knew she was not asking the impossible of this child.

"Well, you see, ball bearings are little tiny balls inside the wheel so when it turns,—well—it turns on those little balls."

"And what is that rod called that goes through the center of the wheel, where the ball bearings are?" asked Miss Rose.

"That is the axle," said Eugene.

"What would you think of looking up different kinds of axles and wheels and telling us more about them?" asked Miss Rose.

"I'd like that," said Eugene.

"You have been checking out books at the library, haven't you?" recalled Miss Rose. "When you go to the library, Eugene, look for a book about wheels. I will give you the name of one to ask for before you leave today."

"My dad will read it to me," said Eugene.

Tommy had located the book and now came forward to show it to the children. "What color would Eugene's red and yellow truck be if the two colors were mixed *before* the truck was painted?" asked Miss Rose.

Eugene was appointed to find out and show the others the next day. The question arose about mixing colors to make the shade of green like Tommy's shirt. It was decided that Tommy should find out when he worked with paints soon afterwards by experimenting with the colors.

Jeffrey had a barn, with animals made to scale. He put them into their pens, and told about them. Miss Rose quoted an original poem about a farm.

Children's Needs Change in Regard to Sharing Ideas

As he grows in his security before the group the individual child may gradually learn to evaluate his presentation. He may consider such points as:

What did I do well?

Did I talk directly to the group?

Could everyone hear me?

What made my talk interesting?

How could I improve on it?

As growth through sharing takes place, there is a shift in emphasis. Many teachers feel it is wiser to have the "sharing experience" center around what has been done at school. There is a time and place for encouraging the children to relate their out-of-school experiences, but these should contribute to the expansion of what has transpired at school.

When children come together to discuss and exchange ideas and plans at school, they get the same value in language expression and still have the benefit of the social living that goes along with it.

Conversation Associated with Children's Art Work

The child's first use of art media may bring little communication of his ideas except as he talks about the paper, the brushes, the paint, or the way he is working. His verbalizations may give some indication of his mental processes and are worth recording from this standpoint.

With enough experience and opportunity to create in art media children reach the stage at which they convey ideas through paint or clay, and readily express in words what they have in mind. The painting or ceramic work is as much a means of communication as is the language, and showing what he has done can be a source of satisfaction to the child. In the early experiences, however, he may need to work undisturbed without trying to communicate ideas. When interest is expressed in what the child is doing, whatever statement he is ready to make should be accepted in the spirit of genuine appreciation. His first remarks may be a casual, "I am painting," or "This blue is pretty." His attention is obviously centered on the manipulation of the material.

Later, after he has had more experience, the same child may be happy to tell how he achieved a certain effect with his brush, or his hand, as the case may be. He may pass through a period in which he is interested in the form, design, and color combinations of his work. In due time, he may be able to represent people and familiar objects, in a crude way, but satisfying to him. Still later his work may illustrate a complete story or scene from a play. At whatever stage, you can help him recognize the worth of his effort and the interesting effects of his unique combinations of line, color, and form. Questions to help him express verbally the significance of his work are justified.

Six-year-old Charles found true delight in the "whorls" he captured in his handpainting. His teacher's comment, "How did you get it to look like that, Charles?" gave recognition to his stage of development.

Ruth, in upper primary, discovered that the repeated rhythm of her outstretched thumb in a circular motion gave the effect of a third dimension. She was delighted to tell how she moved her arm in order to produce this in her painting. "It makes it look as if you could reach way back into my picture and pull something out," she explained.

Advancement in Language Through Enriched Activities

Much language expression comes out when the complete depth of the child's art experience is recognized.

When he has reached this stage in the communication of ideas there will be a rich flow of language as he engages in block building, home center, clay modeling, and construction, just as there is in his painting activities. These spontaneous conversations and interchange of ideas and experiences are an important by-product of the experience itself.

All these types of activities where you follow the leads of the children and direct their thinking into problem solving are really giving them the foundation for being good conversationalists.

Instead of permitting a child's statement to pass unnoticed, an alert teacher will ask questions that will help the child see the implications of what he has said. There is an art in bringing out interesting points, and in creating a learning situation for the entire group, as well as for the individual who is talking.

Surprises

Even the most sophisticated will usually respond enthusiastically to surprises. Some new material or piece of equipment may be wrapped attractively. The children may feel, measure, hold, smell, shake, and listen to its sound, and finally make a conjecture as to the contents. This is an excellent experience in association of words with sensory impressions.

Some objects that might be wrapped by you for a "surprise": a new truck to be used for block building; a vase for flowers; a new tambourine or sand blocks or drum or other musical instrument; a toy animal; a punching bag; a fireman's hat; a new picture for the file; a new book; a puzzle; a sponge for cleaning up.

The children themselves might bring surprises to be shared: a new dress for the doll in the home center; some pine cones; a pumpkin; a story book to be loaned to the group for a time; an abandoned bird's nest; an unusual rock for the rock collection; an interesting shell; there are unnumbered objects which could stimulate interest and a desire for further learning, and serve as a motivation for many types of language activity.

With prior knowledge of what it might contain, the parent might assume the responsibility of wrapping the child's gift or loan, so that he himself could share in the surprise.

This is a media that should be used with discretion so that a "surprise" really stimulates the language of eager curiosity.

V. ORAL DISCUSSION

Discussion implies a more formal type of communication than conversation, but even the youngest members of the school group can learn to participate in discussions if they are vital and within the children's maturation level.

Individual and Committee Responsibilities

There can be much valuable use of language as the children learn to help care for the room, the equipment they are using, supplies, and other details. There is a sharp contrast between rooms where the teacher does such things for the children, and those where the children feel the satisfaction of assuming these responsibilities. Individuals may take over certain definite duties which are rotated from day to day, or week to week. Discussing how this will be done, and who will do it, leads to a common understanding. Much of this is oral, especially with the younger children. Development is gradual.

Opportunities for the More Retiring Children

Your children must realize that there are two helpful ways they may participate in a group discussion; either by speaking or by listening. By far the greater part of discussion is giving attention to whomever is speaking. To the less aggressive child this comes naturally and he may never speak unless you make special note of the fact that he needs guidance in expressing himself as a member of the group.

Remember always that the more quiet children need a limited audience at first. There are many times during the day when you will find it possible to draw together a few children while others are profitably engaged in other activities. This is helpful all through the early childhood years, but particularly in the five- and six-year-old groups. With older groups the retiring child is many times drawn into the discussion if you can help him find something to talk about that adds to the experience of the other children over and above what they can contribute.

The small, spontaneous, informal discussion may be the only occasion when the less aggressive children will take an active speaking part in a group. As they gain more confidence they will participate more in the discussions of the entire group.

Opportunities for Group Discussion

Each day offers endless opportunities for the children to learn the nature and value of talking things over together.

Before going on walks around the school or in the neighborhood, or on field trips, the children formulate a few simple rules. This is language in action expressed perhaps as follows:

Wait at any corner before crossing the street.
Follow the chosen leaders of the group.
Walk on the sidewalk.
Ask before touching anything.

Children may also help state the purpose of the walk, after discussing it together. It need not be for a more specific purpose than to enjoy fresh air and watch for signs of fall, winter, or spring. Afterward, as the children talk, they will ask questions and describe what they have seen and done. Clouds, shadows, and reflections; trees, flowers, plants, animals can be described in many different ways. Words are being used to represent shared experiences, which is a vital purpose of discussion for the young child.

As leader of discussions, it is your responsibility first of all to create a friendly atmosphere; to be sure that the problem is appropriate for the group and worthy of the time devoted to it. What will be discussed needs to come from the group. You should encourage but not force the children to participate. They will talk because they have something to contribute.

The children should know why a topic is being discussed. They will gradually realize that it is for better understanding of a problem. Types of suggested discussions are: Two people want to use the same ball, or other equipment, at the same time. You may say, "Let's talk it over because these two children need to solve their problem." A child wants to find out more about a homework problem. Where can he find it? The group may discuss what research they would like to do or what angles there are to the problem, or they may share common knowledge. What do they want to know about the gas company's installations? Why are the streets torn up? Several group members may have facts to contribute; a member may have questions he wants answered; or a small group may discuss a film they have seen together, some other shared experience, or something they have done with their families or friends. Together you will discover common interests and draw conclusions.

Discussions by children in the classroom are evaluated first of all in terms of individual participation. In the children's earliest discussions each speaker presents what is closest to his own heart. There is a period of growth here in which the trend of the discussion may jump rapidly from one area to another, held together only by a slim strand of association of ideas. Many five- and six-year-olds are in this stage of development.

Guiding Children's Growth Through Discussions

As children grow in ability to communicate there is a strong incentive for written records. You are consciously preparing them to assume responsibility for record keeping when they are ready to do so.

Questions are discussed, also, which may not be directly related to what the children are doing, but they arise through something one of the children has mentioned or an idea that you yourself may bring up. Topics of vital interest "strike fire" within the group and a genuine discussion takes place quite spontaneously.

A discussion may reveal the background of the group members; what they know about a certain topic and what experience they have had regarding it.

There are many types of discussions that draw upon the resources of the individuals within the groups. With guidance, upper primary children are capable of:

Setting up a scientific experiment and following through on it.
Formulating and solving a problem in arithmetic.
Presenting opinions and verifying facts.
Withholding judgments until further data are presented.

Reviewing a story or a book and discussing what the characters did:

What problems did they face?
What did they do about them?
What would you do if you were one of the characters in this story?

Upper primary children will take part in any of these various types of discussion and in others, too, in keeping with their ability, maturation, and experience. As leader, you suggest the next points to consider. You pick up leads. You summarize and bring the group back to main purposes and points which need further consideration. Gradually they learn to throw ideas into the discussion in keeping with the needs of group thinking. As leader of discussions you never lose sight of your role as teacher and guide of children's growth.

Good Questions for Discussion

Questions can be stated in such a way that they call forth more discussion in one form than in another. A question that calls for a "yes" or "no" answer usually does not lead to much of a discussion. "Does water run down hill" can be answered simply by a statement of fact. However, "Why does water run down hill?" calls for more thought.

"Let's discuss coming into the room" is no question at all. It needs to be broken down into several parts; for instance, "What is the best way to come into the room?" or "What are some of the ways we might come into our room?" followed by:

"What would happen if everybody ran in?"

"Why is it best to walk?"

"What happens when everybody walks in?"

The discussion then needs to be followed up with a positive demonstration.

Children can learn to discriminate between questions and decide which ones should be followed through. For example: when the question "What size hole makes the best doorway for a wren?" is brought up during a discussion, upper primary children can decide without difficulty, "Is this question to be answered by opinion or by fact? How can we find out the facts? Is it best for the group to discuss this, or should someone look it up?"

This question has other aspects that might be discussed, for instance, "Why is it important to know the size hole for a wren's house?" and "If we are going to make a house for a wren and we know the proper size for the hole, why is it necessary to make a hole just that large and no larger?" and "How can we do it?"

The answers to these questions depend partly on research or personal experience and partly on reasoning and putting known facts together as they apply to the solution of an immediate problem. Whether or not a discussion of this matter is necessary will depend on the reason it is being considered by the group. Is someone making a place for a wren to live or is he just curious about it? Either way the group can help by thinking the questions through together. Group interest and need enter into the choice.

A question such as "What kind of animals can swim?" will draw directly upon the knowledge your children already have or can get. A specific question would be more within the scope of the group. Suppose your group is developing a story about a certain animal. "When he comes to the edge of the stream can we say that he dives in and swims across unless we know whether this kind of an animal can swim?" Do your children know that the duck can go in but the chicken will have to wait on the bank? What about the dog and the cat? the squirrel and the skunk? As the children discuss these questions they come to the larger more general one, "Which animals can swim and which cannot?" This leads to a lively discussion, and they will seek additional knowledge and bring back to the group the facts they learn for further discussion the next day.

VI. ANNOUNCEMENTS;
RECOMMENDATIONS;
INSTRUCTIONS

Making Clear Announcements

Children like to make announcements to the group and this is an excellent language experience for them. In making an announcement they may tell what has happened or what is going to happen, when and where it is to happen, and who is concerned.

Recommending Candidates for Election

Another similar experience for upper primary children is to give an informal "campaign speech" when nominated for a class office. The children stand up and tell what they will do if elected and why they think they are capable of holding the office. An interesting variation is for a child to tell why a friend or classmate should be elected to a particular committee or office. A discussion of the responsibilities and qualifications needed may precede such a talk.

Giving Instructions Clearly

Requests that necessitate formulating reasonable instructions to be carried out are enjoyed. A child may call upon another to do one thing at first, later two, and progressively more as children in the group are ready for it, as in the following examples:

"Go see if the ivy needs watering."

"Find the drum and make it tell what kind of a day it is."

"Get the red truck and the flat trailer and take them to Larry."

The child who is called upon responds under the watchful eyes of his group. As these directions are gradually lengthened the children become so intrigued that they often carry on the activity in small groups independently. "Take the yard stick in your left hand, go stand in front of the window, and with both hands measure how far it is from the floor to the bottom of the window; then go and stand in front of the green bookcase and measure how tall it is; then come back and tell us which is higher."

With experience the ability of the children to give lucid instructions will be markedly improved. Those who propound the questions gain practice in expressing themselves clearly and in thinking creatively in planning new and interesting things to be done. The spirit of cooperation and consideration for each other must permeate the entire procedure. Your guidance is needed in order to prevent aggressive domination until your children learn how to make the instructions helpful to those who are to carry them out. Skill in listening to language and translating it into action increases with experiences of this type.

VII. ORAL REPORTS

Reporting on Personal Experiences

Children find delight in sharing their personal experiences in the form of an oral report. If such an account is presented in an enthusiastic, graphic way it will call forth a considerable exchange of ideas.

Illustrations at the easel or chalkboard made by the child may highlight the most unique phases. Those listening may ask questions spontaneously that will cause the speaker to tell more.

Even the fives and sixes enjoy reports of a personal experience as:

"One day we went to my grandmother's house.
I skated and jumped rope there.
Two boys next door played with me.
My cousin was there, too.
It was lots of fun.
I like to go visiting."

Barbara, 5/5

Reports of an autobiographical nature require a certain amount of organization. Adele thought over what her friends would like to know about her home before she moved, and gave the following account spontaneously:

When we lived in Texas I had a little calf and my sister had a little calf. When they were hungry their mothers fed them milk. One day one of the calves followed a cow. It never came back. It was my sister's calf. My calf stayed with me. I took good care of it. It followed me all around the lot. It grew up so fast it was as big as its mother.

Adele, 7/1

Many people think of reporting as reading something from prepared notes. A child who is able to stand at ease before a group and present his facts clearly in an interesting way, speaking directly to his listeners, is laying the foundation for a skill that will serve him well.

Standards for a Good Report

As they advance in their ability to organize their verbal expressions, upper primary children are capable of suggesting criteria of good oral reporting:

Stand comfortably and look at everyone
to whom you are talking.
Speak clearly so everyone can hear you.
Make what you have to say interesting.
Think to yourself: "What would I want someone
to tell me about this if I did not know
very much about it?"
Use pictures or draw sketches
to show what you mean.
Answer questions and ask your listeners
what else they would like to know.
If you don't know the answers,
and you think it is a good question,
tell them you will try to find out.
Follow through with a second report
if needed.

The Child with Special Ability

In addition to the reports that any child in the group might be expected to make, there are those of the young genius who has more technical background on a given subject than the average adult.

Every child in Brian's middle primary group was fascinated by this seven-year-old's presentation of what makes the picture appear on the television screen.

A visitor came in and noticed this child had a television primer on his desk. She asked the teacher's permission to talk with him about it. She said, "Brian, I see you have read a television primer. I am very much interested to know something about it. I just can't understand what happens to bring the picture to the screen."

"Oh," said Brian, "if you really want to know you would have to go to the encyclopedia for that." He went over and picked up one of the volumes, then set it down, unopened, whereupon he proceeded to discuss the intricacies of electronics.

"This is the chocolate cake," he said.

"What is that?" the visitor asked curiously, eyeing the painting Brian was sketching to illustrate his point.

"The screen," replied Brian. "The cake is just a figure of speech! The light rays go through a camera lens. After this they go to a tube and there's a photo-electric surface and then immediately when it gets into the tube it changes into electric impulses, and these go through a transmitter and they send out short video waves. Audio means sound; video means light.

"Then the short videowaves go through the antenna; then there's a special wire that goes from your antenna through your picture tube. In your picture tube there is an electron gun (that's another so-called figure of speech). Then the electron gun shoots out light rays and then it goes on to the T.V. screen. The electronic impulses change into light rays and the cake shows on your T.V. set."

The group was about to leave for lunch. Brian offered his sketch to the visitor and went out with the others.

After the children left the teacher remarked to the visitor with a twinkle in her eye, "Brian wants to be an electronics engineer. Do you think he will make it?"

VIII. LANGUAGE THROUGH SCIENCE

Developing Language Through Science

Science discussions, experiments, and displays bring forth all types of communication, verbal, written, and through the arts and crafts. Children are fascinated with this field and appreciate an opportunity to satisfy their desire to know about these mysteries. Their eagerness to explore and their joy in manipulation help them develop an awareness of their environment, encourage analytical thinking, and give them an enlarged scientific vocabulary.

Earth and Water

The six-year-olds who took part in the following experiences with soil and water had already shared many interesting science experiences. They had learned through experimentation and observation that water evaporates into the air, and that this process takes place more rapidly when there is heat present, whether from sun or fire. They had also learned that when water evaporates from a solution, whatever is in the liquid is left behind. They had boiled sea water and had seen the salt that was left.

The week before the soil experiment began they had made jello in the classroom and had noted the grainy texture of the jello that came from the envelope. They had seen the jello dissolve in hot water and had added the word *dissolve* to their vocabulary.

Gathering and Comparing Specimens

There had been a protracted dry spell, and on the way to school, Mrs. Mason, teacher of the group, noted how a claybank in the vicinity had been seamed by rain and then baked and hardened by sun and dryness.

On the day the experiment began Mrs. Mason put her materials on the science table when she reached school early in the morning. She covered them with a heavy cloth, and as the children arrived they were, of course, curious to know what was beneath the cloth.

"Wait," said Mrs. Mason, putting her explanation positively. "The cloth is there to remind you just to feel without looking. This is a time when you will feel with your hands and tell what is there."

"It feels like cans or something," said Jerry.

"This feels like a shovel," said Tom.

When the table was finally uncovered the children saw a number of empty tin cans, two spades, and some rectangular cake pans.

"We are going outdoors to find interesting things about the earth we walk on," said Mrs. Mason. "What will we need to remember?"

David: "To stay in a group."

Emily: "That means we all stay together. Nobody runs ahead and nobody stays behind."

Mrs. Mason: "That is right, Emily."

Janice: "May we have partners?"

Mrs. M.: "It is fun to walk with someone. If you would like to walk with another person invite him to be your partner." Several enthusiastically chose partners, but as is natural with young children, no thought was given to whether boys or girls walked together. The empty cans were carried by volunteers. Mrs. M. carried the spades.

Mrs. M.: "What did we come out to learn?"

Tina: "All about the ground we walk on."

Mrs. M.: (pointing to clay bank) "What is this ground like?"

Mary: "It's cracked."

Mrs. M.: "What do you think made the long cracks?"

John: "The rain."

Mrs. M.: "Why do the cracks all run the same way?"

Lynn: "Where it is lowest the water runs to that place."

Mrs. M.: "Why is the claybank so hard and dry now?"

Greg: "Because we haven't had any rain. The water has all evaporated."

Mrs. M.: "We are going to get some clay from this clay bank to look at and feel when we go back to our room. (She gathered a spade full of clay and put it in one of the cans.) Our feet are standing on soil. We sometimes call it earth or ground." The children placed some of this soil in another can.

They talked about the color of the soil in the claybank. Since their school was next to a sand dune, they filled a can with some of this sand; others gathered pebbles for their cans. When the children returned to the school yard they put gravel into another can and Maybelle asked the gardener for a small amount of rich soil from a flower bed. Then the children returned to the classroom and sat on the rug with their newly collected "treasures."

Mrs. M. (holding up something one of the children had modeled from potter's clay) : "When Peggy started to work with this clay cat it looked like this clay. (Showing a large ball of commercial clay.) What made the cat get hard?"

Mark: "It was the sun. It took all the water out."

Mrs. M.: "Yes, the water evaporated in the sun and the cat made of clay got hard."

"Now, let's look closely at some of the bank clay and some of the clay we use and compare them." (There were several samples of commercial clay and clay which the children had gathered. These were passed among them and discussed so all could hear.)

Mrs. M.: "Let's feel our clay and see how different it is from the clay from the claybank. See what is alike about them. See and feel what is different. Do they feel the same?"

Keith: "They are not even the same color."

Mrs. M.: "No, they are not, are they, but does the color have anything to do with the way they feel?"

Patty: "Our clay feels like ice cream."

Mrs. M.: "Which clay is the smoother?"

Bobby: "The clay we work with?"

Mrs. M.: "Why is it different?"

(More discussion of this point.)

Mrs. M.: "Yes, our clay is pure clay. It has been purified—made pure—by having all the sand and dirt taken out of it." (Mrs. Mason mixed some sand in with the commercial clay and passed it around for the children to feel. She also put some clay on a tray without the sand added.) "Feel how different our clay is when we add sand to it. Rub each of them between your fingers."

After the children had felt of the different soil mixtures, they experimented with wet sand, wet commercial clay, and wet bank clay.)

Mrs. M.: "What happens to our own clay when we wet it?"

Vicki: "It gets smoother and softer."

Mrs. M.: "When we added sand to our clay, what happened?"

Cory: "It made it rougher."

The children found that the first water added to the dry soil soaked in almost immediately, but as the soil became wetter the water stood in little lakes. The soil had reached a *saturation* point.

The children tried molding shapes with soil that had not been wet to the saturation point. They found that clay would stick together when pressed into a ball; the soil would stick, too, but not as well as the clay; but the sand hardly stuck at all. They placed their different balls in the sun to dry for a day or two. The clay remained as a hard ball; the soil crumbled some; but the sand did not form a ball at all.

Larry: "The water all evaporated from these soils. I liked this experiment."

Mrs. M.: "We noticed different colors of soil outdoors this morning. What kind did we get from under the flowerbeds?"

Jerry: "We got top soil."

(Mrs. M. passed the top soil around for all to see.) "Feel this top soil and see if it is like the clay or the sand. Is it smooth like our clay, or grainy and rough like the bank clay?"

Mrs. M.: "What color is the top soil?"

Nancy: "It's brown, and some of the bugs running around in it are the same color."

At Mrs. M.'s suggestion the children listened as they experimented with cartons containing sand.

Mrs. M.: "Mary is shaking her carton as softly as she can. Does it make a soft or loud sound?"

The children experimented with gravel and pebbles in a plastic bottle, with soil in various containers, and with rattles and sandblocks.

Mrs. M.: "Tomorrow we'll talk more about the interesting things we have found today. Now we will put the pebbles and the sand you have collected over on the science table. When you are free you may experiment with the things we have collected. Your homework for tonight is to get some soil from your yard and put it in a tin can or a milk carton or a plastic container and bring it to school with you tomorrow."

Second Day: Earth Helpers

Clark: (Producing carton) "I remembered to bring my homework."

Mrs. M.: "What did you bring, Clark?"

Clark: "It's earth from our garden. Daddy told me that earth, soil, ground, and dirt are all words for the same thing that I have in this carton. Everything that is natural that we walk on outdoors is soil or dirt."

(Other children showed their contributions of soil. Discussion as to color, feel, bugs in the soil, where the soil came from.)

John: "I brought some things that live in the earth. These are special earthworms that my Daddy bought to have in our flower-garden. These are red worms. They have been working in the ground around our flower garden. This is some of the soil they have enriched."

Mrs. M.: "These worms eat lettuce after it has rotted. They love cooked cereal and tomato peelings and any soft food after it rots. These worms will make flowers grow better. They will make vegetables grow greener and trees grow faster."

Larry: "Any earth worm that lives in our soil enriches it."

Mrs. M.: "Did you dig for these worms, John?"

John: "My father dug for them. But he watered the ground first. Sometimes they come out of the ground."

Mrs. M.: "On what kind of a day?"

Larry: "When they come out of the ground at my house, it is never a hot day when the sun is shining. They come out when we water our yard."

Mrs. M.: "The earth worms come out after it has rained, too."

John showed the children how his worms looked through a magnifying glass.

Mrs. M.: "John will put his worms and soil and the magnifying glass on the science table. You may look at them whenever you are free."

(Without further comment Mrs. M. said the following:)

My Garden Helpers

Why is my garden so fresh and green?
Why are the flowers so big?
Down in the ground where they can't be seen
Are worms that work and dig.

They work deep down without a sound,
And when I go tripping by
I don't hear the helpers under the ground
But my plants grow strong and high.

The children enjoyed the "Earthworm Poem" and asked to hear it again. Then they said it with full body movements, making an action play of it, and afterward Vicki tapped out the rhythm with a pair of sticks.

Third Day: Observation and Experiment: Rain Water

The third day it rained. This morning on the table near the door were a glass bowl, a colander, and a piece of thin cloth. As individual children arrived their main conversation was about how wet the rain made everything. A few of the early arrivals made an action play with Mrs. Mason's guidance:

Drops of water dripping
Fall down from the sky.
Water outdoors everywhere
But in the house it's dry.

Later, when the group gathered to plan for the day, the children who helped make their new poem with actions shared it with the others.

There were several comments about the rain, but the main theme was that rain is really water and makes everything wet.

"Our garden helpers will like that," said Wesley.

Mrs. M. caught some of the rain in a flat pan. The children wanted to know where the water in the pan came from.

"Yesterday, *you* did *your* homework. Today *I* did *mine*," explained Mrs. M. "There are some things we can all do together to help with my homework.

"We are going to find out something about water and sand and soil. The water in the first pan is clear rain water. I put the pan out under the eaves of the shed and the rain water ran off the roof into the pan. This water is clear. You can see the bottom of the pan through the water. What does the water in the other pan look like?"

"You can't see through it. It is brown."

The children decided it looked like muddy water.

"Where could this muddy water have come from?" asked Mrs. M.

"It looks like the water in the puddles," said John.

"We had so much rain it ran down off the roof and off of the trees and made puddles in our garden."

"The ground reached the 'saturation point,' " recalled Jerry.

"You are right. The water in this pan did come out of one of those puddles. It really is rain water, but it doesn't look like it, does it? What makes this water look so muddy?" asked Mrs. M.

"It has dirt in it," said Billy.

"This mud is the soil from our garden," Mrs. M. explained. "The rain water picked up some of the soil, and it made the water all brown.

"Here are two jars. One jar is for the rain water I caught in the pan. Bobbie, you come and pour some of the clear water into the jar. This other jar is for the muddy water. Ann, pour some of the muddy water into the jar for us."

"Now," said Mrs. M., "we'll let the muddy water stand while we go for a walk. We'll see what it looks like when we get back."

As they walked along, the children noticed there were many little rivulets as a result of the rain; also, that there were more of these rivulets where the ground was bare and not so many where there was grass or rocks.

"Rivulets are like little rivers. See where the rivulets have washed the soil away where there are no plants to hold the earth. We call it soil erosion. Soil erosion in gardens and on farms is not good because plants need soil to grow."

"Notice which way these little rivulets are running," said Mrs. M. "Where are they going, Mark?"

Mark: "I think they are going to the ocean. They are going toward a low place."

Janice: "Here is a low place. It is all filled up with water."

David: "Look! Here is one place where the water is running over."

Mrs. M.: "It is running just like the other little streams. They are all trying to find a low place."

Gregg: "Will the water get to the ocean after a while?"

Mrs. M.: "Some of it will evaporate and go up in the air, but many of the little rivulets will go on and on and join larger streams. And many of the small streams will go on until they flow into big rivers. Then the rivers will travel on and on until they come to the ocean."

Tina: "All except the water that goes up like steam into the air."

Mark: "When I get hot, I don't go up in the air."

Mrs. M. smiled. "All of you doesn't go up in the air, Mark, but something does. What is it?" she asked the children. "What does Mark do when he becomes very warm?"

"He sits down," said Vicki.

"He fans himself," said Lynn.

"He sweats," said John.

"Yes," said Mrs. Mason, "and when he fans himself, what happens?"

"He cools off," said John.

Mrs. M.: "What happened the day we hung the wet cloth in the wind?"

Mike: "The cloth we hung in the wind dried more quickly. It made the water in the cloth evaporate."

"That is good thinking, Mike," said Mrs. M. "What does the fan do?"

George: "It makes wind on Mark and he evaporates, whish! right up in the air!"

Mrs. Mason laughed: "You mean the perspiration or sweat evaporates and Mark feels cooler. Let's look once more at the little rivers that are still running."

"And at all the little seas they are making," said Lynn.

Mrs. Mason made a spontaneous rhyme:

> The rain comes tumbling down today,
> And little rivers race,
> Cutting gorges to the seas
> They're making every place.

The children liked the verse and used it for an action play as they returned to the classroom.

"What happened to the muddy water we left in the jar?" asked Mrs. M. when they were all back in the room.

Betty: "The water isn't muddy any more. It is clear. We can see through it."

Mrs. M.: "It is clear rain water again, like the rain that falls from the sky before it gets muddy. But where is the mud that was in this water we put in the glass?"

Billy: "The mud all went to the bottom."

Mrs. M.: "The soil *settled* in the bottom. If we stir up the mud what will happen?"

Billy: "It will get brown again."

Mrs. M.: "Martha, you stir the water and let's see."

"Now, if we let the jar stay quietly here will the mud settle again? Will it all go to the bottom? Let's go on with our work and after while let's come back and see what has happened."

Later in the morning the group found that the mud had settled again. At Mrs. M.'s suggestion the children poured the water off the top of the mud and had clear water in another jar.

"It looks clean, now, but would this water be good to drink? Would the water that filtered through the sand be good to drink? Would the clear water in the pan be good to drink?"

Gregg: (Whose father was in the City Health Department): "It wouldn't be good to drink. They put chemicals in water to make it clean so people can drink it."

Mrs. M.: "Yes. Also, if they catch the steam that has come from boiling water and cool the steam so it turns back to water, that water is very pure. We call it distilled water. Good drinking water comes from springs in the ground. Sometimes it comes from wells. People who are not where they can get good water sometimes boil their water and cool it before they drink it. Then the water doesn't make them sick. Tomorrow we will make some distilled water out of some of this rain water and see what it looks like."

Fourth Day: Distilled Water

The sky was overcast and clouds looked threatening. Mrs. M. and the children boiled water and caught the steam in an inverted washpan where it condensed and dripped down into another pan.

The children noted how clear the distilled water was in comparison with the amber color of the clear rain water. They learned the words "condensation" and "distilled."

Fifth Day: Buoyancy

The next morning was bright and sunny again and Mrs. M. filled the plastic pool with water. "We are going to find what will float and what will sink in water," said Mrs. M. "I have brought several things to use in our experiment. You can probably think of others. I have two types of things—heavy things and light things. Here is a magnet. Is it heavy or light?"

David: "It is heavy."

Mrs. M.: "Is this feather heavy or light?"

John: "It is very light."

Mrs. M.: "What about this little boat?" (The children didn't know.)

"Let's experiment," said Mrs. Mason.

George dropped a key in water and it sank at once.

Mary dropped the feather in water and it floated.

George dropped a piece of cotton on the water. "What is happening, George?" asked Mrs. Mason.

"At first the cotton floated," said George, "but when it got wet it went to the bottom of the pool."

"Yes, the cotton absorbed the water; then it sank," agreed Mrs. M. She dropped a closed bottle in the pool and it floated. "The bottle has air inside," explained Mrs. M. "Air always keeps things up."

"Madge, you drop this nail in and see what happens."

Madge dropped the nail and it sank at once.

The children found a balloon would float if it had air in it.

"Let's get our boats and sail them," said Tina.

The children got the accessory toys. They placed the big freighter in the water. They loaded it lightly and then heavily, evenly and unevenly. They tried a canoe and a sailboat.

Tina: "The canoe always comes up."

John: "That's because wood floats."

(Children notice a leaky boat filling with water.)

Mrs. M.: "Why does it sink?"

Ann: "Air all goes out and water comes in and makes it heavy."

The children continued experimenting with boats in the pool.

The Next Week: Foot Painting and Mud Activities

The day dawned clear and hot. As the morning grew hotter, Mrs. M. had two large flat pans ready. One had wet mud: the other wet sand. Two children at a time took off shoes and socks, stood in the pan of mud or sand and rubbed their feet in the contents—holding on constantly to a rail. Then they stepped out onto a large sheet of paper and made foot prints.

Janice: "The mud feels slippery and gooey—much more slippery than the sand."

Mrs. M. had children describe the difference in feeling and texture of both the two pans and the foot prints.

As the children were preparing to come inside afterward, Mrs. M. had them follow her in a "shuffle parade," and she shuffled around and around the yard until all the mud was off their feet. She asked them what the sound was like and they answered "sandpaper."

After the children washed their feet in a bowl of warm soap suds, and then rinsed them, they did a foot painting with starch tempera and paints (same as hand painting).

"This feels like skating," said Tina.

A Day Later: Absorption and Suction

As the group returned to the classroom Mary said, "It's my turn to water the plants."

In performing this task she accidentally spilled some water. Mary started to the closet for the sponge to wipe up the water.

"Let's see what kinds of things will absorb water," suggested Mrs. M.

They discovered sponge would soak up water; also cloth. They found certain pieces of paper would soak up water. Oil paper and cellophane would not; newspaper would, but not immediately. A paper towel, blotting paper, and facial tissues absorbed it more quickly than other kinds.

In connection with this experiment, Mrs. Mason brought small paper cups, paper drinking straws, and some lemonade to serve to the children. When they sucked the straw the lemonade came up into it. "That is because you sucked the air out of the straw," explained Mrs. M., "and the suction pulled the water up where the air had been."

In the Days that Followed: Continued Interest

Mrs. M. noted for a number of days after the culmination of these experiments that the children continued to be interested in them.

Various individuals brought different kinds of sand, earth, and clay and put them in plastic bottles where they could compare them as to color and texture. They found by shaking them that they would sound like their musical instruments. They noticed the same kind of sand or soil in different containers had various sounds, similar to sandblocks and rattles. They found that varying amounts of sand or gravel, and whether it was damp or dry made a difference in the sound.

Charles brought his rock collection. Other rocks were brought in by the children and compared. Mrs. Mason cracked some of the rocks. Some of them crumbled, others split, and still others would not break. They noticed that rocks that came from stream beds were smooth from the action of water. They had much practice in comparing the weight of various rocks and other objects and in working with things that were "heavy" and "light."

The children had acquired considerable background for interesting discussion. Many words were added to their vocabulary. Such words as soil, clay, adobe, cement, erosion, rivulet, suction, pulverize, absorbent, saturation, evaporate, dissolve, grainy, pebbles, filter, were wholly meaningful in the light of their experimentation.

These six-year-olds gained a deep appreciation of earth and water, but perhaps most important of all they were learning to observe, to think, and to draw conclusions.

In an older group in middle primary the children's interest along similar lines led not only to much oral language development but also produced many charts and written reports and stimulated reference reading. They experimented in making adobe and in using cement for construction.

Over a picture of Bryce Canyon, where some of the children had spent their vacation, a committee wrote the following chart based upon their own summary of discussions:

What Is Soil?

Good soil grows food for us.
Soil is made of rocks, insects, rotted leaves, and plants.
Nature takes many, many years to make soil.

IX. CLOCKS AND SHADOWS

Duration of Time

Mrs. Pauline Sanders and her student teacher, Mrs. Judy Diaz, had a beginning primary group of children in a county school, modern in every respect from curriculum to physical plant.

A number of the children were brought to school each day by bus. Others lived within walking distance. Among the children who walked were three who were usually tardy. This led to a group discussion of the importance of being on time. Mrs. Sanders was determined to help these children want to be on time.

She asked the children how they knew when it was time to leave for school. Katherine replied, "My mother tells me when to start."

Kelvin said, "I can tell by looking at the clock."

Mrs. Sanders remarked that Kelvin had one way to tell time. "What other ways are there."

The children mentioned watches, clocks of various kinds, and the timers that some of their mothers used for cooking.

Mrs. Sanders introduced a clock model and an opportunity was given for the children to share their background on "telling time."

"The hour hand is the shortest."

"The long hand tells the minutes," they said.

Mrs. Sanders explained about the minutes in the hour.

"How long is a minute?" asked Mrs. Sanders.

Wendy said, "Sometimes I think a minute is a long time, and sometimes it is real short."

"Why do you think that, Wendy?" asked Mrs. Sanders.

"Well," said Wendy, "if I am doing something I love to do, a minute is too short. But if I am tired doing something I don't like and I have to do it anyway, a minute is a long time."

"Let's sit still for one full minute," suggested Clayton, "and see how long it really is." The electric clock clicked off the seconds as the children sat absolutely still for one minute. They all decided Wendy was right; a minute can be very long.

The children enjoyed experimenting with other blocks of time. How long does it take to sing a happy song?, dictate a chart? choose activities for work time? How long do we spend in our reading experience each day?

These and many other activities convinced the children that when they were having happy experiences, time seemed to go fast.

Mrs. Sanders arranged a bulletin board with two rows of five clocks each.

All had movable hands. Much learning, both as a group and as individuals at independent times was in evidence as the children fixed the clocks to tell the correct time for the routine duties and activities of the day.

Mrs. Sanders explained that there are other ways of telling time. How could they find out what they are?

The children suggested that they could have this for their homework problem and do some "research" on it.

The following morning all the children were eager to share the results of their research. Some had learned about the sundial clock. To clarify this for the children who had not seen one, Mrs. Sanders used the easel and painted pictures to show how this type of time recording worked. Then all participated in dramatizing the sundial.

Mrs. Sanders illustrated on the easel as the other children told of other ways they had found to tell time; the burning of a candle, the tying of knots in a rope to indicate time intervals, the water clock, the hourglass, and measuring the shadow cast by a tall stick.

Using Shadows Effectively

As an outgrowth of their study on clocks these children developed an absorbing interest in shadows. On the outdoor patio they observed, first of all, their own shadow, and then those of their classmates and teachers; also the shadows of many objects, large and small.

Doug was walking behind Glenn when he noticed that his own shadow was following Glenn's shadow just as he was following Glenn. The children were fascinated as they compared the length of their shadows and tried to discover how shadows are formed. At different times of the day they watched how the shadows fell, and outlined some of them with a stick on the soft ground beyond the patio. They discovered that when something solid gets in the path of light rays it casts a shadow. Their shadow screen, used for dramatic expression these many months, now took on new meaning. This was an excellent way to demonstrate that when someone was close to the light source the shadow was large, but became smaller and smaller as the object was moved farther from the light.

All the children experimented with making shadows on the screen with their hands. There was much imagination evident and a rapid flow of language as each child had a turn making on the screen whatever shadow figure he chose, while the other children told of the various things it might be.

The research committee volunteered to look up all the information in the picture file and picture books that the teachers had chosen for their beautiful illustrations and simple reading context. This resulted in the committees constructing a shadow clock.

A piece of doweling was driven into the ground where it would cast a shadow. Small stones were collected to represent the numerals of the clock. Kelvin and Timmy, both very mature children, decided that the stones should be painted to help them remember the numbers. After much discussion, it was agreed to paint the stones representing 3, 6, 9, and 12. Easel paint was used for this purpose.

During the evaluation of this project all of the children checked the time with the school clock and helped the committee arrange the stones so that the shadow clock corresponded in time with the school clock. Many recommendations were made for improving the clock and since this interest continued for nearly two weeks, other committees had an opportunity, with the approval of the original committee, to make changes, each time making a better clock.

These children noted as they observed their shadows that as the sun moved up in the sky, the shadows become shorter, and are very short when the sun is directly overhead. They used a yardstick to measure these and soon could do it with exactness. They also learned that as the sun moves down in the afternoon the shadows become longer again but that they are on the opposite side of the person or object. They discovered, too, that shadows fall in a different position on the patio floor. This was made more concrete by tracing the shadows of various children at different times of day.

Mrs. Diaz made an easel painting depicting the sun's travels across the sky. If the sun is on the east side of the picture in the morning, where would the shadow be? Charles volunteered to come up and paint the shadow on the right side of the picture.

Mrs. Diaz told an original story about Danny and his day at school, where his shadow was when he was walking to school in the morning, how he looked everywhere for it at noon on his way home for lunch and finally found it was underneath him, and how in the afternoon Danny's shadow played with him and his friends in the little red wagon.

East and west and north and south were no longer an enigma to these children, and it was revealing to overhear them giving directions of how to reach specific places.

Each child made his own shadow stick on paper so that he could paint the shadows each hour. This helped clarify the fact that the sun moves across the sky causing the shadow on the clock to move.

It was the children's own idea to have the stick stand up in a clay holder.

The responsibility for marking the shadows of the patio clock from hour to hour was delegated to two children in the morning and a different two in the afternoon. In this way each child had an opportunity at one time or another to serve on a committee of two for this purpose.

It was a satisfaction to see how alert these children were to their responsibility. It was amazing to see how well they learned to estimate time by noting the position of the stick's shadow at different times of the day.

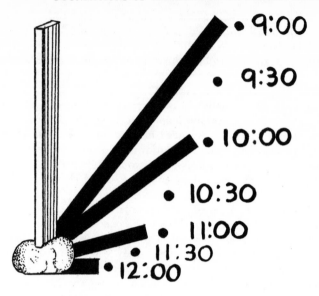

Other Related Experiences

The story "Shadows" by Larry William Kittel Kamp, William Morrow and Co., 1957, was greatly enjoyed. Some time later the children dictated a delightful original story about "Shadows."

Mrs. Diaz quoted the poem "Shadow Children" from *Stories to Begin On*, by Rhoda Backmeister, Dutton, 1941.

Steve immediately responded with Robert Louis Stevenson's, "My Shadow."

The group discussed this poem and when it came to the line, "I see him jump before me, when I jump into my bed," they experimented and discovered from which side the light was coming to make the shadow get into bed first.

These poems were said many times by the children as they went about their work, and on the playground shadows were discussed with great enthusiasm. Many of the children from other primary grades in the school became interested and joined in the activities at this time.

Shadow games were originated and played and the children romped and danced happily with their shadows both with and without musical accompaniment. Drums, tambourines, and rattles were used which increased the fun and mystery of the experience.

As Wanda swang back and forth she chanted happily:

> "Everytime I swing
> in the swings,
> I get two rides,
> One for me
> And one for my shadow."

It became a game to find all the places where shadows could be, and different ways of making them. They found and painted shadows from trees and buildings. Even clouds made wonderful changing shapes.

Alice summed it up this way:

Shadows on the Ground

"Over the hill
the sun comes up.
The shadows are long.
At noon the sun
is high overhead.
What little shadows
it makes."

Beth expressed it as follows:

"Shadows are silhouettes
made by the sun.
My shadow is a dark silhouette
on the ground.
My body keeps the sun
from shining where my shadow is."

Carol, who was especially interested in this activity, went to Lake Tahoe during spring vacation. Her mother wrote down Carol's verbalization as she watched captivated and speechless for several minutes and then exclaimed:

"Look there on the water
See the gorgeous colors.
They are like pictures
in the water.
They are reflections
like our own shadows
from the sun at school."

Other children discussed their experiments with shadows at home, and like Carol, brought back profound observations.

Wayne said, "Moonlight is only a reflection of light from the sun."

Evelyn brought a mirror to school and demonstrated how it would catch the sun's rays. This was a popular experiment, and the children found that when light bumps against a bright smooth surface, it bounces off in another direction. As the children moved the mirror they noted how the light moved also.

Mark brought up the fact that the electric eye on the door of many stores is operated "by the person's shadow that breaks the beam of light and sends a message to the motor which opens the door."

Mother's Day was approaching, and the children and Mrs. Diaz talked over what they could do to help each child's mother have a happy day.

Freddie suggested making her an easel painting; Debbie said, "We give her our books of paintings all the time, I would like to make a card for my mother." Dickie wanted to write his mother a note.

Mrs. Diaz asked the children if there was any way they could do all these things.

Katherine demonstrated how she would make a card from a large piece of construction paper. She folded it in half and suggested decorating the outside and putting an original poem about mother on the inside.

Henry said, "But my mother's interested in our study of shadows. I'd like to make my own shadow for her."

There was hearty accord with this, but the problem arose as to how to get the whole shadow on the card. Solving this dilemma demanded much planning, discussing, and experimentation. The children decided that instead of a card, the shadow would have to be on a larger piece of paper. Each child chose a partner to work with. One child stood in the sun so his life size shadow was cast on a large sheet of wrapping paper. His partner painted the shadow a solid gray or black. The shadow pictures were successful, and each child wrote his own personal message to his mother to attach to the picture.

To My Mother

It is Mother's Day.
This is a picture
of my shadow.
It is just for you.
I love you.
Wendy

Louise, 7/6, wrote inside the cover of her shadow paper:

My Gift for Mother
on Her Day

My gift to Mother   I want to work
On Mother's Day   And do my best
Is to give up all   To make her day
my hours of play.   A day of rest.

The following year Mrs. Sanders carried on a similar experiment with another group of lower primary children. Their interest in shadows had a different inception: the children had been doing clay work and put their completed forms in the sun to dry. Then they went to work with other things. When they returned they found their clay objects were in the shade. They were much puzzled and thought someone had moved them from the sun. This led to a series of experiments and the discovery of how the sun moves across the heavens each day causing the shadows from the building to move. From the shadows cast by inanimate objects to their own shadows was an easy and natural transition.

Out of this the children learned how the shadows change direction and size because the earth rotates on its axis, at the same time that it revolves about the sun.

QUESTIONS ON FOUNDATIONS IN VERBAL EXPRESSION

1. As the child reaches out to grasp and appropriate new words for his own vocabulary, why is it important to avoid laughing at him over the misuse of a word, even though it may seem extremely funny to you? Illustrate.

2. Discuss ways of increasing language fluency and vocabulary growth during the sharing of school plans and classroom experiences. Give examples.

3. Why is it well to guide many of your group discussions so that they relate to the child's own "growing up" experiences, such as safety precautions in street crossing and traffic rules; what makes a good breakfast; being on time; John's lost tooth? Cite further illustrations of this.

4. a. Originate five questions you might bring into a discussion of one of the points in No. 3 above, that would stimulate children's thinking. b. Suggest the maturation level of the group and their possible verbal or other responses to each question.

5. Discuss how the goals of early childhood help children develop their ability in the use of words.

6. How does the democratic classroom provide an environment for verbal expression? Describe such an environment and give examples of oral language of children.

7. Discuss the bearing various types of classroom control have upon the child's growth in language expression.

8. a. Assume that your lower, middle, or upper primary group (select one) is largely from a certain community where some interest predominates, such as fruit growing, trucking, mining, climate or weather, fishing, manufacturing. Select something from the community life about which your children are informed outside of school, or which you might gain from a field trip, and suggest the possibilities for verbal expression that might arise through the sharing of common knowledge and experience. b. Give verbatim examples of the types of verbalizations you would expect to hear from various children.

9. Plan to record the verbalizations of a child of your acquaintance, or those of various children in an early childhood group which you have

observed. Describe the circumstances under which the child was speaking in each instance, and whether you recorded his words with his cooperation, or without his knowledge.

10. Discuss the inter-relationship of science and language in the education of the young child. Give classroom examples.

11. What influence does the teacher's own speaking voice have upon the child's developing patterns of speech? Give examples.

12. Under what circumstances can children learn to speak and listen to each other effectively without raising hands?

13. a. Discuss the influence of the teacher in making snack time an occasion for constructive verbal expression. b. Suggest ideas arising from current interests and experiences that may be discussed as the children eat together.

14. Assume that a child with special ability is making a report on a subject on which he is informed. How will you guide this so that it will be an educational experience for the other children in your group?

15. a. How can a colorful vocabulary be brought into use by an upper primary group of children who have experienced a fierce, windy electrical storm. Illustrate. b. Select some other impressive, unforeseen experience and discuss creative language possibilities.

16. Discuss the relationship of sensory impressions to language development in early childhood education.

SELECTED REFERENCES

Akin, Johnnye, AND SO WE SPEAK, Englewood Cliffs, New Jersey, Prentice-Hall, 1958.

Bailey, Matilda, Edna M. Horrocks, Esther Torreson, LANGUAGE LEARNINGS, kindergarten, Grade I and Grade II, New York, American Book Company, Revised, 1960.

Eisenson, Jon, THE IMPROVEMENT OF VOICE AND DICTION, New York, The Macmillan Company, 1958.

Greene, Harry A. and Walter T. Polly, DEVELOPING LANGUAGE SKILLS IN THE ELEMENTARY SCHOOL, Boston, Massachusetts, Allyn and Bacon, 1959.

Herrick, Virgil E. and Leland B. Jacobs, Eds., CHILDREN AND THE LANGUAGE ARTS, Englewood Cliffs, New Jersey, Prentice-Hall, 1955.

National Council of Teachers of English, Commission on the English Curriculum, LANGUAGE ARTS FOR TODAY'S CHILDREN, Vol. I and II, New York, Appleton-Century-Crofts, Inc., 1954.

Nichols, Ralph G. and Thomas R. Lewis, LISTENING AND SPEAKING, Dubuque, Iowa, William C. Brown Company, 1954.

Piaget, Jean, THE LANGUAGE AND THOUGHT OF THE CHILD, Translated by Marjorie Gabain, New York, The Humanities Press, 1959.

Pronovost, Wilbert Lucien, THE TEACHING OF SPEAKING AND LISTENING IN THE ELEMENTARY SCHOOLS, Wilbert Pronovost with Louise Kingman, New York, Longmans Green, 1959.

Shane, Harold G., Mary E. Redden and Margaret C. Gillespie, BEGINNING LANGUAGE ARTS INSTRUCTION WITH CHILDREN, Columbus, Ohio, Charles E. Merrill Books Inc., 1961.

VERBAL EXPRESSION THROUGH

Part Seven

CREATIVE STORYTELLING

I. WHY TELL A STORY?

The story is one of the great opportunities you have for giving language the power to call up images and impressions. You have only to read what children have dictated or written to become aware of how much stories enrich their vocabularies and influence their speech patterns; also to appreciate how the young child is learning to tell of his experiences through related sentences.

However, listening to a story is, first of all, a joy, and a story is justified if for no other reason than to give pleasure.

If your children hear stories related to their interests they come to look upon storytelling as a natural means of expression. Creative spoken language is spontaneous for them and leads them, later, to written expression and the necessity of spelling accurately in order to write what needs to be said.

Spontaneous everyday stories woven into the day's experiences are a genuine part of the child's life and of the curriculum. There are numerous opportunities through-

315

out the day to tell stories about current happenings.

As the child grows he comes to understand how other people feel. This is a gradual process, and stories that are sincere expressions of life are powerful influences in helping him see the other person's point of view. If you have an extensive repertoire of stories, poems, and songs to use at appropriate and meaningful times, you will do much to inspire, encourage, and stimulate children's creative expression. Children do not create stories and poems until they have heard and enjoyed many lovely ones that others have written. The world of children's literature in prose and poetry furnishes the springboard for creative effort.

What Stories Will You Tell?

The earliest stories are about what happens. Stories can be short, and although it is a real art to tell a story well, the best told story is often just an enthusiastic, vivid account of an experience. Words flow freely, particularly if it is your experience and you are the one who is telling about it.

Creative storytelling requires appreciation of the story by the teller. You should avoid ever telling a story that does not appeal to you. However, your children are fortunate indeed if you can tell a good story that is simple and direct and appropriate to their thinking, discussions, and activities.

You need to recognize the importance of your own extemporaneous stories, and the child's own stories, including his spontaneous verbalizations and the stories he consciously plans and tells.

Through recalling experiences in story form, the child can relive them in his imagination. Later he projects into scenes and situations the things which closely resemble what he already knows; but as his horizon of comprehension broadens these projections gradually move out beyond his own circle of experience.

Children are enthusiastic about helping piece stories together when they realize you welcome their cooperation. Clues help, and logical ideas are better than relying altogether on pure imagination.

Background for a story may come from a factual book such as one about helicopters, or a main character may be chosen and step out of a book into a story of his own. This type of activity is more suited to children in upper primary. The book suggests the setting and the background of facts. For this there will be few, if any, pictures, but children in these upper primary groups can now enjoy a story without the need of story props to stimulate their interest and attention. The possibilities of this type of storytelling are limitless.

The Need for Selectivity and Screening

The world of books and published stories can supplement the stories which you and the children develop. In many parts of America today the child is deluged with resources. There are more stories than he could hear; more books than he could ever read. What *is* used becomes a matter of careful discrimination, so that the child's time will be employed to best advantage. This makes a careful searching essential, in which you, as teacher, can recognize the wide variety of sources for stories, and include those which the child should not be deprived of. It also necessitates screening out poor material, for in these days of over-abundance, how can time and attention spent on the detrimental or even the mediocre be justified?

Technique of Creative Storytelling

Yours to Tell

All genuine storytelling is creative. Stories for the young child should be simple and purposeful.

You may hear a good story, remember it, and retell it. However, if the author of a story gives it to you in written form your inclination may be to read it aloud to the children; but reading a story is not telling it. To tell it, you must bring the story before the listener in the spoken word that has the breath of your own life in it.

The purist uses the author's every word, believing when he pronounces the language aloud he is presenting the story exactly as the author intended it to be.

To the purist *form* is the great reality.

The question which you must decide is whether to you the spirit and the life of the story are the greater reality. If you firmly believe they are, then you can capture these so vividly that your own spontaneous words serve best to recreate the story and make it yours to tell.

The best way to learn to tell a story is to *tell* it. Spontaneity is important; an outline to steer you is helpful; but if you make the story your own, the exact words will spring into being as it unfolds.

Make the story live; put yourself into the scene. Visualize the characters and action as though you were really there. Tell what happens in your own words. Only a few sentences need ever be word for word quotes from the author. The story is *yours* when you tell it.

The Voice of Experience

Simple, purposeful, creative stories grow with the telling. Just as every bird has to find out it can fly, so each individual must discover his own creative ability. Children are naturally creative when they are in a climate which encourages them to express their thoughts and in which these expressions are appreciated.

In like manner, the children's delight in your own creative efforts is your best reward for telling a story. Here it can literally be said, "Experience is the best teacher." Your natural enthusiasm and genuine sincerity are appreciated by the children. True to life characters that think and feel and experience things the child meets in his own life have a strong appeal to young children.

Your facial expression, your manner, and your tone of voice will convey more than the words of the story tell. Children listen closely as the voice drops to a whisper. The change in tone signifies something so important that they wouldn't want to miss a word of it. The artistic story teller utilizes many different shades of loudness and softness, of quality in tone and pitch, but these are done with genuine expression. The artificial is detected at once by the child; the voice that oozes sweetness lacks conviction and does not command respect either from adults or children.

Vivid Impressions

The significance of learning through the five senses has been stressed in Part IV. No discussion of storytelling, however, is complete without considering these.

Color, sound, smell, taste, touch are all important. It may not make a difference in the story whether David's shirt is red or green, but it gives a sense of reality. Tell how things taste for the young child. "John's cereal was warm and tasted fresh and crunchy. He could hear his teeth bite into the crumbling hot toast and feel the cool milk on his tongue." Your young listener relives the experience he knows so well.

For the older child there is more significance in vivid descriptions than in mere sensations:

"Roger had waited so long outside the closed door. The sunshine was bright. It beat down on Roger's head, and he could feel the hot pavement almost burning his bare feet as he stood there alone. Would his friend never come?" Here the sensory impressions help the child place himself in the situation you present, and he appreciates what the story character is facing.

Life-Like Approach

Use quotations freely: Bill thought, "I wonder where I lost my ball! Could I have left it under the tree?" This lends much more reality than to say, "Bill wondered where he had left his ball. He wondered if he had left it under the tree." Since the direct quotation personalizes the story more, it has stronger appeal for the child.

Select a character and present his viewpoint all the way through. Report fully what he said, thought, or did. A one viewpoint story is usually more readily followed by both children and adults. You might say, for example:

> "Skipper watched Jerry climb into the bus. He whined softly to himself as he heard the bus drive away. Skipper could still smell the heavy fumes even after the bus was far off. The little dog stood until he heard the bus turn the corner. He had learned not to chase after the bus the way he did the first day Jerry went away to school in it. Skipper knew he must wait patiently, but it would be a long day with his master gone. How well he could remember that grey morning when he thought Jerry would never return, but now he knew that Jerry would always come skipping back when the warm sun was high overhead and the shadows on the ground were short. Then Skipper and Jerry would have the long afternoon to run, and explore, and do things together."

Children are learning what life has to offer. Stories help them appreciate how people feel, and what they think. Your descriptive, picturesque words help give these impressions. Statements of fact alone do not begin to offer the possibilities in this respect that stories do.

Stories with No Props

A storyteller and a listener are the two main requirements for a good story, and the most practical story is the one that can be told through spoken words, without props. Through directly told stories you avoid having your children become so conditioned to looking at pictures or some other graphic material that they cannot hear without seeing.

Short creative stories suited to the discussion and interests of the children are a daily occurrence. For these you need no materials. You should not hesitate to use aids when indicated, but ideas are your most valuable asset, and ability to tell the story directly to your children at the moment when it means the most should be your goal.

For instance, the day Mary loses her blue sweater and asks everyone to help her find it, your own creative story is about a girl's blue sweater that waited all night on the ground under the bush where the black and white dog carried it. You go on to tell about the little grey kitten that was cold and lost and curled up on the warm sweater and how he followed the girl home the next day when someone brought the sweater to her. You tell how her joy in finding her sweater made her seek the owner of the kitten because she knew how glad he would be to find his pet.

Aids to Creativity

Objects Suggest Stories

Things the children bring in or objects in the room environment often suggest a story. Take, for instance, for the fives and sixes, the sponge that is used to wipe off the easels. How did it get to our classroom? How does it want to be treated? How can it help us and what does it expect from us?

One morning when John's lunch box lid breaks off, the bus driver repairs it for him with a deft twist of the pliers. You tell the story of the little blue lunch pail that waited a long time in the store for someone to buy it. The white lunch box was bigger. The milkman came and bought it for two dollars. Other boxes were purchased but still the little blue box waited. Then John came into the store and tried to decide which box he wanted. How John chose his box makes a tale of comparative size and color, and illustrates money values. John finishes the story by telling about how Mr. Jordon repaired the lid today.

Accessory materials in three dimensions, such as trucks, planes, space craft, people, and animals may be the center of spontaneous stories.

A child in the five- and six-year-old group gleefully selects from the wooden dolls those that compose a family, his own or a hypothetical one. These characters can be used to start him telling the interesting things they do at home. Stories of this type have strong appeal for the younger children.

The same principle can be employed with more advanced materials for the upper primary, such as: *The Story of the Life of the Broken Liberty Bell on the Shelf.*

Then, too, there are the flexible scenes, such as a shoe box peep show, a museum in a carton, *ad infinitum.*

Pictures in Storytelling

Pictures suggest many things, and as you and the children look at a well chosen picture and bring it to life a story takes shape.

A picture file is an invaluable asset to the storyteller. Stories need to be based on clear concepts. A picture presents, for instance, what a raccoon is really like. Many book illustrations are too faint, small, or indefinite for group presentation. Others are in black and white only. Your own file of pictures will supplement the illustrations you find in books.

A story told from an open book with pictures is standard procedure for young children. Here, telling is far superior to reading. The pictures present the continuity and from them you describe in interesting words what happens in the story.

Colorful words are needed, even though the picture shows clearly what the characters look like, and what they are doing. Putting impressions into fitting words is an important part of story telling. Later, the pictures may be eliminated and the story told without them.

One picture may be a starter from which an entire story may develop. Hear the sounds and describe what you see in your own mind. Remember how blue the lake really is on a bright sunny morning. "The blustery wind puffed and blew. It blew dust into the air and sent the white clouds flying. It was a perfect day for kite flying. Billy's red and white kite went up with a tug on the string, up and up into the blue sky. Billy thought it was a big kite, but it grew smaller and smaller as it went up until finally it was only a tiny speck way up there in the blue."

Your words become far more descriptive than the pictures ever could be, for they present what would be difficult to paint. So the story with word pictures only, comes into its own. Familiar things lead out toward the unknown as imagination is developed. Pictures widen horizons and bring the world closer to the child.

Children's Own Paintings in Storytelling

Many of the earlier paintings of young children have no definite story. The individual is concerned with spreading the color on the paper either with brush or sponge or with his own hands. Interesting designs take form and his attention is centered on the experience of putting paint on paper. Gradually, as he works at the easel or with handpainting (often referred to as finger painting), his painting begins to represent ideas. There is often a period in his art work where he is discovering what he can do, and interpreting what his work looks like after he has made it. He may enjoy telling about a picture and finding it shows something more than he intended. Here, language and art are combined in creative expression. These experiences may be the beginning of story telling, but cannot be forced. The child who has a sympathetic listener may speak freely, but too much prodding may force him to make up something just to please you.

As the child grows in art expression he attains sufficient growth to produce a picture at the easel illustrating an idea he has in mind before he starts to paint. He is now ready to illustrate his own stories, and to tell them after the pictures are finished.

You should encourage him, but do not expect more of him than one of his maturation level can produce.

Other pictures are also made by individual children from time to time, as an independent activity, and may be used as the basis for a creative story which the painter tells, or which is developed after group discussion as a composite story.

Picture Roll

A roll of wrapping paper 24" wide is good material for painting a series of pictures that, together, tell a story. The roll may be pulled through or around the end of a box so that only one picture shows at a time; or it may be wound from one roller to another by means of a handle. Such a strip may have pictures to illustrate some well-known, beloved story, or may suggest the making of an original story as the pictures come to view. The group will find a never-ending delight in turning the roll and telling the story.

This plan is helpful in guiding children to follow a sequence of events, since young children often skip from one thing to another in telling their own stories. Many adults find the incongruity and irrelevancy a part of the charm of children's stories. However, to be able to tell a story in proper sequence is one of the goals of oral language.

The picture roll lends itself to practically any type of story or experience, particularly in upper primary and beyond. The children may paint the pictures on the roll, stretched out on the floor, or each picture may be painted separately at the easel and then fastened in place on the roll of paper. This is effectively done by a committee planning and working together. The story may be a follow-up of a field trip or a supplement to the social studies area of experience. A group of lower primary children, after visiting the bird refuge, painted the bus trip and the homes of some of the birds the children saw there. As the roll was turned, the committee told about the excursion as they had planned to do, then other children told their version of the trip, adding details from their own experience.

The stick figures you paint on rolls stimulate children's oral expression. Stories are told spontaneously and evaluated by the storytellers and the group.

Felt or Flannel Board Stories

The felt board is useful in many ways in telling a creative story. You may move the characters about as you talk or place them on a background of scenery which you trace on a piece of flannel stretched over the board.

Children of any age enjoy manipulating the objects on the felt board, either telling new stories or giving their own version of the stories you have told.

Pictures from your file may be backed with a strip of sandpaper or flannel which will make them adhere to the felt board. Paper doll characters of heavy material may also be mounted in this fashion. For many uses felt or flannel figures will suffice.

Your felt board picture file should contain the sun, moon, and stars, vehicles for transportation, figures of children and adults in different poses and costumes. Felt animals and toys, shapes in many colors and sizes, as triangles, squares, and rectangles all prove helpful. Both you and the children will use them in many creative arrangements to suggest story ideas.

After the children have had much experience in hearing and seeing you tell flannel board stories, they will be ready to participate in constructing stories; first, perhaps, retelling their version of yours, but later creating their own. In this capacity, work at the felt board becomes a constructive independent activity for the more mature children.

Creative use of the felt board is excellent for the child in that he is speaking in a natural sequence of events. He is recalling past experiences and drawing upon backgrounds of knowledge. Also, he gains recognition from the group in an acceptable manner. Another valuable feature of this activity is that it provides for the more advanced children to do their best, while at the same time it brings a feeling of success at almost any level of maturity.

Dramatic Expression of Story Ideas

Dramatization of a Story or Song

The child's zest for living, his delightful ebullience, his inclination to dramatize, to bring things to life, make him particularly able to learn from his environment. Through his imagination, whatever he does is alive and takes on the aspect of reality. At home or at school he dials a number on the unconnected telephone and carries on a conversation. A fireman's helmet sets him off on a train of adventure in which he is the fireman going to the fire. However, dramatic expression is not confined to props at all. The young child can be the character or the animal, even without words, and he can also be a tree, fence, garden, or almost any other object which represents something of importance to him in the story. His wholehearted participation in dramatization offers many avenues for learning.

Dramatization cannot be forced. The child needs time to react to the story. After the story is told it is better to go on to something else rather than to expect an immediate response from the children. If, however, the children are enthusiastic in their requests to dramatize, it is well to discuss the story, giving as much background as possible on one character, with everyone assuming that role first before any of the parts are selected.

Pantomime with or without musical accompaniment is a child's natural response to a story. The words of a song may also be considered an invitation to dramatization, but the song should be sung and enjoyed *per se*, first; then the story is presented afterward, rather than having everyone try to act and sing at the same time. The story when acted goes far beyond the words of the song as the children think what might happen to the characters.

The song or whatever is to be dramatized can not only be reviewed beforehand, but the children can also make their own story from it. Take, for example, "Jack be nimble, Jack be quick, Jack jump over the candlestick."

Who was Jack? Why did anyone say, "Jack be nimble"?

One group of sixes made the following story which they played in shadows behind a sheet in the sunshine.

> Jack is building with blocks and Daddy is reading his paper in the same room. The scene changes. Mother is upstairs getting the bed fixed and Jack's bath ready for him. When she is all finished she calls, "Come on, Jack; everything is ready for your bath now."
>
> (Changing scenes is no problem for the five- and six-year-old. Characters walk on and off the screen repeatedly.)
>
> Jack is happy with his blocks and pays no attention. Mother calls again, "Jack! Jack! Your bath is all ready for you."
>
> Jack still does not want to go. Daddy stops reading the paper. "Jack!" he says, "be nimble, be quick; jump over the candlestick and get up to your bath!"
>
> On the table are two candle holders.
>
> Jack sees the shadow of one of them and jumps high enough to clear it.
>
> Jack jumps over the candlestick again and then he and father go upstairs together. Jack gets into a warm bath and he and mother have a good visit while she bathes him. Then he gets into bed and they have a song and story and then mother tiptoes away and Jack goes to sleep.

The principle being emphasized here is that dramatization of any kind is the last form of expression for the children. They do a painting of the character or something about him, discuss how he feels, what happens to him. You avoid having the children memorize lines or follow a scene verbatim. Always the story becomes their own through their creative efforts in adapting it to their own experience.

Sometimes there will be such a diversity of background within the group that there may be several versions and the experience keeps growing and growing until sometimes a visitor entering the room, even one who knows early childhood materials, would not recognize the original source of the dramatization.

Creative Puppetry

When puppets move about and talk there is a strong sense of reality. Here drama and story are combined into one medium.

The puppet stage is the traditional setting for the story in three dimensions, but puppets need not be confined to the stage. The young child delights in putting his fist into a paper sack with a face drawn on it, or into a sock with a head and clothes. Imagination brings the puppet to life and even the shy child is often delighted to make him move about. Puppets available in the room provide a fascinating work center where the children make the characters talk and sing spontaneously. A loosely knit story develops as other children come to listen while the puppets play it out.

A puppet can tell the children a story, too, on your hand, but if done behind a screen there is no direct contact between you and the child, such as in straight story telling. However, you may be immediately in front of the children, and still manipulate the puppet and give him the appearance of life.

Five-year-old Linda and Kathy had been working with the fist puppets and invited the other children to come over and watch their play. The puppets they held up behind the screen said, "Hello! How are you today?"

Some of the children who were the "audience" asked the puppet, "What's your name? Why are you here?" and the puppets replied.

There was friendly banter back and forth, but Linda and Kathy were not satisfied. They withdrew to confer behind the screen, completely ignoring the audience.

Mrs. Moulton went quietly to talk with them. Soon Linda and Kathy returned and the puppets began their play.

Linda's little clown poked his head up and said, "I used to be real little." He doubled himself up into a small ball and laughed and waved his hands, much to the delight of the other children.

"After I grew a little bigger, I was big enough to get my eyes open." (Again much laughter.)

"I used to be real little, too," said Kathy's puppet. "But I'm a big boy now." He stretched up to his full stature and danced up and down. Then the clown and the boy danced together.

The inquiring visitor asked Mrs. Moulton later, "Is this something they have seen, or is it their own?"

"This is their idea. They wanted to know why the boys and girls wouldn't listen to them a while ago and all I said to them was, 'Your puppets were asking questions and of course the audience is going to answer. If you want the boys and girls to listen, you have to give them something to listen to. Tell them a story with the puppets.' "

Older children will plan the general continuity of their creative story and then make the puppets talk as though they were characters in a play. Many times the story is a reconstruction of the children's experiences and becomes autobiographical. Often it is pure fictional, but there is also a service which puppetry may give in helping the child to project the thoughts which he is unable to express directly in language; and he is able to see a problem more clearly as the characters portray the situation. It may mean much to Barbara to play the nagging, bossy child because through this she is able to release her feelings toward her mother or sister or playmate who dominates her in real life.

A group of upper primary children were interested in transcontinental travel, but had shown much concern over the welfare of passengers and crew of planes that were lost *en route*. This feeling grew from a tragic incident that involved a relative of one of the members of their own group. With puppets they presented the survivors of a plane which went down in mountainous territory. While this would not be a subject which the teacher would have chosen for them, she felt that the children were able through the puppet characters to bring their anxieties into a realm where they could work with them and resolve them. The story which the children developed followed the immediate family until they were reunited. The search was extended but the children's Uncle John was never found. The philosophical manner in which these children met this life situation was conveyed to the others by means of the puppet characters.

Shadow Screen

For the young child, the fascination of shadows is captured by a few dress-up clothes and a stretched sheet in the sunshine. More elaborate screens with artificial lighting may be developed for the older children.

The fun of seeing and hearing their friends behind the screen intrigues them. The creative story made by the children and played in shadows gives much opportunity for spontaneity of expression. Children plan the general plot, but leave details to the characters who act them.

A small committee or interest group may work out a story in shadows and present it to their friends. Evaluation helps bring standards into being. The children want to hear what is said, and they can think of ways to make the story more interesting as they go along.

Primary children may use stiff silhouette figures of people and animals to make shadow pictures that move, dance, sing, and talk behind the screen. This is a delightful medium for creative stories for the children with the maturity to work profitably in this area. Manipulating the dolls to produce clear, sharp shadows demands a certain amount of coordination, and the audience seems more remote. This discourages the immature child who has no background for such, but upper primary children are challenged by these factors.

One group presented a delightful story based on the knowledge gained from their social studies about Pueblo Indian life. In their own version of an old legend the dog, Star, ate a chunk out of the moon and wondered what had happened to it.

The shadow figures lent themselves well to the mystery and symbolism of the myths, which the children read with understanding as they played that they were modern Indian children reliving the olden days.

II. EXAMPLES OF CHILDREN'S OWN STORIES

Dictated Stories

Children who are accustomed to spontaneous language expression have little difficulty in telling an original story. Many of these are loosely constructed narratives, but the child has a sense of beginning and concluding his efforts.

"I have a new baby brother and I get to see him tonight. He weighed 9 pounds and 4 ounces, the biggest baby in our family. I want to tell everyone his name so they won't think we named him after Bob in our class. I got to name him myself, and I named him Robert."

Chris, 6/2

Lou, in the five-year-old group, volunteered the following:

Pussy Cat

This is a story of a pussy cat. A little kitty who was always alone and the little pussy cat told the Mother Cat "What are you going to do now?" "I'm going to the grocery store," said the Mother Cat. She went and bought milk for the kitty and bread. So when they finished with that the little pussy cat said "Mother, can I go play?"

You listen and record the stories word for word just as the children tell them. However, in reading their work back to them the correct grammar is used so the child will become familiar with it. You never call to his attention that his usage is incorrect, but by hearing the right expression he will soon use it in his own vocabulary.

Randy's fluent expression was caught by his teacher whom he asked to record for him the following story:

Lost in the Fog

Once upon a time my friend was lost in the fog. And he was my best friend. And I saw him and I brought him home. He thanked me and we played games. His name was Packhy. I was glad he was safe.

Randy, 6/1

Autobiographical Tendencies in Creative Stories

Frequently a child will key his story to one that some other child has told, but there will be variations to fit his own experience. Also, children will often modify and "adopt" their favorite stories to make those of their own. By listening to these stories you can determine the things they find significant—the kitten who ran away and came back home to his mother; the little girl who couldn't have a puppy because there was no room for it; the puppy who found someone to care for him—each of these presents attitudes as well as actions. Perhaps all of them have an autobiographical import.

My Black and White Kitten

I have a little kitten. She has a black and white spot on her tail. One day she ran away.

I went to the baker's and I went to the house of a little old woman. She was not there, so I went back home, and what do you think?

I saw that she had come home.

Dean, 5/1

Terry, age 6 years, 2 months, dictated the following story about:

Molly and the Puppy

A little girl named Molly wanted a puppy very much, but could not have a puppy in her house because she lived in the city and there was no room for a puppy. Her family moved to the country where they could have a puppy. Molly got a letter from her uncle who was going on a trip and wanted to know if they would like to keep his dog, Wags. Molly was very happy and sent a letter back telling her uncle, "Yes." Her uncle wrote back that the puppy would be arriving on the Santa Fe train.

Molly and her mother went to a pet shop to get the puppy a box to sleep in, a blanket, and some dog biscuits. They had some trouble getting a box which was the exact size. Finally they found just the right one and bought it. They went down to the station to pick up the puppy.

They asked the baggage man about a little puppy. Then they heard a large noise, like a lion roaring. The baggage man said that the noise belonged to a puppy. He brought the puppy, and Molly and her mother took him home.

The children liked to play with the puppy, and so one day they decided they would teach him to roller-skate. They got the skates and since the straps would not fit the puppy they got pieces of material to hold the skates on the puppy's feet. The puppy didn't move and so they took them off. Molly's uncle came back and he took the puppy home.

Provision for Differences in Ability

Children who are capable of initiative in story telling need not be restricted because others in the group are not ready to proceed without direction. Some individuals reveal a sensitivity toward words that is encouraged through many opportunities to tell stories, without restriction as to subject or content.

An eight-year-old in a middle primary group produced the following:

The Puppy Who Had No Mother

Once upon a time there was a puppy who had no mother. He lived in a box. One day he went for a walk, and met another dog who wanted a baby. That puppy had a mother once again, and they lived happily ever after.

Michael's story, above, is no less acceptable because of another created by a child in the same group who was eleven months his junior.

Oliver caught the strange mixture of pathos and humor which is typical of the young philosopher in a story which he called:

Tommy Goes to Church

Tommy was a very black cat. He was very young and he did not know much. His mother told him not to go far from home. But one day she did not come back in time to give him his supper. Poor Tommy was very hungry. He cried and cried. A little boy was in the house but he did not know how to feed him. The little boy had to go to church and Tommy, still crying, followed him there. Nobody saw Tommy slip in and before they knew it he was on the altar. His tail was straight up in the air and he looked as if he thought he was the preacher.

Oliver, age 7 years, 6 months

Creative Stories Reveal Influences on Children's Thinking

There are many environmental factors which will affect children's stories. The constructive influence of television and cartoons, for example, as a medium for interpreting desirable concepts and extending children's general background is tremendous; however, the dubious import of certain of the concepts presented in news reports, cartoons, and television within the hearing of the children may be evidenced in the creative expression of various individuals who otherwise have little knowledge of the bizarre in their own homes or neighborhood.

Linda, seven-and-a-half years old, is a highly intelligent, imaginative child. Her story shows how some of these concepts color and influence her thinking.

The Four Little Cats

Once there were four little cats. And their names were Blackie, Max, Pinkie, and Dinkie. And they were robbers! They robbed banks! They robbed gas stations! They robbed stores! Now, what will they rob next?

They looked around for new hideouts. Finally, they found an old house. So they decided they would go over there, so they did. They opened the door and said, "Anybody home?"

"I am," said a little Sun cat in a window. It was yellow.

They said, "Can we have something to eat?"

"Yes," said the Sun cat. "Come with me."

The Sun cat gave them some meat to eat and they stayed.

One day the garbage truck came. The cats were in the house. So they jumped into the garbage can.

The garbage man took them away. They didn't know he took away the garbage. When they dumped the garbage they found the cats. They had learned their lesson so the man let them go.

Linda, 7/6

Influence of the Imagination

A touch of the Midas greed, but no one can say this upper primary child lacks imagination or facility with words:

Chapter I

One day I wanted to invent something. So I got all sorts of gadgets. I didn't know what I was making. I started to put them together. When I was finished it looked sort of like a rocket. So I got an engine for my rocket that I invented. And I didn't know what the controls were. I put the controls on any place. It looked crazy. I called my best friend to come in my rocket. My best friend is Melvin Ho. So I pulled all the switches and Melvin pulled all the controls and we were off. We set off for the moon.

Chapter II
The Monster

I saw planets. I saw Mars. I saw lots of planets. Then I saw something. Melvin thought it was a star. I thought it was a falling star. Melvin thought it was a monster. IT WAS A MONSTER! It was green and purple, yellow, black, orange, brown, tan, white, red, gray, reddish brown, and all sorts of colors. We were brave. We were frightened. "But wait," I said. "Is he our foe or is he our friend?" He looked scary. He looked pretty. Melvin said, "Maybe we can catch him for the Zoo. Then we will get lots of MONEY. About $10,000 dollars. Then we will be rich. We can buy what we want."

Chapter III

Catching a Real Monster

We were thinking about catching him. "But how can we catch him?" said Melvin.

"Any way," I said.

Then we started to float up. Melvin said, "We don't have any space suits."

We hit so hard that we broke the rocket ship. But it's lucky I had ten bottles of sleeping pills. So I opened the bottles of sleeping pills and threw them in the monster's mouth. He went to sleep. He fell and he fell, and finally he landed on earth. We went down to earth and brought him to the Zoo. And we got $10,000,000 and one cent.

The End

Larry, 8/11

QUESTIONS ON VERBAL EXPRESSION THROUGH CREATIVE STORYTELLING

1. Discuss how a good storyteller makes the characters live.

2. a. List the requirements for good illustrative material for young children. b. What types of pictures would you collect for a picture file for your fives group? c. How would you assort these for filing and ready access?

3. Discuss No. 2 above in terms of older children.

4. Analyze a television series that many children enjoy: a. What is the general type of the story? b. Point out some of the truths to be gained from the various episodes. c. Discuss briefly how viewing such programs might affect the following phases of language development and social attitudes: (1) Clear auditory impressions; (2) Speech difficulties; (3) Inflection; (4) Acquiring word meanings incidentally; (5) Conservation and appreciation of nature; (6) Appreciation of law and order and respect for those delegated to enforce the laws; (7) Respect for and consideration of the rights, attitudes, and feelings of other people; (8) Viewpoints, if any, to be carried over into the child's pattern of living.

5. a. Present a story in which an animal does something within the realm of possibility, and contrast it with a fanciful story of animals dressed up, talking and acting like humans. b. Discuss each from the standpoint of the child's background of knowledge by which he may distinguish between fact and fancy. c. Why, therefore, is the fanciful type not recommended for the young child who has little firsthand knowledge of animal life? Discuss.

6. Discuss the principle, "There is no impression without expression."

7. Create a puppet story for: a. A beginning primary group. b. A middle primary group. c. An upper primary group.

8. Discuss ways of bringing far things near and the past to life for the older child when a familiar object tells its story: a. Discuss how processes can be made concrete in this way: the pencil tells how it was manufactured; the Christmas tree tells how it grew to be a Christmas tree; the robin flies in and tells how the apple blossoms finally became a pie; the letter tells how it was written and mailed, and how it was delivered to John. b. Discuss how the past can be brought to life, as: The old well in the churchyard tells the stories of things it saw when it was young, and how people came to drink its water in the olden days before the new church was built; the violin tells how it was built and played and cherished by different persons through the years; the bridge tells of the horses that were ridden over it, the carriages, the early automobiles, the modern cars. c. Discuss the background the storyteller may need to create this type of story, and how it may help develop the child's concepts of time and people and the changing world. d. Discuss the matter of the child's background of experience and readiness for broadened horizons, and the values of older children doing research to create stories of this type "on their own."

SELECTED REFERENCES

Anglund, Joan W., LOVE IS A SPECIAL WAY OF FEELING, New York, Harcourt, Brace & Co., 1960.

Durland, Frances C., CREATIVE DRAMATICS FOR CHILDREN, Yellow Springs, Ohio, The Antioch Press, 1952.

Larrick, Nancy, A TEACHER'S GUIDE TO CHILDREN'S LITERATURE, Columbus, Ohio, Charles E. Merrill Books, Inc., 1960.

Siks, Geraldine B., CREATIVE DRAMATICS: AN ART FOR CHILDREN, New York, Harper & Bros., 1952.

Tooze, Ruth, STORYTELLING, Englewood Cliffs, N. J., Prentice-Hall, Inc., 1959.

Walker, Pamela P., SEVEN STEPS TO CREATIVE DRAMATICS, New York, Hill and Wang, Inc., 1957.

Woods, Margaret S., CREATIVE DRAMATICS, Washington, D.C., National Education Association, 1959.

BLOCK CONSTRUCTION IN DEVELOPING

Part Eight

SOCIAL CONCEPTS

I. DEVELOPING SOCIAL CONCEPTS

Social concepts are only part of the total development which the child receives through guided experience in block construction, yet within this and other aspects of childhood education (see also Parts Nine and Ten) lie the foundations for many significant social understandings and skills.

The Universal Inclination to Build and Learn

Undoubtedly the caveman's child dug out caves fashioned after the crude structure of the adults in his environment. The child of the tree dweller tried to reconstruct in his play the woven shelters which protected him; the nomad's child stitched together bits of skin with a bone needle so that he, too, might have a tent. Or possibly, each, according to his environment, appropriated the abandoned cave, the discarded shelter mat, or the worn-out skin and called upon his imagination to supply whatever was lacking.

Inherent in the child is this love of manipulation, of experimentation, and a joy in imitating what he observes of adult behavior in his environment. This is one of the major ways in which he acquires the skills that prepare him to carry on according to the mores of his people.

The modern school takes cognizance of this characteristic of the child and strives to create an environment that provides him an opportunity to explore, to investigate, to experiment, and to test; a climate in which he learns to listen, to talk, to share, to respect the right's of others; to make choices that are progressively significant; to participate in rhythmic activities, song and dramatic expression; an environment in which creativity is encouraged and cherished and his worth as an individual is genuinely appreciated.

Blocks should be an important media in creating this learning environment in the school of early childhood. They are often the initial step in a long series in the educative process and may be a vital factor in helping the child to master the academic subjects.

Froebel was the first to capitalize upon the child's intuitive urge to build and reproduce. He introduced a series of small blocks which were referred to as "games of skill" and as "gifts and occupations."

Those who conducted the early kindergartens, although they accepted Froebel's theories, insisted upon rigid patterns of procedure and tended to lose sight of the play spirit which Froebel had capitalized upon in teaching children.

Gradually, however, in the more forward looking schools and teacher training centers the wisdom of utilizing the child's play spirit as an aid in teaching was accepted, with blocks an important exponent of this philosophy.

Children naturally build with three-dimensional materials at hand—boxes, boards, crates, become dens, houses, tepees. Robert Louis Stevenson revealed his understanding of children and his vision and insight into their joy in building structures in:

> We built a ship upon the stairs,
> All made of the back bedroom chairs.

This type of dramatic expression is enjoyed by the children of each succeeding generation. The make-believe house reflects the type of living that has caught the child's fancy. Pat and Marian often lived in a tree house, or a tepee, but they are not surprised that for their grandchildren the draped grand piano has become a space ship.

Numerous opportunities for intrinsic, controlled actions and social competencies arise. With understanding teacher guidance, experiences of this type nurture cooperative group living in which the individual contributes his just share and democracy in action truly exists. The child gains a social awareness and learns that planning and working with others is more fun than working alone. Other children have good ideas and each listens to the other's suggestions. Together they make a decision and carry it through. Sharing the blocks with one another, the children build a larger, more complete structure. Respect for another's work is developed. Each unique personality must adjust to each other personality in the group. Each child will give and receive and thereby understand and appreciate democratic principles.

To assure the above, guidance and "on the spot evaluation" are essential in block building. Without immediate evaluation by the children the entire program of self-directed block construction would fail. If evaluated "on the spot," the children can make further progress by capitalizing on the discussions and thought-provoking suggestions and putting them into immediate action.

Block building is a medium through which the child's mental images take form and which provides practice in life situations through reproducing the world in which the child must orient himself.

Objectives and Value in Block Building

Children need to be brought together in ways which require social adjustment, which encourage purposeful activity, which aid in muscular coordination and control. Many of the materials for use with the younger children are limited in their flexibility. There are infinite possibilities in the various types of painting, modeling, carpentry, puzzles, and the like, but these bring only limited if any group action with its potential for individual adjustment and cooperation. Equipment most contributory to self-expression is that which invites investigation and manipulation and out of which a satisfying product emerges. Block construction constitutes one of the most fruitful sources of learning in its contribution to the child's basic needs and total growth.

Physical Development—A Necessity for Growth

Children delight in being active, and block construction demands getting up and down, bending over, reaching, pushing, pulling, and carrying blocks.

Some of the large hollow blocks have grip holes in the ends so that the child can get his hand in and carry blocks from either side. There are two schools of thought on the value of these grip holes. Many teachers favor them. Others, among them the authors of this book, believe that the grip holes eliminate much of the purpose behind the hollow blocks, because the holes remove the necessity of stooping and lifting, which are among the larger muscle activities that aid materially in the physical development of the child. Eye and hand coordination is developed through reaching and lifting hollow blocks without hand grips, and motor dexterity is acquired since the arm and hand are used rather than the fingers alone.

Working with blocks helps children develop equipoise. In order to build some of their complicated structures the children must acquire the ability to balance the blocks so as to assure stability of the structure.

Block manipulation also supplies the child with a variety of sensory impressions which at this period in his life provide one of the major avenues to learning. There is much satisfaction in movement and touch as day after day one block after another is put into place, with each new structure varied according to the promptings of a developing creativity.

Blocks Implement the Six Goals

Block construction is a concrete medium for furthering the six goals of early childhood education to the extent that your ingenuity allows you to take advantage of limitless possibilities.

Attitudes

Wholesome attitudes are an integral part of all the other goals. The spirit in which a thing is carried out is often more important than the activity itself.

There is an attitude of consideration for others' rights to space, and the child learns he must often compromise and relocate his building to avoid crowding someone else's work. "Am I leaving enough space to walk between Ralph's airport and my restaurant," or some such consideration must be given before a new building is launched. Thus the child comes to recognize the need for careful thinking before he begins to build. It is your responsibility to strive toward positive attitudes and couch your suggestions in positive terms.

Blocks offer innumerable opportunities for helping children gain a well-rounded personality. Throughout block construction and the accompanying dramatic expression, there is a need to develop concepts and to help children gain appreciation of community relationships, and there is an opportunity for cooperative planning and sharing of materials. How this is guided will depend upon the maturity of the children. With beginners you may emphasize, "We use just our share and only the blocks we need. Bobby and Louise want to build with blocks, too."

Your guidance leads each child to make his own contribution to the enterprise, to pool ideas, and to try various procedures until everyone is satisfied. Thus, by first-hand experience each child learns that greater things may be accomplished through sharing than he alone could do.

Eddie, Arthur, Brenda, and Stephen were children who usually grabbed for what they wanted, each a law unto himself. One day, however, their teacher learned from their conversation they were going to build houses and be neighbors. Each had so many ideas that the building changed several times. Each brought his own blocks from the shelf, and then the four thought out the best place to build.

It was good to see these children working together toward a common purpose.

Behavior Patterns

Automatic behavior patterns grow out of democratic rules for behavior; from sharing, planning, and building together. Consistency in guidance is essential in the establishing of behavior patterns. If there are no guiding principles to help him, the child will vacillate from one behavior to another.

Among the essential behaviors to be established for the good of the individual and of the group in which he participates are activities such as planning work before starting to build; carrying one block in each hand, or one at a time for the younger children; getting only the blocks needed for the construction; walking with the blocks and avoiding bumping into anyone else; finishing the construction before bringing out the accessory materials; stopping for "on the spot" evaluation whenever necessary; after construction and before clean-up, evaluating work; putting the accessory materials away first; returning the blocks to their proper places according to the outline shape on the wall or the shelves.

The responsibility of each child in the orderly stacking of the blocks at clean-up time reinforces the behavior pattern of returning things to their proper places after use.

Appreciations

As has been emphasized again and again throughout this book a child needs to *appreciate* himself and others and the abilities, strengths, and needs of each, if he is to have a happy life.

Through building with blocks the child learns to appreciate the equipment with which he works.

When arranging the blocks the children express a natural feeling for repetition, rhythm, design, and symmetry, which are inherent in each one's environment. They learn to judge line and balance as they build, and many intricate and elaborate constructions result.

Blocks stimulate imagination and contribute to a more discerning appreciation of good workmanship in balance and design.

Creativity

Creative expression is fostered through block construction as the child comes to realize that he and his friends can work out their own ideas in shapes and structures.

Blocks are so flexible that they can become almost any structure; hence they provide unlimited opportunity for creative dramatization. This necessitates your having a large and varied repertoire so that you can integrate a song, rhythm, poem, action play, or story at the opportune moment. This leads the child into creative expression as he recreates his own experiences and then reaches out into vicarious ones that relate to him. Creative stories are a natural by-product of block building.

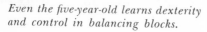

Even the five-year-old learns dexterity and control in balancing blocks.

Independent Thinking

Independent thinking is stimulated through problems constantly arising in block construction. The children solve these problems through discussion, evaluation, interviews with authorities, scientific experiments and observation, and through the use of reference materials (pictorial for the younger children).

When the children's blocks were falling Mrs. Moulton showed a picture of a child balancing with a parasol. "What will the parasol do for Janice?" asked Mrs. Moulton.

Vivian said, "It balances her. Janice leans this way and one side is heavier so she holds her arm way out with the parasol and it keeps her from falling."

Mrs. Moulton placed a parasol in the home center. The children found it and experimented in balancing as they walked on the narrow edge of a two-by-four plank. The sense of balance was discussed in some detail, and then Mrs. Moulton showed pictures of how John had solved a problem about balance. John explained how he had placed an extra block to help support the overhanging block. Much experimentation with blocks followed. Later, during the work period Danny said about his block structure: "It's well balanced. It can't possibly fall. See how I used these extra blocks to balance my bridge."

The enthusiastic interest in balance was stimulated even further when Mrs. Moulton placed a balance scales in the environment, with numerous materials of various weights for the children's use in experimentation.

Even for older children clarification of details may require only a good clear picture, but to create life-like structures often demands real research to find the details which a child wants to represent with his blocks.

Building with blocks also provides opportunity for the child to relate previous solutions to the current problem. He needs to solve the problem of estimating the space required to build in the direction he wants to go. Consistent evaluations demand independent thinking, ability to weigh facts and opinions carefully, and to develop discrimination.

In presenting thought problems you will, of course, make sure they are a challenge, but one that is within the child's ability to solve. Particularly in the representative and constructive stages of block building, children encounter problems in completing an idea. They may solve these problems through creative thinking, experimentation, and ingenuity. For example, several children built a house and when it was finished Glenda said, "Our house doesn't have a window." In their effort to make a window the children pulled out a block. The entire structure collapsed. They then rebuilt it and this time they spaced the blocks in a way that left the desired window.

The more mature child will be able to suggest a possible solution of a problem in cooperation. In one case some of the children wanted to build a bus, while others wanted a house. When a vote was taken they discovered there was an even number on each side. The children discussed the matter and decided that both a house and a bus could be built. The people in the house could go for a ride on the bus. Later the children who voted for the house decided to use it as a bus terminal.

A "truck problem" arose when John wanted to use the truck for his produce farm and Bill wanted it for his gasoline station. The teacher asked the boys to think what they could do about it. They talked it over and decided that John would take his turn and continue to use the truck to carry his "produce," and then he would let Bill have it. In this way they were learning to share and to exchange various rights.

Understanding, Knowledge, and Skills

Dave and Sandra were building with Ivey blocks. They needed another long block but none was available. "Here," said Dave, "we can take two blocks this size and they will be the same length as the long one."

Billy and John were constructing a platform from Ivey blocks. They placed long, narrow blocks down side by side, but there were not enough of that particular length to make the platform the size they wanted. Through thoughtful manipulation they found how many shorter ones laid side by side were the length of one of the larger blocks they had first used.

When he was placing the floor blocks on the shelves according to the shapes of the blocks Larry discovered that when the blocks are put away properly the grain of the wood in the blocks runs the same way as that of the wood from which the shelves are constructed.

Block building gives the young child experience with concrete form, size, and spacial relationships. He also finds blocks a means of expressing his newly formed understanding and knowledge of the life around him. It is possible for him to create realistic forms in his block building much earlier than with paints and clay. In his constructions he will frequently omit something essential to a structure which is not yet a part of his concepts. Pictures are a means of clarifying and extending his understanding as are well-timed and carefully planned field trips. The child's observations can be gradually heightened but never forced. Block construction will help him understand his experiences and retain them in his memory. It is a vital factor in helping him develop ability to make wise choices.

Blocks as Raw Material Throughout the Primary School

How blocks are used depends upon the child's efforts, ideas, and maturation, as well as upon you, his teacher. In building with blocks the child is unhampered by what others have done and uses his own imagination to put them together as he chooses. He learns incidentally through trial and error, and through evaluation of his efforts.

Blocks never lose their appeal as a medium of expression because the child never reaches the limit of their possibilities. They challenge his creative powers, his ability to plan ahead and think constructively and independently; they challenge his power to solve problems as they arise; to concentrate on one problem at a time and follow it through to a triumphant conclusion; they challenge him to interact with his peers in a spirit of "give and take." Blocks also encourage a child to demonstrate his concepts in a concrete and personal way. Thus through block construction the child acquires deeper perception. Since experiences are the source of ideas and ideas are the basis of expression, an idea does not become an integrated part of the child until he has applied that idea in a meaningful situation. Therefore, through the child's block construction you are alerted to, and have an opportunity to rectify, his lack of understanding, his misconceptions, and can know where his ideas and concepts are incomplete.

Building with blocks has definite value for the younger children because it makes the shift from the concrete to the abstract more realistic for them. If the necessity arises to discuss an abstract idea, reference can be made to concrete experiences that have occurred in block building. Some of these may illustrate, for example, the concept of before and after, above and below, wide and narrow, flat, thick, and thin, and the like.

When children are building with blocks they are putting into concrete form their ideas and knowledge of a certain subject.

As the child's attention span widens, his ability to concentrate increases. In like manner his block structures become more elaborate and complicated. Younger children, with their more fleeting interests, usually put away their blocks each day. Older children who have more sustained interest will frequently take a number of days to complete a structure.

Blocks are a natural medium of expression for the five- and six-year-old. The sevens, eights, and nines also find release through block building. Concepts are increasingly more complex and new learnings are constant as the children build with more dexterity and control of block balance. Their structures have greater complexity in keeping with their increasing ability to grasp concepts.

More mature children not only build cooperatively according to the area they are studying, but under teacher guidance they set up their own learning situations.

Emotional Values

Block construction meets children's emotional needs. Frustrations are often released through block building. The tense, hostile child becomes more relaxed and channels his negative, destructive feelings into constructive expression. The shy child becomes less withdrawn as he gains confidence through success with first himself, then one other, and later several other children through block building. He feels a sense of belonging and security. In the same way the child who hesitates to try can feel success in as simple a way as stacking one block on top of another, without in any way interfering with other children; their complex building is not altered by the simplicity of his. Still another child who has been utterly dependent and needs help in every action and decision comes at last to create a structure all his own.

Happiness is a child's inherent right, and the majority of children delight in block construction and find joy and satisfaction in this opportunity for self expression at their particular stage of development.

II. DEVELOPMENTAL STAGES IN BLOCK BUILDING

As in other phases of the curriculum there are developmental stages in the child's block construction. You as the child's teacher can determine his stage of advancement through observing his approach to block building.

The Manipulative and Experimental Stage

Through his manipulation of blocks, with no premeditated purpose in mind, the child familiarizes himself with the characteristics of blocks. He examines them and observes their different sizes and shapes. His activities probably are entirely individual and spontaneous, and the play motive most dominant. He enjoys carrying the blocks from place to place, or he may line them up end to end only to tumble them down to hear the sound of the crash; or he may pile them up indiscriminately, one block on top of another.

The child first familiarizes himself with the charac- teristics of blocks.

No matter how simple his first building may be, this manipulation of blocks is an important part of his development. Even older children who have not previously had experience with block construction will go through this manipulative and experimental stage, but their work usually results in intricate designs, and they are ready to progress to the next step and the next far more rapidly than the less mature child.

Diana, in a five-year-old group, was fascinated with the floor blocks, but was perfectly happy just to pile them up one on top of the other until they collapsed. Then she would clap her hands and laugh with glee.

The same day Tony carried one block after another from the shelf to the center of the room. Then he put them back in their proper places when the time was over.

Phyllis took the pyramid blocks off the shelf. She took each block out and set them all down in a row in front of her. She was intrigued with the way each one came out of the others. When it was time to put the blocks away, Phyllis didn't know how to do it. She did discover that the smaller blocks would go inside some of the larger ones, but she did not attempt to put them back in order, but dumped them all on the shelf. With the teacher's guidance Phyllis solved the problem of nesting them together according to size and was pleased when they all fit together inside the largest one.

Later, these children were interested in using all the different shapes and sizes of blocks and piling them high in a teetering tower. They were beginning to feel the need for balance and design and were striving to make the blocks respond as they continued with their stacking. Phyllis discovered the tall stack she could make with the pyramid blocks.

The teacher made notes of the children's activities from day to day. It was evident that all the children in the group engaged in manipulative, solitary play. There were many blocks being used here and there on the floor, but nothing definite was built. Experiment with shape, size, balance, and design was evident.

The Representative Stage

As the child enters the representative stage he builds from an idea stimulated by his manipulation of the blocks. He creates a structure by piling the blocks on top of one another or out to the side. He may name his towered pile or compare the different shapes and sizes of blocks. Gradually his structure takes on the appearance of what appears to him to be a bridge or a house, a road or some other familiar item, and he continues to build with this idea in mind; or he will look at what he has built and devise a story or explanation of his structure. Particularly with the hollow blocks at this stage, the child will change his mind as the building develops, depending on what fits the structure that is progressing. There is no incongruity for the same structure to be a plane at one time, a boat at another, and then change to a house or a tree within a period of a few minutes.

Although at this stage of building the uninitiated adult can seldom recognize the thing the child says he has built, the child himself has profited because he will have gained the same type of satisfaction as the

At the representative stage, the child's structure gradually takes on the appearance of

a road,

a house,

a bridge,

or some other familiar object.

artist who has painted a beautiful picture, or the poet who has written a lovely poem. The child, too, has created, and has satisfied his own need.

It is during this stage of block construction that routine and fundamental behavior patterns are established as a preparation for larger learning situations.

Richard, Gloria, Doris, and Raymond, a group of five-year-olds, had made a solid structure with hollow blocks. They climbed on top of it and called it a house. Then they made a few adjustments in the structure and actually made it look like the walls of a house. A few minutes later they called it a truck, climbed on top of the front wall, piled blocks in it, and drove away.

Arthur was building with hollow blocks. He put two together and called it a motorcycle. That is what it became to him. Satisfied with himself he proceeded to bring out some more blocks and repeated the same simple pattern. Now he had "two motorcycles."

Fred made an interesting, tall, abstract building with the floor blocks, using curves and cylinders along with the rectangular blocks. He apparently had no idea in mind, but when George asked him what it was, Fred hesitated a moment and then called it "a radio station."

The Advanced Stage

As the child matures he grows into the more advanced stage of block expression. He now begins to work with a purpose in mind. He shows individual styling in his building; he is learning to organize his facts, information, and observations, and is getting ready to extend his experiences. You must remember, however, that his growth in these respects is just as individual as his physical development.

If the block construction is a group undertaking, as it generally is in the constructive stage of development, the children discuss and plan before they start to build. Unlike the representative stage, if the group meet an obstacle in building, they meet it by changing and adapting the structure accordingly, instead of revising their plan to fit the structure.

The child should be encouraged to talk about his construction and to explain his ideas. He goes from the known to the unknown in this way; and from one idea may grow others for further building.

When Danny, Sharon, and Mike built a foundation they said the reason they had to make their building so strong and sturdy was because it was a storage place for cars and furniture.

III. TECHNIQUES OF GUIDING BLOCK CONSTRUCTION

The educational values of block building justify its inclusion as an integral part of the early childhood education curriculum, and as such it demands your careful thought, planning, and guidance; also your interest and enthusiasm.

As in everything else, children do their best work in block construction in a calm and happy environment, free from tension and strain.

The time devoted to block building needs to be long enough to develop whatever individual or group project is in progress, allowing the children to build without a feeling of pressure; yet equally important is your alertness to signs of fatigue, lack of ideas, and the misuse of blocks, which indicate that the children need a change of activity.

Guidance During the Manipulative Stage

In the manipulative stage of block building your guidance is limited to suggesting ways of stacking blocks and putting all of one size or shape together. Each restacking gives the child motor, visual, and kinesthetic experience which helps to develop an awareness of the elements of number, size, weight, and proportion. The child is left to his own devices as long as he is working purposefully. When he ceases to do this, you either help him find new possibilities for work with blocks, or else a new task.

Each child should be encouraged to choose his own material and to select the size and kinds of blocks which he wishes to work with. He should feel free to express whatever idea he has in mind. You need to guard against being overly-ambitious for the child to progress from the manipulative to the representative stage of building. He needs to experiment in order to discover the possibilities of his materials and to exercise his creative powers.

Pictorial and Verbal Records

In the beginning, some teachers build with the children to give them security. These teachers gradually move out of the picture, but sit on the floor or in a low chair and make sketches of the block structures or record the children's verbalizations. As the sketches and verbalizations are presented to the children later on, the individuals involved become vitally interested, and your participation in this manner encourages thoughtful and enthusiastic building. Emphasis is on the work and interest in building with blocks rather than in the finished structure. The child appreciates this attention to his work. The sketches, if recorded regularly, are sufficient evidence of the growth that is taking place, and are also an excellent point of departure for individual parent conferences. They may become a delightful contact between home and school. They also do much to stimulate the child to further growth.

Block Construction Dependent on Background of Experience

Most necessary for expressive and meaningful block construction is a background of vital and widely varying experiences. These are, of course, best gained through personal experience in the community, but stories, the discussion of books, pictures, and film strips may also stimulate interest and give ideas. It is through representation and re-creation of life experiences that the young child learns to understand them; hence you will want to encourage him to talk about and relive the life around him.

A seven-year-old shows imagination and skill in her construction of an old-time castle.

When the child has reached the constructive stage, your guidance should constantly stimulate thought which will lead to creative and more effective use of the blocks.

A chance remark, a sudden need, or an unusual insight on the part of a child can be captured by you and either guided into further expression or called to the attention of the entire group for evaluation, appreciation, or solution.

> Several five-year-old children were constructing a ferry boat and began by building a pointed bow. Julie, who was working with them, protested, "Ferry boats don't come to a point like that."
> The children would have ignored Julie if the teacher had not picked up the lead. She asked Julie to repeat her statement, and then they referred to a picture in the file. They found that ferry boats are open on both ends so the cars can drive on and off at the docks.

You need to be ever alert to clarify misconceptions by asking questions, by capitalizing on the knowledge of children who have the background for particular topics by calling attention where possible to the object the children are attempting to represent, and when this is not possible by referring to books and pictures.

A group who had taken a trip to the airport to see the terminal building, the hangars, the look-out tower, and other features, re-created the entire experience with block construction. They found they needed to do some research. For one thing they had no lights for the pilots' use in landing at night. The children went to books and to reliable pictures in their file to find out about landing lights.

Discussion of Plans Helpful

More meaningful and thoughtful block construction takes place when there is a discussion of plans before the children begin to build. This requires more maturity of purpose and applies particularly to those who have reached the constructive stage.

> A teacher asked a group of six-year-olds, "What are your building plans for today?"
> Ricky: "We are going to build a hangar."
> Sally: "And put up a control tower, too."
> Lucy: "Where will our plane go?"
> Teacher: "The plane can't roll out of your hangar for a trip until after you finish building your hangar." (What the teacher meant was that before accessory materials can be used the block structure must be completed and the builders be ready for dramatic expression.)

On the Spot Evaluations

As is true of all other activities, evaluation is an essential facet of the block building program.

From time to time there needs to be "on the spot" evaluation of a construction which will offer a challenging point to a particular group, or possibly to all of the children, especially if the group is at approximately the same stage in their building. Even children working in other centers on a given day may evidence a clear concept of vocabulary and sound thinking as they participate in the evaluation of block structures developed by other children.

A problem which confronts every beginning builder who has reached the constructive stage is what to do about corners when a train is on the track.

Ricky, John, and Bob in the six-year-old group were building a railroad track. They wanted to turn the corner, which was a sharp one. They put the train on the track and when it went around the curve it fell off. Every time the train was put back on the track it fell off again at this point.

The boys went to their teacher for help, and she suggested they look at a picture of a railroad track that curved. The group studied the picture but still couldn't decide how to build their track.

All the children were called over to study the problem. They looked at the picture and finally Ricky himself decided they could make the track with arched blocks and then the train wouldn't have to make such a sharp turn and would remain on the track.

The boys went ahead and built the track; the train went smoothly around the bend and the boys were proud.

The next morning when Ricky came into the room he went right to the blocks and said, "I'm going to build a train track and make it go around the corner."

He built the track without difficulty, due to the learning experience of the previous day.

A few days later Ricky was building a track again. He said, "I need a train picture." He selected one from the reference file that showed an arched bridge. He studied the picture carefully and remarked, "I could use the arched block for this, too."

One group of children had built a runway with a wind sock. During evaluation, Paul, who had been doing some research, commented, "Your wind sock is going the wrong way. An airplane takes off into the wind."

Several children built a structure and called it a sailboat, but it was square. The teacher suggested that they get a picture of a sailboat and study it carefully. They did this and discussed how they could make their boat more lifelike. Later, they built a more realistic sailboat.

Another group was building a boat with hollow blocks, using a picture from a book, but they were not following a definite plan. The teacher called the group together to decide what kind of boat they wished to build. They chose an ocean liner. They referred to the picture in the book, finished their boat, and had time left to take a ride in it before clean-up.

Helpful evaluation cannot develop spontaneously unless the attitude is one of friendly give and take. Children need to consider the feelings of others in offering suggestions, and those receiving help must be ready to recognize the spirit in which the recommendation is offered. Guidance in this direction is gradual.

When Walter's barn was evaluated and suggestion made for improvement he said, "Yes, that barn of mine isn't very good. That's why I brought David back to work with me so we could make a better one."

Jerry and Arthur were building a long, low, rambling object. It looked like a fence. They used long narrow blocks (approximately $1\frac{3}{4}''$ x $2\frac{3}{4}''$ x $22''$). In their conversation the teacher heard Jerry tell Arthur that his range would hold "1000 acres of cattle."

Later, they put partitions across and divided the enclosure into three parts. One was for the cows, one for the horses, and the other for food.

The construction for Jerry had purpose and meaning. He had lived on a ranch for two years and apparently loved it because it was revealed not only in his block construction but in all other creative efforts. Arthur was an immature child, and for him it meant much to dramatize the experience with Jerry, getting into the construction and sharing a little of the viewpoint of a family other than his own.

In the evaluation of their work the teacher asked Jerry how the food for the animals was stored on the ranch. The children all learned the word *silo* and talked about why the food needed to be stored and where it came from before it was put into the silo.

When a child is guided in his thinking by the teacher's questions he is usually able to reach a satisfactory conclusion.

Ronald was building a tunnel for a train track. The tunnel wasn't tall enough for the train to go under. The teacher paused to comment on his good idea of building a tunnel. "Why didn't the train go under?" she added.

"It's not tall enough," said Ronald.

"How could you make the tunnel higher?" asked the teacher. "Which blocks would you use?"

Ronald thought about it and then finished the tunnel using larger blocks in an upright fashion.

You should be ever alert for opportunities to guide the children into better understandings through block construction.

> One group of six-year-olds had made a theater; another group had built a church. When it came to final details in the construction of the church there was an argument as to whether there would be a cross on it or not. Then the children argued over the pulpit.
> Martha said, "Our priest does it this way."
> Carolyn said, "Our minister does it this way."
> The teacher heard the children and went over to them to explain: "There are many churches," she said. "In the Catholic church you would do as Martha has said, but in the Protestant church you would do as Carolyn said. So you are both right."

The children continued their dramatization, but part of the time they had a cross on their church and did as Martha directed; then Carolyn was in charge and they did as she directed.

Adequate Guidance Summarized

As children work together in block construction they need adequate guidance in order that they may learn to: 1. enter into simple group planning; 2. carry their own blocks in a safe way; 3. work with a purpose in mind; 4. assume responsibility as a leader or a follower; 5. carry through a responsibility; 6. share and express ideas; 7. make use of pertinent information; 8. use material for what it was intended; 9. take care of school and personal property; 10. respect the rights and feelings of others in the group; 11. listen courteously to other children; 12. enter into group discussion; 13. think through group problem solving; 14. clarify concepts and extend ideas; 15. follow good housekeeping procedures in care of equipment; 16. use time wisely.

IV. PROVIDING FACILITIES FOR BLOCK BUILDING

Two difficulties often confront the teacher in providing opportunities for block construction: One is insufficient space and the other is an inadequate supply of blocks. The area in which the children build should be relatively free from distracting objects. If there is inadequate space or an insufficient number of blocks and it is impossible to obtain more, then it will be necessary for you to limit the number of children engaged in block building at any one time, so that each child has enough blocks for the unhampered development of his ideas. By making a record of those who participate on various days you can be sure the block building facilities are made available frequently to every child.

Storing Blocks

Proper storing of blocks makes for efficiency and avoids needless expenditure of time. If at all possible, blocks should be stored on low shelves, adjacent to the block building area. The low shelves are easily accessible to the children, who learn to be wholly responsible for getting out the blocks and putting them away according to an agreed upon plan. If there are no shelves in the room the blocks may be piled on the floor close to the wall.

It is essential that the child be able to see at a glance what material is available and make his choice accordingly. Learning from the beginning that the blocks are to be put away carefully eliminates the problem of the children dumping the blocks together, irrespective of size and shape, and develops a behavior pattern of neatness and order.

Care of Blocks

Care in handling blocks needs to be established from the very first, not only for the good of the blocks, but from the standpoint of the education of the children. The care children take of blocks will be determined by the standards you set up. Hollow blocks and floor blocks are sturdily built to withstand with reasonable care any amount of usage demanded in construction and creative dramatization of children.

On the first day of school, when you acquaint your children with indoor and outdoor environment, you have an opportunity to introduce them to the block center. Some of the children can demonstrate, while the group evaluates getting blocks out, locating a place to build, and replacing various shapes and sizes on the shelves from which they were taken, so they will be ready for use next time.

You may display an old splintered block that has suffered misuse and ask the children to compare it with another which has been used considerately over a long period of time. This comparison of an abused block with one that has been properly handled will show children the choice that is theirs to make in block care. From time to time you may discuss and evaluate the acceptable use of blocks from the standpoint of carrying, placing, and lifting, rather than throwing them about, or knocking or dropping them. Your emphasis will be on the positive rather than the negative use of blocks.

It may be possible for you to take your children to visit the workshop or laboratory where blocks are being built and let them see the pride and care with which they are made.

Blocks may be built by the industrial arts classes in the secondary schools or by the fathers; in both cases the visit by the children will be welcomed. An alternative is to have someone capable of making the blocks come in and bring materials and tools to demonstrate the process of constructing them.[1]

Children will appreciate the blocks, and with your guidance in establishing attitudes and behavior patterns, handle them accordingly.

You can strengthen impressions of how to care for blocks by drawings and pictorial caption cards for the younger children, and through caption cards and bulletin boards in primary groups where children are reading. A wholesome respect for the blocks themselves will go a long way toward eliciting from children the consideration deserved by any piece of equipment of this type.

Selection of Blocks

The selection of blocks requires thoughtful consideration. All too frequently the purchase of a set of blocks is governed by the cost, but the so-called original selection of cheaper materials may be more expensive in the end through warping, cracking, or chipping.

You should make certain, too, that there is a varied assortment of specified sizes and shapes, and if possible, there should be a sufficient quantity so that adequate structures can be built, allowing children to develop their ideas satisfactorily.

Blocks that can be combined in a variety of ways, and remain together by the weight and stability of each part, allow for flexibility of use by the child and encourage more creativity than those which must be fastened together. Rods, bolts, tongues, or other devices are difficult for the five- and six-year-old to manipulate and make block building laborious or tedious. The young child is not interested in the fixed permanent building and should be encouraged to put his blocks away for the day with the idea that they will be ready for use again later, either by himself or someone else.

---

[1] Ivey blocks are not commercially made but you can have them cut to specifications. Hollow blocks may also be built to given dimensions.

An essential quality of blocks is that they can be cut accurately so that all edges are even and that the multiples and divisions of the unit are exact. Blocks are the child's building medium and desirable structural patterns can only be established if the materials are precise.

All blocks should have aesthetic value; their design should be interesting and conducive to the development of architectural principles.

Types of Blocks

It is well for children to have access to two basic types of blocks: a set of large hollow blocks which are fairly heavy to lift, and a set of solid floor blocks.

Numbers, sizes, and shapes will of course be adapted to the age and maturity of the children who are to use them.

Hollow Blocks

Because of their size and weight, hollow blocks are ideal for large muscle development. There is much bending, stooping, and lifting even in pure manipulation of these blocks, and they stimulate sitting, standing, and climbing.

The hollow block is symmetrical in shape, built to specifications which assure free interchange of one size with another in every conceivable manner. The possible combinations are endless. One, two, and three block structures result when two- and three-year-olds use them, while children in the five- and six-, seven- and eight-year-old groups find them excellent for building large constructions such as airplanes, trains, houses, stores, and other community centers.

A dimension of approximately six inches or multiples thereof is highly satisfactory for this type of block. A minimum set of hollow blocks contains the following pieces:

   10 blocks 6″ x 6″ x 12″
   10 blocks 6″ x 12″ x 12″
   10 blocks 6″ x 12″ x 24″
    3 blocks 6″ x 12″ x 24″ with one open face and one, two, or three shelves.

The number of each size may be increased, and a few larger blocks built on the same unit of measure may be added for the older children, for example: 12″ x 12″ x 12″ and 12″ x 12″ x 24″.

Construction with hollow blocks is flexible and brings a variety of building. Even with fewer sizes and shapes than floor blocks, the children can build firm structures larger than themselves. The choice of rectangular and square surfaces based on a uniform unit of measure provides material which is safe and solid. No matter what combination of hollow blocks the child makes he arrives at something firm enough to bear the

weight of his own body, and of such proportions that several children at once can use it effectively for spontaneous dramatic experiences in which they are the life-size participants.

Hollow blocks serve effectively for spontaneous dramatic experiences in which the children are the life-size participants.

Solid Floor Blocks

Floor blocks, so-called, are considerably smaller than hollow blocks, and have a greater variety of sizes and shapes, which may be placed together flat, end to end, side by side, or piled on top of one another. They will also stand on end. Usually made of white pine, they are smooth, unpainted, but well-finished.

Ivey blocks are representative of this type. They stimulate the child's imagination and creativity, and are considered among the best of all blocks designed for children in this category of equipment.

Ivey Block Specifications

Early childhood teachers feel that deep appreciation is due Henrilu Ivey and Ethel I. Salisbury, the originators of the Ivey blocks, for making available at no charge the block specifications on the following page. (While the total number of blocks to be made to specification may be decreased or increased, careful study of the children's use of them should be made before changing the relative proportion of the sizes and shapes in a set. You may wish to start by providing for your group half or a quarter of the number here suggested, and later add another equal amount.)

Ivey blocks provide three-dimensional materials that give the children fundamental concepts of space, line, proportion, and relative values which are basic to mathematical thinking.

For primary children, gears, pulleys, inclined planes, big triangles, and a variety of curved shapes and large cylinders could be devised that would make the value of these floor blocks even greater than the suggested set.

Pyramid Blocks

So-called pyramid blocks have an entirely different use as problem solving material for younger children. These blocks are built on a given shape, with one side open (usually a hollow cube) : each block being just enough larger than the next in size so that they fit inside each other, and the whole set is contained in the largest block.

The child can take them apart and turn them upside down, one upon another, to make a large pyramid (hence their name). Other uses may also be discovered by the child as he manipulates them.

Putting them together again in proper order requires a certain amount of skill and problem solving for the immature five-year-old, or younger child.

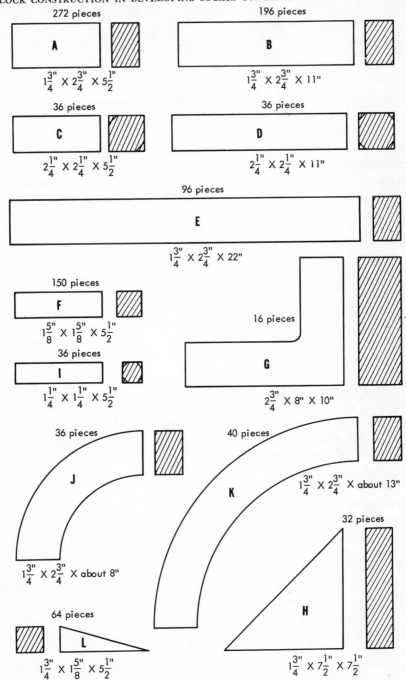

272 pieces

A

$1\frac{3}{4}" \times 2\frac{3}{4}" \times 5\frac{1}{2}"$

196 pieces

B

$1\frac{3}{4}" \times 2\frac{3}{4}" \times 11"$

36 pieces

C

$2\frac{1}{4}" \times 2\frac{1}{4}" \times 5\frac{1}{2}"$

36 pieces

D

$2\frac{1}{4}" \times 2\frac{1}{4}" \times 11"$

96 pieces

E

$1\frac{3}{4}" \times 2\frac{3}{4}" \times 22"$

150 pieces

F

$1\frac{5}{8}" \times 1\frac{5}{8}" \times 5\frac{1}{2}"$

16 pieces

G

$2\frac{3}{4}" \times 8" \times 10"$

36 pieces

I

$1\frac{1}{4}" \times 1\frac{1}{4}" \times 5\frac{1}{2}"$

36 pieces

J

$1\frac{3}{4}" \times 2\frac{3}{4}" \times$ about $8"$

40 pieces

K

$1\frac{3}{4}" \times 2\frac{3}{4}" \times$ about $13"$

32 pieces

H

$1\frac{3}{4}" \times 7\frac{1}{2}" \times 7\frac{1}{2}"$

64 pieces

L

$1\frac{3}{4}" \times 1\frac{5}{8}" \times 5\frac{1}{2}"$

IVEY BLOCK DIMENSIONS

V. ACCESSORY MATERIALS

Accessory materials, such as animals, trucks, planes, boats, people, stimulate dramatic expression with floor blocks. As children develop in their ability to build representative structures the need for accessory materials arises. However, supplementary materials should be used only when the need is apparent, usually after a structure has been completed and there is a definite purpose for using them; unless, for example, a child is building with blocks and during the course of his construction takes up a single block and calls it a train, a boat, a truck, or other accessory that has a direct relationship to his structure. Then the real object may be made available to him as he is free to choose a replacement for the block he has been using for the purpose.

An exception to this general rule is justified when you feel that a child needs stimulation to build. If he has a car he may need to build a garage for it. Similarly, a fire engine may create the desire to build a fire station.

The first accessory materials introduced might be big flattop boats, trains, and trucks, or other vehicles that may be used to transport blocks. If you observe the children closely over a period of time you will note the readiness for accessory materials. When this occurs you may place a few about the room but say nothing concerning them. A child sees and gets the boat, train, truck, people, animals, and trees as the case may be, and is delighted. Then during evaluation the merits of the newly acquired piece of equipment are discussed, as well as its place in dramatic expression.

Six-year-old Judy early in the fall brought three toy horses to school. Patty helped her build a stable and pasture for them using floor blocks. Four half arches were placed together on their sides to make a hollow center to serve as a watering trough and the horses were fenced in by longer blocks laid on edge.

When Mrs. Jensen's five-year-olds constructed a train of hollow blocks, it remained a center of interest for the better part of an hour through the addition of a bell, sandblocks to simulate the sound of a moving train, an engineer's and a conductor's hat, and tickets.

Many times you will find that your group is in need of something that need not be purchased. By applying ingenuity you can usually make something which the children will accept eagerly even though it may be far below your own standard of perfection.

Accessory Materials for Hollow Blocks

Accessory materials will vary from one locality to another, reflecting the life of the community and the culture. Among these materials may be the following:

Discarded steering wheel mounted on a dash board. (Older children make their own.)

(Introduced when needed for cars, buses, trucks, and other vehicles.)

Discarded license plates

Telephones and ear phones

An old radio (does not have to work) ; an old television cabinet

Circular wooden discs, diameter 14″ to 16″ for wheels

Gas or water pumps

Barrel kegs with attached hose for service station or fire engine

Large sheets of heavy cardboard for roofs, and light two-ply wood for use as counters (not for climbing)

Triangular sheeting mounted "sail-wise" on a pole supported in a stand or by some other means, to be used for sailboats

Bells for train, buoy, church, firehouse, and engine

A megaphone

Cash register and old style balance scales

Empty food cartons, cans, and paper boxes, clean and sanitary, for use in houses and markets

Hats and other identifying garments worn by persons in vocations within children's scope of knowledge, such as chef, fireman, doctor, nurse, conductor, engineer, pilot

Containers of various shapes; boxes, smoke stack, chimney

Paper punch, scrap construction paper for tickets

Toy money, coin and bills

Cloth for flags and so on

Ladder

Propeller, approximately 2 feet in length

You will want to add many more accessories to this list during the year, but what you add will depend upon the interests of your particular group.

Accessories for Floor Blocks

Following is a suggested list of accessory materials for floor blocks in use by children in lower primary. A number of the items included come under the category of discard materials:

Drapery and rug samples

Small house furniture

Trucks, buses, automobiles, aircraft, watercraft, trains, railway signals, and traffic signs

Tractors, cranes, derricks, and other equipment

Various farm animals, stanchions, fences, water tanks

Doll people with movable arms (several families including parents, children, babies, grandparents)

Community workers

Trees

Telephones (at least two)

It is important, too, that you make your visual aids available, also your picture files, books, and reference materials, and that you have access to films.

Field trips taken to places of interest help clarify ideas for children in primary groups and enrich block building by furnishing new content.

If your school has a supply of peg boards which were such an essential part of the equipment for the fives in the traditional school, you will find an excellent use for these as an accessory material for blocks. Without pegs they make excellent roofs and roads and the children find innumerable other uses for them.

Children's Use of Block Accessories

Success with accessory materials is more than merely having a piece of equipment available in the classroom. You must know what to do with it. For instance, an automobile dashboard with a steering wheel is useful for dramatic experiences. If this is placed in the environment the child will experiment in manipulating the wheel and press in the foot pedals, and for him this is the important part of driving. At times the children may place the dashboard at the head of a column of blocks, or build around it to make what is for that particular moment a truck or other craft of which the steering gear is a part. Technical details of operation such as he would need to know in order to drive the vehicle on the highway are not a part of the child's thinking at this age.

Making accessory materials available to the children as they demonstrate a readiness to incorporate them into their dramatic experiences means watching their block building activities closely.

Gary, Ross, Jamie, and Michael displayed an interest in the story of pilots and planes which Miss R. told. They chose songs about flying and participated freely in the body rhythms with musical accompaniment.

Miss R. placed a discarded microphone on a low shelf, along with other materials, as an old radio set and a wooden box with buttons and wheels to turn. The above four children selected these materials from among those that were available and used them as part of their structure of hollow blocks.

With these materials the four children reenacted a plane flight. The box with buttons became radar equipment. A pilot's headgear was worn by Gary who called out, "Pilot to co-pilot, fasten your safety belt."

As the dramatic experience unfolded there was much realistic verbalization. Comments such as the following were heards: "Calling W W W. Come in, come in."

"Pilot to Central Tower. R-r-r r-r! Euga, euga, euga."

"Radio is broken!"

At this point the children jumped out and parachuted to safety.

The cooperation exhibited was delightful. Rapport was excellent. The children took turns using the accessories and all were avidly interested.

VI. DRAMATIC EXPRESSION THROUGH BLOCKS

Listening to Children's Block Activities

The preceding spontaneous dramatization illustrates one value of blocks that sometimes eludes perception: the insight that you, as teacher, can gain by close observation and listening as construction is in progress. This will help you gain a background on the interests, concepts, strengths, needs, and personality of the individuals, making possible a better interpretation of the curriculum in terms of the maturity of each child.

Verbalizations: An Index to the Child's Thinking

During block building children utter interesting verbalizations which you should be alert to record.

John constructed a rectangular column with curved blocks extending from the side onto the base of the main structure and explained: "This lighthouse watches out for boats."

Rusty placed upright cylinders at regular intervals over his building area on the rug and said, "Look at all the posts for the sea gulls to rest on."

Several children were building with hollow blocks. "We're making a service station," Michael explained. "A service station is different. A gasoline station is where they 'dispel' gasoline, and a service station is where you get your windshield wiped and your tires pumped up."

Explanations of this nature bring wide use of a varied vocabulary because there are new terms associated with each construction. There are many opportunities for learning as ideas are exchanged in this manner.

Another group of six-year-olds was building a landing field.

"Where do we keep our airplanes?" asked Tommy. "Shall I make a garage?"

Their teacher explained the word "hangar" to them and they found a picture of one and studied it. The hangar they constructed afterward using floor blocks served in their dramatic experiences, and the impression that planes need servicing and care remained permanently with children, as was revealed by their subsequent dramatizations.

In another part of the room, Randy and Michael chose a boat from the accessory shelves and built an enclosure of floor blocks around it. Randy sang to himself as he worked:

1   1   3   3
Up, up it goes;

1   2   3   4
Up go the sides.

Later, when Billy asked what he was doing, Randy explained, "We're going to paint this boat. That's why it's in dry dock."

Dramatic Expression Reveals Children's Concepts

As your children work independently with blocks they reveal themselves to you. Their activities become an open book as you learn better how to look for significant indications of their growth. Through their dramatic expression you come to know and understand the individuals within your group.

A group of immature six-year-olds working independently with blocks and accessory materials provided their teacher with many opportunities to observe each child without intruding upon their interchange of ideas.

Loren, atop a structure of hollow blocks, said: "I've got to try out the plane and see that it works. Hey, Shirley! If you want to ride on the airplane we take passengers here!"

Another child came in with an accessory plane and started to walk rapidly with it lifted high overhead. Loren said, "You have got to call me up before you can take off." His hollow block plane had changed to a control tower and he was in command.

Here came a big model of a transport plane and John said, as he tried to put the accessory people into the plane: (The plane was approximately fifteen inches long, and the wooden cylinders that represented the passengers were about six inches tall.) "The ladies won't fit in; the man won't fit in, but they must get a turn."

He picked up one of the figures and held it on top of the plane, resigning himself to the fact that he could not get them inside it, and proceeded to take one of them at a time.

Billy called out, "You got to say, 'Pilot to control car! Pilot to control car! Over!"

John: "224 take off. Motors are all warm. Take off! Take off that way!"

Another child came in with a new plane. Jay said, "This is the control tower."

Using floor blocks he laid four arcs down together in such a way that they made a hollow circle. (Each block was a complete quarter of the circumference.) Then he laid two more on top, which left the double decker circle incomplete. Then he said, "We need two more. Bring all the arcs there are."

Here was potential leadership, almost to the point of bossiness on the part of certain individuals. Responses were fairly consistent. The teacher observed this, but also made mental note that all complied, were living the experience, and seemed happy about it as they participated freely in the verbal flow of ideas.

To the young child a block structure is life itself, with all needed details supplied by his imagination, whether it be an airport he envisions or a plane, a house or a room, a barn or a truck, a helicopter or a rocket. People and animals live for him according to his own mental image of them. Mechanical things seem to move, even though they are in reality, stationary. Because the blocks are free of detail in design, and thus not designated as anything in particular, the child is able to endow them with the characteristics of whatever he is dramatizing, and in so doing, he reveals his innermost concepts.

Children are quick to pick up each other's leads when they are working together on a common project. However, there is also considerable parallel activity when individuals are proceeding independently of each other or when one small group works spontaneously in the vicinity of other children. Here the ideas of first one child and then another are caught up and expanded by others. The educational significance of this characteristic of childhood is tremendous. As you observe your own children you will discover how readily their dramatic expression can be directed into channels of constructive learning by your own guidance at the opportune moment.

The Child Reconstructs the World Around Him

The young child readily adapts whatever materials and objects he finds in his immediate environment and uses them according to the dictates of his fancy.

Blocks are unexcelled among materials for your children in the possibilities they offer for self-directed dramatic expression. Dramatizing life situations is a natural, childlike avenue of learning through which the child expresses his understanding of life about him.

Impressions gained from field trips or walks around the neighborhood are often reflected later in block building, and as you observe the dramatic expression which results you have the opportunity to become aware of the concepts that children may have gathered on a field trip or from some other recent experience.

Perhaps one of the chief values of dramatic expression with blocks is that the children, as they relive the adult activities they see around them, become increasingly aware of the world in which they live and thereby gain insight into the purposes and uses of the institutions of modern society. Block building is one of the best means through which the child will learn about his community.

The children who have built boats, trains, airplanes, space craft, houses, garages, and farms then become the boat captains, train conductors, engineers, astronauts, airplane pilots, navigators, passengers, carpenters who build houses, or families living in houses. They drive their cars or trucks into the garages they have constructed, or plow their farms. They blast off into space and return. The dramatic expression that centers about a particular construction depends upon the background and maturity of the children who are participating in it. All the while there is a rich exchange of ideas about how the representative living shall go on, or how the people they have become would act in resolving their problems of sharing materials and alloting a fair proportion of space for construction to different groups. They find that "talking it over" helps them to reach a satisfactory solution.

Dramatic expression often results when children have a new and interesting experience, such as a visit to the firehall, or to the spot where the excavation for a building or the construction of a home is taking place. One child may announce, "I'm a fireman, and I am hurrying to put out a fire." He is immediately joined by others who also become firemen.

These experiences are more realistic if there are a few simple props, such as firemen's hats, big boots, and short pieces of hose, or crude equipment of some kind to simulate a fire truck.

The construction itself need not be elaborate if it is representative of the child's maturity and ability. Some of the simplest structures stimulate much dramatic activity. Two or three hollow blocks placed in the position of a cross on the floor may become for the child the craft which he guides through water, on land, or into space, depending upon his concept of the part he is living. Another child joins him and then another as more hollow blocks are added, until the body of the structure is extended to provide each with a place to sit and ride.

A seven-year-old group wanted to build a plane that they could really get into. They had no hollow blocks, so they used chairs, placing them as follows:

```
              x   x   x
              x   x   x
  x   x   x   x   x   x   x   x   x
              x   x   x
              x   x   x
              x   x   x
              x   x   x
```

After they had their passenger plane built out of chairs there was dramatic expression with each child participating.

The stewardess served the food.

The pilot and co-pilot flew the plane.

The passengers enjoyed the ride.

A ticket office was set up by using a classroom table. Paper tickets were made.

Roberta, John, and Jackie made an airplane of hollow blocks. Roberta was the stewardess and went up and down the aisle serving food. She went to the "cockpit" to serve the pilots. John was the co-pilot and told Roberta, "No thank you. I don't want any food. I'm the co-pilot and the pilot is sleeping, and I can't eat while I'm on duty."

Children's Dramatic Expression a Reflection of Their Maturity

Ross, Michael, Jamie, Denise, Helen, and Gary made a pier and later they built a boat. They pushed their boat back and forth across the "water" in rhythmic motion.

Jamie and Gary used "people" from the accessory materials and walked them on top of the pier, saying as they did so, "Walk, walk, walk, walk, walk."

The next day Billy, John, Randy, and Stanton built a harbor, which included a lighthouse, a pier, and a ferry boat. The pier had a rope which they explained was to haul the boats up for dry dock when they needed repair. Their activity was much more elaborate. Instead of "pushing and pulling" the ferry boat, the children brought their "ocean liner" in the dock, loaded it, and repaired it. They pushed a "ferry boat" to the dock with a tug boat. They sang an original song as they did so about the tug boat.

5	6	5	6	5	6	5
Chug	a	chug	a	chug	a	chug

5	5	5	5	3
Here	comes	the	tug	boat.

The lighthouse gave out warnings:
John: "Lighthouse to ship—1—1—1—" (Imitating code).
"Better go to dock. It's foggy."
Billy: "SOS—a storm is coming! A storm is coming!"
Randy: "A chug-a-chug-chug" (pushing little tug boat).

Only Loren worked by himself, placing and replacing the moorings. Through observing these children's dramatic expression the teacher noted that it would be well to encourage Loren to work with someone—perhaps with Randy who was not so domineering.

Teacher Participation

Some teachers feel they can guide their children by entering temporarily into some of the children's dramatic experiences and then withdrawing soon afterward. This does not interrupt the continuity of the dramatization.

During the first few weeks of school the teacher of one group of five- and six-year-olds participated briefly, here and there, in spontaneous dramatic experiences. She felt her presence would help keep interest high and encourage participation by some of the children who needed an opportunity to feel the value of dramatization. By lending enthusiasm to the enterprise Miss Adams kept the spontaneous dramatizations alive until the children's initiative could be developed. However, the children themselves thought of most of the developments, and the block construction was theirs.

In the course of several weeks the hollow blocks became a fire department, ships, buses, trucks, and the teacher, by participating, led the children into more extensive and meaningful dramatic expression. When the first fire truck was built, for instance, she produced a bell to ring in the fire station and reported several fires to the chief, asking him to come quickly.

Again, by jumping onto the truck and becoming a fireman she was able to bring in different ideas and enrich the children's knowledge as they lived the experience.

When the children are able to proceed alone, the teacher's influence may be withdrawn, or may be needed only at the start of an activity, or she may enter in temporarily by invitation.

Miss Kellogg became a participant in one such dramatic experience when Terry, Cindy, and Roland invited her to take a train trip with them. They had arranged the hollow blocks so there were rows of seats for the passengers. The children made the sound effects, and Miss Kellogg, sitting in one of the seats, introduced a train song. After their teacher left the train, the children continued on their journey. Other children came for a ride, and left.

Mrs. Ruggles told a story to her group of seven-year-olds about a boy who visited the automobile factory where his father worked. He saw all the different processes that go into making a car.

The next day Roy brought a flashlight to share and during block construction he built a flashlight factory. Then he built a factory that made whistles. This factory was a large square building with a tall apparatus in the middle. In each corner he had a bench with a man behind each one. Roy said the middle part was where the whistles were made and that the men in the corners were operating the machine that made the whistles blow.

Other buildings were constructed around the factory: dwelling houses, service stations, stores, a bank, and a hospital.

In the dramatization there was an accident at the factory. The patients were taken to the hospital where they were put to bed and bandages were applied to their wounds. Soon the people were well and went back to the factory to work.

The Teacher's Evaluation of the Block Activity Program

You must constantly be evaluating and improving your block building program, and your success in this may be measured by the following questions:

1. In what way are the children enjoying their work? The value of the experience is lost if the children do not attack it enthusiastically and joyously.

2. How are they expressing their own ideas?

3. In what way does the construction evidence good thinking, originality, and thoughtful planning?

4. How do the children evidence social development in such areas as cooperation and consideration for each other?

5. Are they using the materials legitimately?

6. Are the blocks used to the best advantage structurally, considering such things as curved blocks for corners, firm foundations for structures, good balance and proportion?

7. How safe is the construction?

8. How are accessory materials utilized toward dramatic expression?

9. Is problem solving evidenced with individual groups? How?

10. How is each child becoming more able to work with others?

11. In what ways is he communicating his ideas? What vocabulary growth is evidenced in his verbalizations?

12. How are his concepts being clarified?

13. Were adequate pictures available for reference? How were they employed?

14. What books, if any, were consulted? (To be read by child if he is learning printed symbols; otherwise he refers to pictures.)

15. How was cooperation evidenced in the sharing of space, blocks, and accessory materials?

16. How were others considered when the location of the buildings was chosen?

17. In what ways are individual children increasing their own self-control?

18. How were the clean-up responsibilities distributed?

Your answers to questions such as these will indicate the degree to which you have attained an effective block building program, one which will prove to be a major force in developing creative, imaginative, and well-adjusted children, able to work with a balance of independence and cooperation.

QUESTIONS ON BLOCK CONSTRUCTION

1. How do blocks help meet the child's need to investigate, to experiment, to manipulate, and to test? What foundations do you see in this for later learning?

2. Justify the statement that "Block construction constitutes one of the most fruitful sources of learning in its contribution to the child's basic needs and total growth."

3. Explain in detail what is meant by developmental stages in block building. Discuss how the child's growth is gradual and continuous here as elsewhere.

4. How will you explain the value of block construction to parents: a. from the standpoint of their child's own personal development; b. from the standpoint of academic learning; c. from the viewpoint of social living?

5. Give examples of children's block construction to illustrate the six goals at work in your classroom.

6. a. How does the democratic classroom provide a desirable climate for the use of blocks? b. Discuss adequate guidance of block construction for the five- and six-year-old children. Give examples.

7. Explain how your picture file may be used by the children to clarify concepts and help guide block construction.

8. What will be your policy in guiding children's dramatic expression through block construction? Explain in detail.

9. What criteria will you use in your selection of blocks? Describe and illustrate as to size, shape, material, and consider the structural possibilities for manipulation, dramatization, and other uses by children.

10. What behavior patterns will you seek to establish in your group on the use of accessory materials? Justify.

SELECTED REFERENCES

Bureau of Elementary Education, TEACHERS' GUIDE TO EDUCATION IN EARLY CHILDHOOD, Sacramento, California, State Department of Education, 1956 (Compiled under the direction of the State Curriculum Commission.) .

Garrison, Charlotte Gano; Sheehy, E. D. and Dalgliesh, Alice, KINDERGARTEN FOR FIVE-YEAR-OLD CHILDREN, New York, Teachers College, Columbia University, 1937.

Heffernan, Helen and Todd, Vivian, THE KINDERGARTEN TEACHER, Boston, D. C. Heath and Company, 1960.

Johnson, Harriett M., THE ART OF BLOCK BUILDING, John Day Company, 1933.

Kaurn, Ethel, THE WISE CHOICE OF TOYS, Illinois, University of Chicago Press, 1938 (Second edition rev.).

Leonard, Edith M.; Miles, Lillian E. and Van der Kar, Catherine, THE CHILD AT HOME AND SCHOOL, New York, American Book Co., 1944.

SOCIAL DEVELOPMENT THROUGH CENTERS OF INTEREST AND

Part Nine

AREAS OF EXPERIENCE

I. SOCIAL STUDIES IN THE EDUCATION OF THE YOUNG CHILD

When the total development of the child is considered the social studies assume a role of major import. Today's child must live in a world where other people are a factor in his life even before he learns to talk. Social values become meaningful to him in so far as he experiences them himself.

Technological advancements bring diverse cultures close together in today's world. Even the very young child must learn to live in harmony with people who differ from each other and from him. His horizons are broadened at an early age to include an interest beyond his own community. His understanding of the social values in his own personal relationships with family, friends, school group, neighbors, serves as a foundation for his growing appreciation and understanding of the values he finds in situations further removed from his circle of living.

Social Studies Defined

Social studies are not just a subject of the school curriculum. Broadly speaking they embrace all the social experiences in the school that help prepare the child first to understand and know himself, and second to gain a total understanding of the interrelationships of people and the physical world in which they live. Gradually he must learn to be a good citizen in his own right and on his own maturation level through democratic living with his fellows. In this way he is prepared to take his place in a complex, social culture.

The influence of the social studies permeates throughout the entire school day. Through the experiences gained in the social studies core, the child comes to feel a sense of the unity and the relationship of human lives as well as of his school curriculum. Thus "social studies" is an intricate field of study. It incorporates the development of desirable social attitudes and behaviors; the assimilation of information and skills which deal with the many aspects of human relationships of home, school, neighborhood, community; the appreciation of present and past cultures of the nation and world. It begins with the present and goes back into the past, always starting with the known and going to the unknown. Each of these aspects enriches the others. Therefore social studies in no way neglects basic facts, knowledge, and skills. Instead, it blends or amalgamates the once isolated subjects of geography, civics, and history into real life situations and helps the children to discover the *who, what, when, where, why,* and *how* of life through meaningful experiences rather than by rote memorization. These are the over-all goals. During the primary years the emphasis in social studies is on the child's present interests and needs, while at the same time the foundation is being laid for the more analytical and abstract study of the social sciences and related fields which will follow in the child's later education.

The social studies are fundamentally concerned with the children's understanding of human values. Social relationships are understood by each individual first of all as they pertain to his own life.

Learning About Social Relationships Through School Experience

In your classroom you can provide innumerable opportunities for your children to learn the art of working in company with others, each pursuing his own interests without interfering with the interests of others. The joy of sharing and taking turns needs to be balanced with the child's ability to stand up for his own rights. Later comes direct cooperation in working with others toward common goals.

The mainspring of courteous and civil dealings with neighbors and friends, as well as strangers, lies in the ability to sense and respect the feelings of the other party. Here again the child needs to recognize, understand, and control his own feelings and reactions. There is continual need for progress along these lines all through the school of early childhood.

II. CENTERS OF INTEREST FOR THE FIVE- AND SIX-YEAR-OLDS

Five- and six-year-old children are developmentally equipped to learn from participation in flexible interest groups.

Environmental Centers

As explained in the preceding definition of Social Studies, one phase not to be overlooked is the importance of children learning to work side by side and to observe each other's rights. This is achieved for the fives and sixes largely through setting up environmental centers in which the individual child can do something constructive either alone or with a small number of his peers.

The term "Centers of Interest" may be used to designate these environmental centers in which your children undertake various activities according to their changing interests and developing maturity. All the work centers voluntarily chosen by your children from day to day come under this category. The books on the library table, the clay, the blocks, the easels, and the musical instruments, the home center, puzzles, scientific experiments, all may be considered *environmental centers*. Their exact location in the immediate physical environment may be flexible. For example, hand painting is an environmental center although it may be done either indoors or outside. Each child needs experience in a well diversified selection of these centers.

This type of teaching can be done with practically any size group. With larger numbers of children environmental centers are even more urgently needed than with smaller ones. It is possible to use these centers successfully with 35 or even 45 children under circumstances of dire emergency, although a group of from 20 to 25 children is much more desirable.

Ideas as Centers of Interest

There are two ways to think of a "Center of Interest" for the fives and immature six-year-olds: the environmental centers just explained and the relationship of ideas listed below. In the latter connotation the term may apply to any topic or category around which a child's attention centers for a time, as revealed through his activities, his conversation, his choices and preferences.

For example, an interest in air travel may develop spontaneously while one or several children are building with blocks or painting at the easel, but may quickly shift to boats or some other interest.

Children have the happy faculty of really living the thing they are doing. One group had been dramatizing a hospital scene in their spontaneous block construction. The interest was followed through when the next morning Sally announced as she skipped into the room bringing one of her favorite toys, "I've brought my pig to 'happy up' the sick children, today."

A more pronounced "Center of Interest" may stem from one of the universal interests of childhood: birthdays, homes and families, toys, as dolls, teddy bears, tricycles and bicycles, cars, trucks, buses, sea, water, and air craft, space travel, their own pets, zoo or circus, service station, or church. Children are also interested in different kinds of food; in gardens, orchards, farms, and weather. Any of these things may make a productive center of interest if treated in the light of the child's maturation level. Also, at their maturation level—which means without historical emphasis—the interest of five- and six-year-olds can center briefly around holidays, such as Halloween, Thanksgiving, Christmas, Valentine or Friendship Day, Easter (Wake-up Time), May Day, Mother's Day, Father's Day, and other holidays peculiar to the region or the religion of the children.

The above are typical Centers of Interest that may continually pop up with the fives and the immature sixes, but a child at this age seldom keeps one interest uppermost in his thinking to the exclusion of others. The interest of a particular group will depend on the type of community and neighborhood, the family backgrounds, the maturity of the children, and your own guidance.

Misusing Centers of Interest

With many teachers there is a tendency to put children into skills for which they are not developmentally ready. Consideration of the children's ability and readiness is needed before any attempt can be made to plan the program. You need to guard against holding a child to an activity for which he lacks skill or attention.

Just because the children in one group are ready for a thing is no reason why other children can do it. This is one problem the teacher encounters in making a long time plan in the summer before she knows the ability and maturation of her children.

A good environment provides the type of experiences and activities needed for each individual. In groups of fives and immature six-year-olds these activities are carried on simultaneously by individual children or small groups, not by committees.

You should be ever alert to continuity of learning in your group and recognize centers of interests as they appear from time to time instead of attempting to limit five- and six-year-olds to any one "unit of work" or "area of experience." By its very nature "a unit" implies an organization of subject matter that requires an extended period of time. This demands an attention span which far exceeds the limits of the young child.

> Beverly was in a group of five-year-olds whose teacher was "developing" a florist shop in an effort to introduce more "activity" into her program. Beverly's experience illustrates in a negative way how a young child's interest may be forgotten in attempting to hold the group to a given plan of action regardless of individual differences.
>
> The children were all divided into committees by naming their favorite flowers. Many flowers were suggested, as carnations, roses, daffodils. Beverly was especially fond of pansies, so when asked to choose what committee she wanted to be on she said, "The Pansy Committee."
>
> Unfortunately, she did not understand all that serving on this committee involved. When she found it was making crepe paper pansies she did not want to be on it. But the teacher was also a believer in "sticking by your word." Beverly had said she wanted to be on the pansy committee and on it she would remain.
>
> The next day Beverly had a stomach ache and couldn't go to school. During the days that followed she developed one illness after another until finally the mother sensed the situation and took a screaming and protesting Beverly back to school.
>
> It was not until the teacher sought consultation from an administrator who understood children that this teacher was able to see she was asking more of these five-year-olds in skill than they were able to produce.

Effective Use of Centers of Interest

Voluntary choices of activities need to be made by the individual children. Those who choose the same center often work there side by side in company rather than in social groups. However, some children will work together cooperatively in these centers, especially as they become better acquainted and feel security within a small group. Group work comes gradually, and in time the children learn to share ideas and materials. Spontaneous, informal groups develop, and interests remain flexible for the five- and six-year-olds.

Though fleeting, centers of interest manifest themselves again and again in different ways and with different children. Some centers are of comparatively short duration; some are longer, and often more than one center of interest may be followed through simultaneously on the same day, or over a period of several days.

> For many days Max was not interested in any center. His teacher made every effort to encourage him but did not force him to enter into the activities.
>
> One day, without any apparent reason, Max said, "I'm going to build a restaurant with the hollow blocks."
>
> This interest lasted two days, and four other children joined Max. They dramatized a restaurant in operation.
>
> Just as suddenly as it began, Max said, "Aw, I don't want to run a restaurant anymore. I'm going to go paint," which he did. (He painted a fire he had seen in the neighborhood.)
>
> The restaurant broke up—but it had been a living reality to the group, and from then on Max was an active participant in the various centers.

The implication of a real center of interest is that the benefits of a truly democratic classroom climate will enhance every learning situation and the curriculum will be an integrated one.

If the goals are being achieved, behavior patterns are being developed to make it possible for the children to work independently and creatively in the various centers. As you move among them wherever you are needed, you observe, note, and evaluate the children's responses, realizing always that a child's response is a barometer of his readiness to learn. This helps develop Attitudes and Behavior Patterns—Appreciations and Independent Thinking—and much creative expression is the result.

Clarification of the children's concepts, rather than pursuit of the subject as such, is always uppermost in good planning, and the starting point in any Center of Interest is *"wherever the child is."*

Mrs. Vigus Follows Up on Immediate Interests:
A Center of Interest Develops[1]

Mrs. Vigus, teacher of fives and immature six-year-olds made her program so flexible that she continually capitalized upon the children's immediate interests. A vivid description of what happened one morning follows. Early this day as Mrs. Vigus checked over her notes from the preceding morning she felt she was ready to follow through on the ideas that had come up in the children's activities and discussions should the same interests continue today. There had been Dick's station constructed from blocks, the airport Jim had been enthusiastic in building, Alice's joy in her daddy's new car. Mrs. Vigus had songs and poems and stories and action plays ready for each of these interests, as well as those about George's new baby sister and Marnie's turtle. Intruding upon her busy thought was the insistent mewing of a kitten outside.

Andre and Pete were the first children to arrive. As they began arranging flowers for the room, they told Mrs. Vigus about the tiny kitten they had heard up in the palm tree.

"He will probably come down when he gets ready," Mrs. Vigus assured them. "Kittens like to climb trees."

As others arrived the kitten became the topic of conversation.

"How do you suppose the kitten got up there so high?" Mrs. Vigus asked.

"He climbed up there," said Andre.

"Could Marnie's turtle climb like that?" asked Mrs. Vigus.

"My turtle stays on the ground," said Marnie. She ran to bring the turtle.

"Could the turtle dig his claws into the tree the way the kitten does?" asked Mrs. Vigus.

The children crawled to show how the turtle walks. Then they stood up, made claws with their fingers, and pretended to climb like the kitten.

"My dog walks like this," volunteered Charlie, demonstrating. Several of the children began to walk like dogs.

"Why doesn't Peter's puppy or Charlie's dog climb up the way the kitten climbed our palm tree?" questioned Mrs. Vigus.

"My pup has claws but they are not as sharp as the kitten's," offered Genevieve.

"The kitten will get tired of hanging on like that and then he will come down. He isn't very happy up there."

"What makes you think the kitten is unhappy, Robert?" asked Mrs. Vigus.

"He's crying," the boy replied.

"Kittens can let you know how they feel, can't they?" offered Mrs. Vigus.

---

[1] Adapted from an article, "Typical Experiences in the Kindergarten Day," by Edith M. Leonard and Dorothy D. VanDeman in the *California Journal of Elementary Education*, California State Department of Education, August, 1955.

"Maybe he wants us to help him," suggested Dudley.

"What could we do to help the kitten?" asked Mrs. Vigus.

The children talked this over and finally suggested calling Mr. Ryan, the custodian. "Mr. Ryan is our friend. Maybe he would help us get the kitten down."

Three children volunteered to go find Mr. Ryan who was working in the yard on the other side of the building. But when Mr. Ryan came he did not have a ladder long enough to reach the kitten. "I believe he'll come down when he's left alone," counseled Mr. Ryan.

The children went about their morning's work, but interest in the kitten remained high. The group decided to stay away from him and see if he would come down of his own accord, but various ones kept going cautiously to the door and peering into the tree. They talked in subdued tones: "He's still up there," and "He's crying harder now."

"It's a good thing it isn't a stormy day. The kitten would be cold and wet if it were raining," said Alice. A recent heavy rainstorm had made a vivid impression on these five-year-olds.

"I know a poem about two little kittens one stormy night," volunteered Robert. Several children were in a casual group by the door. Mrs. Vigus had joined them and was listening.

"We would love to hear your poem, Robert," said Mrs. Vigus, speaking for the others.

Robert began the poem, one he had learned at home. Mrs. Vigus recognized it, but it was not one of her memorized repertoire. Robert quoted most of it, but there were parts he couldn't quite recall. Seeing the child's distress, Mrs. Vigus commended him. "You did well to remember that much of the poem, Robert. It's a long one. My mother used to say it to me when I was a little girl. I have it in a book. Let's find it."

Half a dozen children followed Mrs. Vigus over to her bookshelf where she kept materials for her own use. The other children, who were at work in environmental centers located in various parts of the room, did not seem to notice. Mrs. Vigus took down one of the volumes and found the selection.[1] By glancing at the book now and then she was able to complete the verses for Robert who joined in with her on the familiar lines. The rhyme told how the two kittens argued over a mouse, were swept out into the cold, and eventually found it better to lie down and sleep than to quarrel and fight."

"I know a song about three little kittens. They lost their mittens," said Charlie.

"I do too," and "So do I," were general comments.

Seeing the interest in this, the children shared the old nursery rhyme, "Three Little Kittens." Then Mrs. Vigus got the drum and while she tapped softly the children around her were kittens looking for lost things. Various

---

[1] "The Quarrelsome Kittens." *Let's Read Together Poems*, selected and tested by Helen A. Brown and Harry J. Heltman, Evanston, Ill.: Row, Peterson & Co., 1949, p. 84.

children suggested a ball, a bell on a ribbon, a piece of string, a catnip mouse—things kittens might easily lose. Other children gathered around and joined in the rhythms. They were kittens playing, then lapping milk, then asleep, then climbing a tree.

Mrs. Vigus called the remainder of the group to leave their work and come. They gathered around and were kittens to her accompaniment on the piano. After the children were all seated on the rug, Mrs. Vigus quoted a poem, "The Pussy that Climbs to the Top of the Tree."[2] The children were delighted.

Mrs. Vigus then began to tie things in with the problem at hand. She threw out a leading thought and waited: "The kitten in our palm tree has been up there a long time. He must be getting tired." But the children were not to be rushed into a discussion of the point. Seeing they were not quite ready to pick up her lead, Mrs. Vigus did not force a response.

Margaret Ann volunteered to share another poem she knew. It began, "Once there was a little kitty, whiter than snow." It told how he was able to catch a mouse.[3] The children heaved a sigh of relief when the mouse got away at the end of the poem.

Then followed a familiar action play, "My kitten tried to bat my ball."[4] The children all joined in and afterward Mrs. Vigus played the piano as they continued to be kittens.

Many teachers might have gone ahead without referring to the kitten the remainer of the day, but Mrs. Vigus knew this was an absorbing interest with many learning possibilities. The children returned to their work centers, but later, after they had put away their things and cleaned up the room, they sang several songs about kittens[5] and quoted poems they knew. They recalled another action play about a big grey cat,[6] and Mrs. Vigus helped them make a new action play:

---

2 Helen Hay Whitney, "The Cat," *The Golden Flute, An Anthology of Poetry for Young Children*, Selected by Alice Hubbard and Adeline Babbitt, New York: The John Day Co., 1932.

3 Elizabeth Prentiss, "Long Time Ago," *op. cit.*, p. 22.

4 Edith M. Leonard and Dorothy D. VanDeman, "My Kitten and My Ball," *Say It and Play It: Fifty-two Action Plays*, Evanston, Illinois: Row, Peterson, & Co., 1950, p. 18.

5 "Doggy and Kitty," *The Kindergarten Book*, Lila Belle Pitts, compiler, Boston, Ginn & Co., 1949; "A Kitten in School," p. 10, *Another Singing Time*, Satis N. Coleman and Alice Thorne, John Day, New York; "My Kitty," by Ada Richter and Constance W. Camp, p. 25, *New Music Horizon No. B*, Silver, Burdett & Co., 1944; "Playful Little Kitty," p. 93, *God's Wonderful World*, by Agnes Mason and Phyllis Chanian, Random House, 1955; "Pretty Pussy," from *Songs for the Little Child*, by Clarabelle Baker and Kohlsaat.

6 "Big Grey Cat," p. 13, *Say It and Play It*.

Kitten in the palm so high
  You climb and climb and climb.
Up you go, but never down,
  You stay a long, long time.

Come down, kitty, please come down,
  You mew and mew and mew.
You're high enough, so just come down,
  That's all you have to do.

The children liked their new poem so well that they repeated it with actions several times. Once when they came to the end of it, Arleen went right on with words of her own. She said, "Climb down, down, down," then added, "That shouldn't be hard for you." She said the "downs" very slowly, moving her whole body to a squatting position on each of them.

Mrs. Vigus and the children were enthusiastic over Arleen's contribution. They did it again and added it to the end of their new action play.

At mid-morning snack the kitten was the main subject of conversation, along with other interests that were naturally brought up.

As rest time approached, Mrs. Vigus noted a growing feeling of excitement and concern among the children, so while they were gathering and preparing for rest, she sang a soft lullaby about a kitten asleep by the fire.

Some of the children noticed that, curiously enough, the kitten had stopped crying and was lying on one of the strong palm fronds in the top of the tall tree. "The kitten is resting now, too," Janet commented as she lay down on her blanket, so Mrs. Vigus changed her song to make it about the kitten "asleep in the palm tree."

After rest the group went out into the yard and made free use of the outdoor space and equipment for large muscle development, but various individuals showed an interest in the kitten from time to time. Before long, they were all over under the palm tree looking up. The little kitten was now hanging by his claws. He seemed to be really making an effort to climb down. He would start, hesitate, and then cry pitifully.

Mary Ellen said, "I think that kitten is lost. Maybe he doesn't have any home to come down to."

Light broke on Andre's face. "I tell you what," he said. "If that kitten's lost, why don't we tell the Humane Society to come and get him?"

Mrs. Vigus' face lighted up too. "Tell us about the Humane Society, Andre," she said.

"Mr. Myers runs the Humane Society," said Andre, drawing on his background of experience. "Mr. Myers brings in lost animals and takes care of them. He tries to find homes for them."

"We got our dog from Mr. Myers," said Peter.

"The Humane Society could get the kitten a home, maybe," said Alice.

"Are we sure this kitten is lost?" asked Mrs. Vigus.

The children agreed they really did not know much about the kitten except that he was unhappy and could not get down from the tree, and he was probably hungry and tired and maybe cold.

Two of the children went to the office to ask the principal to help them call the Humane Society. When they returned they reported that Mr. Myers was out on his route but would call when he came in that afternoon. But the children thought the kitten needed help now.

After talking it over they decided that someone could go with Dudley to the office and ask the principal if Dudley might call his Uncle Bill. This mission was successful.

When Dudley's Uncle Bill came he thought they could get the kitten down if they had a long enough pole and something the kitten would like to eat. So John, who lived near, offered to run home and get some cat food from his mother. Dudley and his Uncle Bill went with John. Soon they returned with a long pole.

"It's the pole my daddy uses to get avocados down," explained John. "Mother sent this piece of fish in this can. Cats like fish."

"We'll fasten the can to the end of the pole and put the fish in it," explained Dudley's uncle.

Inch by inch the kitten was enticed by the smell of the fish. He managed to lower himself down to it, but each time he reached it Uncle Bill lowered it a little more. When the kitten was in reach of Mr. Ryan's ladder, Uncle Bill climbed up and brought him down the rest of the way. "Surprising how a tiny kitten could mew so loud," laughed Uncle Bill.

"And cause so much fuss," added Mr. Ryan.

But the children and Mrs. Vigus were busy wrapping the shivering little creature in a castoff sweater from the spare clothing supply Mrs. Vigus had in readiness for emergencies. In spite of the fish he had managed to eat, the kitten lapped milk the children obtained from the cafeteria and warmed for him. Soon his "mews" changed from pitiful cries to contented purrs as he curled himself up in the carton the children gave him for a bed.

One of the women from the cafeteria came by. "That must be the Wilton's cat," she said. "They have gone on a trip for several days. Their neighbors have been putting out food, but I suppose the little creature has been lonesome without his folks. But they'll be back tonight."

Mrs. Vigus went to her felt board file and selected some felt figures of a kitten, a tree, a house, a ball, a ladder, and a long narrow strip that would represent the pole. She placed these on the felt board as she told the children a new story about a kitten who found a home and then thought he had lost it again when the family went away for a few days. The children helped tell the part about how the kitten climbed into their tree at school and just stayed up there. A discussion followed about how hard it is to make some things go up and how easily they come down again. They realized it had been different with the kitten. As Frances pointed out, "It was easier for this kitten to go *up.*"

Mrs. Vigus ended the story with the new action play they had made that morning, and the children joined in wholeheartedly in both action and words.

A Teacher's Interpretation of Educative Experiences

The foregoing account shows how unforeseen opportunities present themselves to the teacher who is alert to possibilities for learning. It illustrates the quality of patience required to lead young children to learn at their own rate of speed; how necessary it is to guide the young child toward each succeeding step in his thinking and growing without forcing him.

There was a regular meeting of the parents of Mrs. Vigus' room a few days later. The parents had all heard about the kitten from the children. Now Mrs. Vigus interpreted the happenings of the day in discussing it with the parents.

"My preparation for that day was not wasted," she said. "Even though I did not follow my plans, real learning was taking place. The kitten interest provided a natural incentive for many common experiences. We had more language expression, songs, action plays, stories, rhythmic experiences, and more science and number concepts developing than we would have had if I had attempted to follow through on what I had planned for that day. The children thought together about an urgent need. They not only talked over what they might do, but made definite plans of action and attempted to carry them through. Then they evaluated these and made new plans on the basis of what happened.

"These were truly educative experiences," she continued. "They carried over into their painting, their clay, their block construction, their music, not only that day but in days that followed. The rhythmic activities to music were drawn from our discussion about the kitten and about other kinds of well known animals that climb or walk, crawl or swim, waddle or fly. The experiences we had in trying to think of ways to get the kitten down furnished us with ideas for activities that could be done to music.

"We talked about community helpers; about firemen who put out fires, and then we were firemen going to a fire. We remembered how traffic guards help us, and then we were traffic guards helping people cross the street. Since Dudley's Uncle Bill was a Boy Scout, we were Boy Scouts, too, going to camp and helping people and animals. We were Mr. Myers, going out to find dogs and cats that were lost. We thought how these animals would look and what they would do. We were Mr. Myers bringing the animals in, caring for them, feeding them, and finding homes for them. We were people looking for a dog like the one Peter got from the Humane Society. We were John's father using the pole to get avocados down from his tree; we helped Uncle Bill reach with the long pole. We were re-living what we had experienced as a group. We played we were climbing Mr. Ryan's ladder and bringing the kitten down; we wrapped it in a warm sweater; we washed our hands in preparation for handling food; we recalled how we went to the cafeteria and heated milk for the kitten. We acted out the things that the children brought out as they discussed the morning's experience. They suggested what we might do to the accompaniment of music, guided sometimes by my suggestions. Each child interpreted the ideas in whatever way he thought best, and everyone entered into the experiences with enthusiasm."

In this illustration the situation arose in the children's school environment. It came to the children. At other times, the teacher plans to take the children out to find something not in the immediate environment.

Mrs. Vigus realizes that a walk for the five- and six-year-olds can provide many learnings. It need not be long or time consuming. A trip through the school building and grounds, or around the block, or to a home or store may bring a host of truly educative experiences for the young child, while more extensive field trips are left for the older children.

Planning Subsequent Learnings

After their experience with the kitten in the palm tree, the children continued to talk about pets. One day Bud brought his puppy to school. That evening Mrs. Vigus stayed to plan her program for the next day. As she worked about the room she thought of the different pets that had come to school. "How could I increase the learning from these experiences?" she asked herself. Using paper and pencil she jotted down ideas as they occurred to her.

"The children could recall which animals have fur," she thought. "The kitten, the puppy, the bunny, and the hamster would qualify here. They could remember which pets have feathers. Let's see. There were the duck, the chicken, the parakeet, and the canary they brought to school. There were two other pets, a turtle and a snail. I might ask the children to think about the pets that have a shell. That would tie these last two animals into our discussion."

The children registered much interest when Mrs. Vigus spoke of pets next day. They started comparing pets as to color, size, and ways of moving. Mrs. Vigus guided their thinking away from adverse comparison of one pet with another, and they soon saw that what one pet might lack in one way, he made up for in something else. In appraising the day's experiences Mrs. Vigus realized that all the discussion that day had been based on the children's remembering. She knew they also learn from observing, from asking, and from looking at pictures. From her picture file Mrs. Vigus selected colored pictures that had to do with pets; clear pictures that showed the whole animal without distracting factors to confuse the children.

She planned how the children might talk about these pictures. She wanted them to do more thinking, analyzing, learning the meanings of words and how to put thoughts into language, rather than memorize facts about the animals. She wanted to draw out various children's ideas about the pets, as this would reveal what they would need to learn next. She thought of stories and poems to use in connection with the pictures; also action plays and songs about bunnies, kittens, dogs, turtles, snails, and canaries.

Mrs. Vigus finds that planning ahead helps her to be more at ease and more spontaneous with the children. Thus she is able to think of appropriate ways to use materials and appropriate things to say when the time comes.

Field Trips into the Homes

The next day Mrs. Vigus showed the pictures and followed through as she had planned. But she still felt the children needed more experience. She wanted them to be more alert.

Bud, who lived near, had brought his puppy to school. Why not take the children over to his house so they could see the yard where the puppy lives! Mrs. Vigus called Bud's mother who happily consented to the children's coming.

Mrs. Vigus thought of the many ideas she would like to stress and decided to put them in the form of questions so the children could answer for themselves: Where did Bud get his puppy? Where does Gyp sleep? Where does he play? What does the little dog like to chew? Who feeds him? What does he eat? Where and when? How does his tongue go when he drinks milk? Where does Bud keep the puppy's water dish? Why? When would he be thirsty for a drink of water?

Bud could answer many of these questions for the children. They could see other things for themselves when they arrived. What kind of a tongue does a dog have? How is it different from our tongues? The children would have to watch the puppy's tongue closely to see how he used it. What would happen to the milk he was trying to swallow if he could not make his tongue go so fast?

Other questions the children could answer from watching Bud and Gyp together might be: "How does the puppy let Bud know he is happy? How does Bud know when his dog is tired? How do the puppy's feet move when he runs? What toys does he have? How does he play with them? What dishes does Gyp use for his food? What does his bed look like? What kind of house does he have? What do his pen and fence look like? What are they for? Why does he have a collar? A leash? What is his license for? How old does he have to be before he must have a dog license?"

"Why couldn't they also go on over to Billy's yard and see where he keeps his hamster?" Mrs. Vigus thought. This involved a telephone call to Billy's mother who said she would like to have the children come.

So another opportunity to learn from direct observation was arranged. Mrs. Vigus listed vocabulary the children might acquire in contrasting the puppy and the hamster:

Bud's puppy has a "heavy *coat* of fur." His fur is *long* and *curly*. The hamster's fur is *short* and *straight*. The puppy's ears are big and long and they *droop*. Grumpy's ears are little and short and *pointed*; they stand up. Both have *warm* fur.

Much language expression would follow, and the children would gain vivid concepts from the experience.

Mrs. Vigus found poems, songs, action plays, and stories which she might introduce spontaneously during the trip or weave into later discussions.

She decided to remain silent at times during their trip and wait for her children to react. She realized that truly educative experiences for these five- and six-year-olds meant not only her own active presentation of ideas, questions, and materials, but her quiet alertness and observation of the children's responses to their environment and to her.

Redirecting a Center of Interest

A spontaneous center of interest may need redirection into constructive channels.

> Three five-year-olds built a military base. Their dramatic activity was centered on combat planes in action and the experience was gaining in emotional tension and overstimulation.
>
> Mrs. Vigus, their teacher, wanting to divert the interest into more constructive channels joined Allen, Joe, and Jeanne and called their attention to pictures showing the various types of civilian activities in which airplanes are needed. The children were interested at once and as they talked the group became intrigued by a picture of an airplane being used to spot and

fight fires. The children immediately changed their army environment to the headquarters of the forest rangers. They built trucks to carry fire hoses and said their planes were carrying sodium borate to spray on the fires.

Other children became interested in Joe, Allen, and Jeanne's work, and for several days the entire class discussed forest rangers before work time. This led to an understanding that foresters do many other things besides fighting fires. Mrs. Vigus brought in picture books and procured a film called "Rainbow Valley," which is about the life of a forest ranger and his family. To supplement her own background she obtained information from the Conservation Bureau and Forestry Departments of the state and federal governments.

This activity carried over into easel painting. The children depicted the spraying of the forest trees, the cutting of trees that were in need of being felled, and with their blocks they built a lookout tower and a saw mill. They also built a lumber truck to carry the lumber from the mill to the lumber yard.

The forestry interest waned and the children became absorbed in boats, with particular emphasis on the bell buoys and the lighthouse, but never again during that year did violence or destructive gun play consume their thinking.

III. AREAS OF EXPERIENCE FOR PRIMARY AGE GROUPS

Definition of the Framework and Scope of the Curriculum

Long time planning in the school of early childhood necessitates a thorough study of the *framework of the curriculum*.

The *scope* includes the whole gamut of activities and learnings which bring growth for the children in behavior patterns, attitudes, appreciations, insights, understandings, meanings, concepts, knowledge, and skills, as well as independent thinking and creative expression.

The *sequence* is the succession of activities, learnings, and experiences cited in the "scope."

In order to make more effective teaching possible and to provide a balance of learning experiences without duplication, some states, counties, and cities have developed a framework usually beginning with the here and now of home and school life, then on into the neighborhood, the town, community, and finally the outside world. Within this framework lie many areas of experience rich in educational possibilities.

An Area of Experience Defined

The basic principles of social studies have their beginnings for the primary years in an *Area of Experience*. The selection and development of an area of experience may vary considerably from one group of children to another. An area is always flexible and within the boundaries of the children's growing interest, needs, and strengths. It should be held together by a problem vital to the children and should be stated in the form of a question whose answer requires much thought, study, research, and discussion. An Area of Experience makes provision for children of varying abilities and maturity to work toward common purposes, each according to his capacity. Through an Area of Experience each individual within the group has the opportunity, the freedom, and the encouragement to solve problems, to learn, and to find his own form of creative expression through the committees he chooses to work on, as well as in the common experiences of the group.

It should be stated here that many far-seeing educators now use the term, "unit of work," with the same connotations that pertain to an "area of experience." It is well, therefore, to ascertain the meaning attached to the terminology in any discussion of curriculum. The term "unit of work" as used in the present discussion connotes an area of experience or area of study as defined herein.

Characteristics of a Good Area of Experience

A good area of experience is not just a vehicle to provide practice in social studies, reading, arithmetic, spelling, writing, and other aspects of the curriculum. It includes all of these, but the children feel there is a sincere purpose in developing their area. The values inherent in an area of experience make it worthwhile, even if there were no reading, writing, spelling, and arithmetic learning taking place. However, a good area necessitates much language development, all types of arithmetic within the maturation of the members participating, and countless opportunities for reading and writing. The children themselves realize that in order to carry out their purposes they need ability in the skill subjects, and their interest creates a genuine incentive or inner drive to grow in these fields. Hence academic learning is a product of an area of experience rather than an end in itself. Life in a room of this type is seldom, if ever, static and there is a constant stimulus to children's awareness of the world around them.

The teacher and the children together develop an area of experience and it has a logical outline of progress and growth.

Above all, the area should be planned so that it presents a challenge to every member of the class. This means keeping in mind the interests and needs of each individual child. Also, it necessitates that the area be developed for that particular group of children in the light of their background, their maturity, and that as the experience progresses each child will put the stamp of his own creativity upon it. While general areas and the sequence of their presentation should be prescribed, the approach should be determined by the needs of the specific group. When children have a voice in the planning of experiences they learn the give and take of privilege and responsibility. Only if the young child's interest is fanned by a factor in his immediate sphere of attention can appreciable learning of subject content be achieved.

You will want to guard against pushing the group beyond its interests and capabilities in an effort to secure a certain amount of progress. Goals for the area of experience should be built on children's needs. Their active participation should determine its length. Satisfaction and accomplishment and the discovery of answers to questions should culminate the area.

Not only do all phases of the curriculum enter into an area of experience planned by you and the children, but personal integration of the individual also takes place as the children develop spiritually, emotionally, socially, physically, intellectually, and creatively while learning to live together happily and successfully. With emphasis upon human relationships and understanding, social education proceeds through every activity of the experience, including research, discussions, committee work, construction, creative expression, and scientific experiment, as well as music, literature, and dramatic arts.

A Case of Teacher-Interest Predominating

Martin's mother noticed that her seven-year-old seemed to lack interest in his school work. When he came in from school one day she said, "Son, I have not heard anything about what you are studying this year. Last year you talked so much about the activities of the school. What are you studying now?"

Martin said, "Indians," in a very disinterested tone.

The mother said, "You did not say that very enthusiastically. Don't you like to study Indian life?"

"No," said Martin, "I don't, and neither do any of the other kids, but the teacher just loves Indians. She loves what they do; she loves what they say; she loves what they eat; and she loves everything about Indians."[1]

---

[1] Compare with "Areas Demanding More Maturity," a few pages hence.

A Parable for All Teachers

An opposite illustration is that of an invalid boy who had lived all his life on a ranch with horses as his only interest, although he was unable to ride. He had never attended either a public or a private school. His father had hired tutor after tutor but the spoiled boy had sent them away. The father decided to make one last attempt to find a tutor for his son. He employed a young man who had traveled all over the world, but because of an injury had to give up his chosen profession for a time. The young man took the position as tutor on the condition that the father would let him handle matters as he saw fit.

The first morning the tutor spoke pleasantly to the boy but made no attempt to teach him anything. The tutor just sat and read a book. Presently he left the room, but his open book showed the picture of a beautiful palomino. When he returned the boy was looking at the pictures in the book. Neither made any comment.

The next morning the tutor had yet another book under his arm. He said a pleasant good morning and sat down to his reading. After a time the tutor started to rise and dropped a number of pictures at the boy's feet. The pictures were all of horses—sheiks on Arabian horses; great horses from Normandy; Spanish ponies of the strain left by the conquistadores in Mexico. The boy stooped painfully and picked up the pictures and examined them with interest. Finally, he reluctantly returned the pictures to the tutor who accepted them without a word.

Each morning the tutor continued his reading and each morning he managed to leave something that intrigued the boy's interest. One morning he brought in a brightly embroidered belt, tossed it over a chair and began sketching the design. The boy could hold back his curiosity no longer, "What's that?" he asked.

"It's a sheik's embroidered belt," answered the tutor.

"What's a sheik?" asked the boy.

"That's a chieftain of the nomad people in North Africa."

"What are nomads and where is North Africa?" asked his pupil.

Seeing that the boy was really interested the tutor laid his book aside and told how his grandfather had been with Lawrence of Arabia in North Africa. He talked for a while, then seemed to be about to return to his book, but the boy's eager questioning spurred him on. With eyes alight the lad kept urging his tutor to tell him about Arabia and the exploits of the chieftains with their beautiful horses.

There was never any more trouble with this boy. Spurred to know more about the horses he loved, he eagerly undertook to learn to read. Partly because of his maturity, but even more because of his awakened interest he mastered reading far more quickly than the average child.

To his surprise and delight he found there were other things of interest in the world. Each time the boy asked a question the tutor managed to inject some remark that stirred the boy's curiosity. In the course of time their investigations led them through the entire subject matter field— science, literature, religion, reading, writing, and mathematics. An interest in astronomy was sparked by stories of the desert skies and how the caravan travelers set their course by the stars.

This tutor listened to the questions of his pupil and answered him in detail, talking only so long as the boy was interested. Instead of continually *asking* the boy questions, the tutor listened and answered questions. He presented problems in such a way that the boy was led to think them through successfully for himself.

The difficulty in this approach often is that in many schools the teachers feel they have too many unsolved questions of their own to be able to answer the children's questions. If this be the situation they should be encouraged to seek for the answers along with their children.

Positive Areas of Learning in Primary Groups

Starting with the child himself, if you follow the widening field of his awareness, you will discover that the factors which influence his early learning are found within his home, friends, neighborhood, and community. As he comes to understand the social relationships existing within these groups of which he is a participating member, he is developing concepts upon which will be built all his future understandings of more remote relationships.

Through surveying the possibilities of his widening horizons, you will be able to discover the areas of experiences through which your children will profit educationally. Your classroom will become a laboratory, a small world in which children live and learn together as they re-create the life around them. Together you will draw ideas from a selected portion of life; and the children will be influenced directly by first-hand experiences, both incidental and planned, and, indirectly through the people they know, the pictures and films they see, the books they read, and through stories, songs, and poems.

In solving their problems children reach out into the home and the community for their ideas, and they grow and learn as they speak, plan, evaluate, execute, re-evaluate, and re-plan. Many of their learnings are academic: records need to be kept and used; problems in space and numbers must be solved; references must be consulted and reports made.

Diversified responsibilities mean opportunities for diversified abilities to be brought into focus.

The children within each group are unique, but it is possible to find within their sphere of influence general fields of interest within which suitable areas may be located for any group. Those most commonly chosen relate to homes and families; neighborhoods; the grocery, market, bakery; a wholesale distributor in a special area such as produce, meat; the dairy; fire control facilities; newspaper; library; postal service; air travel; trucks and trains; a local industry based upon some natural resource or crop such as oil, citrus, cotton, wheat.

Areas Demanding More Maturity

Life in some other community, different from the one in which the children live, offers deeper understanding of their own living conditions. The next step beyond this is to study life in a more primitive culture and then in another part of the world. Conditions which are further removed from the child in location (geography) and in time (history) are reserved for older groups which have more maturity and understanding to bring to the study.

Any evaluation of the children's readiness for such an area of experience must take into account the means by which they will gain the necessary experiential background from which to develop the area.

The life of the American Indian in his native habitat offers a wealth of opportunities to deepen the children's understanding of man's ability to develop a culture in a wilderness removed from civilization as it exists today. However, to engage in such a study which means dropping back into history, children need to attain a background that enables them to appreciate the significance of historical as well as cultural and social values. Readiness for such a study is seldom reached before upper primary or beyond.

A Beginning Primary Group Studies the Construction of Homes

Observing and Reliving the Development of a Subdivision

A large subdivision was being developed near a particular school. There was much leveling to be done and heavy equipment was at work as the children came to school each day. Some fathers of the children in beginning primary were working on this project and other families were waiting to move into the houses when they were finished. Interest in this activity was at high pitch and several walks were taken to the scene to observe the machinery closely. The children were delighted with the talk given by the foreman who clarified the "workings" of the mammoth machinery. The children returned to the school with many new ideas for creating their own subdivision with blocks and boxes. Songs, poems, stories about the experience, found among children's literature, as well as numerous verses created spontaneously by the teacher and the children were used. Creative body rhythms of the machines at work were enjoyed, and several charts were developed with a vocabulary that was difficult but easily mastered by the children because of their enthusiasm for the machines.

The children decided one of the best ways to remember the experience would be to make a big class book. Each of the children contributed an easel painting to illustrate one of the machines, and had a part in the composite literary content which was dictated by them, written in manuscript first on the chalkboard and later in the book in large black lettering by the teacher.

Mrs. R. was delighted by the enthusiasm with which this fascinating creation was read and explained by these primary children again and again.

A few of the pages follow:

Earth Movers
(title page)

Fifty Ton Giant

This "Euc"[1] can carry one hundred thousand pounds of material. It has no tail gate.

Page 1

Heavy Duty Giant

This "big boy" can go thirty miles per hour and carry fifty tons.

Page 2

A Crane and Dump Truck

The crane is loading the fifteen ton dump truck. This truck has a tailgate.

Page 3

[1] "Euc" = excavating machinery.

The Houses Go Up

As Mrs. R.'s children watched the foundation being laid, attention was called to the reason for a firm foundation. As they noted the carpenters erecting the supporting timbers, Victor's father, who was a carpenter, came on his day off and talked to the children at their level of understanding on the general construction of houses and the need for a strong, well-braced structure. The children saw the plumbers and the electricians come, do their job, and go, and they drew upon all their experiences as they built their own tract of houses. There was considerable discussion on the need for the chimney to be hollow so that the fumes could escape. Rather than just making houses that looked, externally, like what they saw, the children would think about the different needs of a house and how they were fulfilled in reality. The class divided into crews rather than committees. The teacher asked stimulating questions to encourage problem solving and commended their successful efforts freely. All along, concepts of building for family living were expanded through songs,

Bull Dozer

This bull dozer
is loading on a flat top.

Page 4

Lightweight Grader

This grader
can move easily.
It can do many things.

Page 5

The Little Train

The little train
can go fast.
It says, "Chug, chug."

Page 6

A Skip Loader

This can
pick up materials
and load them in a truck.

Page 7

stories, poems, dramatic expression, rhythms, and creative charts.

Progress Stopped by a Strike

A general strike of the men on construction occurred when the houses were near completion. The children saw the unfinished structures standing silent, and grieved over the delay of progress that prevented the families from moving in. They could see how vital teamwork is if a project is to be completed.

Back to Work

Finally the strike was settled and hammers and saws began pounding and buzzing again in the neighborhood. The children were delighted and promptly went to their own work of making another book on new houses, each child illustrating with easel painting his own page in the book.

Living in the Home

The next problem was one of moving into the new homes in which some of the children would actually be living. They were eager to share details with other children. Problems incident to moving out of the former house and into the new one brought forth much discussion, new concepts, and a wealth of academic as well as aesthetic and social experiences. There was clarification of the various kinds of houses: cottages, two-story houses, apartments, duplex, triplex, cabins, lodges, hotels, motels and mobile homes; arrangement and purpose of the various rooms in the house; the type of furniture for each and kinds of activities that take place in each. Placement of possessions was discussed; which things go where; and finally, most important of all, what is a family?

Always the most important phases of the discussions were summarized and recorded on charts to which the children frequently referred.

From painting pictures of their families evolved a number experience taking the form of a workable bulletin board. In answer to the question, "How many are in your family?" the individual child inserted the correct number card to represent his family unit.

Contributions of each member of the family were discussed with emphasis on the child's responsibility to the welfare and happiness of the family.

Instead of setting up work committees for this area these six-year-olds established six different family groups of varying sizes, consisting of a father, mother, brothers and sisters. Some families also had a grandmother, grandfather, aunt, uncle, or cousin living with them. Children rotated playing the role of the various family members from day to day.

The families were named and plans were made for the responsibilities each would assume.

Plans also included discussions, representations, and dramatizations of family life and how to achieve it, such as by members' being courteous, considerate, unselfish, with a happy attitude; sharing, taking turns, family unity, and providing for safety in the home; activities of the home, cooking, eating, dish washing, cleaning, laundering, sleeping; family fun, such as reading together, sharing experiences of the day, picnics, vacations, exploring the out-of-doors, celebrating special days and holidays together, going on excursions to the library, museum, zoo, shopping for food, and how the family transports itself.

During the living of family life the children worked individually and collectively, proving through actual experience how interrelation is necessary and natural among people. Often a child broke into spontaneous song:

Barbara's Creative Song

$$\frac{2}{4} \quad \begin{array}{c|c|c|c} 5 \ 5 & 3- & 8 \ 8 & 5 \ - \\ \text{This is} & \text{where} & \text{Terry} & \text{lives} \end{array}$$

$$\begin{array}{c|c|c|c} 5 \ 5 & 3- & 8 \ 8 & 5 \ - \\ \text{This is} & \text{where} & \text{Mary} & \text{lives} \end{array}$$

$$\begin{array}{c|c|c} 3 \ 3 & 1 \ - & 5- \ 3 \ - \\ \text{This is} & \text{where} & \text{I} \quad \text{live.} \end{array} \|$$

The following chart was one of the children's favorites:

On Our Street

Many children live
on our street.
We all know
and like each other.
It is fun to be neighbors.
All of us are good friends.

As the children painted or otherwise depicted the occupations of their fathers (and/or mothers), Mrs. R. stressed "service" rather than "status." For the more itinerant workers represented in the group she emphasized the value of the harvest and the food, remembering that no matter how menial the contribution, it had its importance.

A Supplementary Study Suggested by the Area

The children decided they needed a place for family pets, which led naturally into a discussion and research problem of animal homes. There were numerous verbalizations recorded in the planning and creating of a workable bulletin board. In one column were the animals and in another were their homes. A string attached to each animal was matched to the animal's appropriate home. This demanded discrimination, recall, and a background of knowledge.

Always likenesses and differences were stressed among humans and animals, in their homes, family life, and proper care.

Animal Families

Animals have families, too.
They live in many different places.
The mothers protect their babies.
Some animal fathers help the mothers keep the babies safe.
Mothers help their babies find food.
Sometimes the father brings food both to the mother and the babies.

Children with Special Problems at Home

As the study of family life went on, Mrs. R. was concerned about the personal and emotional reactions of Johnny, who was an orphan, and Jimmy, from a broken home, and Mary, who was a rejected child with an alcoholic father, and Sue, whose parents wrangled much of the time and then took their revenge out on her. Mrs. R. explained her point of view on this as follows:

"The child who is lonely and insecure, with heavy burdens and anxieties about his own inadequate relationship to his family group, or the child who feels inferior or unimportant as a person, may need special consideration. It is difficult for him to be interested, enthusiastic, and expressive when he hears and sees his peers living in a happy, wholesome, and loving family environment. Is it any wonder that he squirms and wiggles and perhaps openly rebels and becomes a resistant isolationist? This child needs assurance of his place in the group at school. You can help him with responsibilities and tasks that bring satisfaction and success and increase his appreciation of his own worth as an individual."

"Some children do seem to accept their unusual home situation philosophically and will make adjustments without any special help."

A Middle Primary Group Inquires
"Why and How Is the Community Around Our School Changing?"

Some idea of the nature of an area of experience in a group of seven- and eight-year-olds may be gained from the following.

Room Environment

The room environment was set up to emphasize the area and facilities available. Moveable desks and chairs were arranged in groups in an "L" shape on both sides of the room. This permitted work areas near the front of the room by the chalkboard. The "community" was built to the left, leaving the right side of the room free for planning and group meetings. The windows gave light for the work area and made it possible for Miss Holman, the teacher, to supervise the children working on the patio. Below the windows were shelves for storing the accessories and on top of this was a display shelf or work area on a level with the windows. To the back of the room were more storage cupboards and drawers. In the center there was a sink and work area which was used for cleaning, experimenting and display purposes.

On the right was a piano, more files, bulletin boards, and charts. All around the room were places for charts, bulletin board displays, pictures of community helpers borrowed from the audio-visual library, notices, notes to the individual children, and things of general interest, such as "Let's Make Trucks, a Truck Builder's Chart," giving detailed steps for building the main body of a truck. The child was free to use other types of construction if he so desired. A caption read, "Who helps us meet our needs?" Evaluation charts for the children's use were prominently displayed:

Busy Worker!

1. What do I plan to do next?
2. How well did I follow through on my plan?
3. Did I stop and clean up well?
4. What chance did I have
   to help a friend?
5. What did I do
   to make our work time better
   because I was here today?

Let's Evaluate

1. We talk things over together.
2. Let's think what we have been doing.
3. What problems do we have?
4. What suggestions can we make
   to solve these problems?
5. Do we have ideas to share?
6. How can we do better next time?

First we work
Then we play,
That's what makes
A happy day!

The room was light, airy, and cheerful. An attitude of interest and a sense of responsibility were everywhere in evidence, which bore testimony to the splendid rapport between teacher and children.

Research Corner

Many books were in evidence, and there was much material and information about electricity which the children had contributed.

Research for these children meant, "How can we find out?" They came to know through experience how to acquire their background from encyclopedias, reference materials, books, periodicals, pictures, and objects, but they also learned how to find out through interviewing people, both individually and in groups, and by going on field trips. The resource people whom they interviewed were: parents, teachers, students, and other people in the community who are culturally conscious and who have traveled; tradesmen, workers, and professional people who are interested in cooperating with the schools; and members of community organizations.

Independent activities also related to the study of the community. One example was a set of cards in which the children matched the names of people who worked in the different shops and places of business with the name of the store or establishment, as

> department store—clerk
> shoe repairs   —shoe repair man or cobbler
> hamburger stand—meat cook
> office building   —typist—book-keeper

The Patio

The patio was enclosed from the playground with a high fence. There were work tables, storage shelves, and cabinets on the patio, as well as plenty of open space. The easels were set up there but space was also allowed for construction work.

Planning

The area began the first day with the children's interest in how their Hope School environment was changing and growing. From this an interesting chart developed about:

Our Changing Community

Our Hope environment is changing,
growing,
        growing,
                growing.
More families come.
There are more children
to go to school.
This makes more cars
on our roads.
We need wider roads.
Our school is growing
bigger and bigger.
Our changing community
brings new needs.

With a stick figure drawing to represent the child as the center, Miss Holman developed a bulletin display of each child's needs:

We Have Many Needs

Food —————————— Shelter
Clothing —————————— Transportation
Communication —————— Protection
Education —————— Worship

Activities

The area was well under way at this time and after much planning, discussion, and evaluation the children proceeded into the community activities which consisted of:

1. Building the community—making the building themselves from cardboard and wooden boxes. (This was necessary before "living in the community" could take place, but Miss Holman and even the children, in this case, were more interested in the phases that followed rather than constructing an exact replica of the community.)

2. Measuring and lining off the streets with white chalk, then discussing names for the streets to submit to the group for vote.

3. Making light poles and using dry cell batteries.

4. Making "Stop," "Yield Right of Way," and street signs (which proved to be tedious work that the children executed beautifully).

5. Constructing trucks from wood.

6. Making a mural showing the sources of gas, electricity, and water.

A community was under development in one corner in the front of the room. The children had done considerable research and had solved some of their problems about the community. They had constructed so far a:
Court House, United States Post Office branch, School, Church, Service Station, Department Store, Restaurant, Fire Station, Super-Market, Hospital, and several homes.
Community Centers still needed:
Library
Bus Station
Park—Trees
Police Station (must be near Court House)
Motel
Bank
Medical and Dental Center
The following committees were at work:

Buildings—	Busily erecting planned buildings.
Trucks—	Constructing the type of trucks that would help the community meet its basic needs.
Clay—	Involved in the process of modeling figures to represent the individuals in the community.

Light-Poles— Working on their own system of lighting, the children had hooked up the batteries. The entire class was interested in the public utilities, such as water, gas, electricity, and telephone, and this committee was attempting to solve the problem of why the lights did not work.

The children, on their own, had come to see four possible sources of difficulty: there might not be enough power in the dry cell, the light bulbs might be too small, the lights might need more time to warm up, or the wires might not all be connected properly.

The children tried the wires first; they found some of the wires were not touching. Soon they had the lights on.

Murals and Utilities— This committee showed remarkable background on the sources of water, gas, and electricity which had been gained from independent research and through their interviews with community representatives from these fields.

Street— This committee was studying the Vehicle Code Manual and learning how the traffic regulations of their city met the basic needs of protection and transportation. From their research the committee developed a chart which read as follows:

Curb Colors

Red—Means no stopping (Unless it is a bus zone)
Yellow—Loading only
Green—Fifteen minute parking
White—Loading or unloading for a limited time

This committee was also intent on naming the various streets in their community, and making labels for them.

Signs— Speed limit signs, "Hospital—Quiet" signs, road signs, parking signs, landmark signs were all under development.

Evaluation

Elizabeth, on the building committee, had worked industriously making a "stained glass window" for the church building only to find that it was going to be too small to fit the window frame. Miss Holman said, "How can you plan so that the next window you make will be large enough?"

The children helped Elizabeth see that she would need to measure and with what and how she should go about this.

Margaret went over to try to work the lights, but when she put one of the wires to the battery nothing happened. One of the children standing nearby stopped what he was doing and explained to her how she would have to touch both of the wires together to make the lights go on. He explained how electricity needed two wires to complete the circuit. Margaret thanked him and put the two wires together and the lights went on.

Another child was busy making clay people. She discovered for herself that fingers and toes would not stay on a clay figure if she just stuck them on. She learned how to manipulate the clay and gradually pull the arms and head out from the main body.

Loyd was painting an ambulance and said he was going to put a cross on it just like the one on their church. Mike sitting next to him said, "The cross on the ambulance is red and not the same as the cross on the church." So the children were learning for themselves rather than being told these things by an autocratic teacher.

When the members of the light pole committee reported, Miss Holman made special note of how well they had worked together. Then she helped them solve their problems of how many $1\frac{1}{4}$-volt batteries it would take to make a 6-volt battery.

Summary

In discussing their work the children mentioned what they had set out to do, and told how nearly they had achieved it. Plans were readjusted as a result of these evaluations.

There was a wide scope of activities in this area which revealed a consideration for the various levels of maturity, capabilities, needs, and interests of every child in the room. There was something for each to do that would challenge and bring him satisfaction.

Each child discussed his problems with all the children, who in turn gave ideas and opinions for their solutions. Triumphs were also shared and appreciated by all. The children were learning to adjust their judgments without being dominated by the opinions of others.

As Miss Holman went from group to group, she quietly made a suggestion here and there; she always recognized worthy individual contributions to the progress and welfare of class members and the success of the activities as they progressed. She made notes on the needs, strengths, and progress of each child, such as Lawrence's need for self expression and his high-strung nervous reaction to everything—this was shown in his splashing paint on the mural, not with any malice or negativism but due to awkwardness and lack of coordination; another child's effort to gain group approbation; still another's need to have courage to go ahead even if her work was not up to standard. Two children evidenced a need for more skill in measuring and in the use of tools, and Mark needed to be reminded to take better care of materials.

All important was the teacher's encouragement to observe the immediate environment and to be alert to interrelated causes and effects.

The environment provided opportunities to explore in other areas. The door was always open to new thoughts and experiences.

There was evidence of a former interest and the beginnings of another which indicated that a well-guided area of experience never really ends abruptly in a class, but rather serves as a main trunk upon which new branches of interest may sprout and grow.

This area of experience was a splendid example of the way a teacher can meet the requirements of a prescribed curriculum and at the same time sustain a child-centered program. Sharp-edged interest, well guided, is the key to genuine and long-term learning.

Where This Interest Could Lead

With the background of experience which the above group had thus far acquired they might develop a new study in any of the following fields:

1. Transportation, which might include such problems for solution as:
    a. How is our daily life affected by transportation?
    b. What would happen to our community if transportation stopped for a period of time?
    c. What kinds of transportation are used in bringing our food?
        1) Why are we able to have the variety of foods we do?
        2) How has science helped the transporting of produce?
        3) How does this help the farmer?

2. Communication, including telephones, telegraphs, the postal system, air mail, signaling by lights, radio, radar, television, short wave.

3. Public utilities, including a thorough study of water, gas, or electric light and power.

4. Community Helpers, including the medical profession, surveyors, postal service, carpenters, city officials, teachers, librarians, and public works, such as sanitation.

IV. DIFFERENCES IN CULTURAL BACKGROUNDS CONTRIBUTE TO SOCIAL STUDIES

My Neighbors

I used to class my neighbor
As the man who lived next door,
While those remote and seldom seen
Were ten miles off or more.

The telephone and daily news
The auto, bus and train
Soon brought our neighbors closer
And shrank the world again.

But now the jet and rocket
Have simply gobbled space;
The whole world is our neighbor—
Yes, every tribe and race.

The Chinese are our neighbors;
More neighbors dwell in Rome,
And Zanzibar and Timbuctoo
Are really close to home.

Appreciation of People Who Are Different

Children can come to be objective, unemotional, and open-minded about people who are different, not only in race, creed, or culture, but in ability and talent, or mental endowment, or because of physical handicap, or because they think and act differently.

Every child can be helped to realize at an early age people's interdependence on one another—that every person has a unique contribution to make and is to be respected as an individual human being.

Marian was in college, some two thousand miles removed from the "home front" before she came to realize that people respond in different ways, and that they are justified in having their own particular customs, mores, religious feelings, work, and recreation; furthermore, that these customs and ways of thinking may be as good for them as hers are for her. She had been reared by overly protective parents who had dogmatically announced in spirit and in fact, "we believe *this* is right and any other way is wrong."

The child will develop greater understanding of other human beings everywhere when led to discover that human nature is universally the same and that outward differences, when compared to inner worth and potential, often become unimportant. There are many differences among citizens of the same country, but the people are still held together by common bonds. It will go far toward making for greater international understanding and more permanent values if teachers and other leaders of children everywhere learn to view the aesthetic arts of other cultures with some of the deep-grained appreciation that those people themselves have acquired through many years of developing them.

A sensitivity and empathy international in scope is encouraged when you discuss likenesses rather than differences in people from other localities. Misunderstandings are minimized when children everywhere realize that their peers in friendly countries in other parts of the world have homes; that they eat, sleep, work, play, go to school, celebrate holidays, have pets, and know similar joys and sorrows, even though their environment and customs may differ.

With all the emphasis on outer space today even primary age children can talk about the world as naturally and even more intelligently than did the adults of yesteryear. They see films and video programs, hear stories from relatives and friends who have traveled widely. Many children are, themselves, well traveled; perhaps they sit next to a child from another country in school, or from another area of the nation. Also many children have teachers of different cultural backgrounds, which does much to bring people together and emphasize fellowship. The greatest barrier seems to be in communication, an inability to relate to others through the spoken or written word.

Guiding Toward Intercultural Understanding

In a large district there is a school in which many races are to be found. There is not only the problem of differences in color, but in language and family background as well. Yet the unity in this school is almost like one big family. When questioned the principal said:

"From the time children enter this school we avoid connecting any indiscretion or negative behavior with the race of the child. If the safety committee representative comes in and reports, 'That Indian boy is fighting on the school grounds,' we ask, 'What is the name of the boy who is fighting?'

"There is a conscious effort made to help individuals appreciate the things in which others are superior. The Negro children in the school do outstandingly fine work in music and rhythm; it is possible to select the art work of the oriental children because of the lines and representative quality in their paintings, and that of the Mexican children because of their feeling for color. These are the racial differences which we help children to appreciate, but we dwell most on our likenesses, the things we have in common. There are few problems here, and whenever one does occur the prejudice stems from the attitude of adults on the outside.

"Sometimes parents who have recently moved here come to us and say, 'I won't have my child holding hands with these children.' When such instances occur we are polite but firm. 'This is a public school,' we say, 'designed for all of the children of all of the people. Every child is treated alike here. We make no distinction. The only remedy we can suggest is that you move into a neighborhood where none but children of your own race attend the schools.' "

Children of foreign born parents appreciate the respect shown their cultural background and the consideration given them as individuals by peers, teacher, and administration. This leads them to feel they have a stake in American democracy. By the same token, children of the "old line" American families develop a truer sense of pride and a less superior attitude. They realize that they must strive even more actively to make good their heritage, to make it a living thing, not just to rest on the laurels of their ancestors.

All these things help the children realize what it means to be an American, to be proud of their country, and to be eager to assume obligations as well as to enjoy the privileges of freedom. It brings, too, a greater appreciation of the contributions of all the people who have built America.

Miss Holman had displayed a bulletin in a prominent position in her middle-primary room presenting the question: "What does America mean to you?" This led to seven-year, six-month-old Jimmy creating and making independently the following chart:

America and What It Means to Me

I love America.
Think of other countries.
People are very poor there.
We need to keep up the good things
we are doing.
Keep America the greatest country.
You are helping right now
to make our country the best.
Every city in America needs
to be kept clean.
Don't wait for other people
to pick up the papers.
Pick them up yourself.
That's how to keep America the best.

Prejudice is not necessarily confined to any one nationality or group. Lolita, of Mexican descent, enjoyed her first day in school. When she returned home she said to her mother, "My teacher is Mexican."

The mother, who knew that Miss M., the child's teacher, had flaming red hair and fair skin, said, "What makes you think she is Mexican, Lolita?"

"No one could be so nice," said the child earnestly, "if she were not Mexican."

Miss M., who was of Irish descent, felt this was a high tribute in that the child had identified her with those she held in greatest esteem.

The Squad from Beulah Land

The artist teacher's concept of social studies as carrying over into the lives of the children is illustrated by what happened to the Squad from Beulah Land. This is recounted by a close friend of Miss Hilton, the teacher who had a major part in it.

During the crucial years of World War II people from all parts of the country as well as from other nations flocked into one of our great industrial cities. This resulted in schools being overcrowded with children from every corner of the globe—many of whom fought with each other outside and glared fiercely at each other inside the school.

It was early in the school year and Miss Hilton's restless, seething upper-primary group had not even begun to "simmer down." She saw Elim, a shy little Hindu boy glance about him nervously and thought sadly, "Ramon has probably been picking on Elim again."

The children were studying the lighting phase of community resources, and some of the committees were doing particularly good work. They had learned how to connect the current in order to light the globes on the electric light poles they had made. When the children came together to evaluate their work Miss Hilton had an inspiration. In the back country from the city were sheep ranches, and she had bought a woolen rug at the mills on one of her vacation trips. She got it out of the closet now.

"We have been studying the uses of electricity in our community. Let's see what happens when electricity is not hooked up to make power," she said.

"Come here, Ramon. We are going to do an experiment. Rub your feet on this wool rug and then touch my hand."

Ramon did so.

"What did you feel?" she asked.

"It felt like an electric shock," Ramon replied.

Miss Hilton turned to the group and asked, "What is this kind of electricity called?"

There was no answer.

"Static electricity is generated by the friction of your feet scraping across the wool rug," she explained.

"If someone kept touching you with a shock like this could you work well?" she asked.

"No," said Ramon doubtfully.

"This shock is weak and cannot really hurt you, but what would happen if someone touched you with a heavy charge of electricity?" Miss Hilton asked.

"It would hurt. And if it was strong enough it could really kill a person," said Ramon.

"But when electricity is conducted through the wires in our experiment what does it do?" asked Miss Hilton.

"It works for us and gives us light," volunteered Jenkins, a badly crippled Negro boy who was one of the brightest children in the room.

"The same thing is true when we irritate our friends and do things to annoy them," continued Miss Hilton. "It prickles and makes us send off sparks. And if the current of anger is stronger?"

"It makes us fight," said Isadore (Izzy), a Jewish boy who possessed a keen dry sense of humor.

"But if we pull together it is like hooking up the current so that all our power goes toward accomplishing something worthwhile."

"Like the lights for our city," added Ramon.

The electric spark illustration seemed to have lighted a new spirit among that class of boys. Pat, a true Irishman, and Seppie, a hot-blooded Italian, who had always seemed to fight "at the drop of a hat" grinned shyly at each other, and Pat reached out, pretending to get a crackle and spark out of Seppie.

That afternoon's conference did not "cure" the situation, but things were never so bad again. Miss Hilton read the children stories and poems and they in turn gave reports on other stories in which the underlying theme was brotherhood.

One boy in her group, Wayne Ralston, hardly seemed to fit into this polyglot group. He was a blue-eyed friendly boy of Scandinavian extraction with a great potential for leadership. Miss Hilton knew that Wayne's father, who had been in the service, had gone down with his ship, and that Wayne's mother had come to the city to work in an airplane factory. Because of the housing shortage they had taken the only place they could find to live—an apartment on run-down Finn Street.

More and more often Miss Hilton saw a cloud on Wayne's bright face. She sensed his loneliness when he lingered to talk with her after school and often encouraged him to help her about the classroom. "Do you have friends to play with after school?" she asked the boy casually.

"I don't play much," answered Wayne. In a burst of confidence he added, "They fight. I don't like to fight. I like to be friends."

"Where do the boys play?" asked Miss Hilton.

"There isn't any place close by we can play," said Wayne. "They won't let you play in the street."

"What do you like to play, Wayne?"

"Oh, football!" said Wayne with a young boy's enthusiasm for an older boy's sport. "My grandfather was going to get me a football for my birthday, only his cotton crop in Texas was a failure. Maybe he can get it next year."

The following week end Miss Hilton went walking on Finn Street, and not far from Wayne's home she found a vacant lot. Inquiry revealed the lot belonged to the baker, a big, good-natured fellow with no children of his own. The lot was piled high with rubbish which the city had been after him to clear, so he said the boys would be welcome to use the lot if they would clean it up. He even offered to haul away the heavy stuff and have the debris picked up if the boys would put it in piles.

Cheeks pink with excitement, Miss Hilton went to buy a football.

The following week end she was on hand at an early hour to help the boys begin their out-of-school project.

Six boys were already awaiting her at the lot, but soon every boy in the neighborhood was either delving in or watching. Miss Hilton counted them—twenty-three in all: Wayne and Izzy, four of her Negro boys, three Chinese, the slender Hindu, a Polish boy, Seppie, the Italian, a Greek boy, a Turkish and two Anglo-American boys. There were seven Mexican boys from six different families. Five of these boys were not only poorly housed but also poorly clothed and fed. The other two boys came from better homes, but because of social barriers that had been erected against their families they were belligerent and unfriendly toward the "whites."

Now they were all working at a hard task together. While they were struggling with the body of a broken-down truck, Rafe, a big husky Negro boy with a Deep-South religious background remarked, "This is going to be a Beulah Land when we gets it all cleaned up."

This tickled the boys and "Beulah Land" it was christened. The very name helped bring peace. When hot-headed Seppie and equally hot-headed Pat started to pick a fight, Izzy drily remarked, "I thought 'Beulah Land' was a happy place! Are we going to have war in Beulah Land?"

The fight subsided.

When they paused to rest and eat the fruit Miss Hilton had brought, they talked about football. "What kind of football will you play?" Miss Hilton asked.

"Regular!" said Pat enthusiastically.

"You would!" thought Miss Hilton, glancing fondly at his saucy belligerent face, and added to herself, "Bless, Izzy!" when she heard him say,

"Will you buy the football suits, Pat? You have to have padded suits to play regular football. Better make it *touch*."

After some discussion the boys decided on touch football until they could buy their suits, which, incidentally, was about six years later.

When the squad was being formed Wayne and a boy named Oehlenbusch—promptly called "Bushy" by the boys (a name he still proudly uses) —were made captains. When sides were chosen, Jenkins, the lame boy, drooped visibly until Izzy asked, "Who's going to referee this jamboree?"

Wayne cast his eyes over the group. "Why not Jinks?" he asked. ("He makes 'A's' in school. Some of us don't," he added wryly.)

"He can study the rules," added Izzy. "Jinks, Referee of the Jamboree!"

Jinks was no longer drooping. For once he was included. He had had recognition from his peers.

The months went by and the boys moved upward to another room and another teacher. But by then they had become fast friends. They had numerous squabbles but no serious difficulties and they always presented a solid front to outsiders.

Wayne's mother found an opportunity to move to a "better" neighborhood, but Wayne protested vigorously. He didn't want to leave the Squad. There was mourning in Beulah Land until the policeman on the corner proved an unexpected ally. "Why, Mrs. Ralston," he protested, "that boy of yours is better than a social worker. There used to be gang fights and petty thefts, and I used to have to keep me eye right on Finn Street, but now," he added proudly, "there's not a better street anywhere. That boy of yours, he's *friendly*. Instead of saying, 'Hello, Chink!' or 'Hello, Pachuco!' he grins and says, 'Hi! Can you come on over?' I tell you, Mrs. Ralston, a friendliness like that is worth more than a club."

So Mrs. Ralston refurnished the apartment and they remained on at Finn Street.

The "Squad from Beulah Land" became known as the toughest football team in the school; tough in the sense of being hard to beat. Occasionally a member of their group moved away, but mostly it remained intact. Due largely to the leadership of Wayne and Izzy, the boys not only held to the high standards of conduct and sportsmanship which Miss Hilton had helped them to formulate, but to scholarship standards as well. As a unit they went from Beulah Land to junior high and to high school. Most of them finished high school and more than two-thirds of them went to college. Many of them went into the service and two boys, a Negro and the Polish boy, lost their lives in Korea.

One of the Chinese boys took high honors at Stanford and is now a bank executive. Another is a doctor, the third a professional football player.

Three of the Mexican boys are teachers, one owns a popular restaurant, one is in the Air Force, and two are day laborers. Two of the original group unfortunately drink to excess and one of these two has been involved in a dope ring.

Of the remaining three Negro boys, Jinks is a judge in the superior court of his state, another owns a men's clothing store, and the other lays linoleum for a firm in his city.

The shy, quiet Hindu is a psychologist; the Italian boy owns a beauty salon; the Greek has a fine restaurant, and the Turk manages a finance company. One Anglo-American is a shoe salesman and the other is in the

Navy. Wayne is an electrical engineer, and Izzy a clever and successful lawyer.

With two exceptions these men are all honorable, respected citizens in the community. Some of them are gaining fame and fortune; others are average, run-of-the-mill citizens. The remarkable thing about them, however, is the strong bond of friendship that still exists among them. Those who live in the same city or in the vicinity frequently visit with each other. There is pride but no apparent envy over another's achievements, and there is an evident feeling of protectiveness toward the two who have gone astray. Once a year they go back to "Beulah Land" for a reunion and re-live the days when they worked and played together. Only dire necessity prevents a member of the Squad from participating in this reunion. They say that Jinks, Referee of the Jamboree, became a judge largely because he just can't get out of the habit of refereeing.

Although their paths are so divided, the participants in this experience respect each other as individuals without regard to achievement or failure since school days. Through the interest of a primary teacher who had the vision to see beneath the rough exteriors engendered by adverse circumstances, an experiment in social living was begun which resulted in life-long friendship and appreciation of the worth of each individual.

This group exemplifies the viewpoint that social studies builds toward true social living.

The human heart and mind are like the keyboard of a piano. A master hand can bring forth inspiring harmony; one who lacks sensitivity makes a cacophony of discord. Someway, for most of these boys, Miss Hilton found the master chord. Fortunately there are other Miss Hiltons in the ranks of the teaching profession with the vision to continue guiding the children of the world.

As a postscript to this story, which is based on fact, (with changes of names, places, and certain circumstances to avoid identification), Wayne and Izzy recently bought Beulah Land and established it for the use of other generations of boys.

QUESTIONS ON SOCIAL DEVELOPMENT THROUGH CENTERS OF INTEREST AND AREAS OF EXPERIENCE

1. a. What is the need for environmental centers in the early childhood classroom? Give examples. b. Justify a second connotation of the term "center of interest" and describe examples.

2. What values would be derived from a center of interest early in the fall based upon summer vacations of the children? With a certain group in mind, describe.

3. Other than your general collection of informational material, why would it be undesirable for you to make a long time plan before knowing something of the ability and maturation of your children?

4. Cite classroom examples to illustrate the function of social studies throughout the school day. How can you, as teacher, know whether your social studies program is achieving its purpose?

5. a. At what maturation level in early childhood may committees begin to function effectively? Why not at an earlier age? b. Discuss the qualifications of a good committee member and the purposes served by committees in middle and upper primary.

6. Describe a mid-primary child whom you consider socially well-equipped.

7. a. Why did the last tutor of the over-indulged boy succeed so well in teaching him? b. What can you, personally, learn from the artistry of his teaching?

8. What is meant by an "Area of Experience," and why is it not found in the fives and immature six-year-old groups?

9. Consider what the resources within your community offer your children as possible areas of experience: for example, you might think of some vital question that is of major importance to everyone, such as:
   "Why Do We Need Our Airport?"
Then ask yourself:
   "How would this touch the lives of these children now?"
   a. List several questions on which your children could contribute ideas at the outset from out their own experience and thinking.
   b. Consider other possibilities of this area of experience for a particuular group of primary age children.

10. How can you make sure your emphasis is on learning experiences in terms of the child's growth and development?

11. What place have easel painting, clay work, verbalizations, and creative music in the development of an area of experience?

12. Why is it desirable to have the children state the title of an area in the form of a question? Discuss, giving illustrations of possible titles and evaluating them in terms of the possibilities they open up for learning.

13. Set up questions through which you suggest evaluating an area of experience to indicate the growth of the children's intellectual, social, physical, and emotional development.

14. Show in what ways an area of experience encourages the children to read and write. Describe various types of experiences in reading and

writing associated with a given area and illustrate with typical examples of children's work.

15. a. On what basis will you evaluate the culmination of an area of experience? b. Show how an area moves naturally toward its own culmination.

16. a. How would you launch an area of experience? b. Discuss how one area of experience may suggest another to follow it, and show how the new area may grow out of the preceding one. c. Must the new area necessarily arise from the preceding one? Explain.

SELECTED REFERENCES

Ambrose, Edna and Alice Miel, CHILDREN'S SOCIAL LEARNING; IMPLICATIONS OF RESEARCH AND EXPERT STUDY, Washington Association for Supervision and Curriculum Development, N.E.A., 1958.

Cartwright, Dorwin and Alvin Zander, Editors, GROUP DYNAMICS, Evanston, Ill., Row Peterson, Co., 1960.

Clark, Kenneth B., PREJUDICE AND YOUR CHILD, Boston, Beacon Press, 1958.

Elkins, Frederick, THE CHILD AND SOCIETY—THE PROCESS OF SOCIALIZATION, New York, Random House, 1960.

Erdt, Margaret, TEACHING ART IN THE ELEMENTARY SCHOOL, Revised ed., New York, Rinehart, 1962.

Estvan, Frank J. and Elizabeth W. Estvan, THE CHILD'S WORLD; HIS SOCIAL PERCEPTION, New York, G. P. Putnam's Sons, 1959.

Giles, H. Harry, THE INTEGRATED CLASSROOM, (RACIAL), N. Y., Basic Books Pub. Co., 1959.

Hanna, Lavone A., Gladys L. Potter and Neva Hagaman, UNIT TEACHING IN THE ELEMENTARY SCHOOL, New York, Rinehart, 1955.

Harap, Henry, SOCIAL LIVING IN THE CURRICULUM, Nashville, George Peabody College for Teachers, 1952.

Hoffman, Elaine, and Jane Hefflefinger, Series of books on Community Helpers: OUR FRIENDLY HELPERS, 1954; MORE FRIENDLY HELPERS, 1954; FRIENDLY SCHOOL HELPERS, 1955; FRIENDLY FIREMAN, 1954; Los Angeles 38, California; Melmont Publishing Inc.

Jarolimek, John, SOCIAL STUDIES IN ELEMENTARY EDUCATION, New York, Macmillan, 1959.

Krug, Edward, ADAPTING INSTRUCTION IN THE SOCIAL STUDIES TO INDIVIDUAL DIFFERENCES, 15th Yearbook, National Council for Social Studies, 1944.

Lane, Howard, and Mary Beauchamp, HUMAN RELATIONS IN TEACHING: THE DYNAMICS OF HELPING CHILDREN GROW, Englewood Cliffs, N. Y., Prentice-Hall, Inc., 1955.

Merritt, Edith, WORKING WITH CHILDREN IN SOCIAL STUDIES, San Francisco, Wadsworth Publishing Co., 1961.

Michaelis, J. U., SOCIAL STUDIES FOR CHILDREN IN A DEMOCRACY, Second Ed., Englewood Cliffs, New Jersey, Prentice-Hall, 1956.

Miel, Alice and Peggy Brogan, MORE THAN SOCIAL STUDIES, Englewood Cliffs, New Jersey, Prentice-Hall, 1957.

National Society for the Study of Education, SOCIAL STUDIES IN THE ELEMENTARY SCHOOL, Nelson B. Henry, Ed., Fifty-sixth Yearbook, Part II, Chicago, Univ. of Chicago Press, 1957.

Preston, Ralph C., TEACHING SOCIAL STUDIES IN THE ELEMENTARY SCHOOLS, New York, Rinehart, 1958.

Preston, Ralph C., TEACHING WORLD UNDERSTANDING, Englewood Cliffs, New Jersey, Prentice-Hall, 1955.

Quillen, I. James, and Lavone A. Hanna, EDUCATION FOR SOCIAL COMPETENCIES, Chicago, Scott, Foresman and Co., 1948.

Stendler, Celia Burns and Wm. E. Martin, INTERGROUP EDUCATION IN THE KINDERGARTEN—PRIMARY GRADES, New York, Macmillan, 1953.

Tiegs, Ernest W. and Fay Adams, TEACHING THE SOCIAL STUDIES, Boston, Ginn and Co., 1959

Willcockson, Mary, Ed., SOCIAL EDUCATION FOR YOUNG CHILDREN, Washington, D.C., National Council for Social Studies, 1956.

Witmer, Helen L. and Ruth Kotinsky, Editors, PERSONALITY IN THE MAKING, (Chapters V, VI, VIII, IX.--Effects of class prejudice, culture, and family on personality development), New York, Harper & Bros., 1952.

Yrager, Helen G. and Mirian Radke Yarrow, THEY LEARN WHAT THEY LIVE, Parts I and II, New York, Harper & Bros., 1952.

A PHILOSOPHY TOWARD

Part Ten

SELECTIVE HOMEWORK

I. HOMEWORK IN THE EDUCATION
OF THE CHILD

The term "homework" as viewed from the traditional standpoint frequently recalls to memory many and varied drill assignments that had to be completed in an allotted period of time. The children who received the assignment groaned within, but came to regard it as something to be tolerated as a necessary evil. They learned to take it as they would a bitter pill with the determination to get it down quickly with the least possible effort. On their part, mother, father, and other members of the family all too frequently thought of homework as something painful which the child must undergo in order to make his grade in school.

Time, however, brings opportunities for changes, and some of the changes which have been made in homework have been for the better. Educators are realizing more and more that everything must be meaningful to the individual if he is to profit from the experience.

Homework, then, if used to advantage, should be carefully selected to meet the needs of the child who is doing it, and should be a part of a learning process that stimulates, interests, and challenges him. Selective homework of this character is an enrichment of the school program and not just a means of gaining more time for meaningless drill.

Well selected homework is an opportunity to extend learnings and to explore captivating new fields with parents who are interested and anxious to share. Whether the terminology be "home-work" or "school-work" the difference is in the connotation of the word "work." Many children today think of work as a golden time to pursue some avenue of investigation and learning which is especially satisfying to them, often chosen voluntarily and carried on independently. No longer is it, "Do these 64 examples at home tonight," or "Tonight you are to memorize this entire poem."

Home-School Cooperation

It may be a fresh idea to teachers as well as parents that homework is an opportunity to build more secure and satisfying parent-child relationships and to cement home-school-child bonds. It is an opportunity to extend the child's knowledge and explore new fields with him, fields which may be new to the parents, also. This "learning together" brings a closeness which is highly prized and makes for greater cooperation and understanding between the home and school.

The attitude of parents toward the homework program of their child is paramount. They can do much to influence the child's attitude through their own active interest and cooperation. Parents need to recognize that learning is continuous and there are no characteristic differences in school and home learnings in helping their child achieve his own unity of action and reaction. It is therefore necessary for parents to be co-guides in the great adventure of educating their child.

Thus, you and the parents are working together to execute a sound homework program which facilitates the steady intellectual development of the child.

When the value of selective homework for young children was discussed with the parents of one five-year-old group, Mark's father said he enjoyed most the "sharing feeling" as he and his son explored, investigated, and discussed a project together.

Donna's mother said, "I feel a new closeness to my child through helping her with her homework."

Others in the group nodded their agreement.

The child's own inner drive for achievement, his natural bent to explore, as well as committee work, group discussions, and individual reports—all of these can easily and fruitfully lead into planning, research, or problem-solving after the day in school is over.

The modern approach to education introduces a new challenge that fairly entices the children into the fascinating land of learning. Perhaps it is not entirely fair to call it a *new* challenge, because some real educators felt it in the traditional days, while some present-day teachers still continue to do formal teaching. However, many teachers now realize that teaching can be more and more creative, and the new spirit can touch and imbue those children whom it reaches with an insatiable curiosity about things to be learned in the classroom.

This desire to know should be capitalized upon, beginning with the youngest learners. This is the reason the area of experience approach to learning, in which the child participates actively, is many times more interesting and the children retain far more than they ever would under the formal approach of looking up assignments and reporting on what they are told to read. Certainly in most situations this influence will later spread to the parents. This in itself would justify bringing the parents in for conferences, meetings, workshops, observations, and participation in the classroom, because in this way they are also reached. Basically, the same procedure can be used with the parents as with the children. This is the reason for inviting them to participate in an area of experience. Having parents ask their own questions regarding a learning experience not only inspires them; it also involves them in the area so much that their interest is absorbed completely. This is ego-involvement of the type so close to the heart of a good psychologist. Through this the individual becomes so engrossed in the project that he wants to argue out his own views and find material to substantiate his beliefs and perfect his discussion. In this way he makes a far greater effort to know his material and present it with conviction and finally make it his own rather than just remembering it long enough to prove his point.

"Custom-Made" Homework

Homework is a form of follow-up drawn from points that arise at school during the day. The learnings can be followed through the next day when the children report back on something they were to find out. Homework may cut across many areas of the curriculum. The child may explore the community or the home environment to find an answer to a question, or may bring in specimens and examples. Therefore homework must of necessity be custom built for the school and the needs of the particular group. The term "selective" embodies this viewpoint. Selective homework arises from discussions in the group and follows a need for expression and investigation. It frequently stems from the children's own initiative. "That can be our homework for today" is often heard as the children become curious about something that intrigues their interest. This possibility can be discussed and agreed upon before the children leave for home that day. Because of their high interest the first thing the children say upon greeting Mother or other members of the family is "Our homework for today is _____." However, you will want to have homework planned in advance in order that, if it does not grow out of the day's discussion, you will still have something available that is related to the interests of the group.

Homework for the Five- and Six-Year-Olds

There are several reasons why beginning a homework program that follows up on the day's leads is exceedingly desirable even with the five-year-olds. It can start with these children and continue on through the elementary school.

With the right kind of homework procedures in the early years of a child's educational career, you and parents as partners will be able to facilitate the best learning possible in the all-around development of the child.

1. After the children have had necessary experience with color, you may talk about colors used in the home, asking the children to name some of them. Some child may say, "I can't think of any more now, but I'll find out tonight."

And others will say, "I will, too."

Thus the homework comes from the children themselves.

Other suggested areas from which homework may be drawn from the children are:

2. Following a discussion on and much experience with shapes: The homework may be to "find as many different shapes around your home as you can." This may be more definite, as to: "find round things," or "find things that are square or oblong."

3. Find all the things at home that the sun will shine through.

4. Stand outside the kitchen when your mother is getting dinner. As you smell the food, have someone in the family write down all the smells you can identify. (*Identify* may be a new word learned.)

5. Go for a walk with your mother or some other member of your family around the neighborhood where you live. Remember one interesting thing you see and tell us about it tomorrow. This may be varied according to the locality and the interests of the group; for example, the suggestion might be more specific as, "Look for all the animals you see and tell us about them" (if there are pets in this area), or "Look at the

houses being constructed," or "Watch the birds flying." The homework should be adapted to the current events, the season or the weather, making sure that what is expected is within reason and probability.

At this level, children may also enjoy painting pictures at home to illustrate the informational material they collect.

Homework in the Lower Primary

Interests and needs are more influential in determining the nature of homework than the child's age.

When Mark's father helped him make a chemical garden at home, he brought it to school to share. Homework for this group was to find out what made the plants grow without soil.

A favorite song, story, or poem may contain an idea which could be followed through at home. There may be something to find out or to verify.

A new word in basic vocabulary may suggest homework. For example, the child may find out all the ways "up" and "down" are used in his house or by his family and tell the others in his reading group the next day.

After reading a particularly funny story the homework may be: "Watch for something funny that happens at home, and then tell us about it or pantomime it for us tomorrow."

In one lower primary group a lively discussion of various types of machines and heavy road equipment was climaxed by a dramatization which the children greatly enjoyed. Afterwards, the teacher suggested:

"Let's have our homework for tomorrow be about all the different kinds of machinery we can think of. We can go behind our shadow screen and dramatize the machines at work. Nobody will see us, but they will see the shadow of the machine we are pantomiming."

Homework in the Middle Primary

Something significant in the neighborhood or community may suggest homework of varying complexities for children of differing maturity and abilities. In a locality where there are various kinds of trees available to the children at home, their homework may be to, "Collect different types of leaves from your yard and see how many shapes and sizes you can find. Choose three or four different leaves. Bring them to school and arrange them according to size."

Another homework assignment might be to find a maple leaf or the leaf of some other tree common to the locality, and hold it up to see what its shadow looks like, then look through the leaf toward the light and see what the veins are like. Bring the leaf to school and fasten it on the window where the light can shine through it. For a less mature group, the homework would end here, but a more thought-provoking activity might be, "Find another kind of leaf that looks different from the maple leaf. Study the contour and the veins and find out what kind of a leaf it is. Bring the maple leaf and the other leaf to school."

Homework for still another group might be, "Find a leaf that is smooth and slick when you feel it. See what the plant looks like and where it is growing. Is it a tree or a bush? Bring the leaf to school and tell about it."

Homework of this nature is adapted to the children. Much depends upon the way it is followed through the next day when the child brings in his report on the leaf, or other concrete object he may have brought. Something about the object may suggest a picture to him that he might paint—its shape, size, or color. If leaves are being studied the children may group them according to likenesses and differences. Older children may do research reading on venation and the life cycle of the leaf.

A middle primary teacher wanted the children's parents to appreciate some of the learning from a recent field trip. She discussed it with her group and it was decided to talk over with their parents the different ways they could express their thanks to Mr. Bradley, the Harbor Master, for his kindness in giving them a conducted tour of the harbor environment.

The next day all but one child brought a letter written in his own manuscript. The one child brought her own painting of Mr. Bradley with a badge down under his belt.

One of the more advanced examples follows:

> Dear Mr. Bradley,
>   Thank you for stopping your work
> to show us around the pier.
>   We enjoyed it very much.
>   Charles

Homework of this type becomes part of the regular class work and is completely voluntary.

Sending home questions and problems for children to talk over or find out in cooperation with parents certainly develops an inquiring mind and an ability to think independently and use reference and research material effectively.

As the children mature in this program there is opportunity for critical evaluation of material shared with the group, an attitude and skill so important in scientific research and democratic government.

Homework in the Upper Primary

The child in upper primary is ready for more extensive educational activities outside the school room. Anything that helps to create a more favorable attitude toward an understanding and appreciation of the world in which he lives is worthy of parental cooperation. As the child progresses in school it becomes increasingly important for every parent to consider seriously his boy's or girl's need for a quiet, peaceful, well lighted place of his own dedicated to study. Reference books and materials need to be readily accessible. A family counsel may help decide the most appropriate times for the child to study, that is, when he will be free from distractions such as conversation, television, radio, or interruptions from telephone calls and friends dropping in. It lends much encouragement if a parent, or better yet both parents, make themselves available for answering questions and helping solve problems. Instead of making this a social time for other members of the family, it helps the eight- and nine-year-old to concentrate if the parents and older children use this time for their own concentrated work and for cooperative work with the child on his project. It is essential if the homework is to prove effective that both child and parents be rested and free from frustrations during the preparation of the homework.

At times the child's homework will necessitate an interpretation of some community resource. The parents need to register a genuine interest in this and go with their child on whatever excursion or field trip is needed to stimulate interest and increase knowledge. This should in no way take away from family recreational pursuits and activities nor interfere with the child's own play time with peers. His time for rest and sleep must be carefully guarded, also.

Homework on this level remains voluntary, and the child gradually assumes the responsibility of getting it done, especially when some member of the family is close at hand to lend moral support and answer questions or lead the child to a source where he can obtain the information necessary to solve the problem himself.

Suggestive Types of Upper Primary Homework

The ideal homework for this level is really a continuation of the independent work carried on in the classroom, such as:

> making worthwhile conversation with family and friends;
> explaining the day's activities and experiences, at school and en route;
> sharing future plans with others;
> giving summaries of stories read;

seeing programs and telling what is appealing in these programs;

making announcements of coming events at school;

participating in clubs or other organizations;

interviewing specific people for definite purposes;

planning and giving a home dramatization with the help of other members of the family;

doing selective reading of a recreational, research, or scientific nature;

reading aloud to members of the family, a younger neighborhood child, a blind friend or shut-in, or a peer;

locating pertinent information in the daily press by using the index;

pursuing some hobby which is of intense interest and reading about it; sharing this interest with friends and finding ways of expanding any collections it may involve;

going to the public library regularly and checking out books (which the child himself has located on the shelves) ;

making a telephone directory of numbers needed for emergency calls;

making a directory of friends and any other people or places that may interest him;

using the telephone for specific purposes;

taking messages, recording accurately, and relaying to proper person;

writing letters to a pen pal;

keeping a daily diary at home;

creating poems, stories, songs, and action plays;

making collections and writing stories about them;

helping with the marketing; checking prices and making change;

playing dominoes and other games that involve keeping score;

keeping an accurate record of allowance and any money earned and how spent;

keeping track of household bills and comparing them month by month;

studying the birds, insects, flowers, trees, and shrubs of the immediate environment;

studying the stars and writing stories about them;

visiting historic and cultural places in the community;

taking "snapshots" and writing descriptions of these;

making a scrapbook of national and local holidays and writing about their origin and purpose;

studying the weather and learning names and data about the clouds;

doing creative art and manipulating experimentation.

The all-important factor is that the experience be meaningful and important to the individual child.

The amount and type of homework must necessarily be geared to the needs, interests, and capacities of each child. The first consideration is the child's present attitude. It will vary considerably within groups, and care must be taken to give this problem thoughtful study in order that constructive attitudes are established and retained.

Policy also is an important factor, and this will vary from school to school.

Checking Homework Results at School

It is your responsibility to see that the results of the children's homework are effectively utilized. This should be done the next day immediately following the experience. Each child's work should receive recognition in some way. Work which has value for the other children at the time should be explained by the child who produced it, and, if feasible, demonstrated, discussed, and evaluated. You should be free with suggestions to stimulate further thought, and give honest commendation when possible.

As parents help their children meet homework projects, they will become more cognizant of the daily problems their child is helping to solve through group effort, and a new respect for education will emerge. The children who have learned to solve problems in this way will continue to educate themselves—and is this not the ultimate end and aim of education?

QUESTIONS ON THE PHILOSOPHY BEHIND SELECTIVE HOMEWORK

1. How does the "Philosophy Behind Selective Homework" differ from the assignments you were given in school?

2. Describe five homework assignments in accord with the philosophy here presented for one or more of the following: a. a fives group; b. a beginning, middle, or upper primary group; c. an older group.

3. Discuss how you would follow through on a homework assignment in one of the goups in No. 2, above. Cite specific examples of work done by the children.

4. What could you do for the child who does not have the family's cooperation and is handicapped by a lack of interest in his schoolwork at home?

INDEX

INDEX

ABOUT THE AUTHORS

Edith M. Leonard earned her B.S. Degree at National College of Education, her Master's Degree at Claremont Colleges and did graduate work at Northwestern University. She has served as Kindergarten-Primary Supervisor in the San Bernardino City Schools, and as Primary Supervisor at Santa Barbara State Teachers College. Miss Leonard is now Professor of Education at Santa Barbara. Edith Leonard and Lillian Miles were co-authors on *The Child at Home and School* (1941 American Book) and *Counseling with Parents in Early Childhood Education* (1954 Macmillan). She has been a contributor on a number of other publications on Early Childhood Education.

Dorothy D. VanDeman received her B.S. Degree at Whittier College and her Master's Degree at Claremont Colleges Graduate School. She did graduate work at Whittier College and Broadoaks School of Childhood Education in Pasadena. She is presently a Professor of Education at the University of California—Santa Barbara. She has served as a supervising teacher in various capacities in guidance and teaching of children.

Lillian E. Miles was with the San Bernardino, California Board of Education for more than thirty years. She has been a free-lance writer for some twenty-five years and has written articles for many educational magazines as well as for a large number of trade publications. She is also known as a poet and writer of children's stories.

This book is printed in Baskerville type, one of the most popular book faces of modern times. It was designed by John Baskerville, a native of Worcestershire, England. A transitional face, its principal characteristics are lightness, openness, and refinement when set in mass. Baskerville is an extremely graceful face; its rounded and generous characters seem designed especially for eye comfort. The text is complemented by the use of Garamond Light and Garamond Bold for part openings and the major headings.

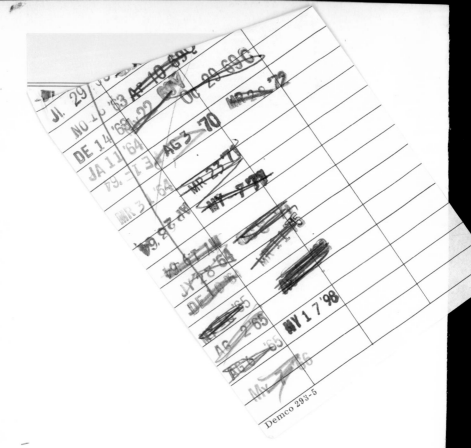